W9-AKB-465

NOISE MAKERS

25 WOMEN WHO RAISED THEIR VOICES & CHANGED THE WORLD

A GRAPHIC COLLECTION FROM

kazoo

Alfred A. Knopf
NEW YORK

WHAT IS A NOISEMAKER?

Take a deep breath, open your mouth, and say your name. Now say it again louder. And again, louder still. You've just proven something big to yourself (and also possibly to your neighbors as well): You aren't afraid to make some noise. Your voice—and your willingness to use it—is exactly what it takes to change the world.

You, dear reader, are a Noisemaker.

Of course, as you probably already know, it's not always so easy to raise your voice, speak out, ask questions, and demand answers. But that's where this book comes in. In these pages, you'll find the true tales of 25 remarkable women throughout history, all told in comics created by 25 of the very best women and non-binary cartoonists today. Turn the pages, read their stories, and you'll soon learn that you are not alone, but instead part of a long line of women who have dedicated their lives to making noise, even when they were encouraged, if not expected, to stay silent.

The Noisemakers in this book were scientists and chefs, artists and activists, engineers and explorers. Many of these Noisemakers lived during times in history when the rules were different for girls than they were for boys. This book is not about how small their lives were supposed to

be but how big their dreams actually were. They flew through the sky and dove into the ocean. They built magnificent things that no one believed could ever exist. They ran faster, climbed higher, and played harder than anyone ever thought possible. They painted, danced, and wrote with beauty and power. They broke stories and broke rules. And they saved lives—and changed lives, including, as a matter of fact, all of ours.

The world is what it is today only because these Noisemakers dared to be strong, smart, fierce, and true to themselves. And hopefully, just knowing that they came before you will give you all the extra courage and strength you ever need to follow your own amazing path, no matter where it may lead.

Your story—the one about how *you* will change the world—has already begun, of course. Now grab a pen or pencil, or a set of crayons, and fill in the rest.

xo,

Erin Bried

EDITOR IN CHIEF
***KAZOO* MAGAZINE**

CONTENTS

Grow

Tinker

Play

Create

Rally

Explore

CROW

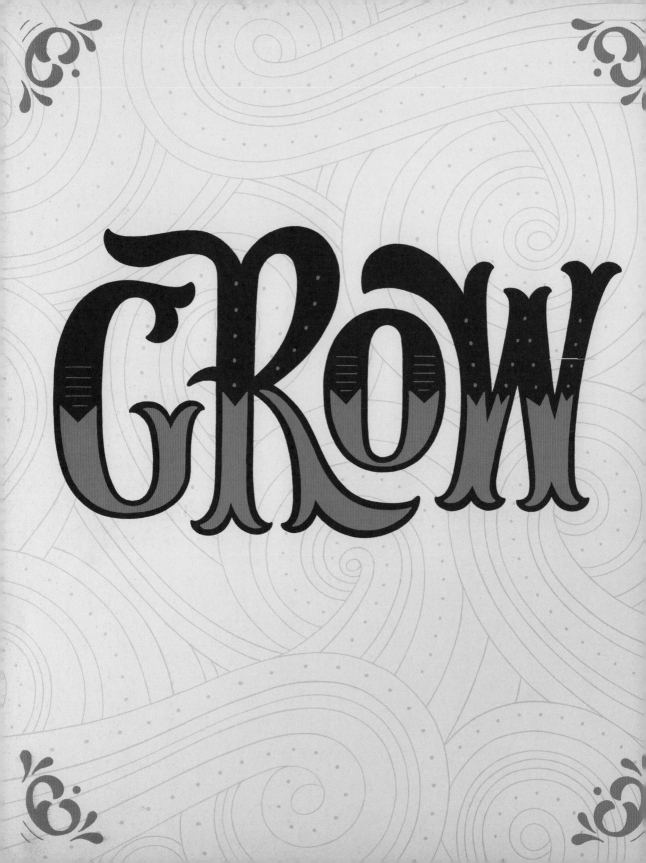

The world is magnificent, and if you sit still for a moment to just look around, it's impossible not to be filled with absolute wonder. Here we stand on this giant planet, spinning around the sun, which is only one of a hundred billion stars in our galaxy, which is one of a hundred billion galaxies in our universe. It's difficult to even wrap your mind around how massive our universe is—and how small we are. But since our earliest days, humans have tried. We've been asking important questions, like *How did we get here and why?*, *What do we do now?*, and *How do we all fit together?* The four incredible scientists in this chapter have helped unlock some of life's great mysteries. They've studied the seas and the stars, our plants and our past, and they've made sense of the world and our place in it.

The SHARK WHISPERER

· · · · ·

EUGENIE CLARK
1922 ~ 2015

Marine biologist Eugenie Clark spent her entire life swimming in the ocean with sharks so that we might learn to love them as much as she did. By diving into the deep, she showed us how knowledge can help turn fear into wonder.

EUGENIE AND ME

COUNT ALL THE THINGS YOU HAVE IN COMMON WITH EUGENIE CLARK.

- I've visited aquariums.
- I like to swim.
- The ocean is my happy place.
- I think fish are fascinating.
- I believe we should be kind to all creatures.
- I can hold my breath for a long time.
- I'd like to discover animals no one has yet seen.
- I'm not afraid of the dark.
- I am brave.
- I am curious.

Photo by Tak Konstantinou. Courtesy of Mote Marine Laboratory & Aquarium

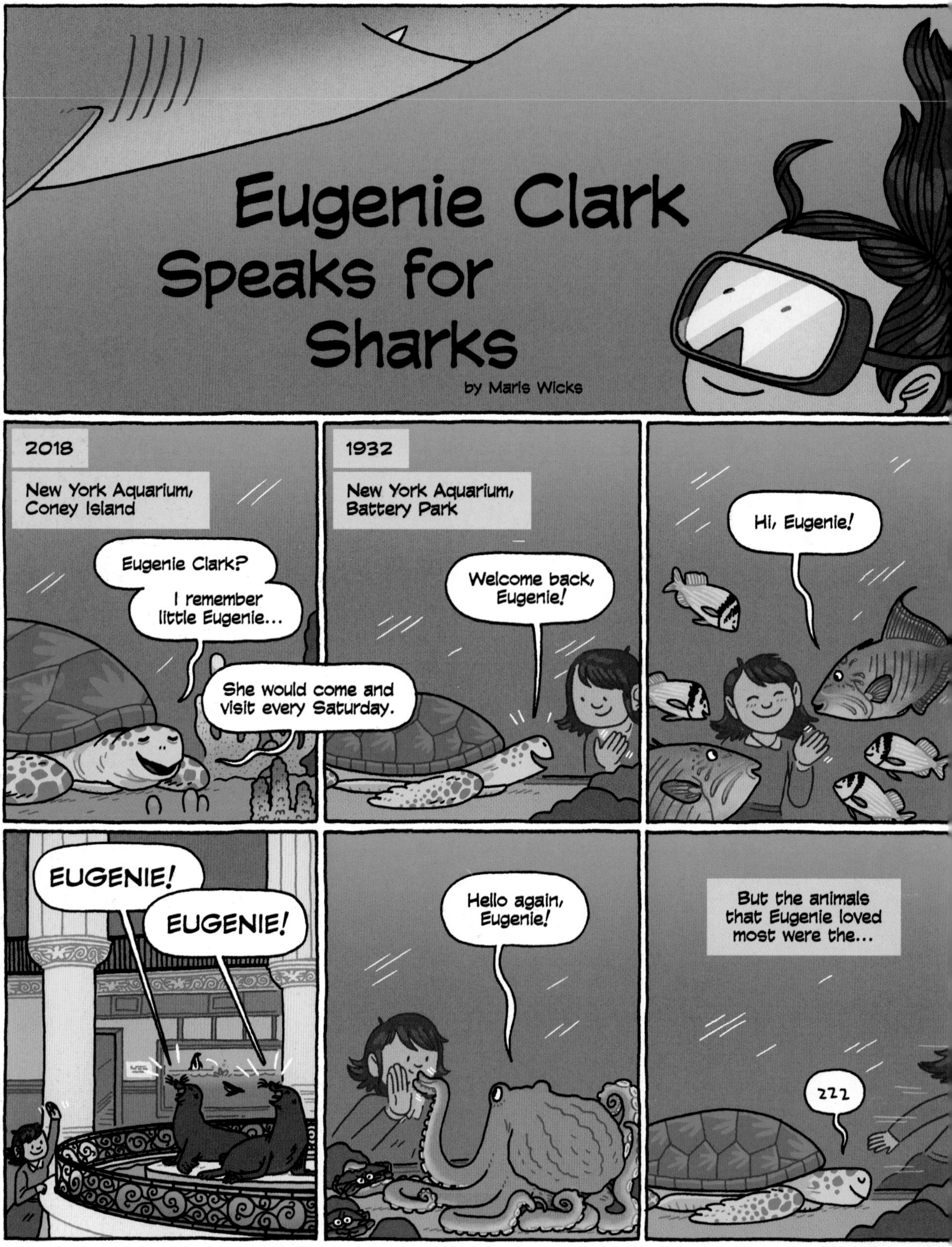

Eugenie Clark Speaks for Sharks
by Maris Wicks
2018
New York Aquarium, Coney Island
Eugenie Clark?
I remember little Eugenie...
She would come and visit every Saturday.
1932
New York Aquarium, Battery Park
Welcome back, Eugenie!
Hi, Eugenie!
EUGENIE!
EUGENIE!
Hello again, Eugenie!
But the animals that Eugenie loved most were the...
zzz

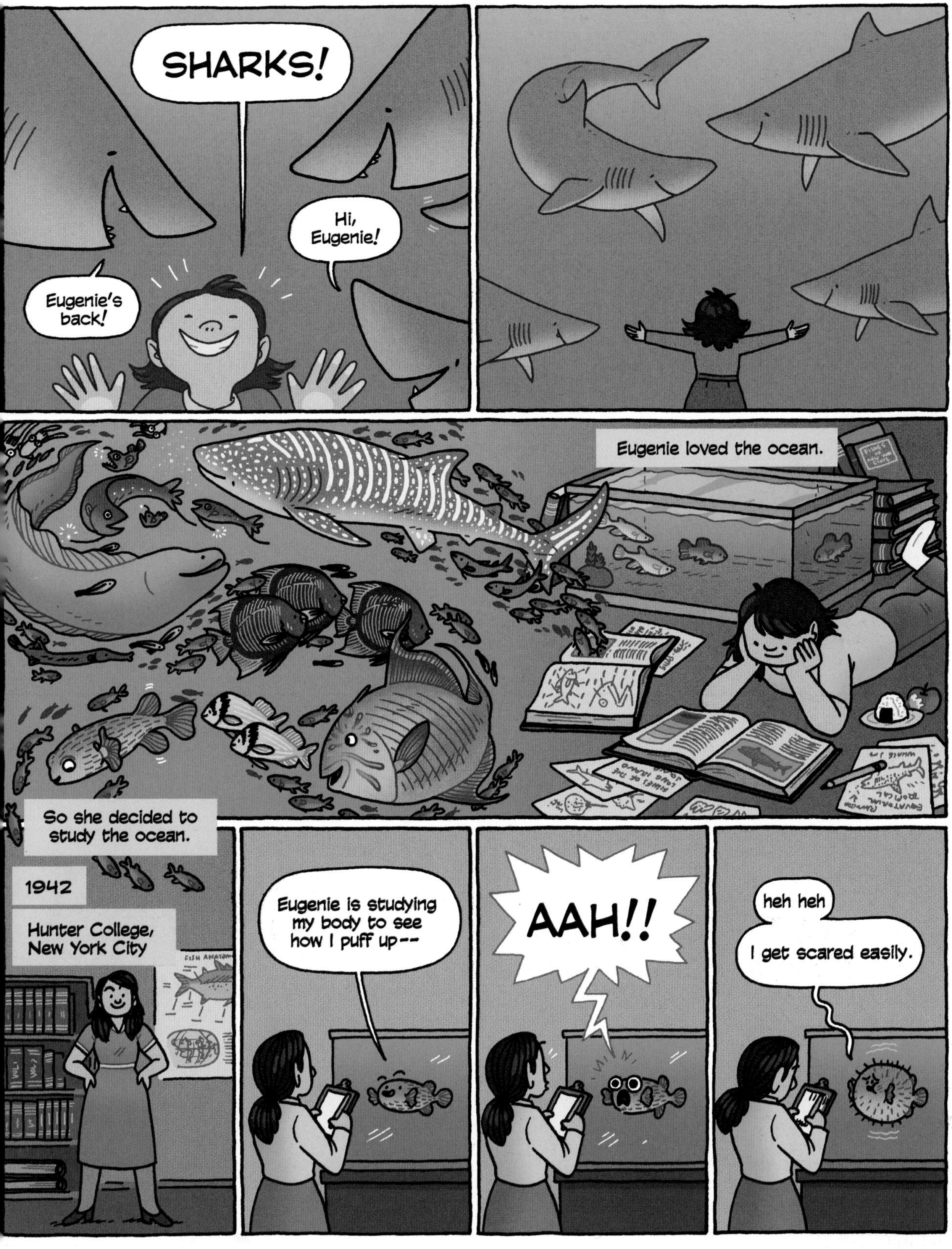
SHARKS!
Hi, Eugenie!
Eugenie's back!
Eugenie loved the ocean.
So she decided to study the ocean.
1942
Hunter College, New York City
Eugenie is studying my body to see how I puff up--
AAH!!
heh heh
I get scared easily.

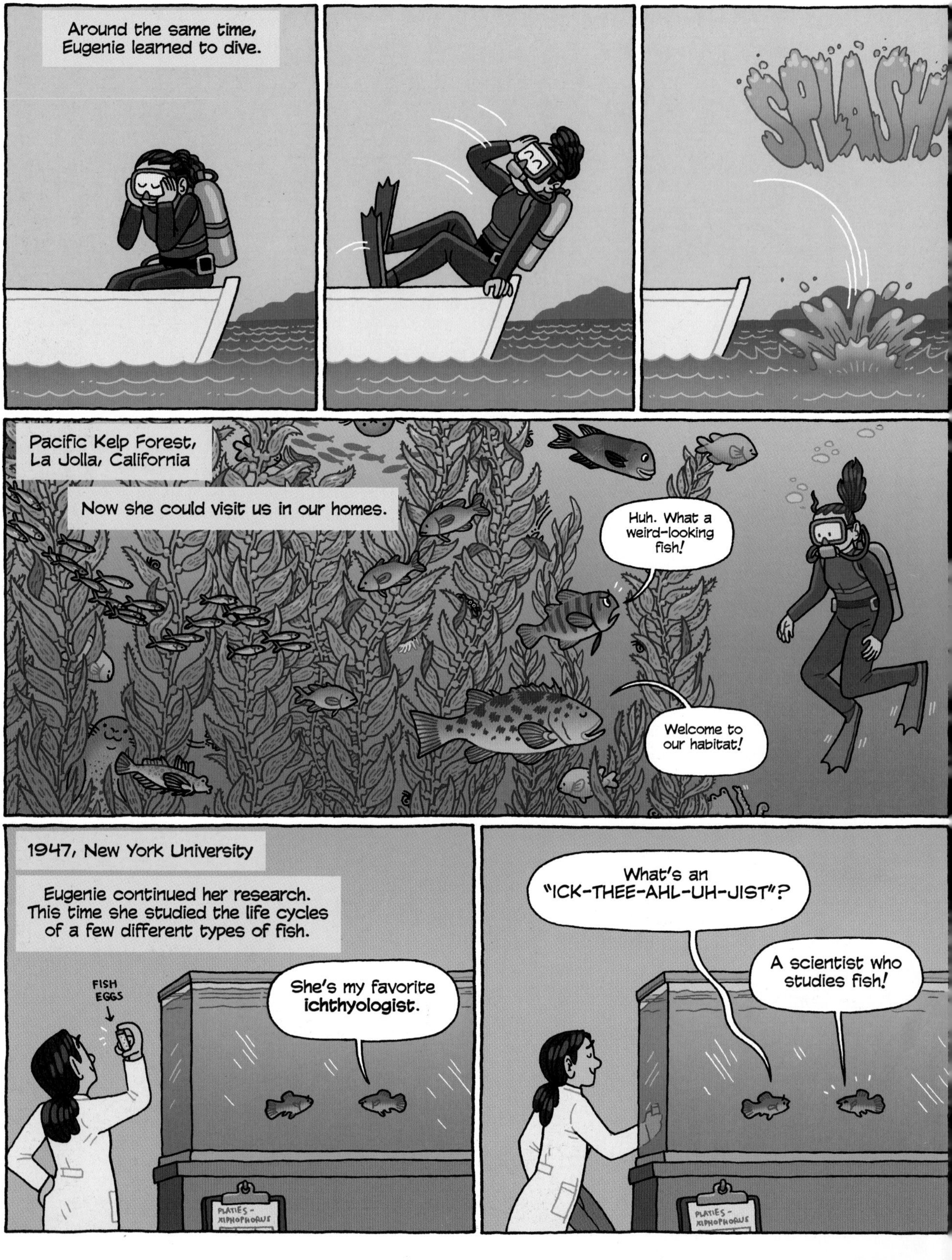

Around the same time, Eugenie learned to dive.
SPLASH!
Pacific Kelp Forest, La Jolla, California
Now she could visit us in our homes.
Huh. What a weird-looking fish!
Welcome to our habitat!
1947, New York University
Eugenie continued her research. This time she studied the life cycles of a few different types of fish.
FISH EGGS
She's my favorite **ichthyologist**.
PLATIES - XIPHOPHORUS
What's an "ICK-THEE-AHL-UH-JIST"?
A scientist who studies fish!
PLATIES - XIPHOPHORUS

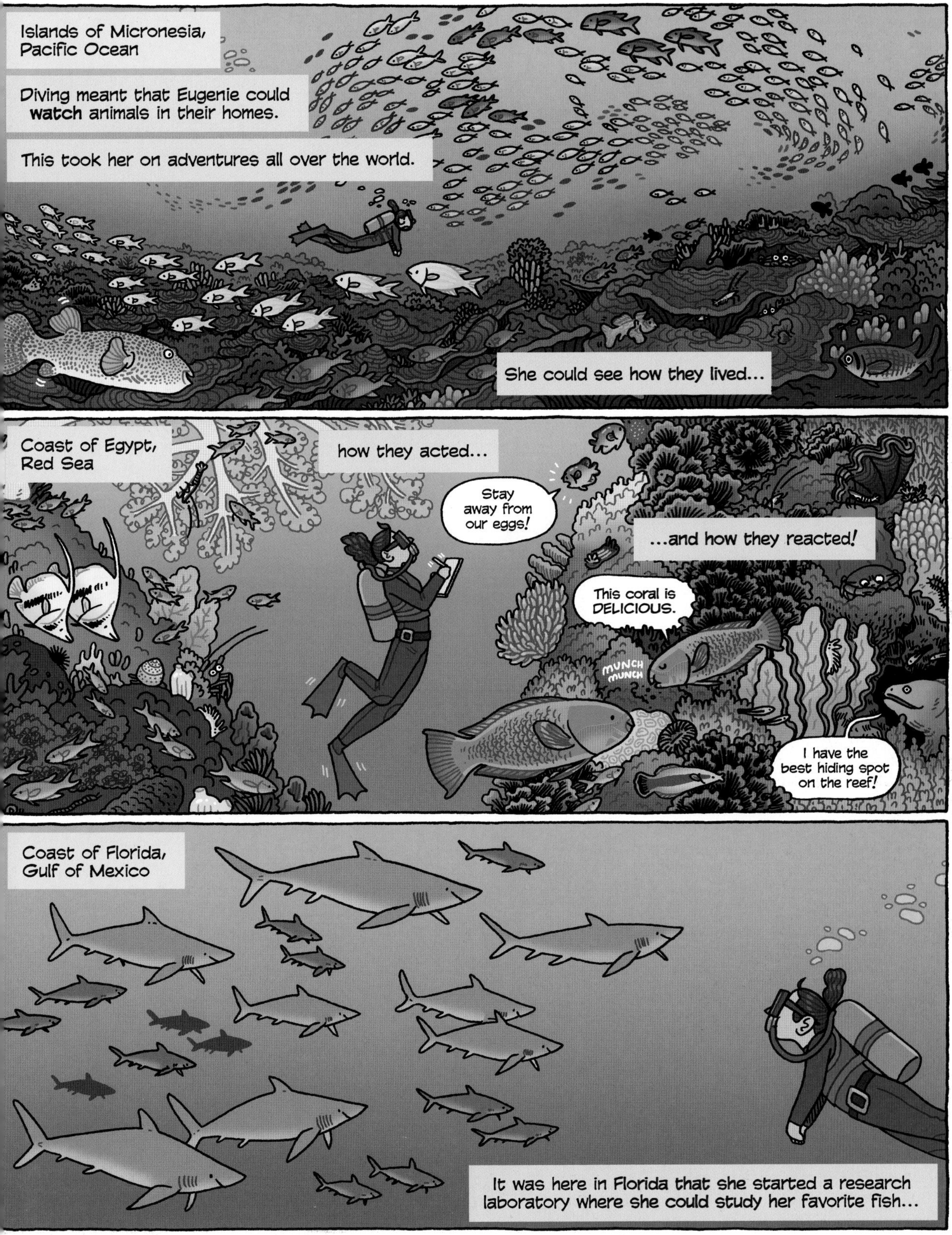
Islands of Micronesia, Pacific Ocean
Diving meant that Eugenie could **watch** animals in their homes.
This took her on adventures all over the world.
She could see how they lived...
Coast of Egypt, Red Sea
how they acted...
Stay away from our eggs!
...and how they reacted!
This coral is DELICIOUS.
MUNCH MUNCH
I have the best hiding spot on the reef!
Coast of Florida, Gulf of Mexico
It was here in Florida that she started a research laboratory where she could study her favorite fish...

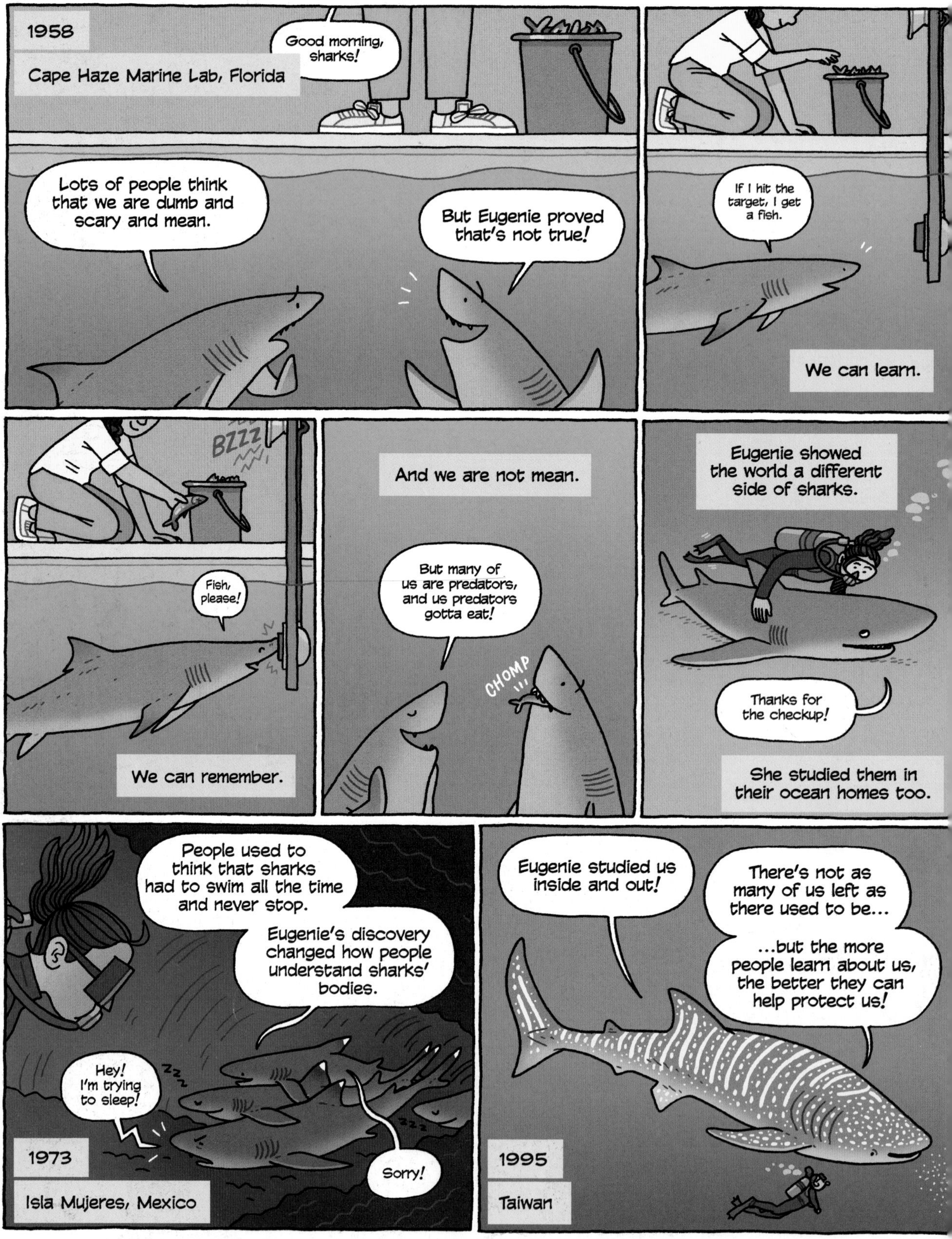
1958
Cape Haze Marine Lab, Florida
Good morning, sharks!
Lots of people think that we are dumb and scary and mean.
But Eugenie proved that's not true!
If I hit the target, I get a fish.
We can learn.
BZZZ
Fish, please!
We can remember.
And we are not mean.
But many of us are predators, and us predators gotta eat!
CHOMP
Eugenie showed the world a different side of sharks.
Thanks for the checkup!
She studied them in their ocean homes too.
People used to think that sharks had to swim all the time and never stop.
Eugenie's discovery changed how people understand sharks' bodies.
Hey! I'm trying to sleep!
Sorry!
1973
Isla Mujeres, Mexico
Eugenie studied us inside and out!
There's not as many of us left as there used to be...
...but the more people learn about us, the better they can help protect us!
1995
Taiwan

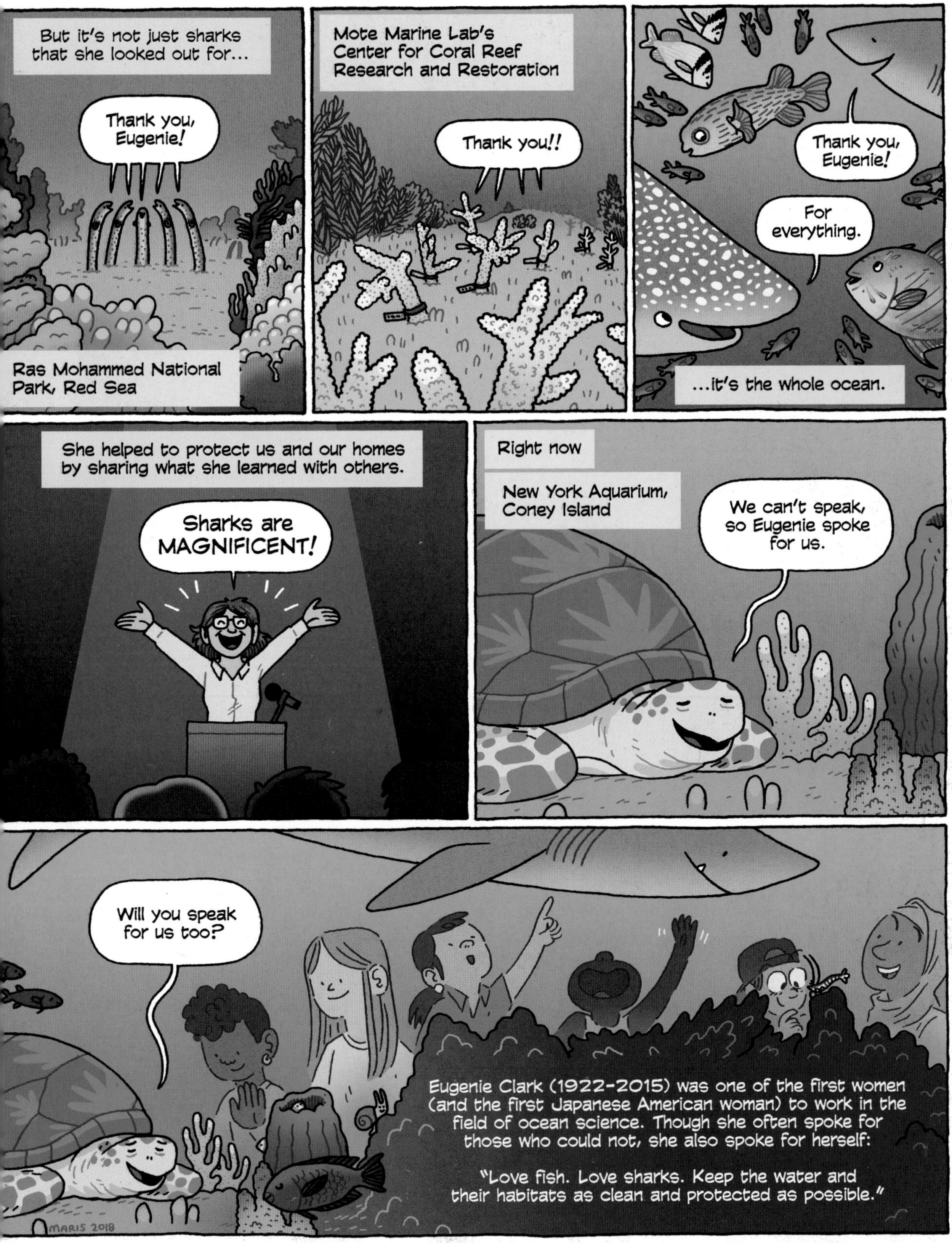

But it's not just sharks that she looked out for...
Thank you, Eugenie!
Ras Mohammed National Park, Red Sea
Mote Marine Lab's Center for Coral Reef Research and Restoration
Thank you!!
Thank you, Eugenie!
For everything.
...it's the whole ocean.
She helped to protect us and our homes by sharing what she learned with others.
Sharks are MAGNIFICENT!
Right now
New York Aquarium, Coney Island
We can't speak, so Eugenie spoke for us.
Will you speak for us too?
Eugenie Clark (1922–2015) was one of the first women (and the first Japanese American woman) to work in the field of ocean science. Though she often spoke for those who could not, she also spoke for herself:
"Love fish. Love sharks. Keep the water and their habitats as clean and protected as possible."
MARIS 2018

The TREE PLANTER

. . . . .

WANGARI MAATHAI

1940 ~ 2011

If you've ever felt like you're too small to matter or what you do can't possibly make a difference, then take a lesson from Wangari Maathai, an environmental political activist, who started a revolution and changed the world by planting a single tree.

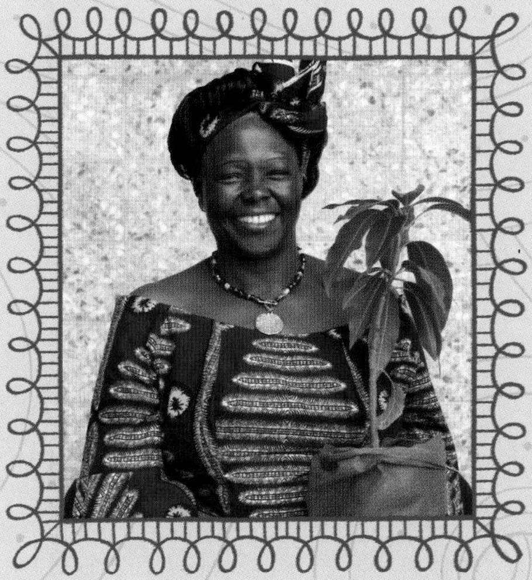

WANGARI AND ME

COUNT ALL THE THINGS YOU HAVE IN COMMON WITH WANGARI MAATHAI.

- I've planted a garden.
- I like to dig in the dirt.
- I care about the environment.
- When I learn something new, I like to share it with others.
- I know people working together are stronger than people working alone.
- I like to work with my hands.
- I like to watch things grow.
- I will always stand up for what I believe.
- I am helpful.
- I am hopeful.

Photo courtesy of the Green Belt Movement and UNEP

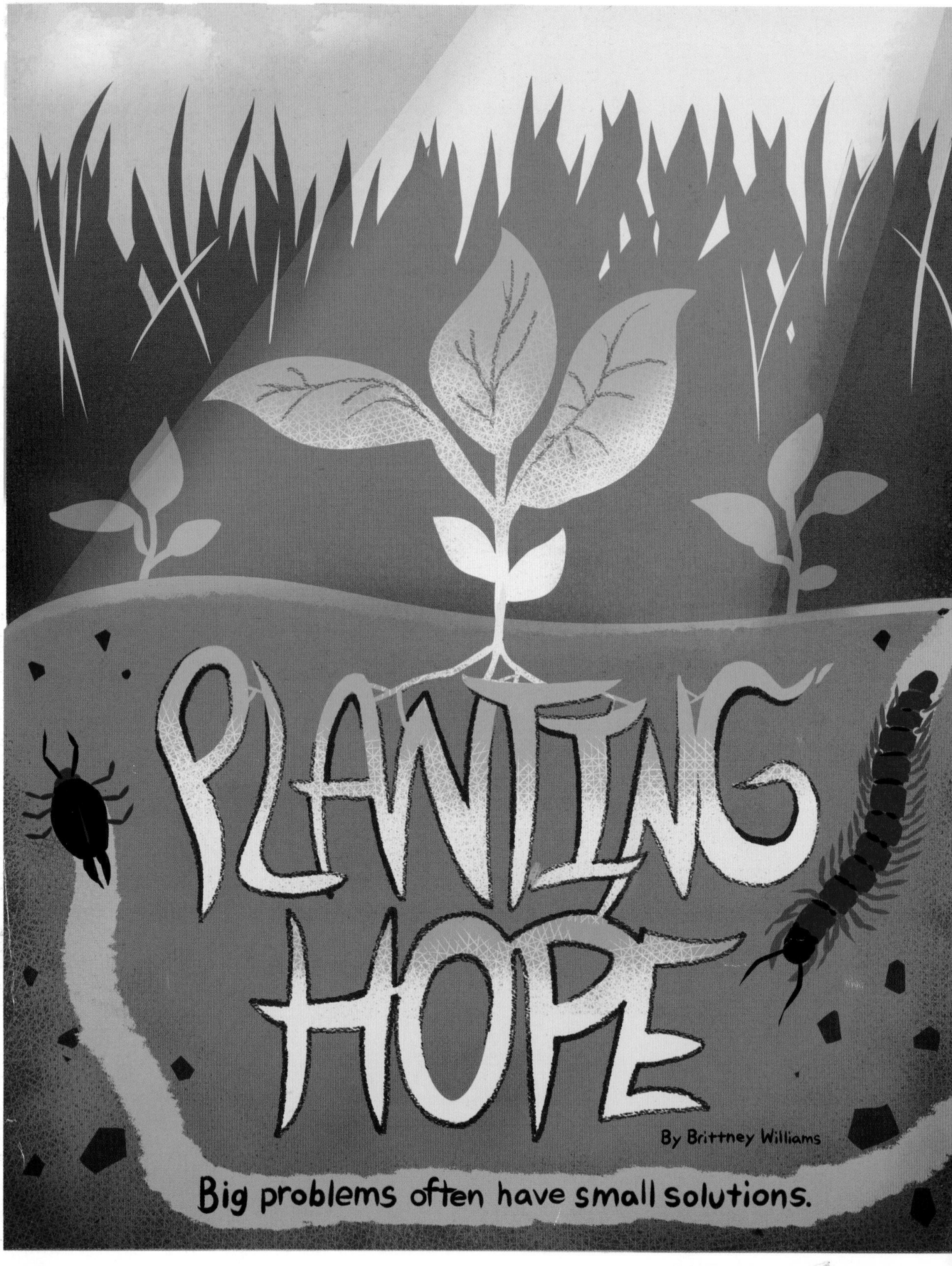
PLANTING HOPE
By Brittney Williams
Big problems often have small solutions.

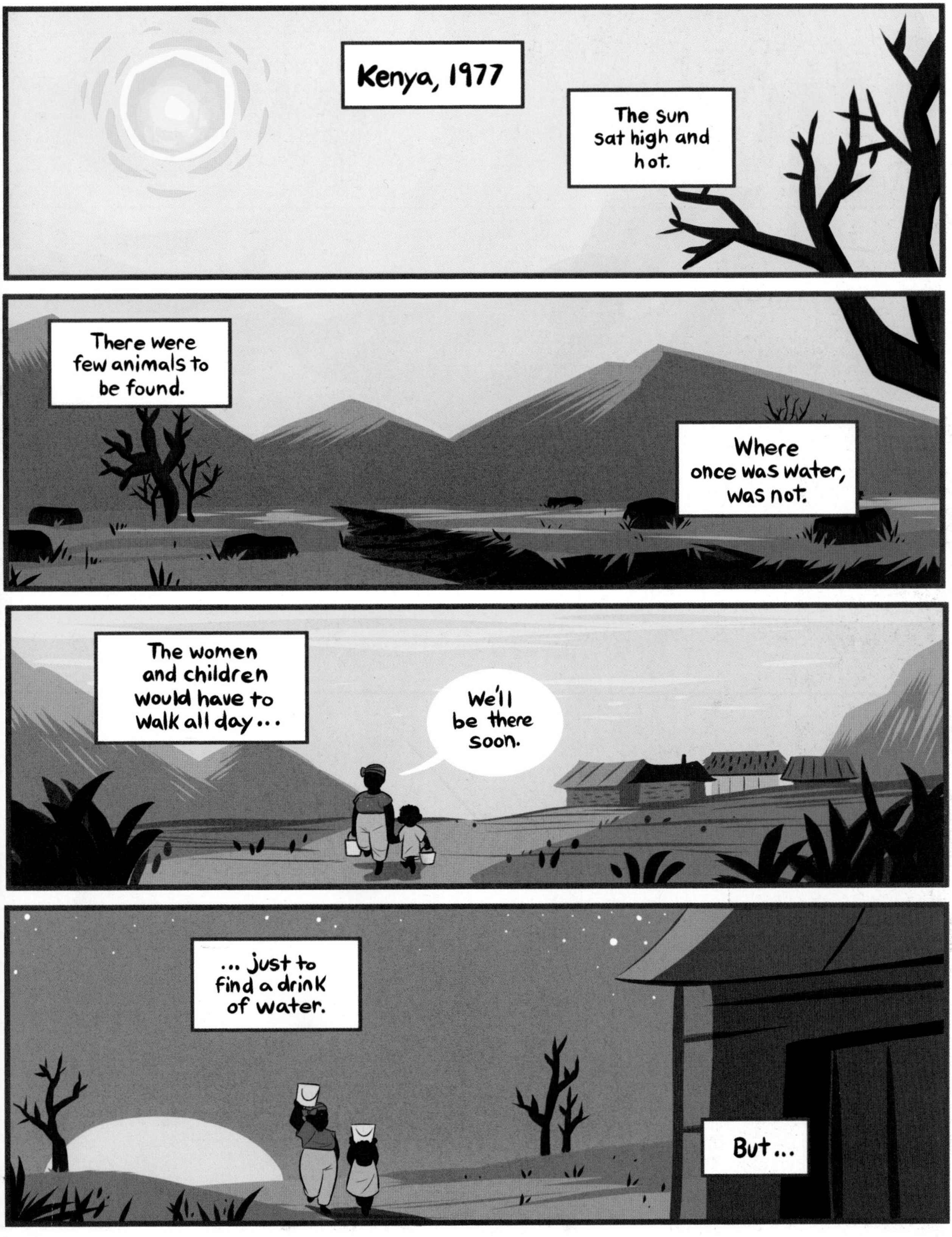
Kenya, 1977
The sun sat high and hot.
There were few animals to be found.
Where once was water, was not.
The women and children would have to walk all day...
We'll be there soon.
... just to find a drink of water.
But...

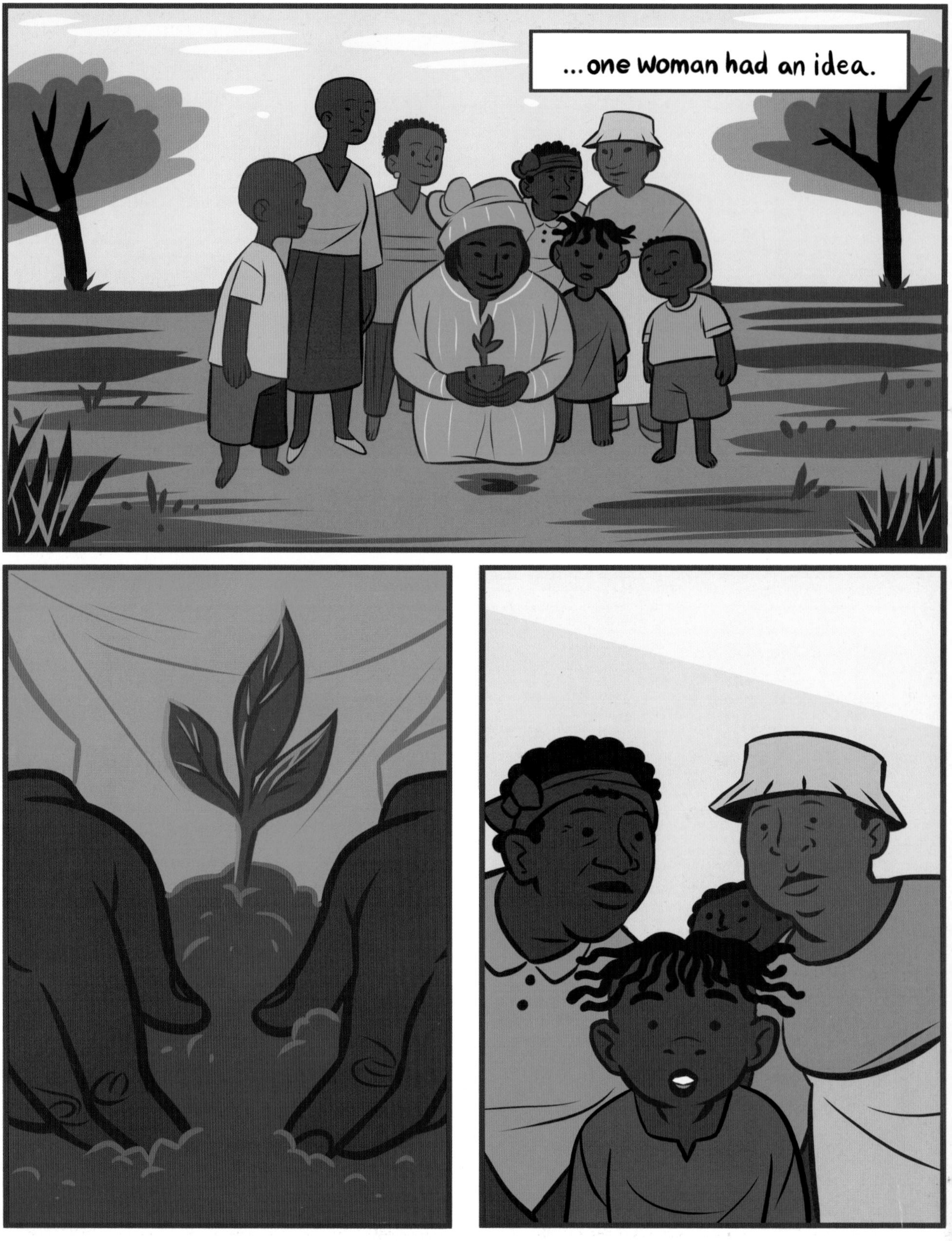
...one woman had an idea.

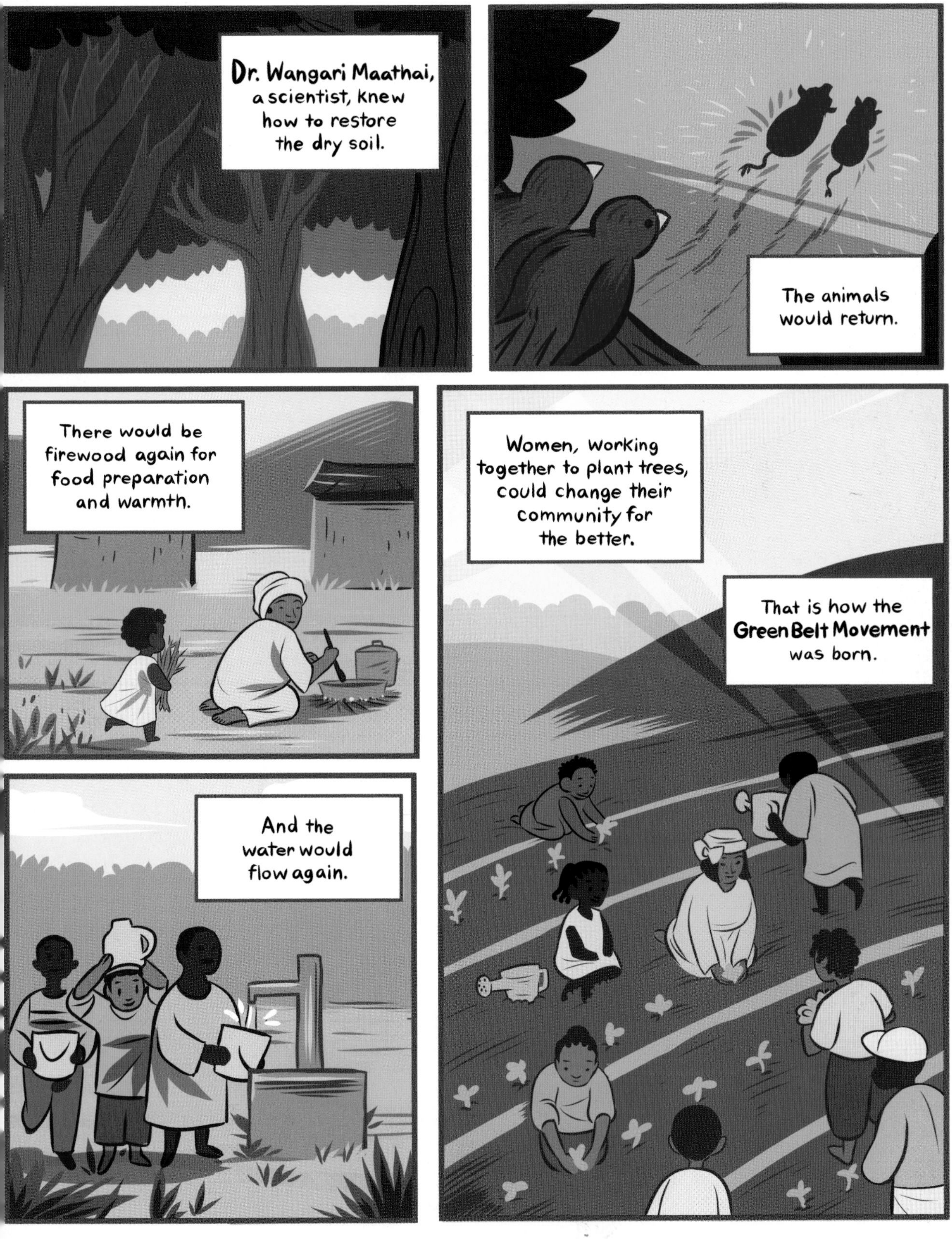
Dr. Wangari Maathai, a scientist, knew how to restore the dry soil.
The animals would return.
There would be firewood again for food preparation and warmth.
And the water would flow again.
Women, working together to plant trees, could change their community for the better.
That is how the Green Belt Movement was born.

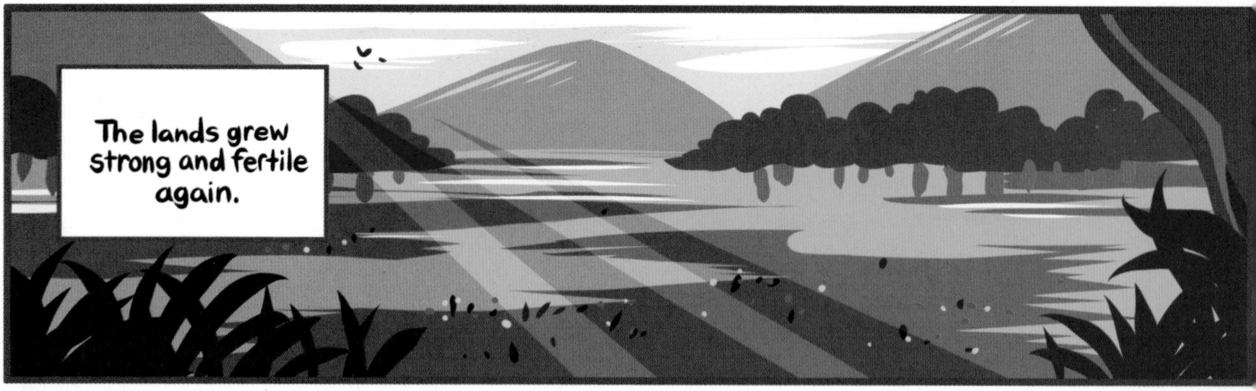
The lands grew strong and fertile again.

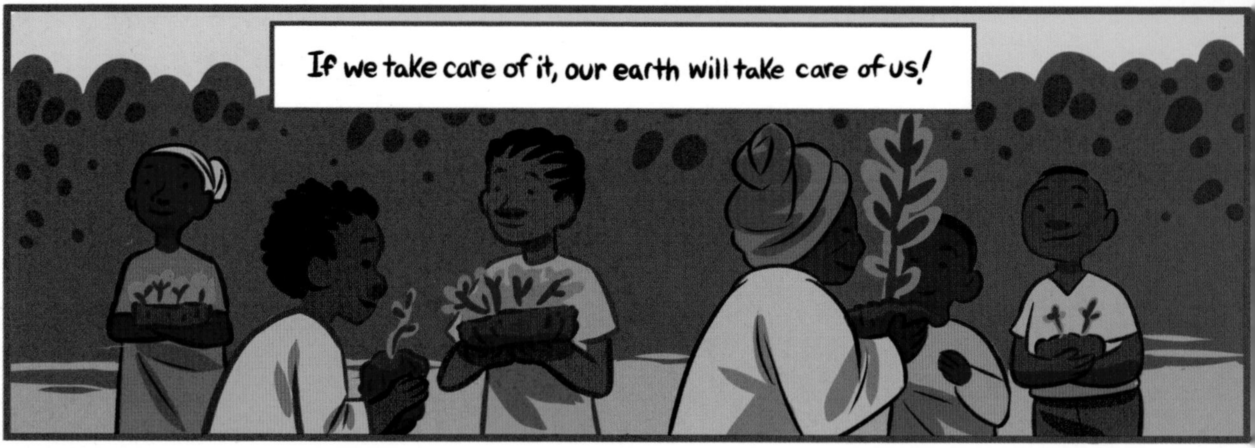
If we take care of it, our earth will take care of us!

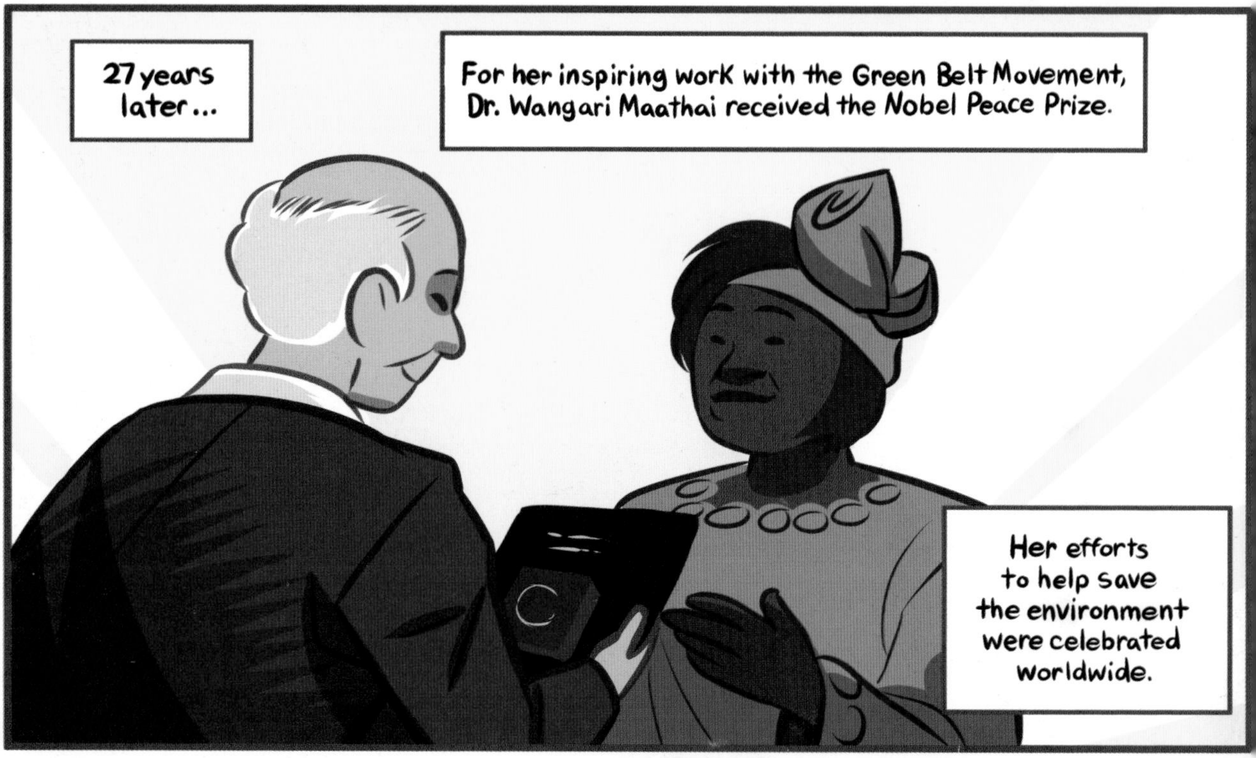
27 years later...
For her inspiring work with the Green Belt Movement, Dr. Wangari Maathai received the Nobel Peace Prize.
Her efforts to help save the environment were celebrated worldwide.

Thanks to her, 51 million trees have been planted in Kenya and beyond.

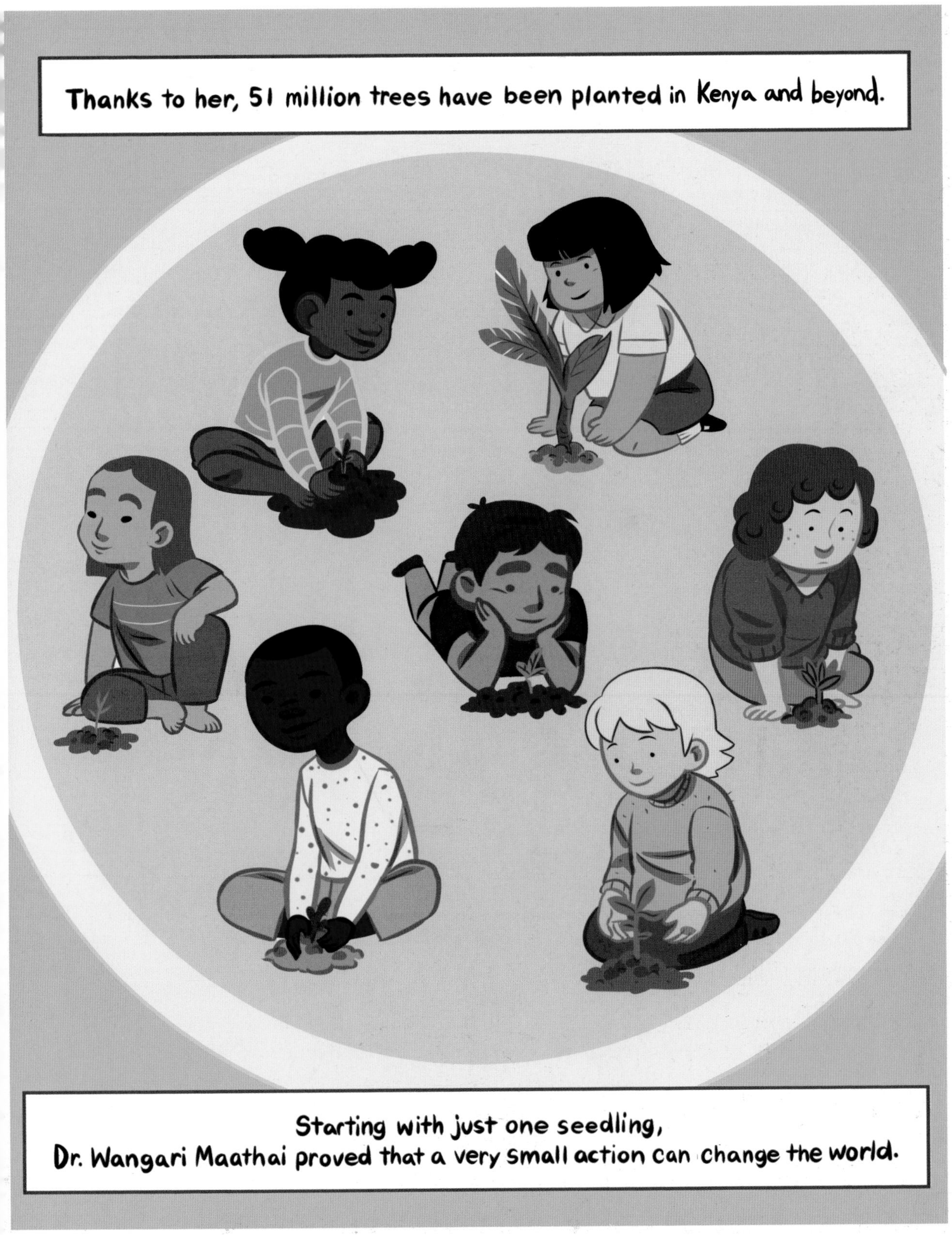

Starting with just one seedling,
Dr. Wangari Maathai proved that a very small action can change the world.

The FOSSIL HUNTER

· · · · ·

MARY ANNING

1799~1847

She sold seashells by the seashore, but paleontologist Mary Anning *also* discovered massive fossils of never-before-seen dinosaurs, helping us understand what life was like on Earth long before humans.

MARY AND ME

COUNT ALL THE THINGS YOU HAVE IN COMMON WITH MARY ANNING.

- I like to hike.
- I'm not afraid to climb.
- I like to imagine hidden treasures.
- I like to figure out how things fit together.
- I like to make new discoveries.
- I like dinosaurs.
- I enjoy organizing objects according to size and shape.
- I like to draw pictures.
- I'm patient.
- I'm dedicated.

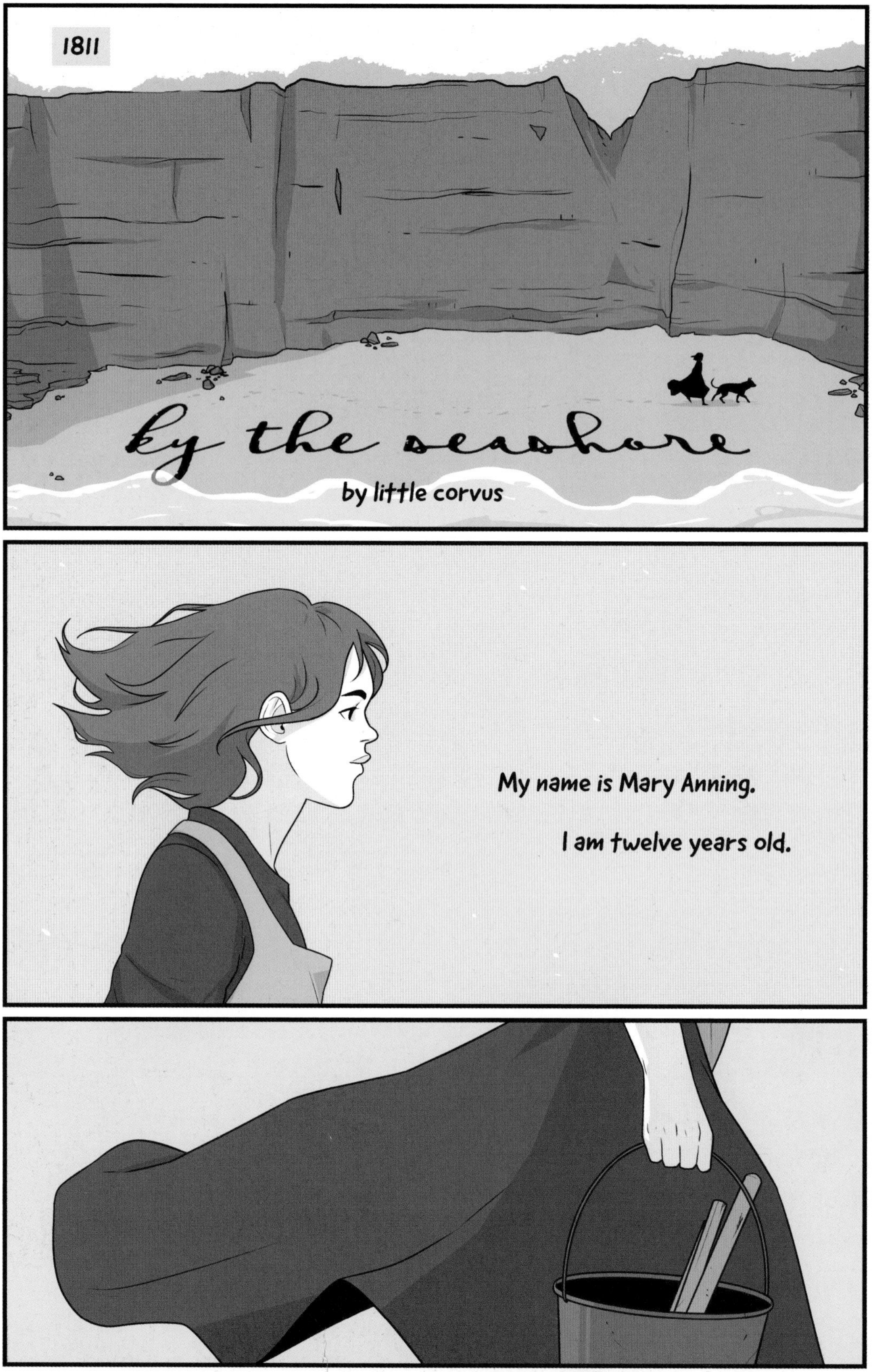
1811
by the seashore
by little corvus
My name is Mary Anning.
I am twelve years old.

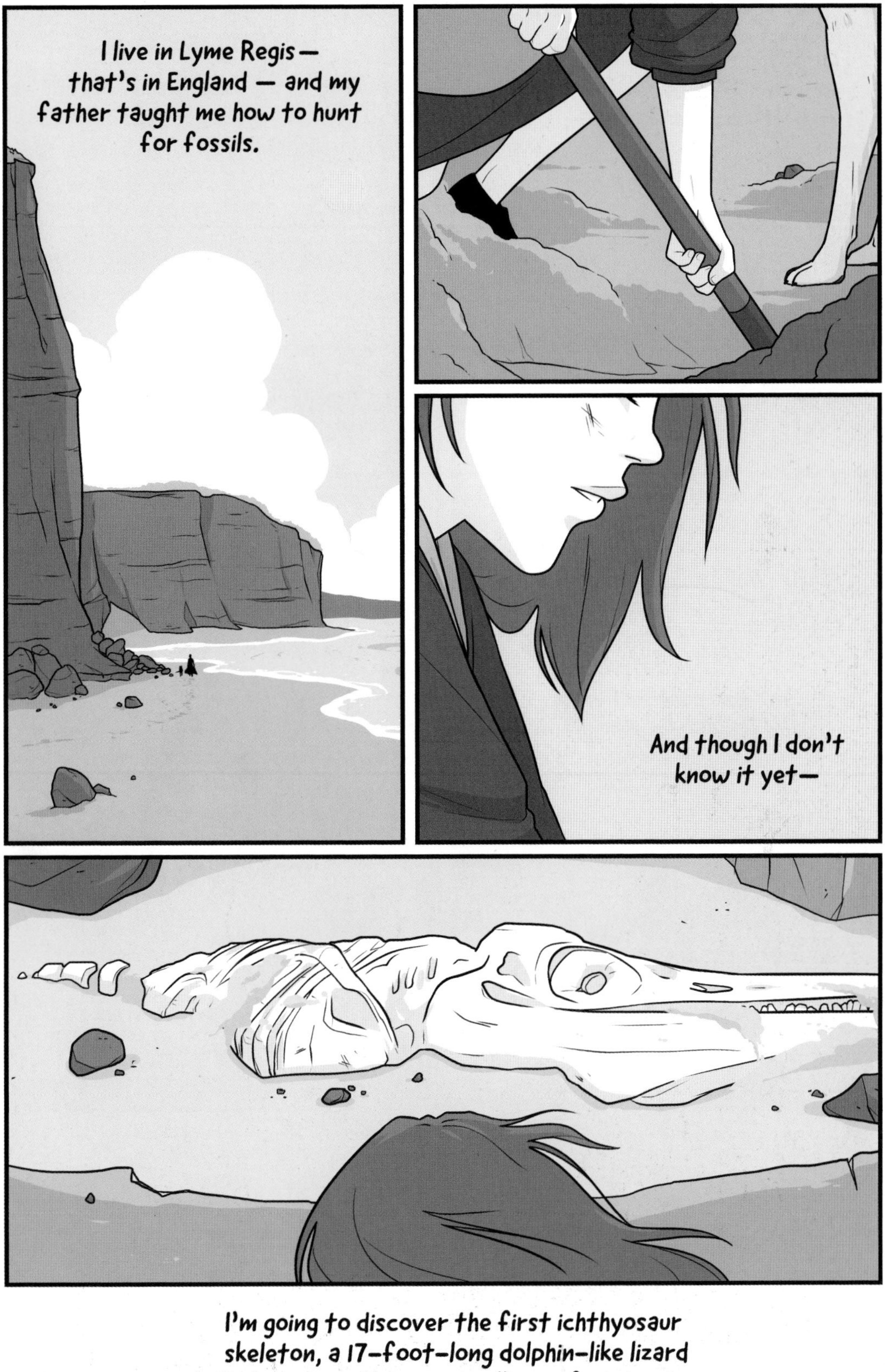
I live in Lyme Regis— that's in England — and my father taught me how to hunt for fossils.
And though I don't know it yet—
I'm going to discover the first ichthyosaur skeleton, a 17-foot-long dolphin-like lizard that swam in the ocean millions of years ago.

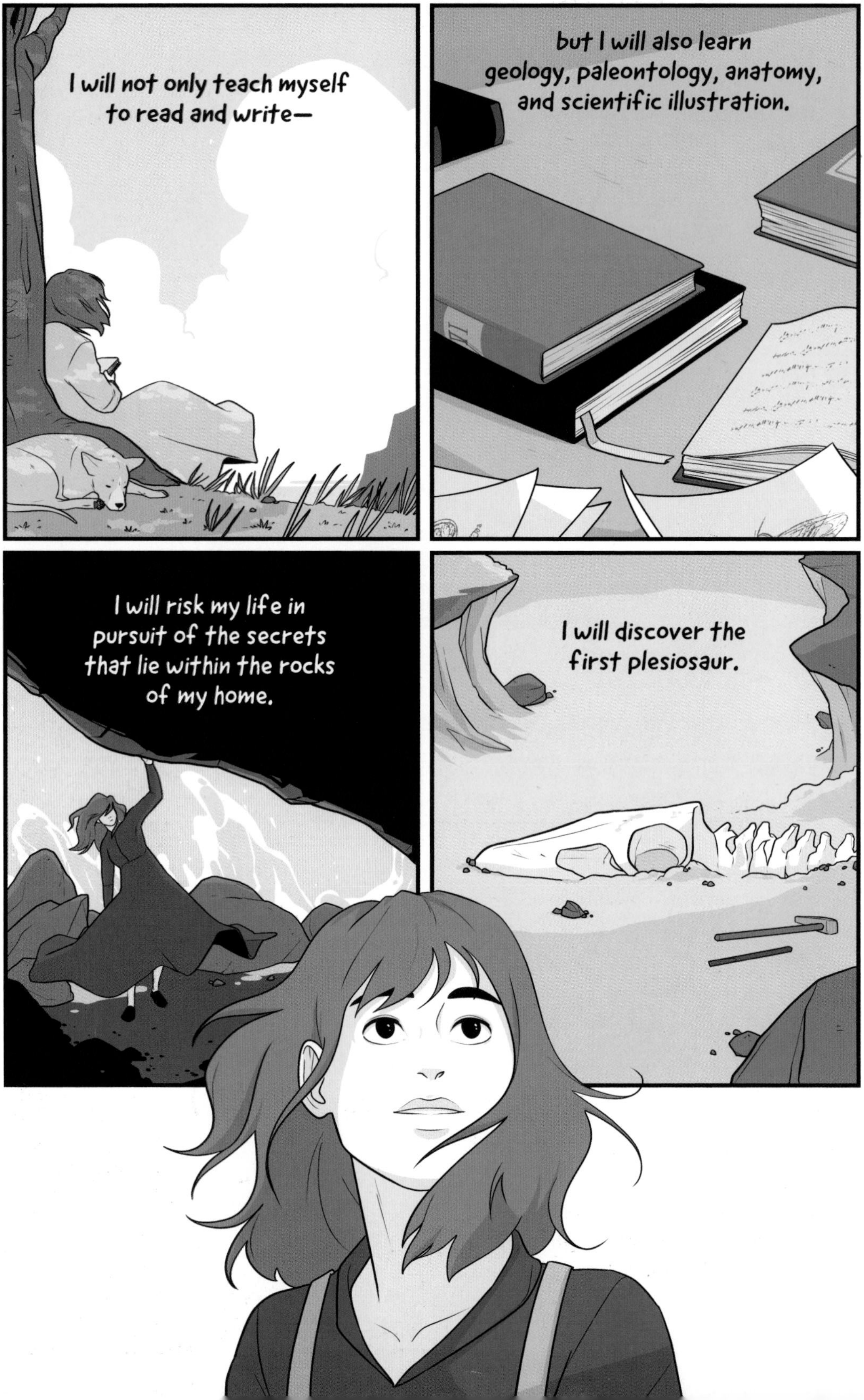
I will not only teach myself
to read and write—
but I will also learn
geology, paleontology, anatomy,
and scientific illustration.
I will risk my life in
pursuit of the secrets
that lie within the rocks
of my home.
I will discover the
first plesiosaur.

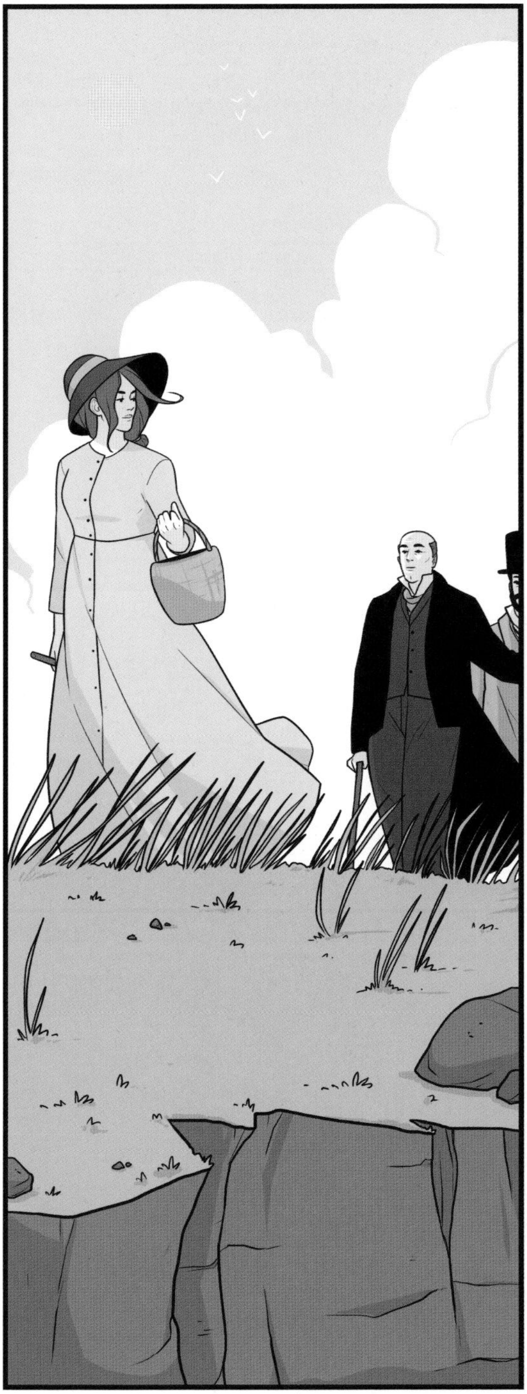

My discoveries will be numerous, and end up displayed across the globe.

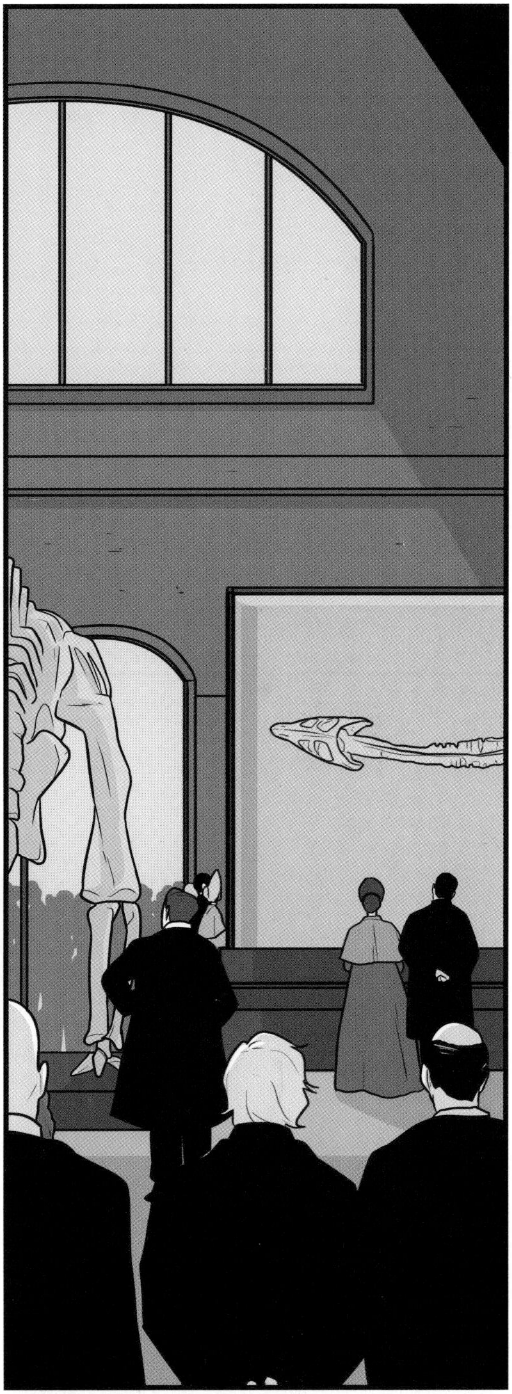

World-renowned male scientists will come to me for my guidance and insight.

Through my scientific contributions will go unrecognized for a time, I won't be entirely forgotten.

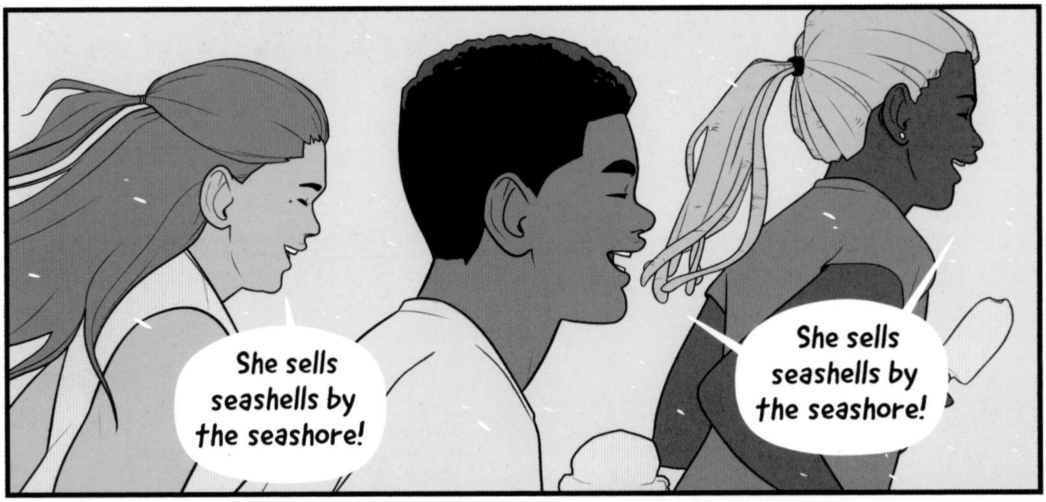
She sells seashells by the seashore!
She sells seashells by the seashore!

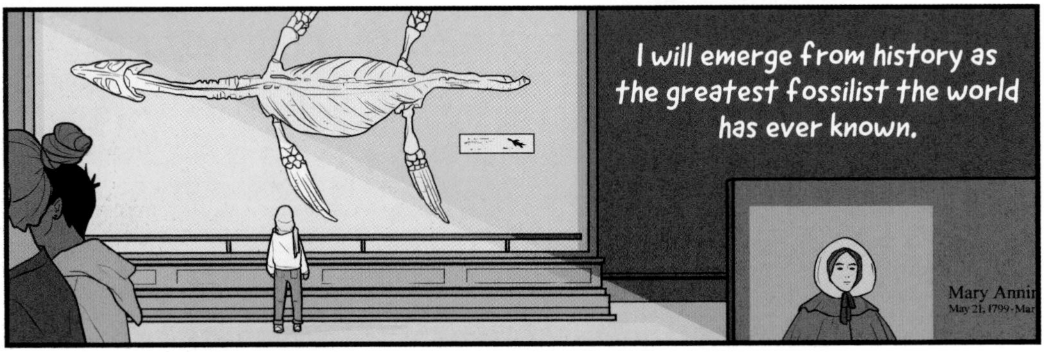
I will emerge from history as the greatest fossilist the world has ever known.
Mary Annin

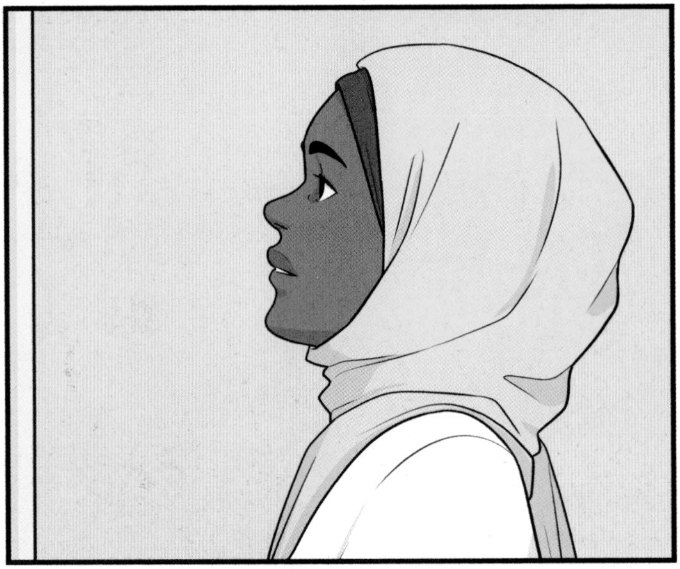

And I will inspire other young girls — maybe even you — to make discoveries of their own.

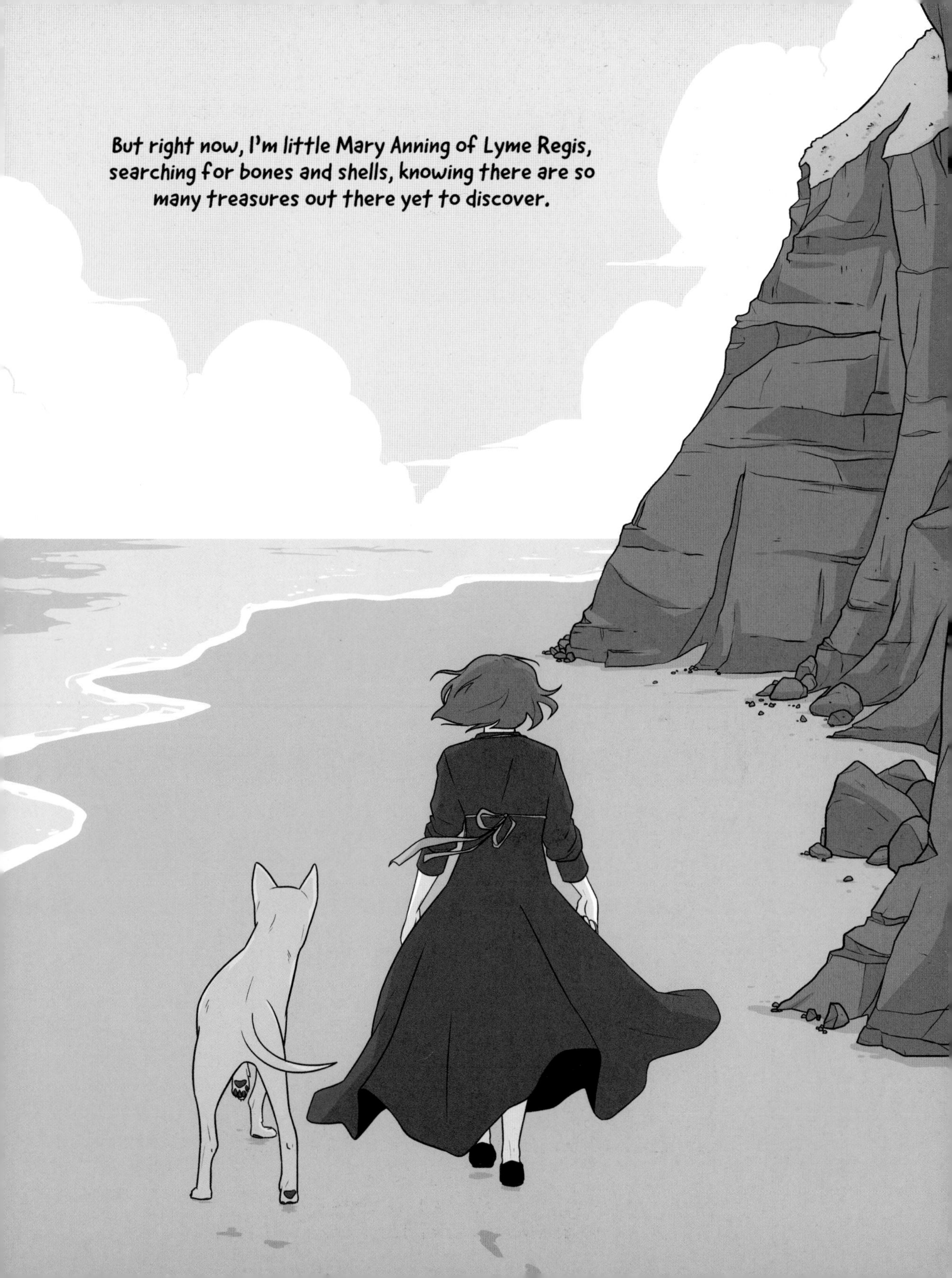
But right now, I'm little Mary Anning of Lyme Regis, searching for bones and shells, knowing there are so many treasures out there yet to discover.

THE SKY WATCHER

CAROLINE HERSCHEL
1750~1848

She dreamed of becoming an opera singer, but as the first woman to ever discover a comet, Caroline Herschel found a different sort of stardom. The maps of the night sky she drew by hand many years ago are so precise that they still guide astronomers today.

CAROLINE AND ME

COUNT ALL THE THINGS YOU HAVE IN COMMON WITH CAROLINE HERSCHEL.

- I like to sing.
- I like to look at stars at night.
- I love figuring out math problems.
- I think maps are cool.
- I like spending time by myself.
- I like to imagine what's out there in space.
- I'd love to build a telescope.
- I enjoy being precise and careful with my stuff.
- I'm observant.
- I love to learn.

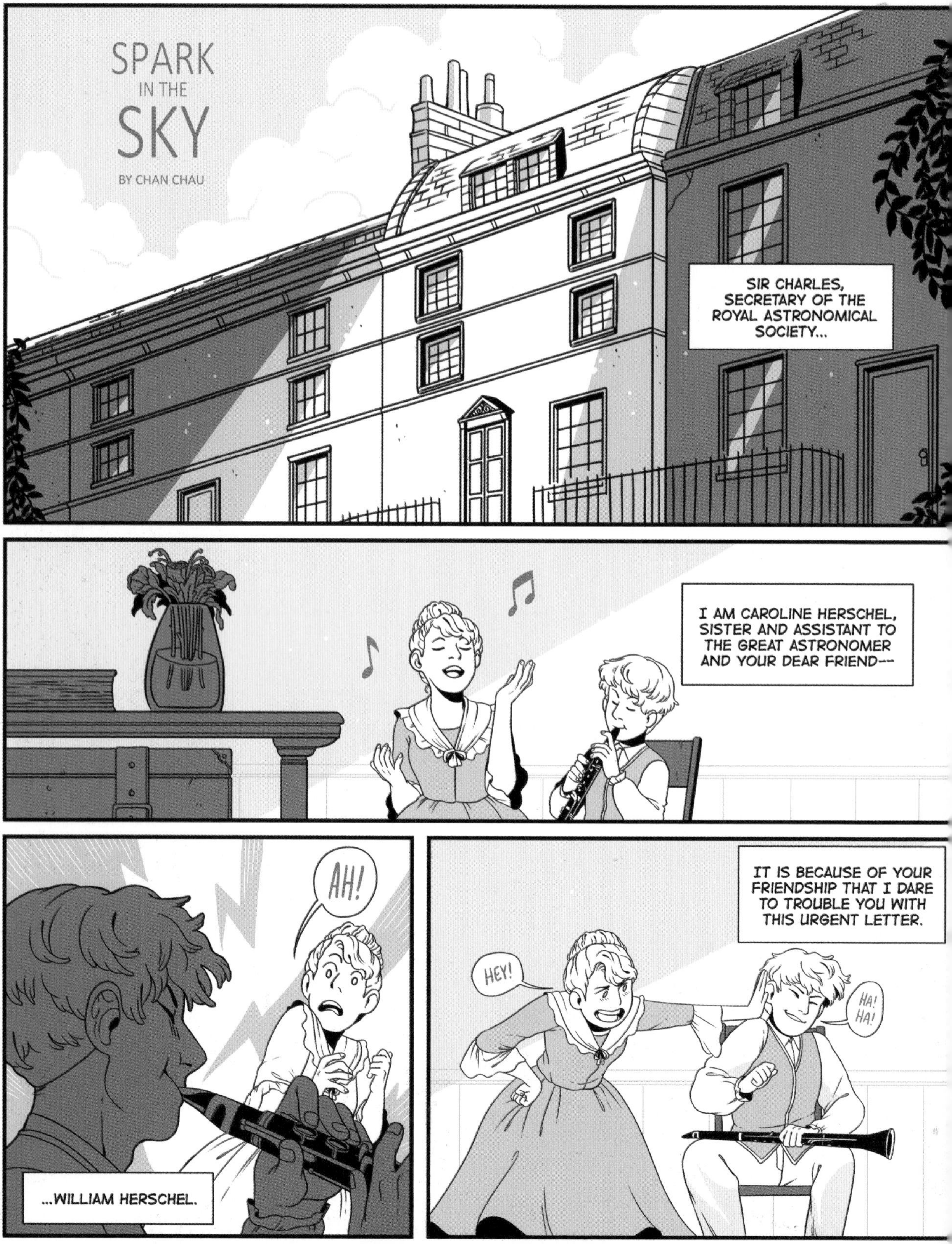
SPARK IN THE SKY
BY CHAN CHAU
SIR CHARLES, SECRETARY OF THE ROYAL ASTRONOMICAL SOCIETY...
I AM CAROLINE HERSCHEL, SISTER AND ASSISTANT TO THE GREAT ASTRONOMER AND YOUR DEAR FRIEND--
AH!
...WILLIAM HERSCHEL.
IT IS BECAUSE OF YOUR FRIENDSHIP THAT I DARE TO TROUBLE YOU WITH THIS URGENT LETTER.
HEY!
HA! HA!

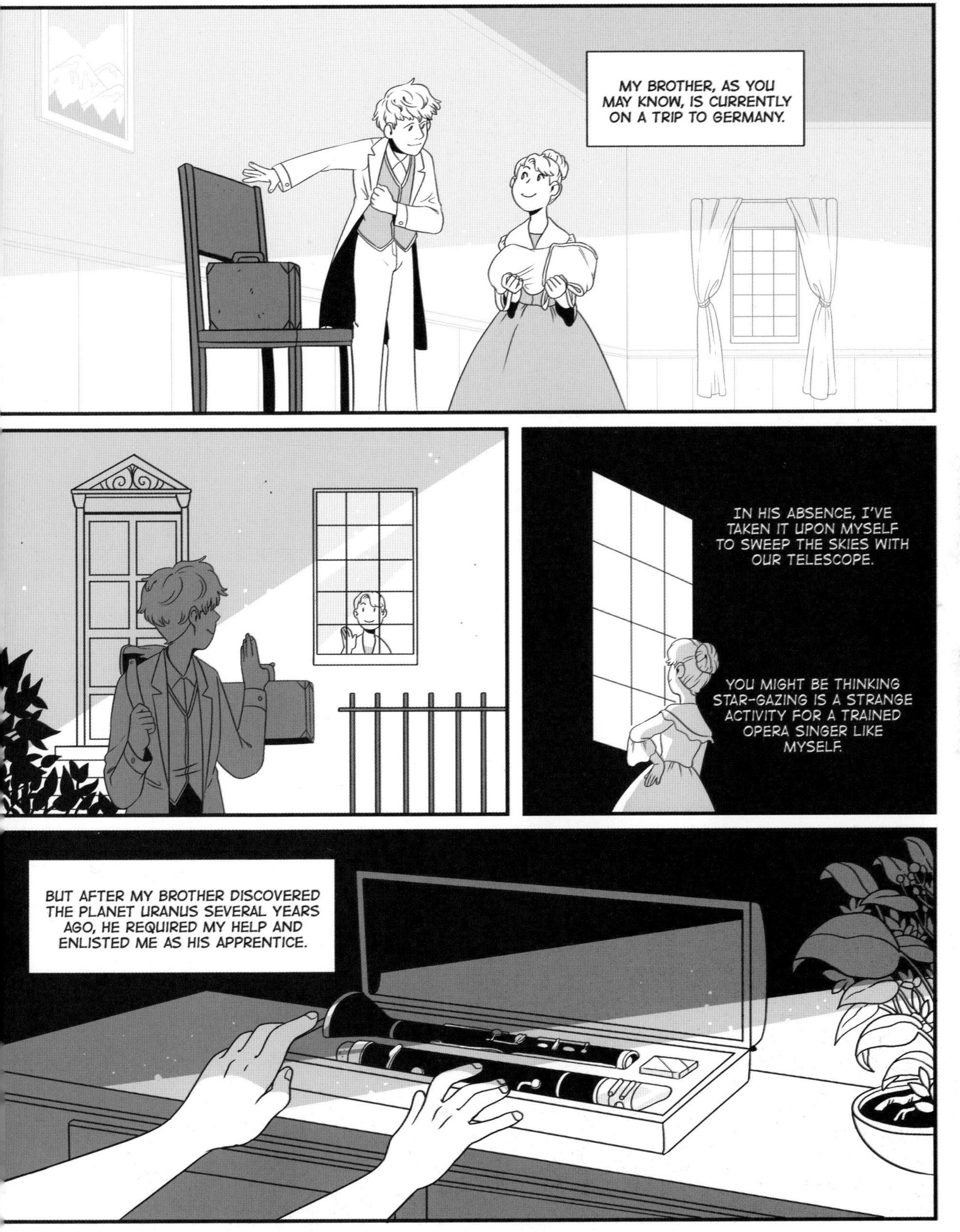
MY BROTHER, AS YOU MAY KNOW, IS CURRENTLY ON A TRIP TO GERMANY.
IN HIS ABSENCE, I'VE TAKEN IT UPON MYSELF TO SWEEP THE SKIES WITH OUR TELESCOPE.
YOU MIGHT BE THINKING STAR-GAZING IS A STRANGE ACTIVITY FOR A TRAINED OPERA SINGER LIKE MYSELF.
BUT AFTER MY BROTHER DISCOVERED THE PLANET URANUS SEVERAL YEARS AGO, HE REQUIRED MY HELP AND ENLISTED ME AS HIS APPRENTICE.

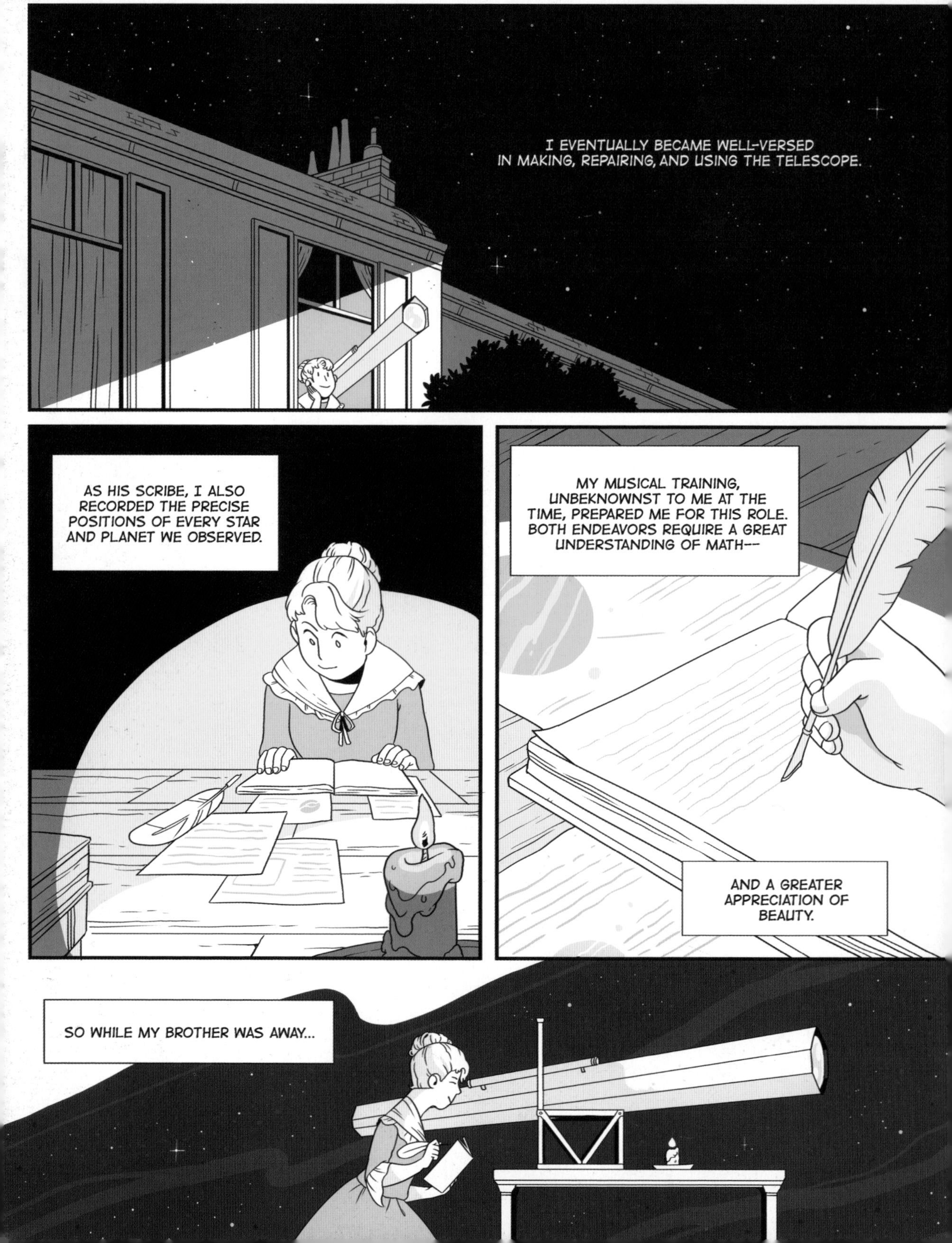
I EVENTUALLY BECAME WELL-VERSED IN MAKING, REPAIRING, AND USING THE TELESCOPE.
AS HIS SCRIBE, I ALSO RECORDED THE PRECISE POSITIONS OF EVERY STAR AND PLANET WE OBSERVED.
MY MUSICAL TRAINING, UNBEKNOWNST TO ME AT THE TIME, PREPARED ME FOR THIS ROLE. BOTH ENDEAVORS REQUIRE A GREAT UNDERSTANDING OF MATH--
AND A GREATER APPRECIATION OF BEAUTY.
SO WHILE MY BROTHER WAS AWAY...

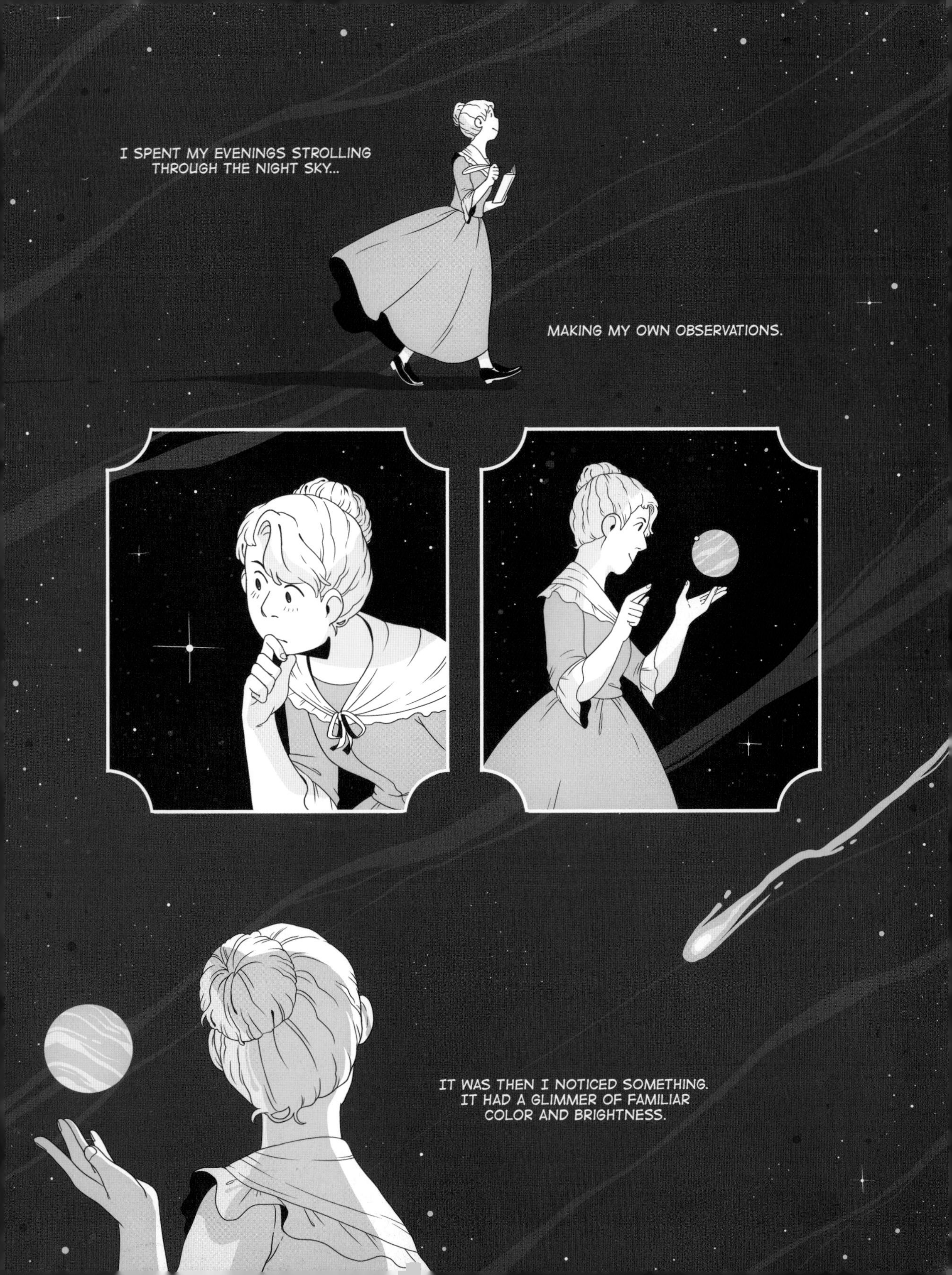
I SPENT MY EVENINGS STROLLING THROUGH THE NIGHT SKY...
MAKING MY OWN OBSERVATIONS.
IT WAS THEN I NOTICED SOMETHING. IT HAD A GLIMMER OF FAMILIAR COLOR AND BRIGHTNESS.

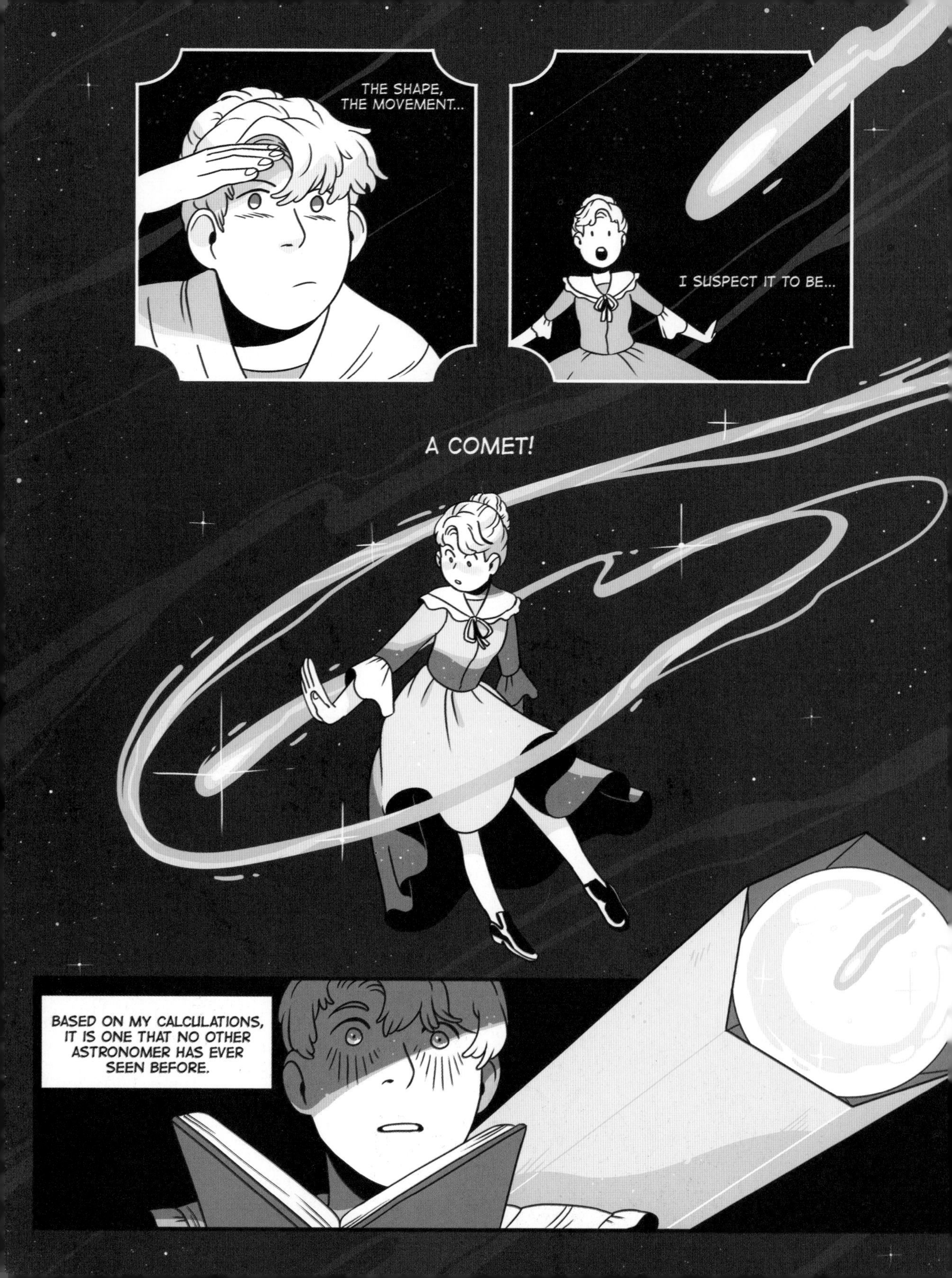
THE SHAPE, THE MOVEMENT...
I SUSPECT IT TO BE...
A COMET!
BASED ON MY CALCULATIONS, IT IS ONE THAT NO OTHER ASTRONOMER HAS EVER SEEN BEFORE.

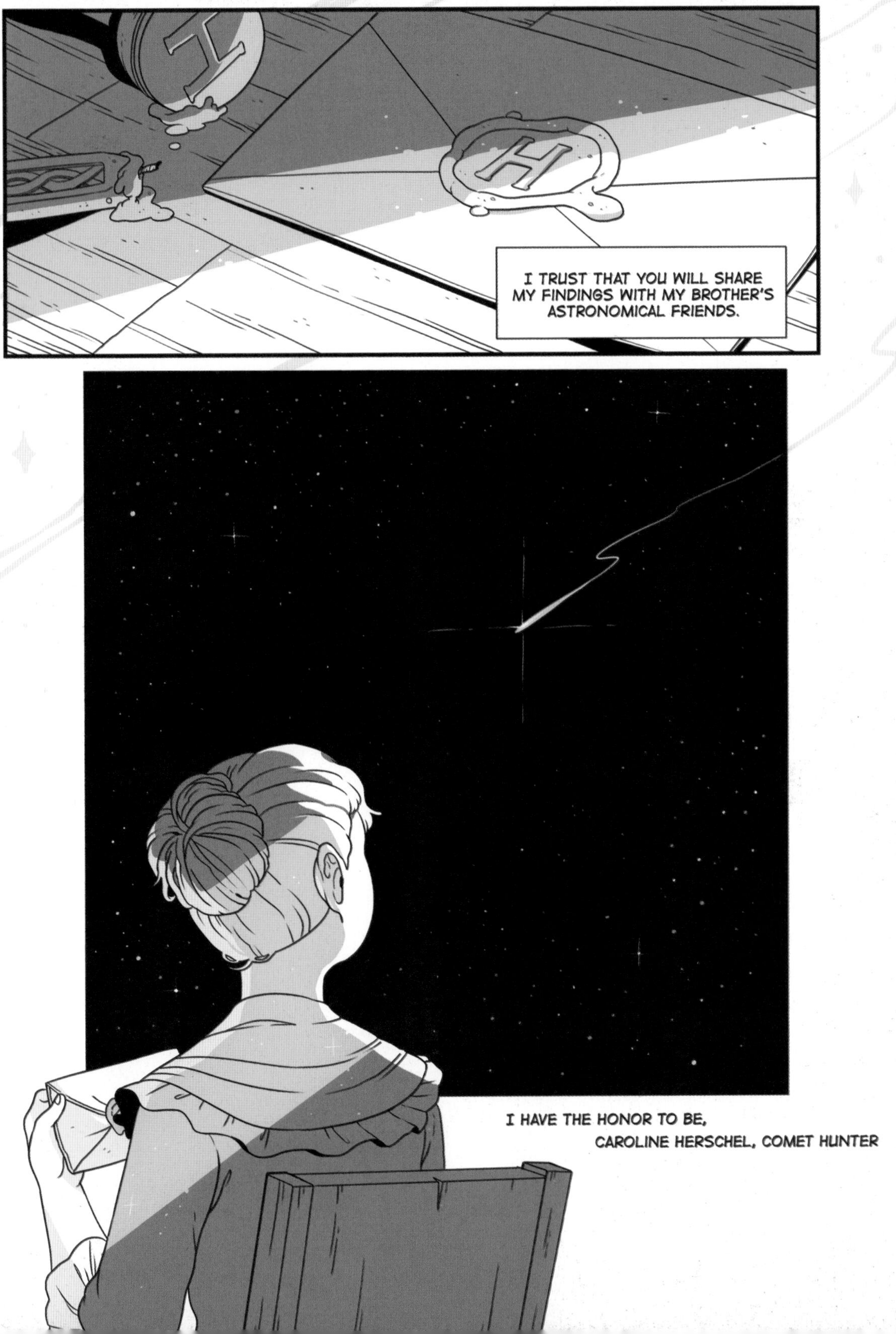
I TRUST THAT YOU WILL SHARE MY FINDINGS WITH MY BROTHER'S ASTRONOMICAL FRIENDS.
I HAVE THE HONOR TO BE,
CAROLINE HERSCHEL, COMET HUNTER

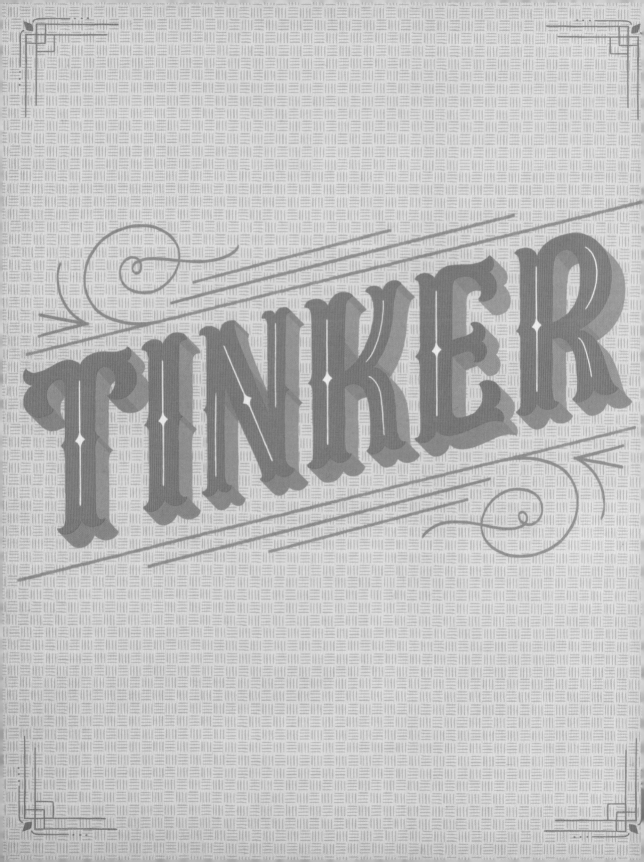

TINKER

Creativity and courage—that's what fuels the minds of great inventors. When faced with a problem, they not only dream up a solution that no one has ever imagined before, but they also then figure out how to bring that dream to life. The four great tinkerers in this chapter have used every tool at their disposal—rock, wood, wires, computers, beeswax, even the scrolls inside player pianos—to build new things to make our lives easier, safer, and more beautiful. What will you invent? Let these fascinating stories get your wheels turning.

The BRIDGE Builder

•••••

EMILY WARREN ROEBLING

1843 ~ 1903

It was NEVER supposed to be her bridge to build, but after its first two chief engineers (her father-in-law and her husband) couldn't finish the job, Emily Warren Roebling took over and got it done. The Brooklyn Bridge was an engineering marvel, and it's thanks to Emily's bravery—and her brain—that it remains one of America's greatest landmarks today.

EMILY AND ME

COUNT ALL THE THINGS YOU HAVE IN COMMON WITH EMILY WARREN ROEBLING.

- I love building things.
- I think math is fun and interesting.
- I like to keep things organized.
- I don't get discouraged when people tell me I can't do something.
- What I start, I finish.
- I know that just because something hasn't been done before doesn't mean it can't be done.
- I prefer bridges to walls.
- I have faith in the work I do.
- I'm a natural leader.
- I'm determined.

EMILY and the BRIDGE

by kiku hughes

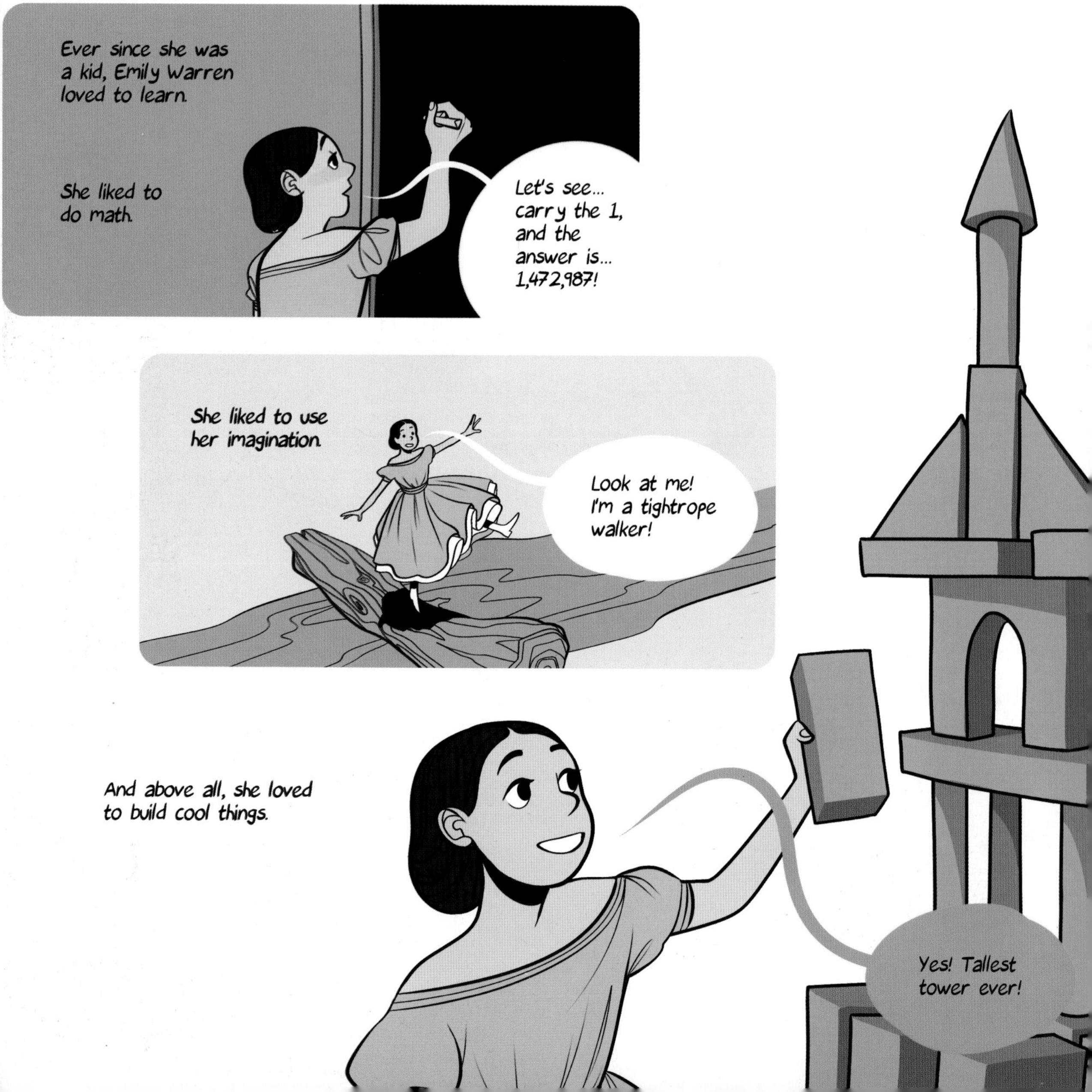

Ever since she was a kid, Emily Warren loved to learn.
She liked to do math.
Let's see... carry the 1, and the answer is... 1,472,987!
She liked to use her imagination.
Look at me! I'm a tightrope walker!
And above all, she loved to build cool things.
Yes! Tallest tower ever!

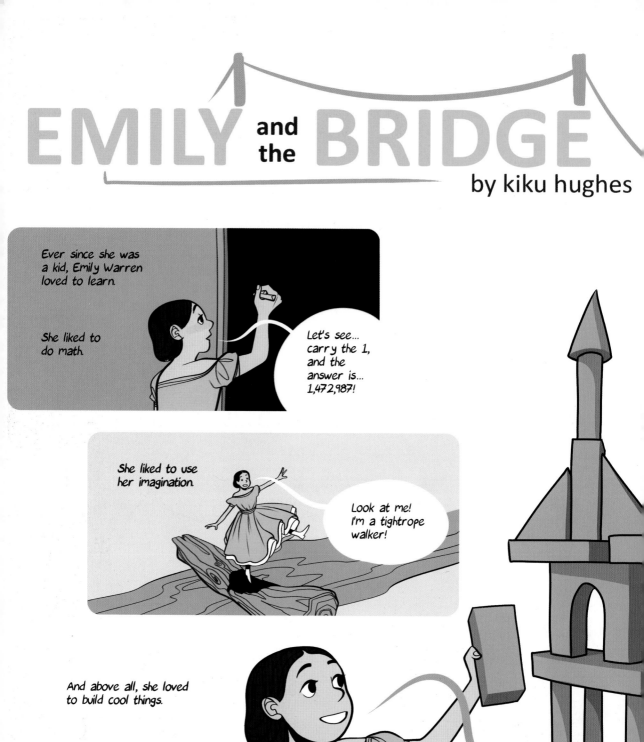

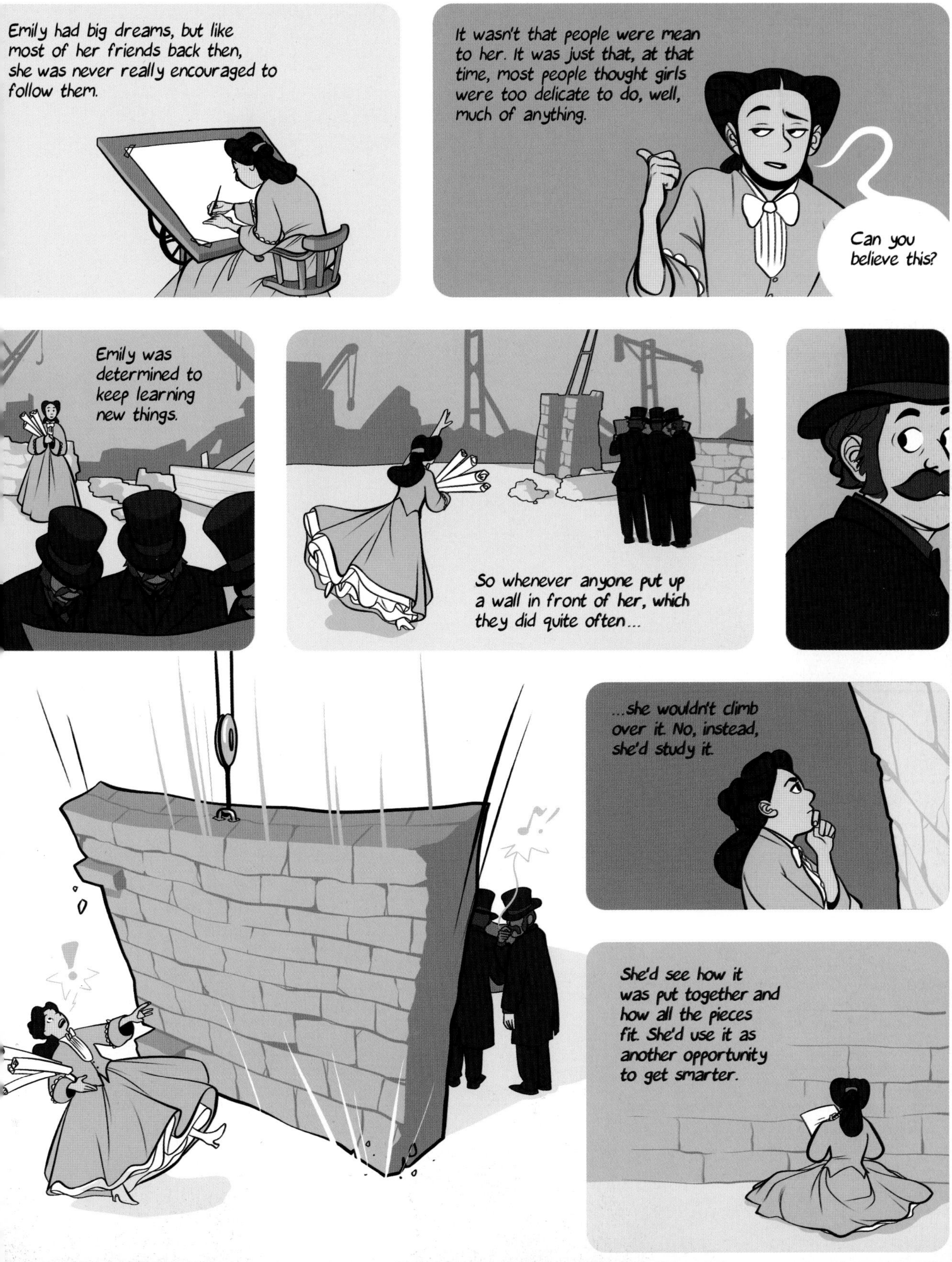

Emily had big dreams, but like most of her friends back then, she was never really encouraged to follow them.
It wasn't that people were mean to her. It was just that, at that time, most people thought girls were too delicate to do, well, much of anything.
Can you believe this?
Emily was determined to keep learning new things.
So whenever anyone put up a wall in front of her, which they did quite often...
...she wouldn't climb over it. No, instead, she'd study it.
She'd see how it was put together and how all the pieces fit. She'd use it as another opportunity to get smarter.

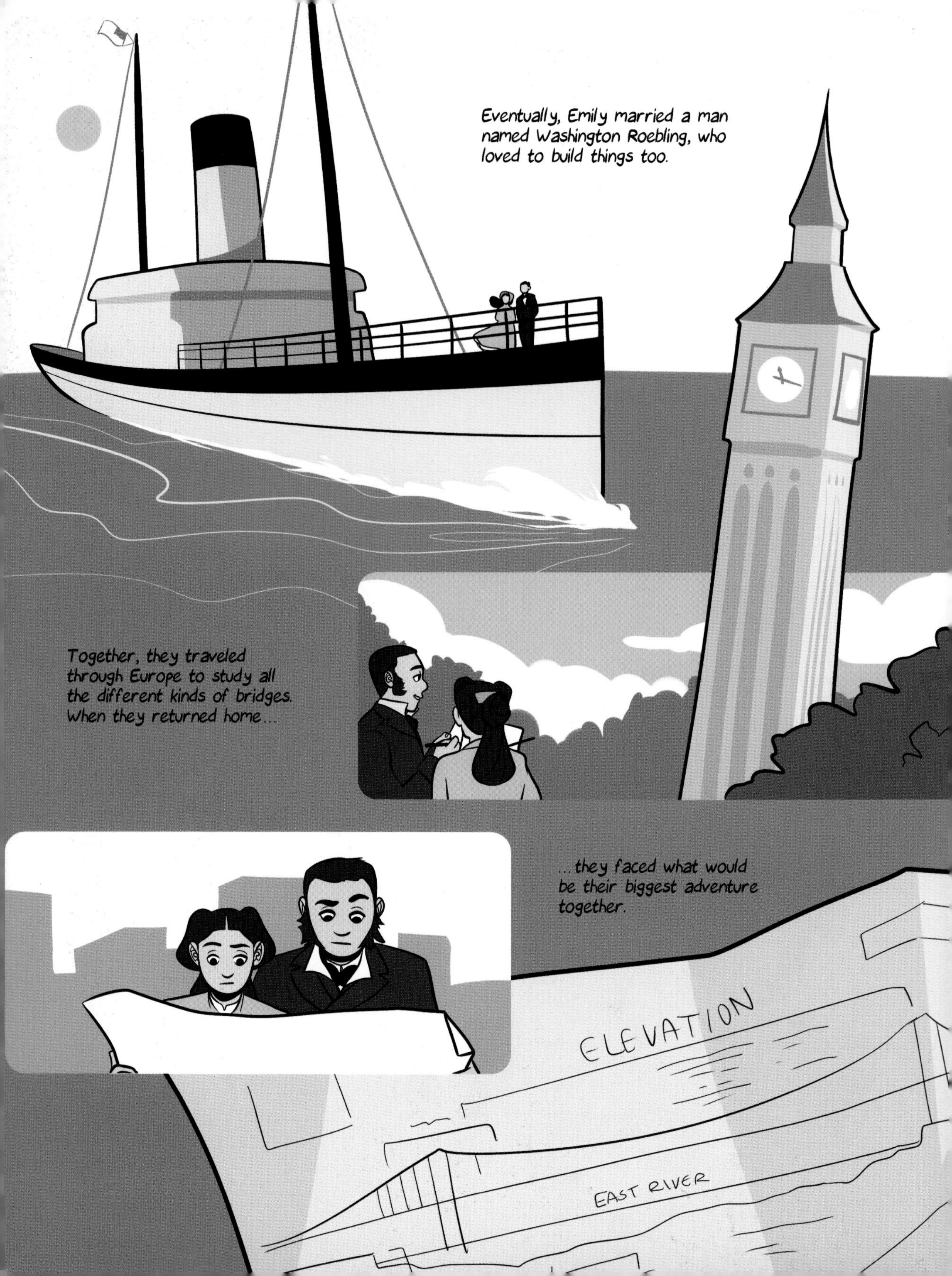
Eventually, Emily married a man named Washington Roebling, who loved to build things too.
Together, they traveled through Europe to study all the different kinds of bridges. When they returned home...
...they faced what would be their biggest adventure together.
ELEVATION
EAST RIVER

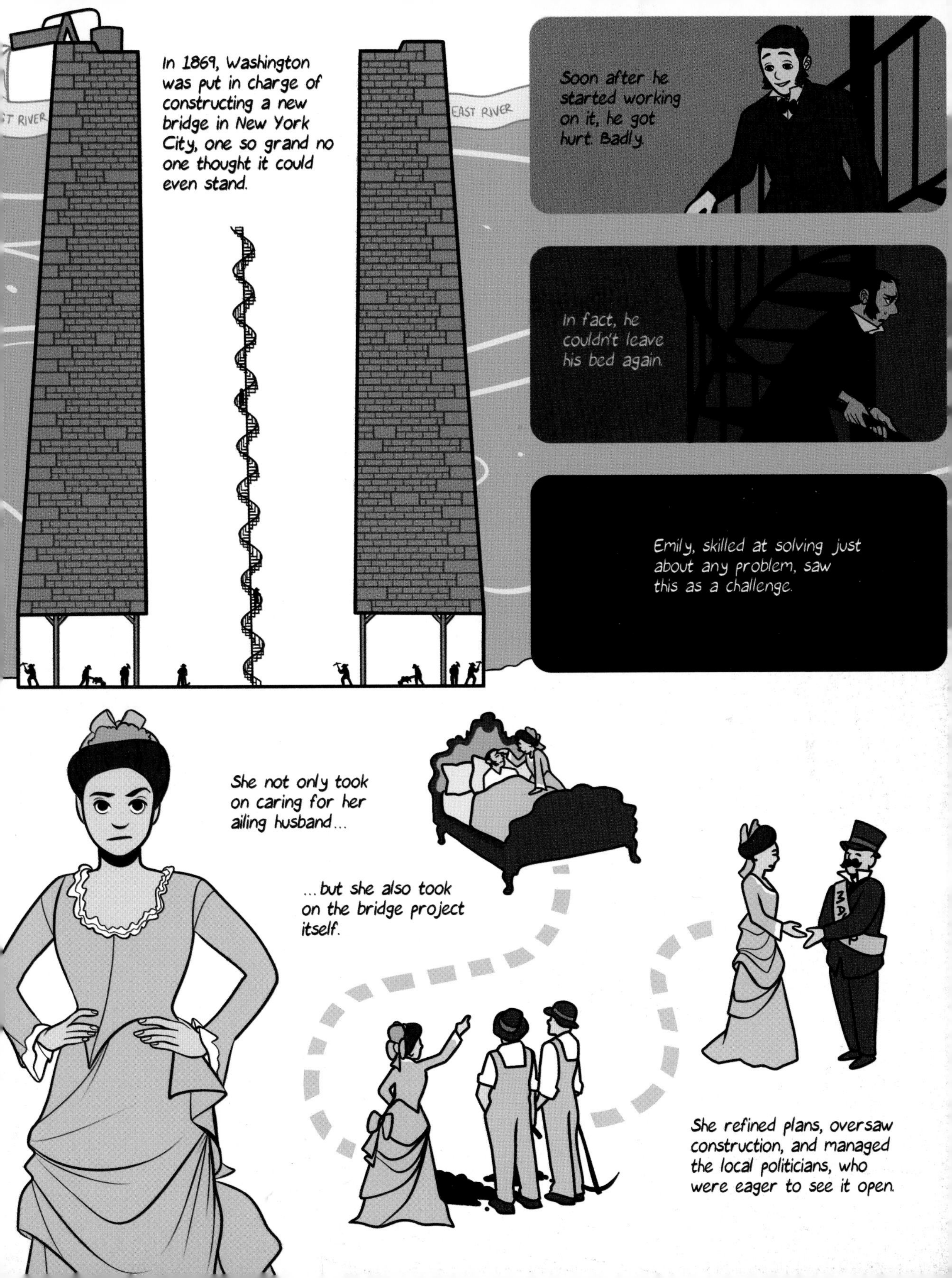

In 1869, Washington was put in charge of constructing a new bridge in New York City, one so grand no one thought it could even stand.
EAST RIVER
Soon after he started working on it, he got hurt. Badly.
In fact, he couldn't leave his bed again.
Emily, skilled at solving just about any problem, saw this as a challenge.
She not only took on caring for her ailing husband...
...but she also took on the bridge project itself.
She refined plans, oversaw construction, and managed the local politicians, who were eager to see it open.

If anyone on the project doubted her at the start, she soon proved them wrong with her quick thinking and hard work.

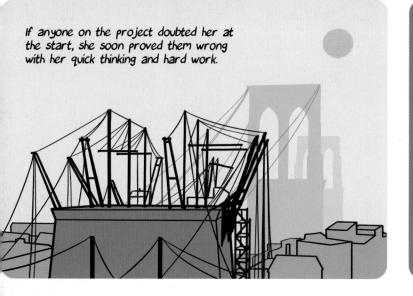

She won the respect and admiration of the engineers who worked for her.

And 11 years later, when the Brooklyn Bridge was finished...

...Emily was given the honor of being the first person to cross it.

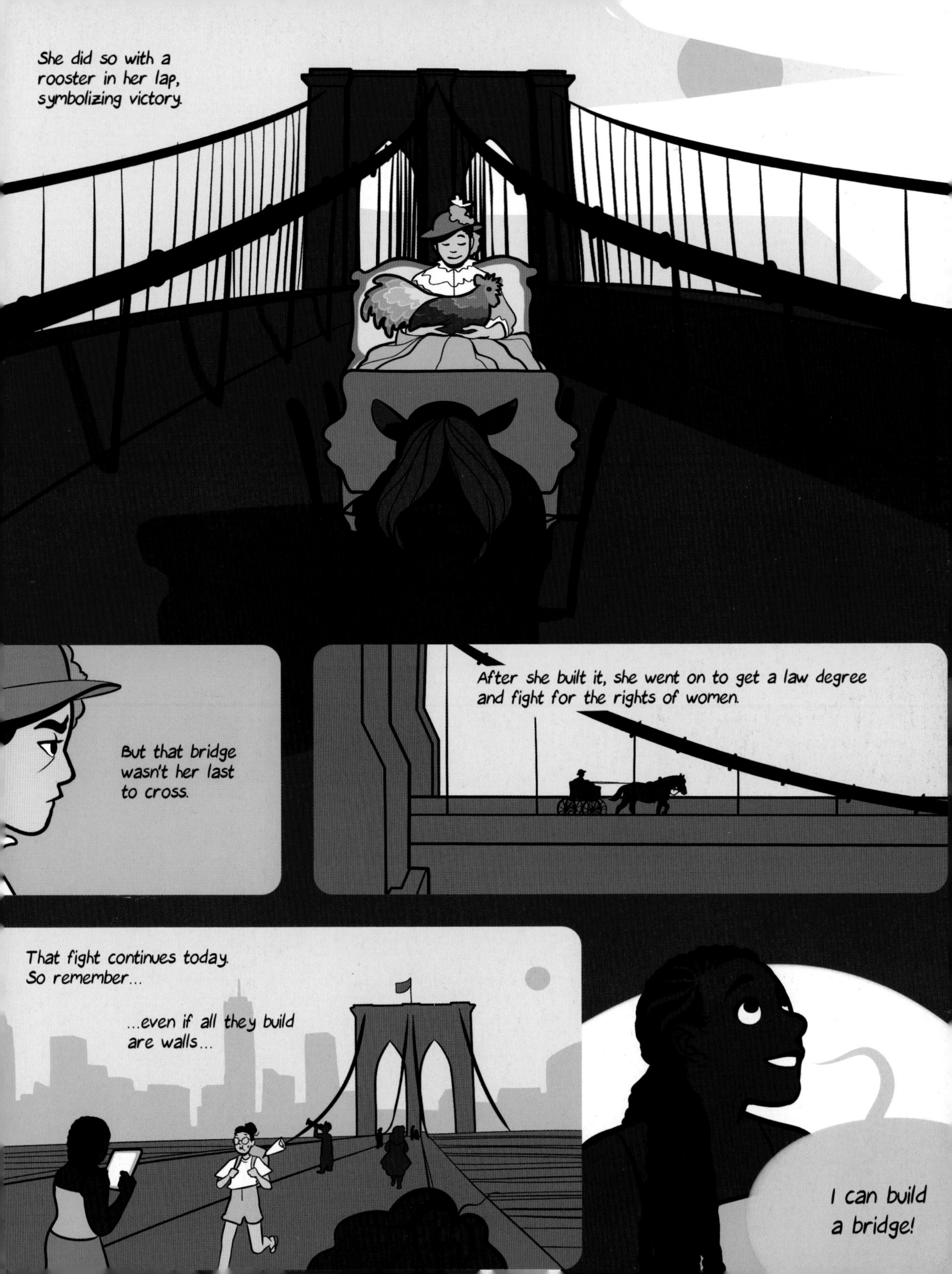
She did so with a rooster in her lap, symbolizing victory.
But that bridge wasn't her last to cross.
After she built it, she went on to get a law degree and fight for the rights of women.
That fight continues today. So remember...
...even if all they build are walls...
I can build a bridge!

THE SHIP DESIGNER
.....
RAYE MONTAGUE
1935~2018

From the moment she saw her first submarine, Raye Montague was fascinated by boats, and she was determined to build her own. She was told she'd never be allowed because she was African American and a girl, but she didn't give up. Raye became a brilliant engineer, and was the first person in history ever to design a ship using a computer. Oh, and she did it in less than nineteen hours.

RAYE AND ME

COUNT ALL THE THINGS YOU HAVE IN COMMON WITH RAYE MONTAGUE.

- I enjoy designing things and making them better.
- I'm a quick learner.
- If I watch very carefully, I can understand how things work.
- I love gadgets and gizmos and anything with moving parts.
- I know who I am, and what I'm capable of.
- When I see an opportunity, I take it.
- I want to learn everything I can about coding.
- If someone tells me I can't do something, I take that as a challenge.
- I'm patient.
- I'm driven.

Photo courtesy of David Montague

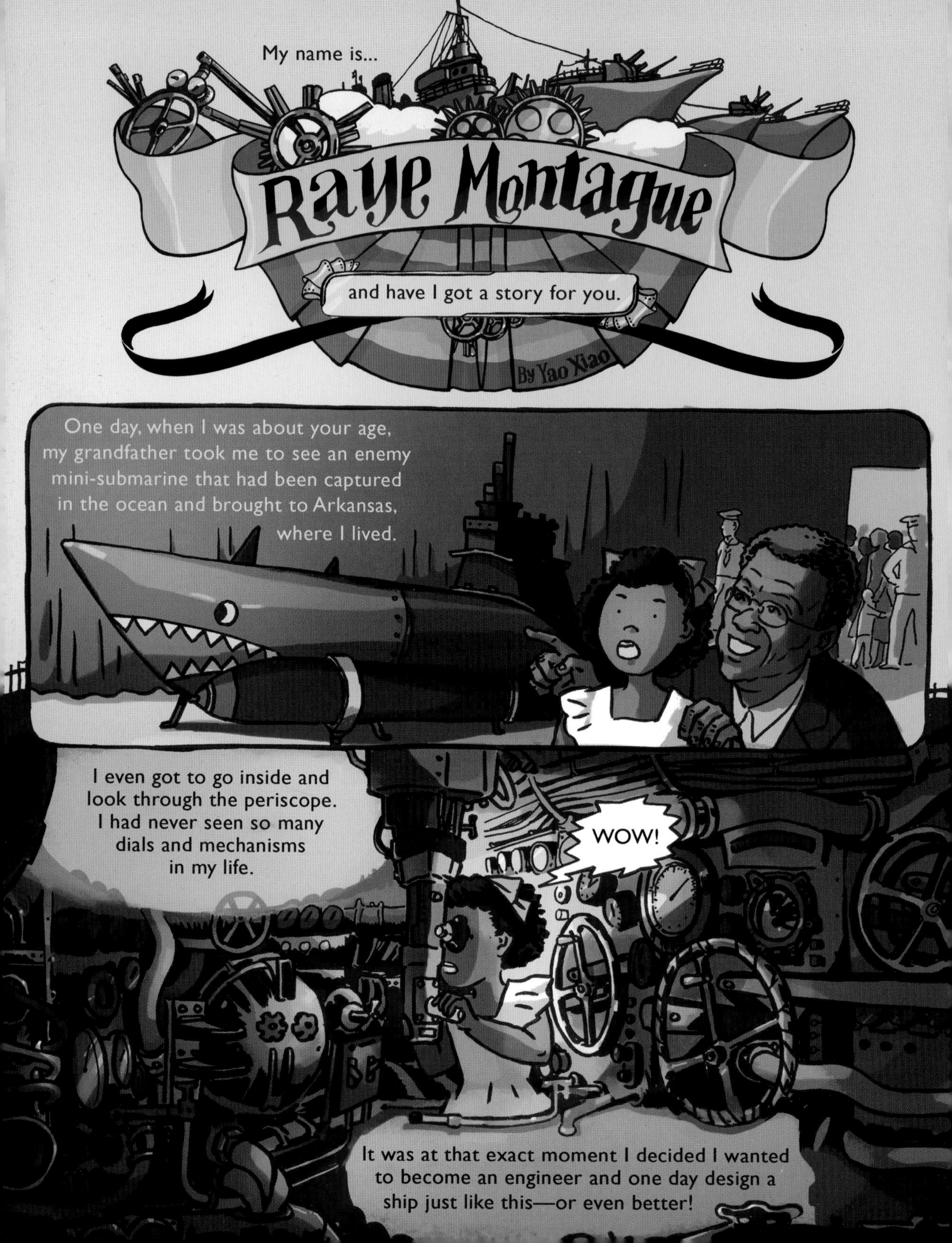
My name is...
Raye Montague
and have I got a story for you.
By Yao Xiao
One day, when I was about your age, my grandfather took me to see an enemy mini-submarine that had been captured in the ocean and brought to Arkansas, where I lived.
I even got to go inside and look through the periscope. I had never seen so many dials and mechanisms in my life.
WOW!
It was at that exact moment I decided I wanted to become an engineer and one day design a ship just like this—or even better!

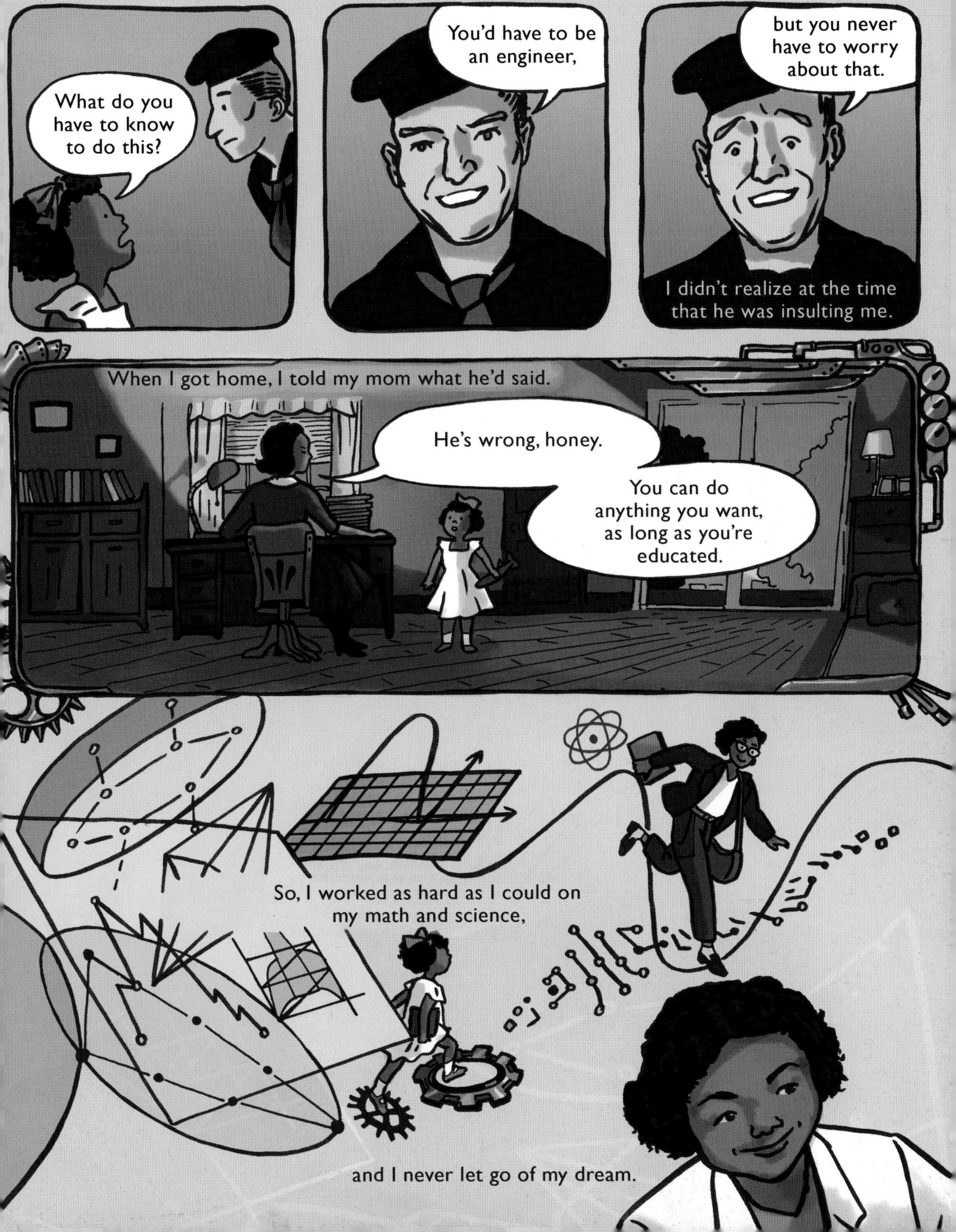

What do you have to know to do this?
You'd have to be an engineer,
but you never have to worry about that.
I didn't realize at the time that he was insulting me.
When I got home, I told my mom what he'd said.
He's wrong, honey.
You can do anything you want, as long as you're educated.
So, I worked as hard as I could on my math and science,
and I never let go of my dream.

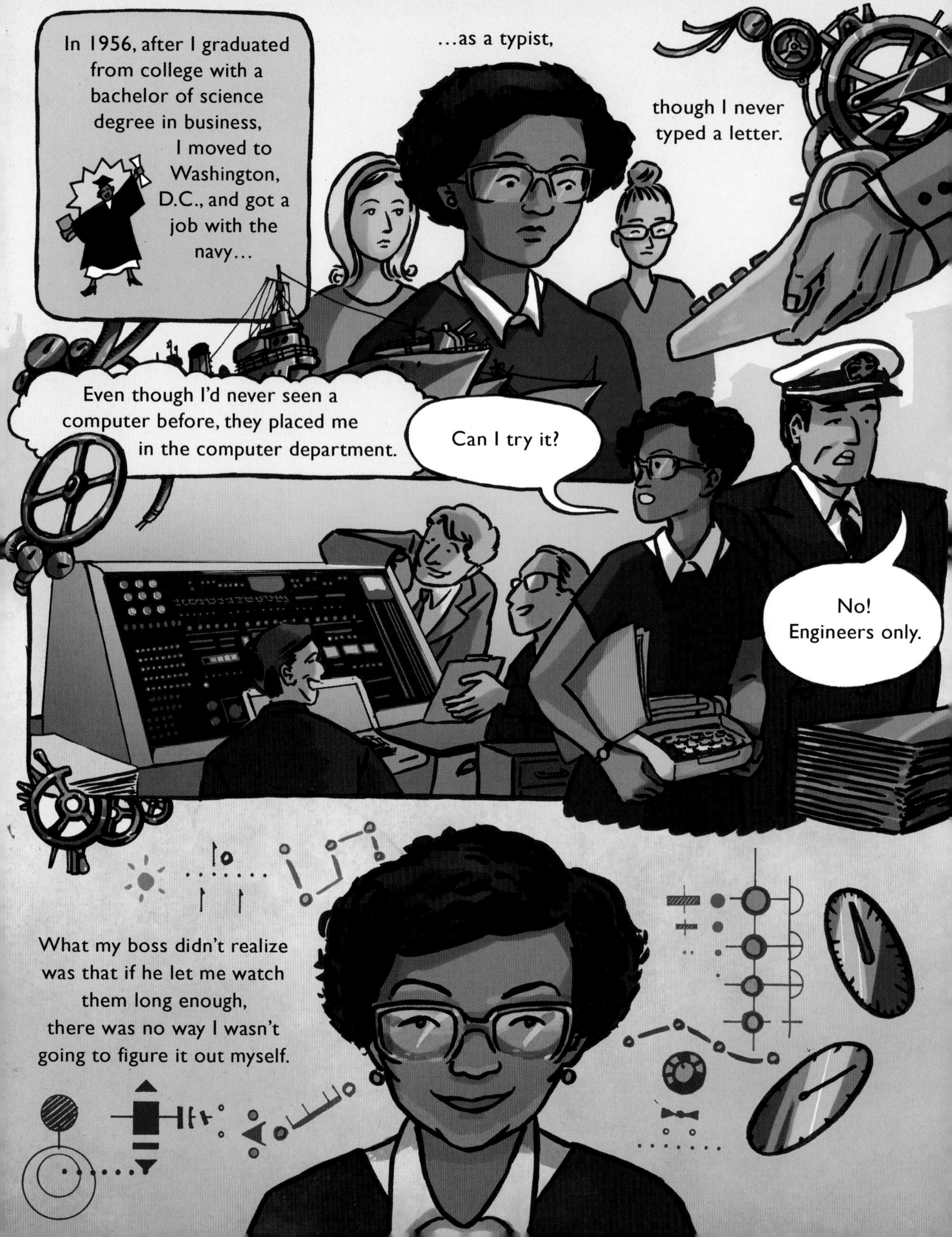
In 1956, after I graduated from college with a bachelor of science degree in business, I moved to Washington, D.C., and got a job with the navy...
...as a typist,
though I never typed a letter.
Even though I'd never seen a computer before, they placed me in the computer department.
Can I try it?
No! Engineers only.
What my boss didn't realize was that if he let me watch them long enough, there was no way I wasn't going to figure it out myself.

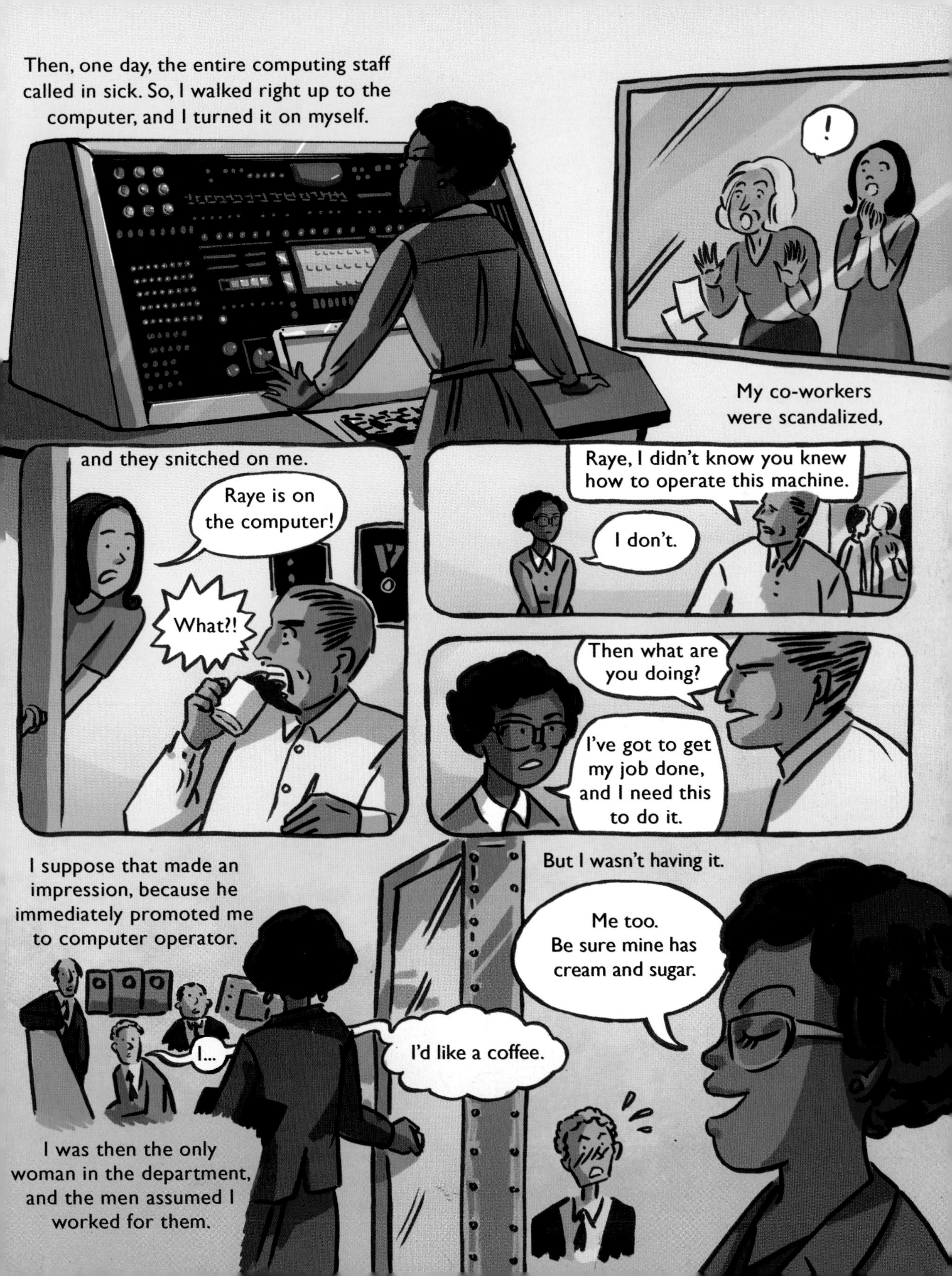
Then, one day, the entire computing staff called in sick. So, I walked right up to the computer, and I turned it on myself.
!
My co-workers were scandalized,
and they snitched on me.
Raye is on the computer!
What?!
Raye, I didn't know you knew how to operate this machine.
I don't.
Then what are you doing?
I've got to get my job done, and I need this to do it.
I suppose that made an impression, because he immediately promoted me to computer operator.
I was then the only woman in the department, and the men assumed I worked for them.
I...
I'd like a coffee.
Me too. Be sure mine has cream and sugar.
But I wasn't having it.

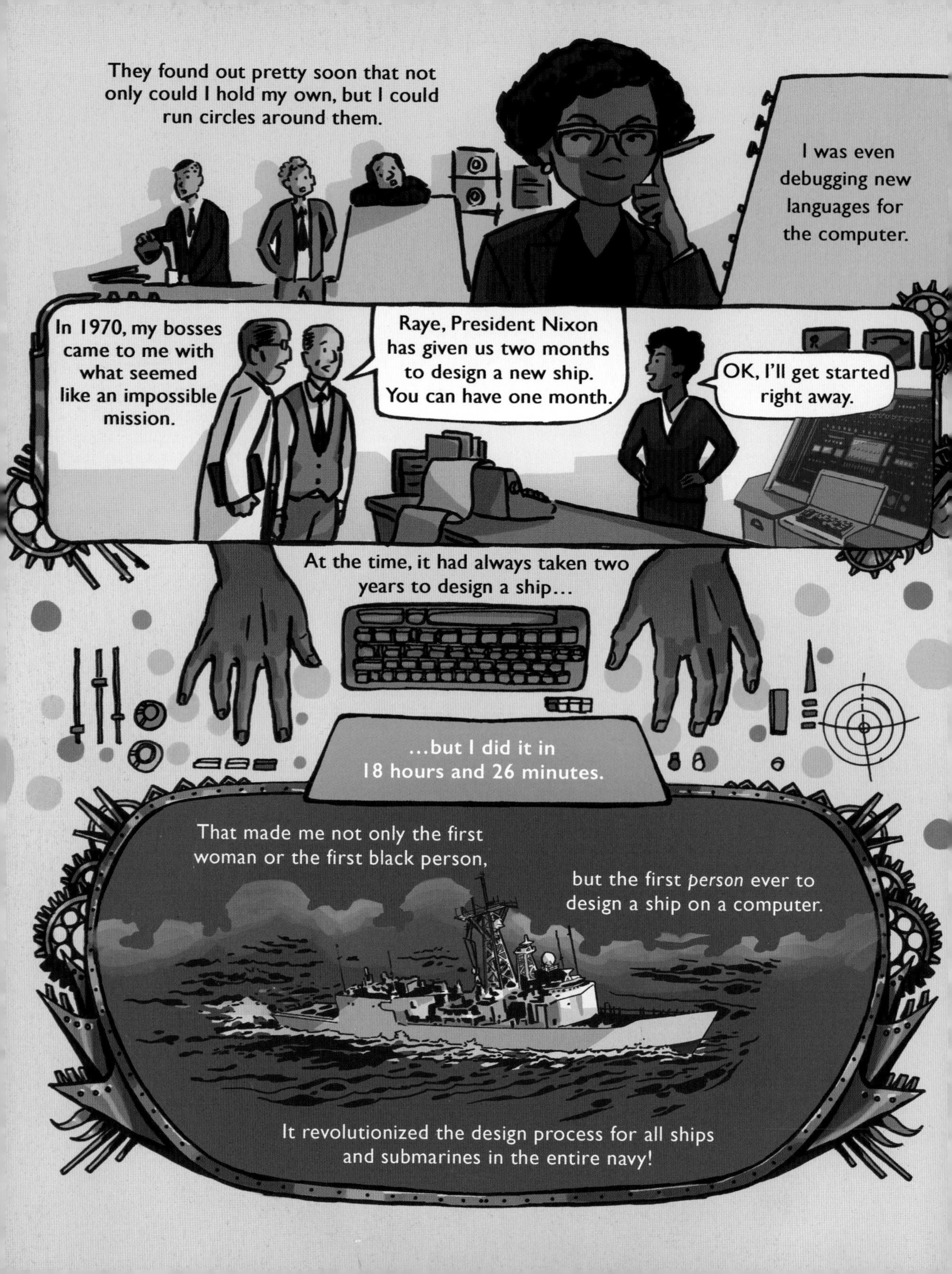

They found out pretty soon that not only could I hold my own, but I could run circles around them.
I was even debugging new languages for the computer.
In 1970, my bosses came to me with what seemed like an impossible mission.
Raye, President Nixon has given us two months to design a new ship. You can have one month.
OK, I'll get started right away.
At the time, it had always taken two years to design a ship…
…but I did it in 18 hours and 26 minutes.
That made me not only the first woman or the first black person,
but the first *person* ever to design a ship on a computer.
It revolutionized the design process for all ships and submarines in the entire navy!

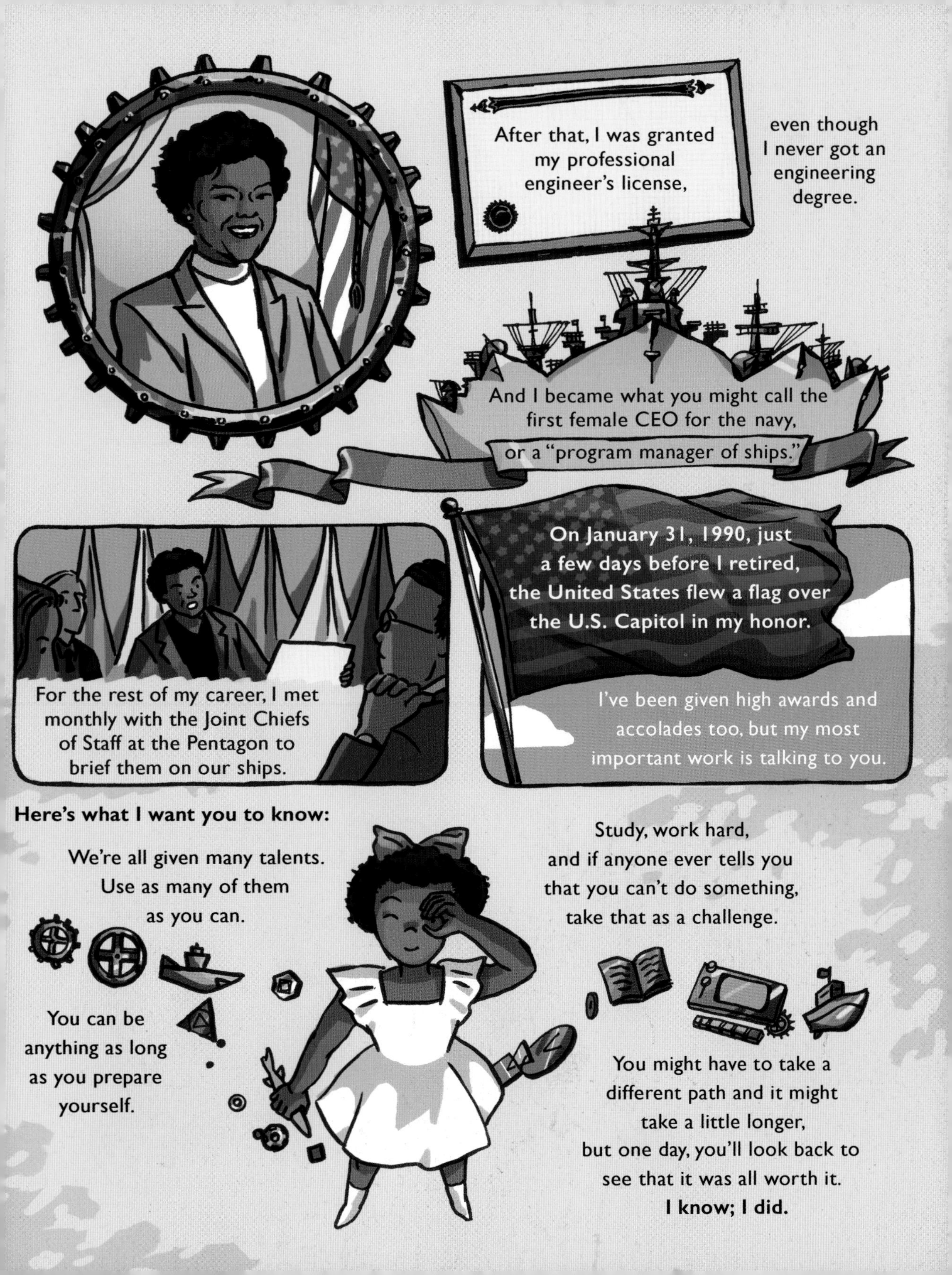

After that, I was granted my professional engineer's license,
even though I never got an engineering degree.
And I became what you might call the first female CEO for the navy, or a "program manager of ships."
For the rest of my career, I met monthly with the Joint Chiefs of Staff at the Pentagon to brief them on our ships.
On January 31, 1990, just a few days before I retired, the United States flew a flag over the U.S. Capitol in my honor.
I've been given high awards and accolades too, but my most important work is talking to you.
Here's what I want you to know:
We're all given many talents. Use as many of them as you can.
You can be anything as long as you prepare yourself.
Study, work hard, and if anyone ever tells you that you can't do something, take that as a challenge.
You might have to take a different path and it might take a little longer, but one day, you'll look back to see that it was all worth it.
I know; I did.

The STAR INVENTOR

· · · · ·

HEDY LAMARR

1914 ~ 2000

If you've ever doubted that you could be two things at once—an athlete *and* a musician, an artist *and* a scientist, a chef *and* an explorer—then let Hedy Lamarr inspire you. She was not only one of Hollywood's most celebrated stars but also a dazzling inventor. She's proof that no matter what others expect of you, you can be and do *everything* your heart desires.

HEDY AND ME

COUNT ALL THE THINGS YOU HAVE IN COMMON WITH HEDY LAMARR.

- I love watching movies—and making them too.
- I like to play dress-up.
- I love thinking up new inventions.
- Even in my sleep, I dream about what I could make.
- Some stuff I've made has worked, some hasn't, but I'll never stop building.
- I like to share my ideas with my friends.
- I want to be known for what I do, not just how I look.
- I want to be useful.
- I'm a problem-solver.
- I'm a star.

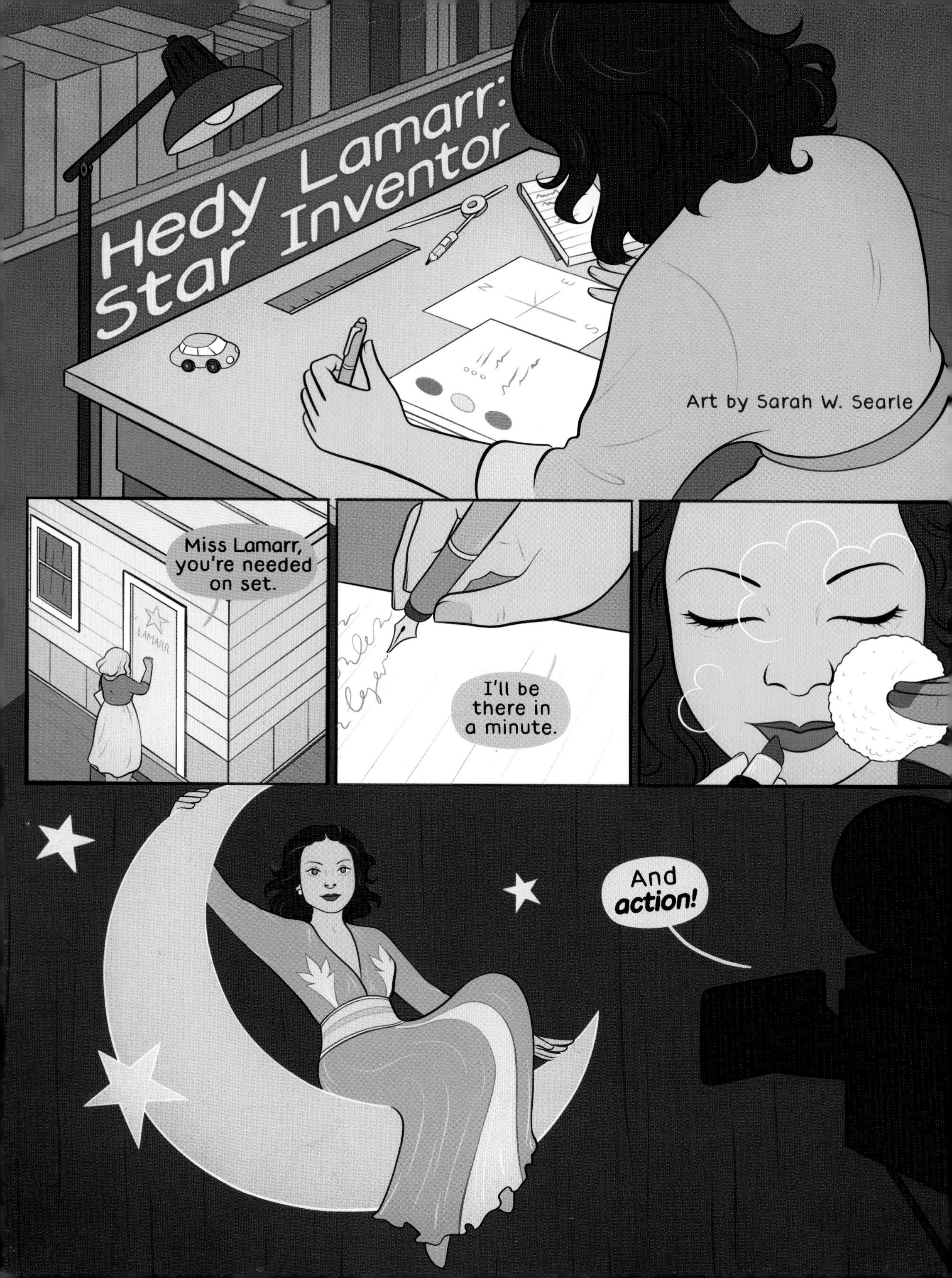
Hedy Lamarr: Star Inventor
Art by Sarah W. Searle
LAMARR
Miss Lamarr, you're needed on set.
I'll be there in a minute.
And action!

Hedy Lamarr was one of the most famous movie stars in the world, and ever since she was a kid growing up in Austria, she wanted to know how everything worked.

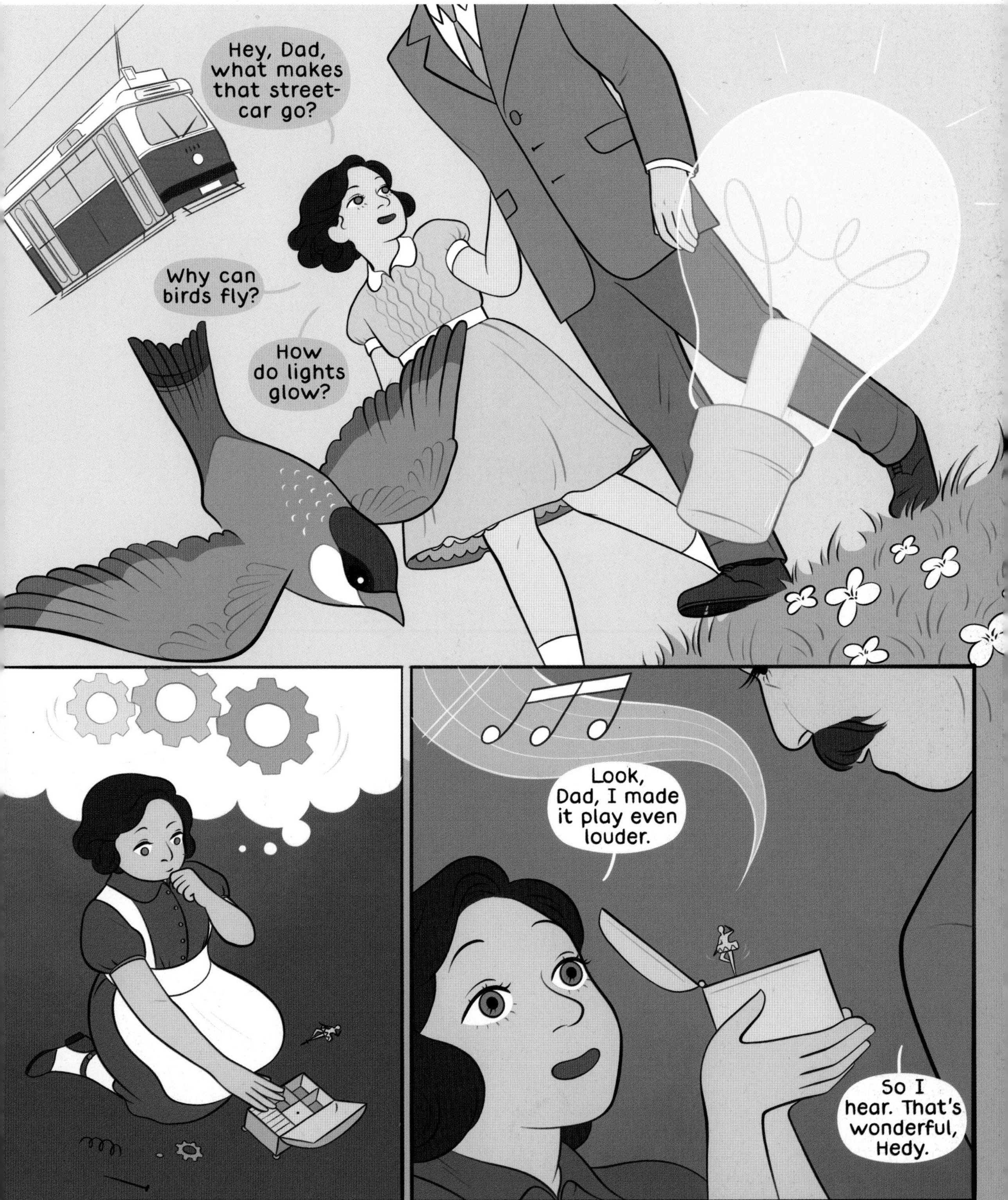
Hey, Dad, what makes that street-car go?
Why can birds fly?
How do lights glow?
Look, Dad, I made it play even louder.
So I hear. That's wonderful, Hedy.

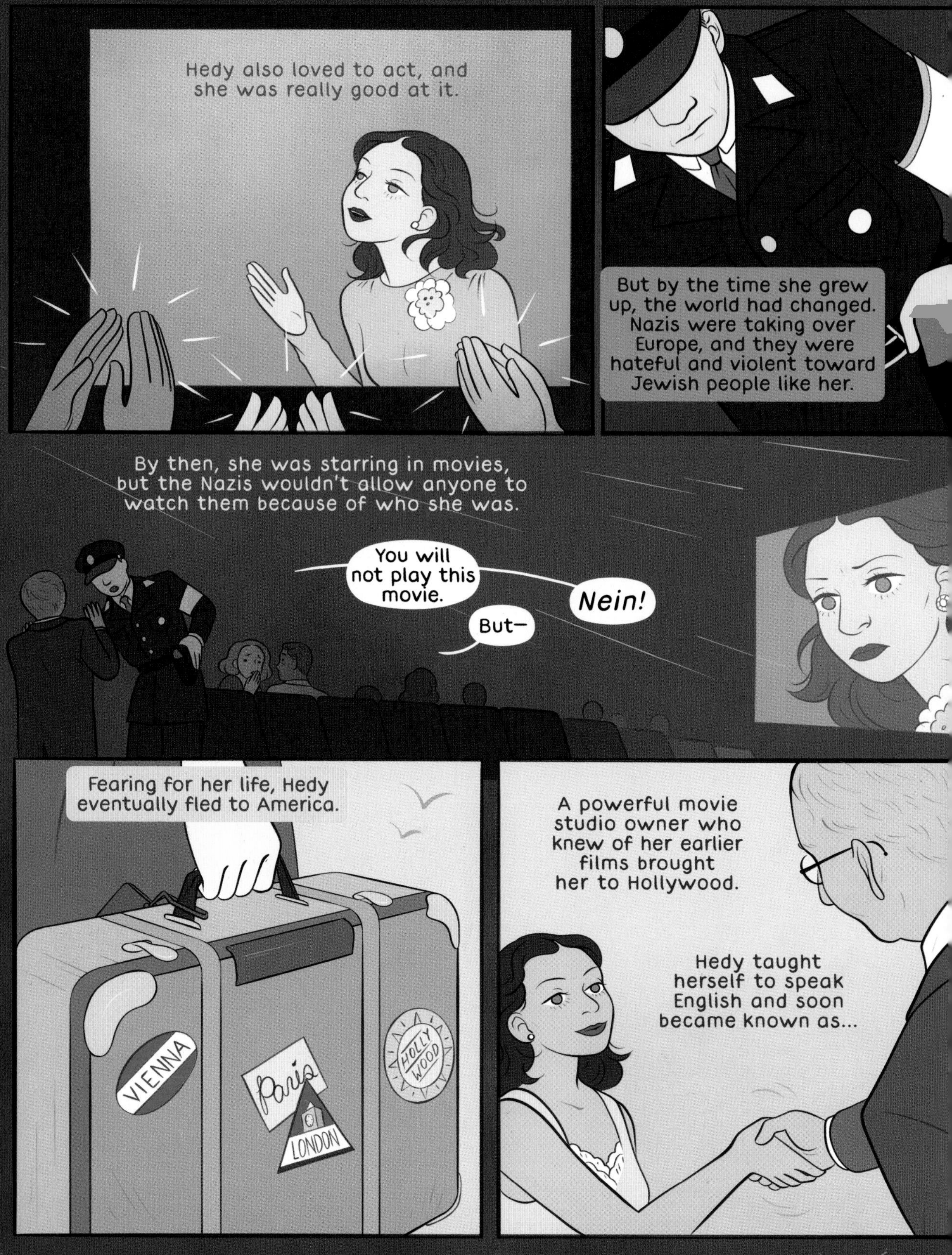
Hedy also loved to act, and she was really good at it.
But by the time she grew up, the world had changed. Nazis were taking over Europe, and they were hateful and violent toward Jewish people like her.
By then, she was starring in movies, but the Nazis wouldn't allow anyone to watch them because of who she was.
You will not play this movie.
But—
Nein!
Fearing for her life, Hedy eventually fled to America.
VIENNA
Paris
LONDON
HOLLYWOOD
A powerful movie studio owner who knew of her earlier films brought her to Hollywood.
Hedy taught herself to speak English and soon became known as...

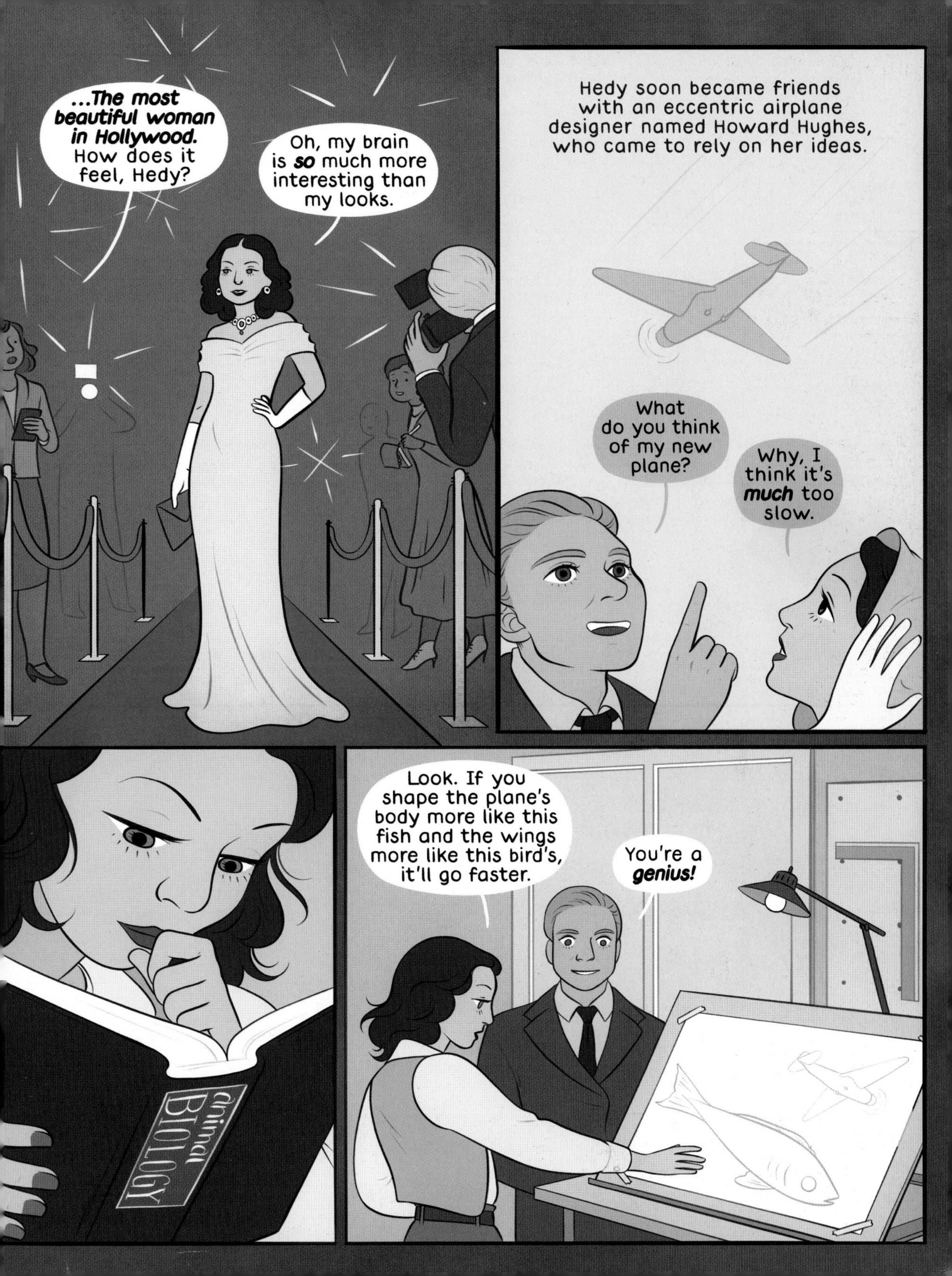
...The most beautiful woman in Hollywood. How does it feel, Hedy?
Oh, my brain is so much more interesting than my looks.
Hedy soon became friends with an eccentric airplane designer named Howard Hughes, who came to rely on her ideas.
What do you think of my new plane?
Why, I think it's much too slow.
animal BIOLOGY
Look. If you shape the plane's body more like this fish and the wings more like this bird's, it'll go faster.
You're a genius!

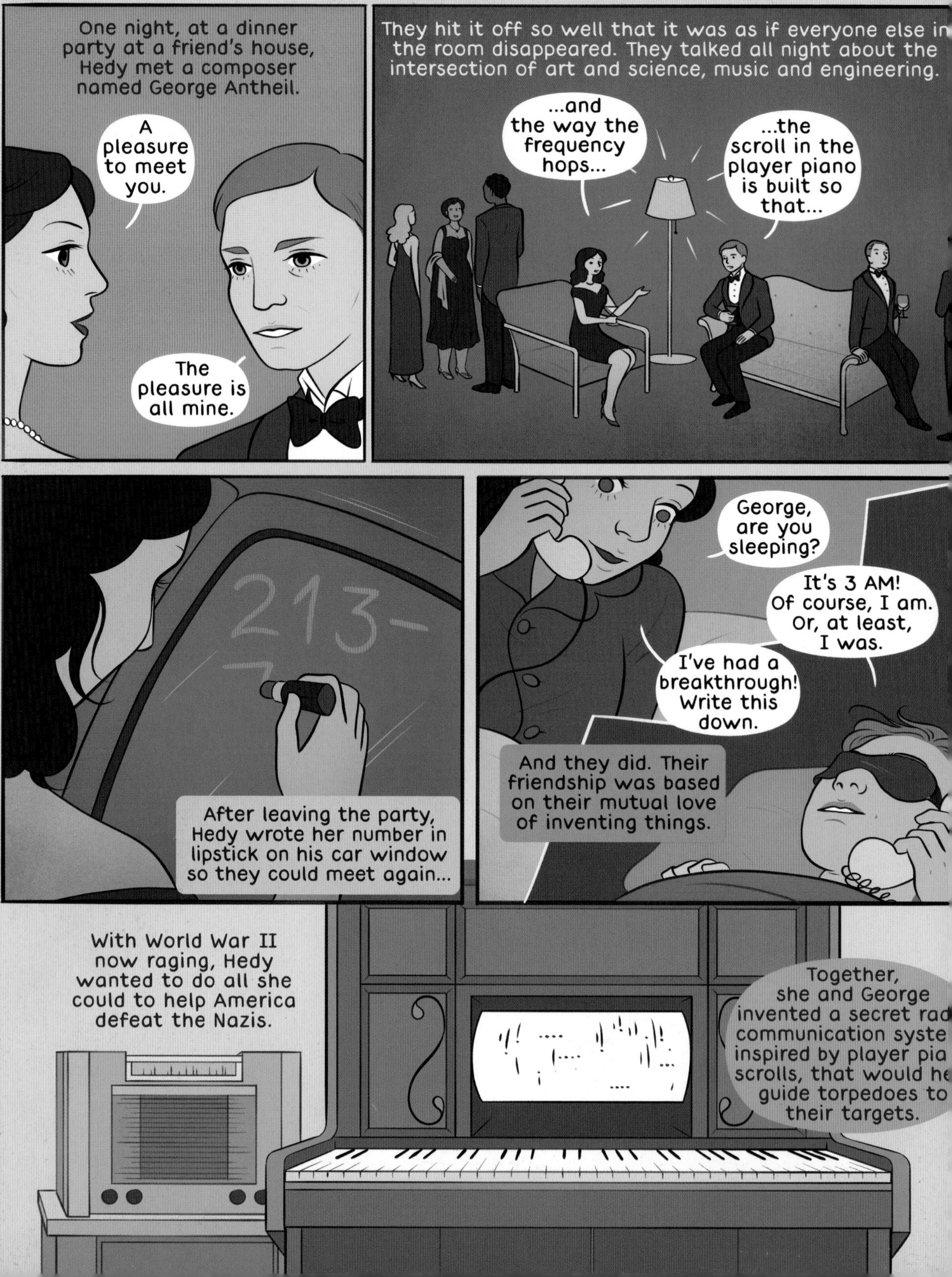
One night, at a dinner party at a friend's house, Hedy met a composer named George Antheil.
A pleasure to meet you.
The pleasure is all mine.
They hit it off so well that it was as if everyone else in the room disappeared. They talked all night about the intersection of art and science, music and engineering.
...and the way the frequency hops...
...the scroll in the player piano is built so that...
213-
After leaving the party, Hedy wrote her number in lipstick on his car window so they could meet again...
George, are you sleeping?
It's 3 AM! Of course, I am. Or, at least, I was.
I've had a breakthrough! Write this down.
And they did. Their friendship was based on their mutual love of inventing things.
With World War II now raging, Hedy wanted to do all she could to help America defeat the Nazis.
Together, she and George invented a secret rad
communication syste
inspired by player pia
scrolls, that would he
guide torpedoes to
their targets.

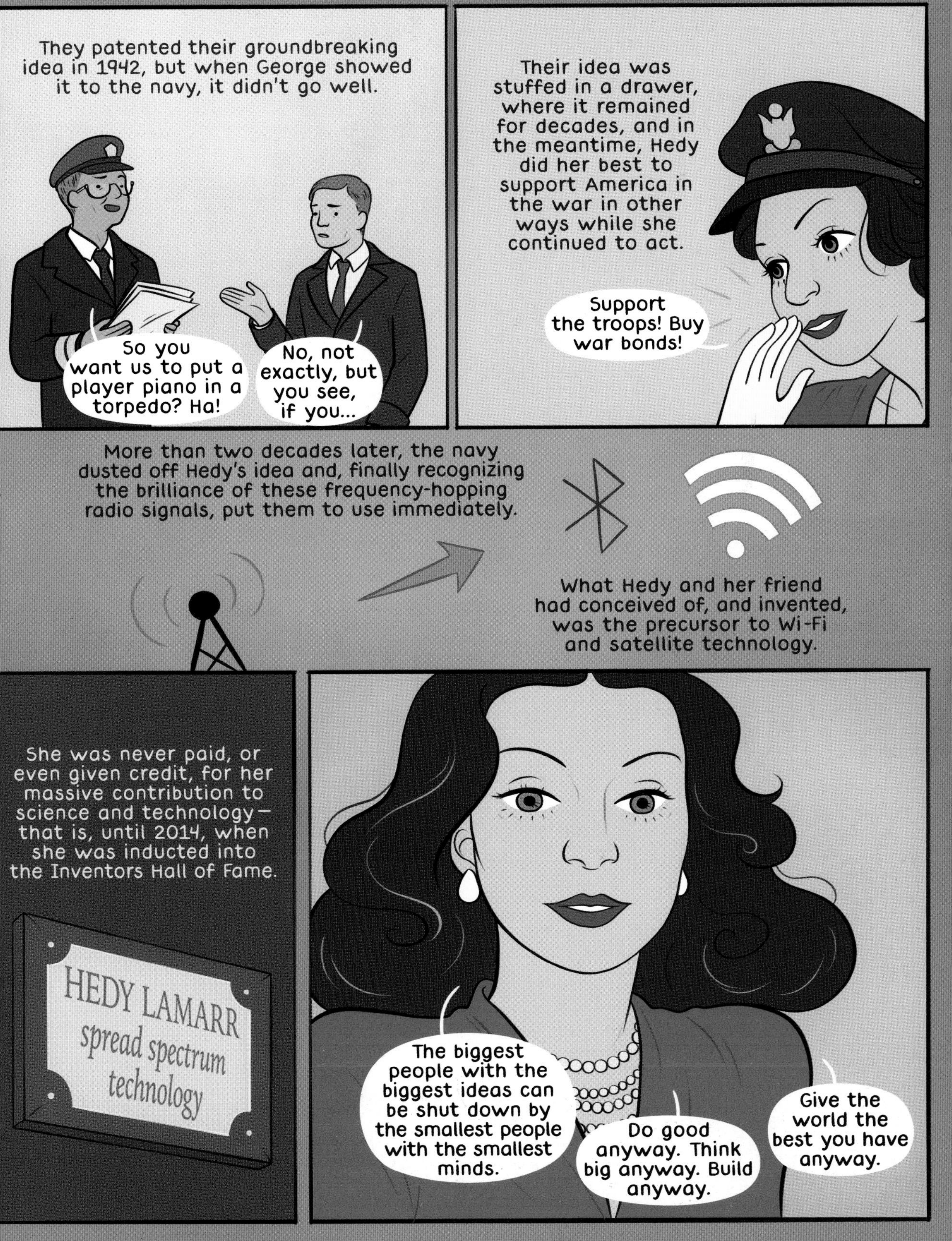
They patented their groundbreaking idea in 1942, but when George showed it to the navy, it didn't go well.
So you want us to put a player piano in a torpedo? Ha!
No, not exactly, but you see, if you...
Their idea was stuffed in a drawer, where it remained for decades, and in the meantime, Hedy did her best to support America in the war in other ways while she continued to act.
Support the troops! Buy war bonds!
More than two decades later, the navy dusted off Hedy's idea and, finally recognizing the brilliance of these frequency-hopping radio signals, put them to use immediately.
What Hedy and her friend had conceived of, and invented, was the precursor to Wi-Fi and satellite technology.
She was never paid, or even given credit, for her massive contribution to science and technology—that is, until 2014, when she was inducted into the Inventors Hall of Fame.
HEDY LAMARR
spread spectrum technology
The biggest people with the biggest ideas can be shut down by the smallest people with the smallest minds.
Do good anyway. Think big anyway. Build anyway.
Give the world the best you have anyway.

THE RADICAL ENTREPRENEUR

MADAM C. J. WALKER
1867 ~ 1919

Madam C. J. Walker, the daughter of former slaves, was the first woman in America to become a self-made millionaire, and she achieved her success by thinking big, working hard, and hustling her way to the top. "I got my start by giving myself a start," she said, and perhaps even more impressively, once she amassed so much wealth and power, she used it to lift up those around her and make the world a better, fairer place.

C.J. AND ME

COUNT ALL THE THINGS YOU HAVE IN COMMON WITH MADAM C. J. WALKER.

- I like to do things for myself.
- I know what it's like to want something I can't have.
- And I know how to work hard until I get it.
- I want to run my own business someday.
- I know I can make something to change the world.
- Giving makes me even happier than getting.
- When I see something wrong, I work to change it.
- I have big dreams.
- I'm ambitious.
- I'm generous.

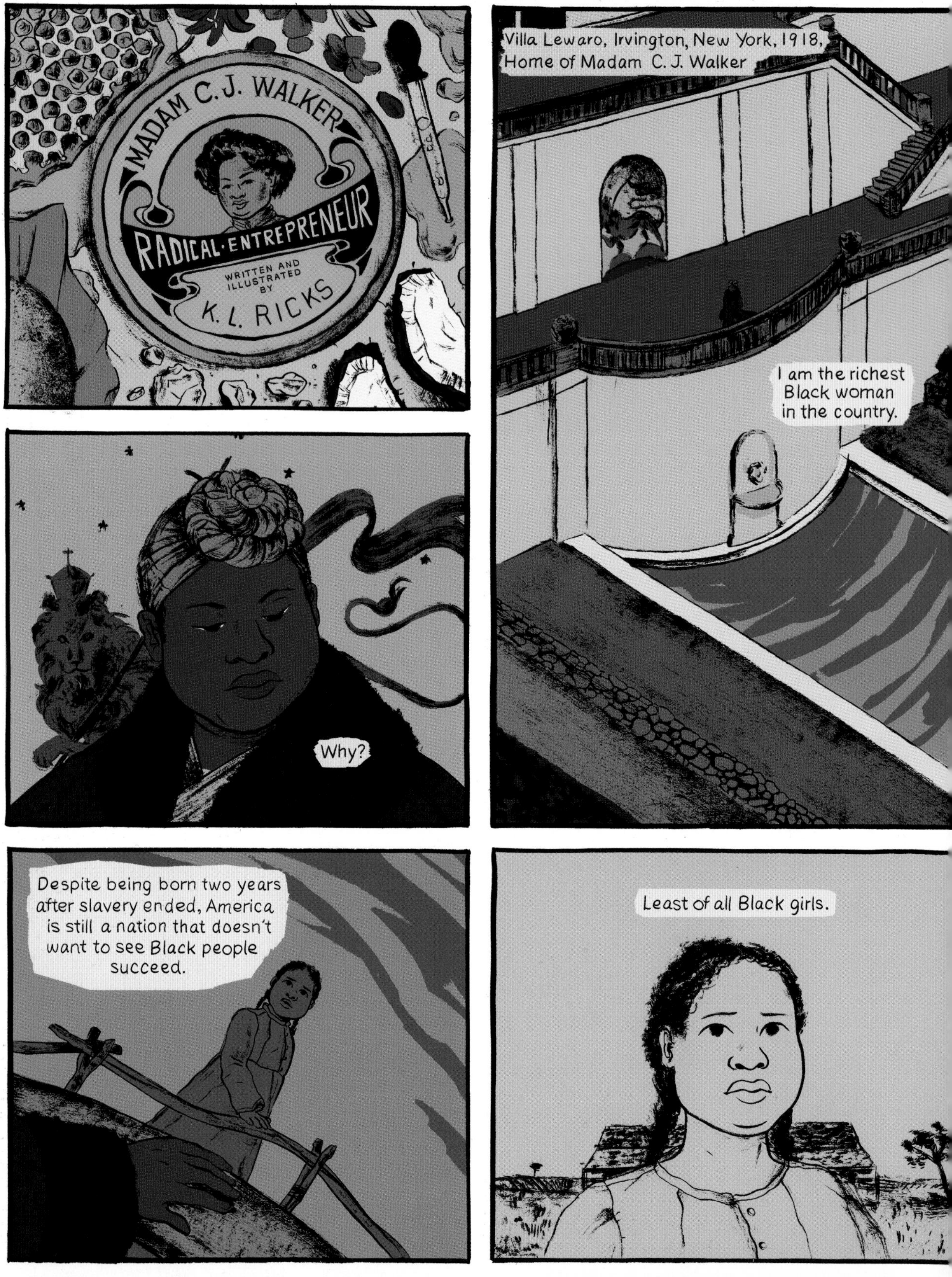
MADAM C.J. WALKER
RADICAL·ENTREPRENEUR
WRITTEN AND ILLUSTRATED BY
K.L. RICKS
Villa Lewaro, Irvington, New York, 1918, Home of Madam C.J. Walker
I am the richest Black woman in the country.
Why?
Despite being born two years after slavery ended, America is still a nation that doesn't want to see Black people succeed.
Least of all Black girls.

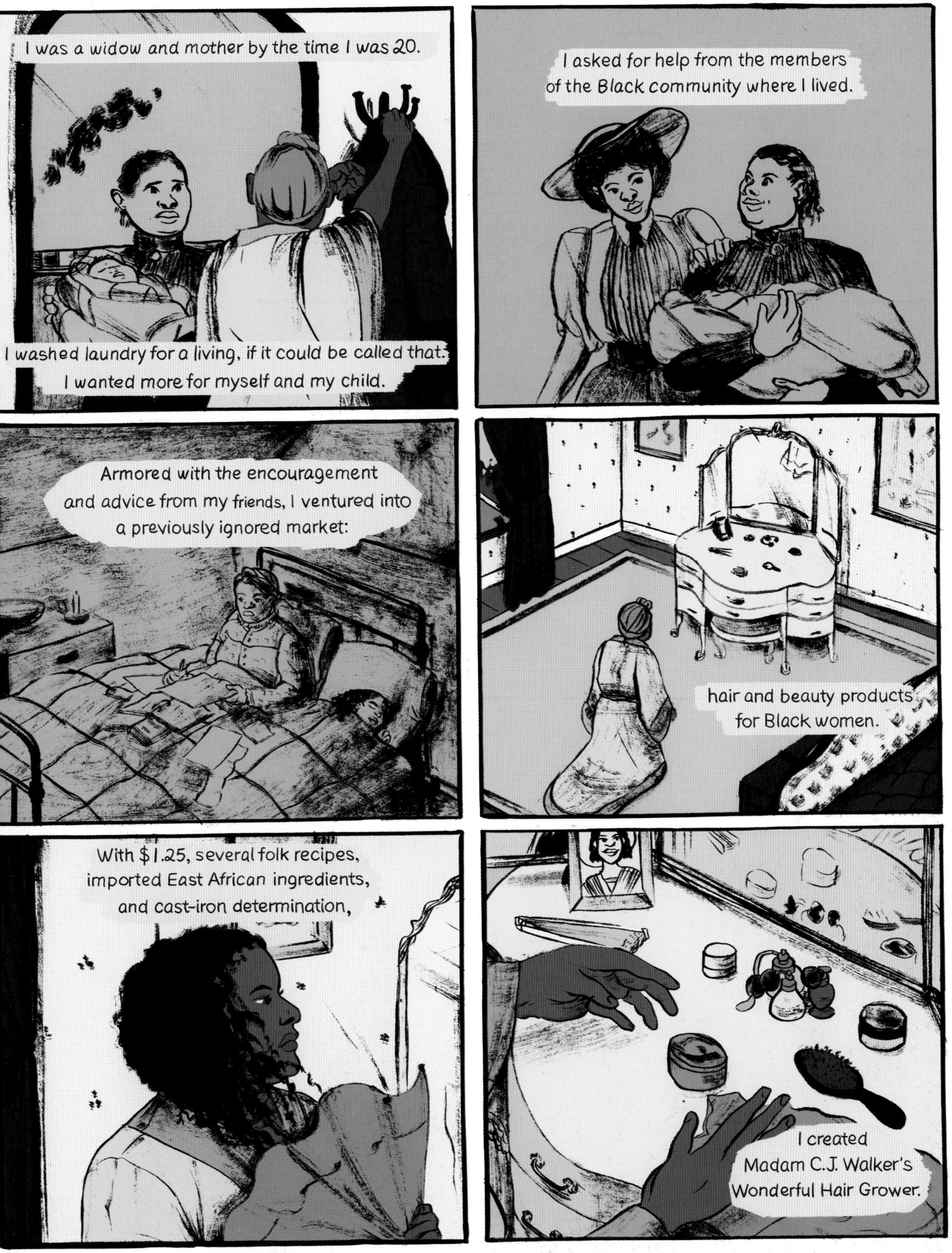
I was a widow and mother by the time I was 20.
I washed laundry for a living, if it could be called that. I wanted more for myself and my child.
I asked for help from the members of the Black community where I lived.
Armored with the encouragement and advice from my friends, I ventured into a previously ignored market:
hair and beauty products for Black women.
With $1.25, several folk recipes, imported East African ingredients, and cast-iron determination,
I created Madam C.J. Walker's Wonderful Hair Grower.

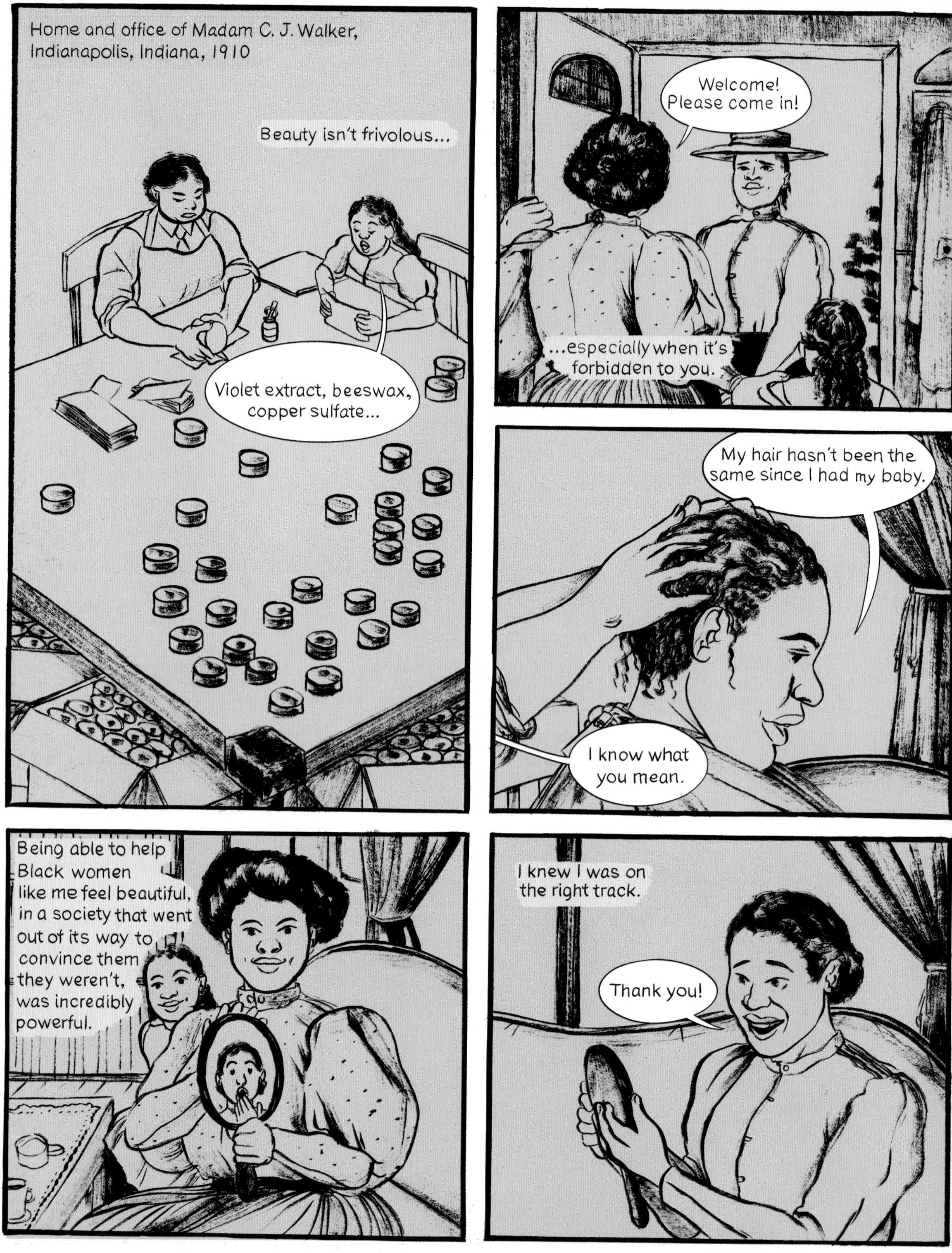
Home and office of Madam C. J. Walker, Indianapolis, Indiana, 1910
Beauty isn't frivolous...
Violet extract, beeswax, copper sulfate...
Welcome! Please come in!
...especially when it's forbidden to you.
My hair hasn't been the same since I had my baby.
I know what you mean.
Being able to help Black women like me feel beautiful, in a society that went out of its way to convince them they weren't, was incredibly powerful.
I knew I was on the right track.
Thank you!

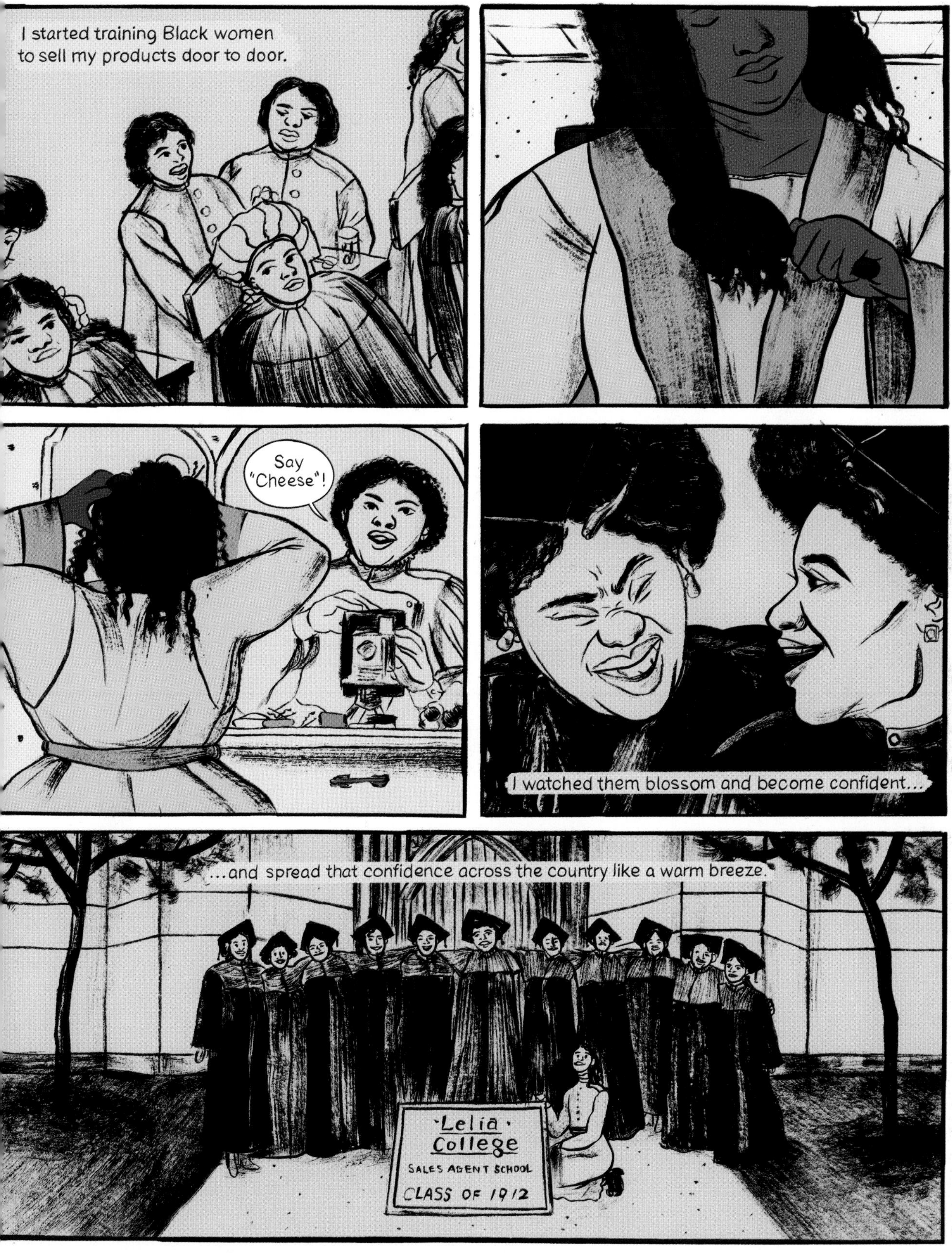
I started training Black women to sell my products door to door.
Say "Cheese"!
I watched them blossom and become confident...
...and spread that confidence across the country like a warm breeze.
·Lelia· College
SALES AGENT SCHOOL
CLASS OF 1912

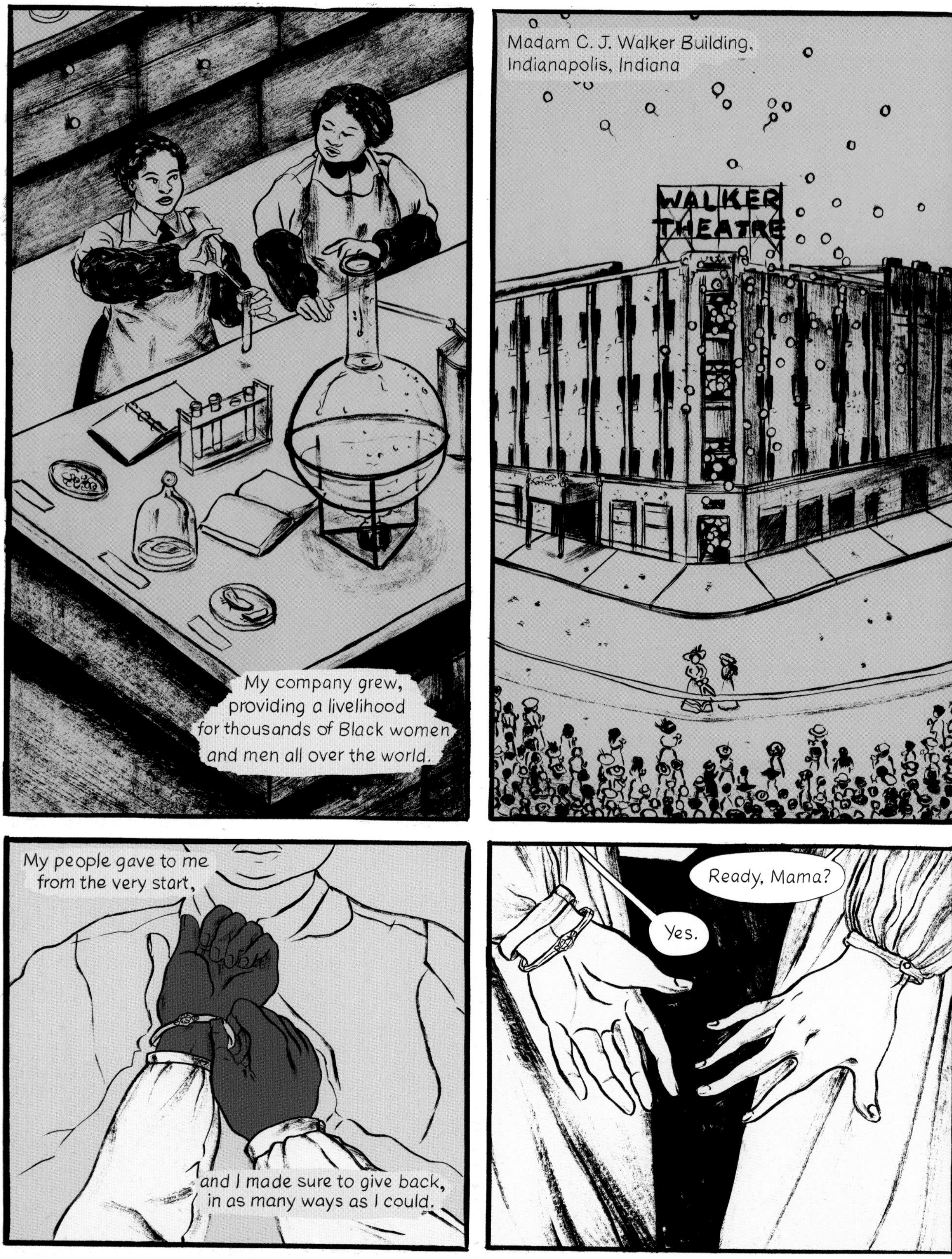
My company grew, providing a livelihood for thousands of Black women and men all over the world.
Madam C. J. Walker Building, Indianapolis, Indiana
WALKER THEATRE
My people gave to me from the very start,
and I made sure to give back, in as many ways as I could.
Ready, Mama?
Yes.

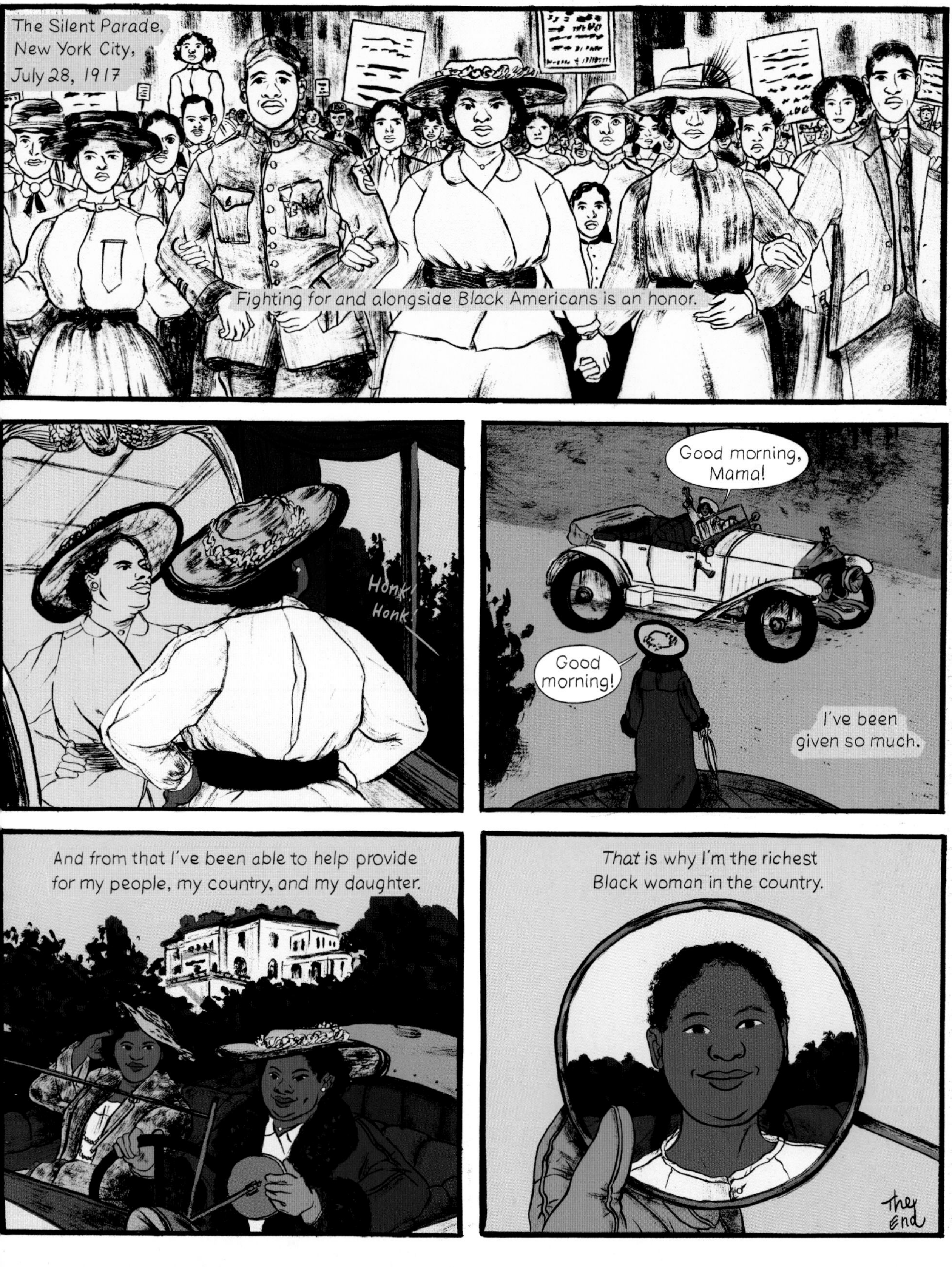
The Silent Parade, New York City, July 28, 1917
Fighting for and alongside Black Americans is an honor.
Honk! Honk!
Good morning, Mama!
Good morning!
I've been given so much.
And from that I've been able to help provide for my people, my country, and my daughter.
That is why I'm the richest Black woman in the country.
The End

PLAY

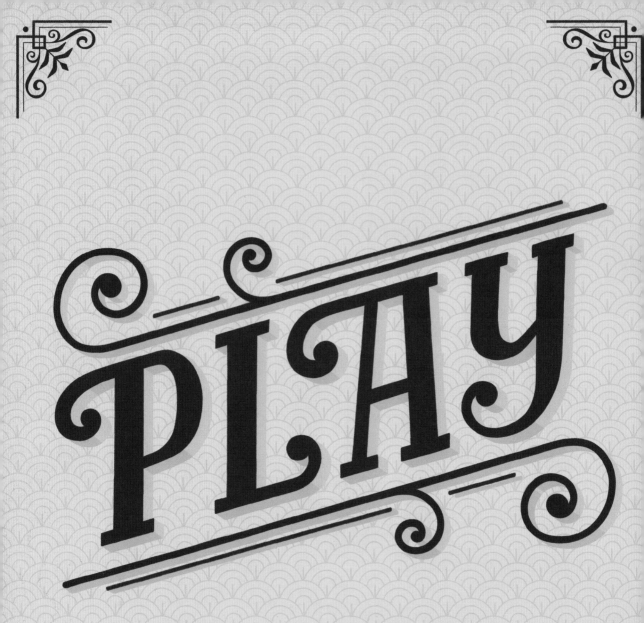

Athletes don't often make big speeches, but every single one begins her journey with the same four words: "I want to play." Once they're in the game, they usually leave it to their bodies to do most of their communicating. We don't have to hear them talk to know what they're telling us with every throw, kick, and leap. Their message is already crystal clear: Embrace your strength. Focus. Work hard. Win. And enjoy every second of it. The three athletes in this chapter—a cyclist, a ballerina, a mountain climber—did all of those things and more. They broke down barriers, not only so they could play, but so you can too.

The GLOBE-TROTTING Cyclist

ANNIE LONDONDERRY
1870 ~ 1947

She wanted to become the first woman ever to bicycle around the world, but before Annie Londonderry could set off on her journey, she had one important thing to do: learn how to ride a bike! She took two quick lessons—and off she went! Fifteen months later, she pedaled home again, having circumnavigated the globe. She's proof that any dream is possible if you're bold enough to pursue it.

ANNIE AND ME

COUNT ALL THE THINGS YOU HAVE IN COMMON WITH ANNIE LONDONDERRY.

- I love to ride my bike.
- I believe in myself.
- I seek out adventure.
- I stay open to all opportunities.
- I want to travel the world.
- I may be small, but I'm mighty.
- I have a knack for finding clever ways to earn money.
- I love entertaining people with my stories.
- I'm strong.
- I'm sensational.

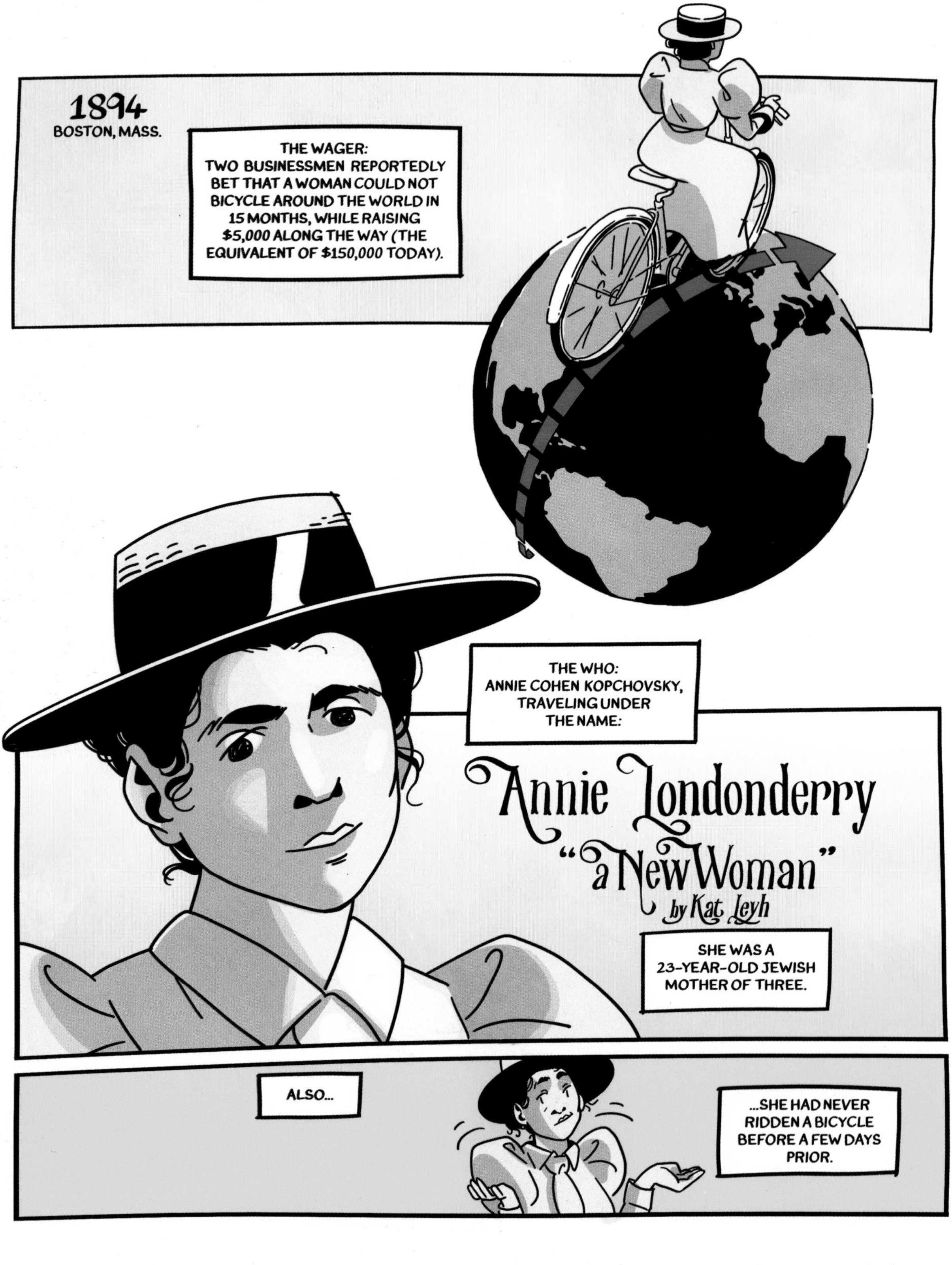

1894
BOSTON, MASS.
THE WAGER: TWO BUSINESSMEN REPORTEDLY BET THAT A WOMAN COULD NOT BICYCLE AROUND THE WORLD IN 15 MONTHS, WHILE RAISING $5,000 ALONG THE WAY (THE EQUIVALENT OF $150,000 TODAY).
THE WHO: ANNIE COHEN KOPCHOVSKY, TRAVELING UNDER THE NAME:
Annie Londonderry
"a New Woman"
by Kat Leyh
SHE WAS A 23-YEAR-OLD JEWISH MOTHER OF THREE.
ALSO...
...SHE HAD NEVER RIDDEN A BICYCLE BEFORE A FEW DAYS PRIOR.

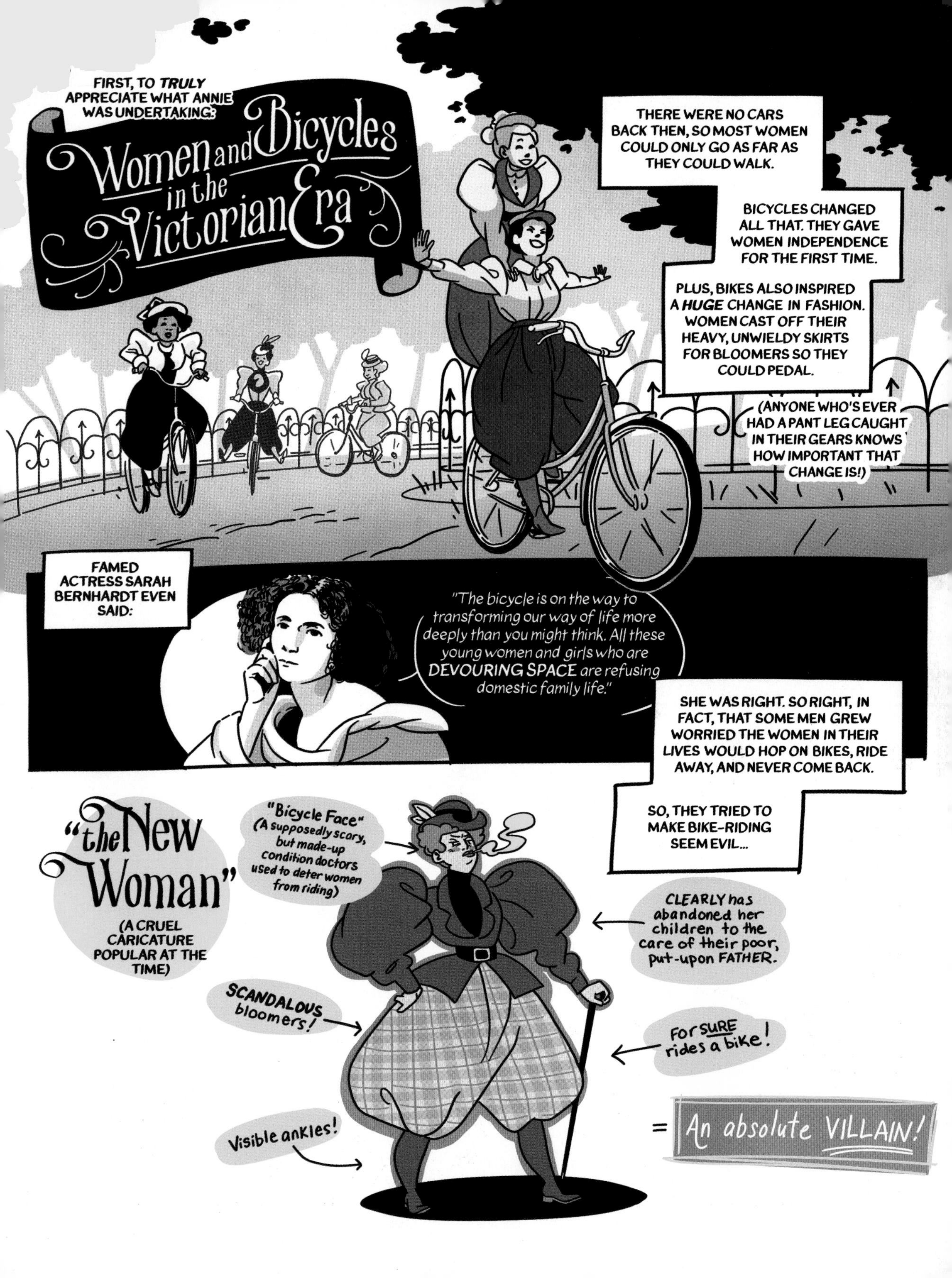

FIRST, TO TRULY APPRECIATE WHAT ANNIE WAS UNDERTAKING:
Women and Bicycles in the Victorian Era
THERE WERE NO CARS BACK THEN, SO MOST WOMEN COULD ONLY GO AS FAR AS THEY COULD WALK.
BICYCLES CHANGED ALL THAT. THEY GAVE WOMEN INDEPENDENCE FOR THE FIRST TIME.
PLUS, BIKES ALSO INSPIRED A HUGE CHANGE IN FASHION. WOMEN CAST OFF THEIR HEAVY, UNWIELDY SKIRTS FOR BLOOMERS SO THEY COULD PEDAL.
(ANYONE WHO'S EVER HAD A PANT LEG CAUGHT IN THEIR GEARS KNOWS HOW IMPORTANT THAT CHANGE IS!)
FAMED ACTRESS SARAH BERNHARDT EVEN SAID:
"The bicycle is on the way to transforming our way of life more deeply than you might think. All these young women and girls who are DEVOURING SPACE are refusing domestic family life."
SHE WAS RIGHT. SO RIGHT, IN FACT, THAT SOME MEN GREW WORRIED THE WOMEN IN THEIR LIVES WOULD HOP ON BIKES, RIDE AWAY, AND NEVER COME BACK.
SO, THEY TRIED TO MAKE BIKE-RIDING SEEM EVIL...
"the New Woman"
(A CRUEL CARICATURE POPULAR AT THE TIME)
"Bicycle Face" (A supposedly scary, but made-up condition doctors used to deter women from riding)
CLEARLY has abandoned her children to the care of their poor, put-upon FATHER.
SCANDALOUS bloomers!
For SURE rides a bike!
Visible ankles!
= An absolute VILLAIN!

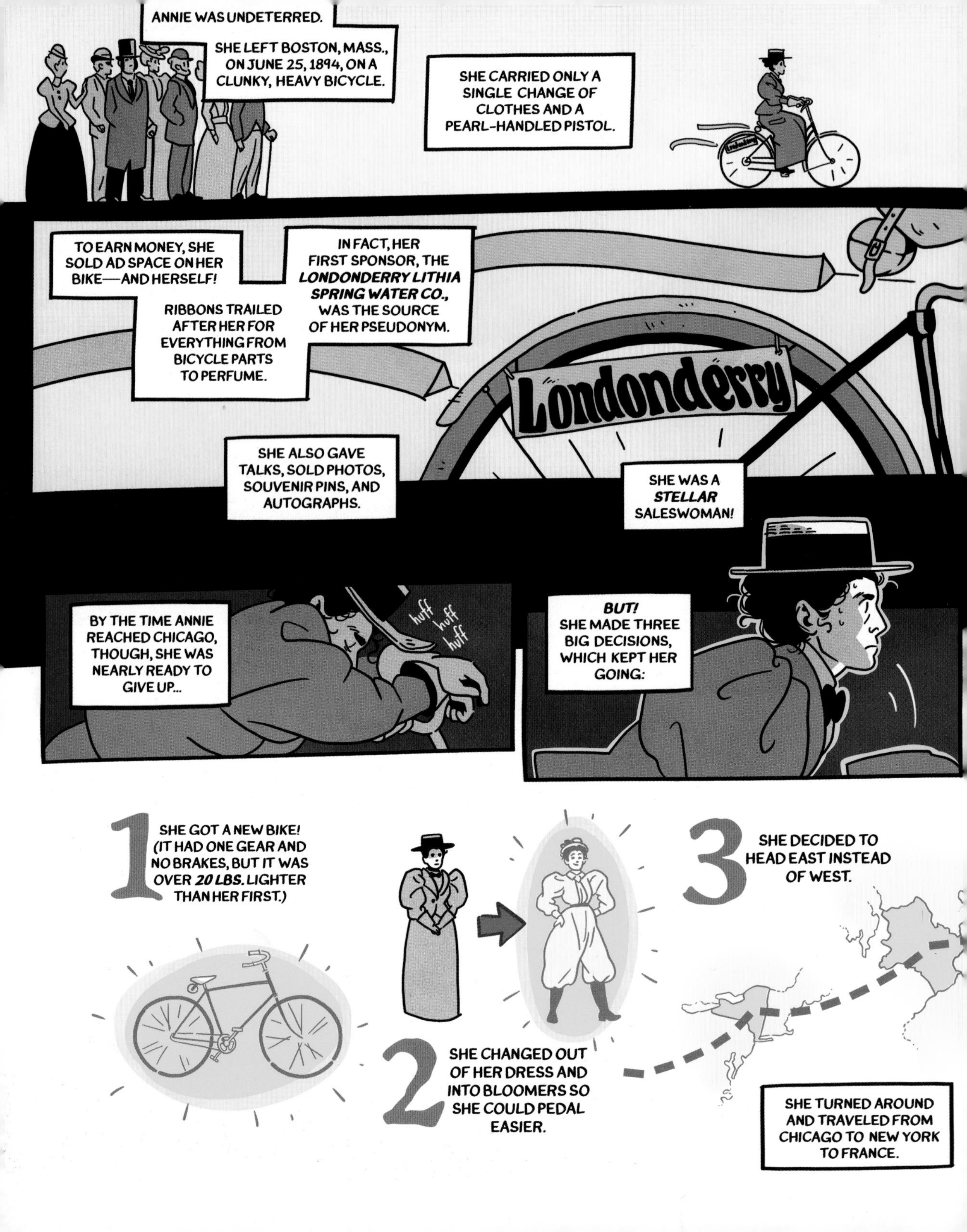
ANNIE WAS UNDETERRED.
SHE LEFT BOSTON, MASS., ON JUNE 25, 1894, ON A CLUNKY, HEAVY BICYCLE.
SHE CARRIED ONLY A SINGLE CHANGE OF CLOTHES AND A PEARL-HANDLED PISTOL.
TO EARN MONEY, SHE SOLD AD SPACE ON HER BIKE—AND HERSELF!
RIBBONS TRAILED AFTER HER FOR EVERYTHING FROM BICYCLE PARTS TO PERFUME.
IN FACT, HER FIRST SPONSOR, THE *LONDONDERRY LITHIA SPRING WATER CO.,* WAS THE SOURCE OF HER PSEUDONYM.
Londonderry
SHE ALSO GAVE TALKS, SOLD PHOTOS, SOUVENIR PINS, AND AUTOGRAPHS.
SHE WAS A *STELLAR* SALESWOMAN!
BY THE TIME ANNIE REACHED CHICAGO, THOUGH, SHE WAS NEARLY READY TO GIVE UP...
huff huff huff
BUT! SHE MADE THREE BIG DECISIONS, WHICH KEPT HER GOING:
1 SHE GOT A NEW BIKE! (IT HAD ONE GEAR AND NO BRAKES, BUT IT WAS OVER *20 LBS.* LIGHTER THAN HER FIRST.)
2 SHE CHANGED OUT OF HER DRESS AND INTO BLOOMERS SO SHE COULD PEDAL EASIER.
3 SHE DECIDED TO HEAD EAST INSTEAD OF WEST.
SHE TURNED AROUND AND TRAVELED FROM CHICAGO TO NEW YORK TO FRANCE.

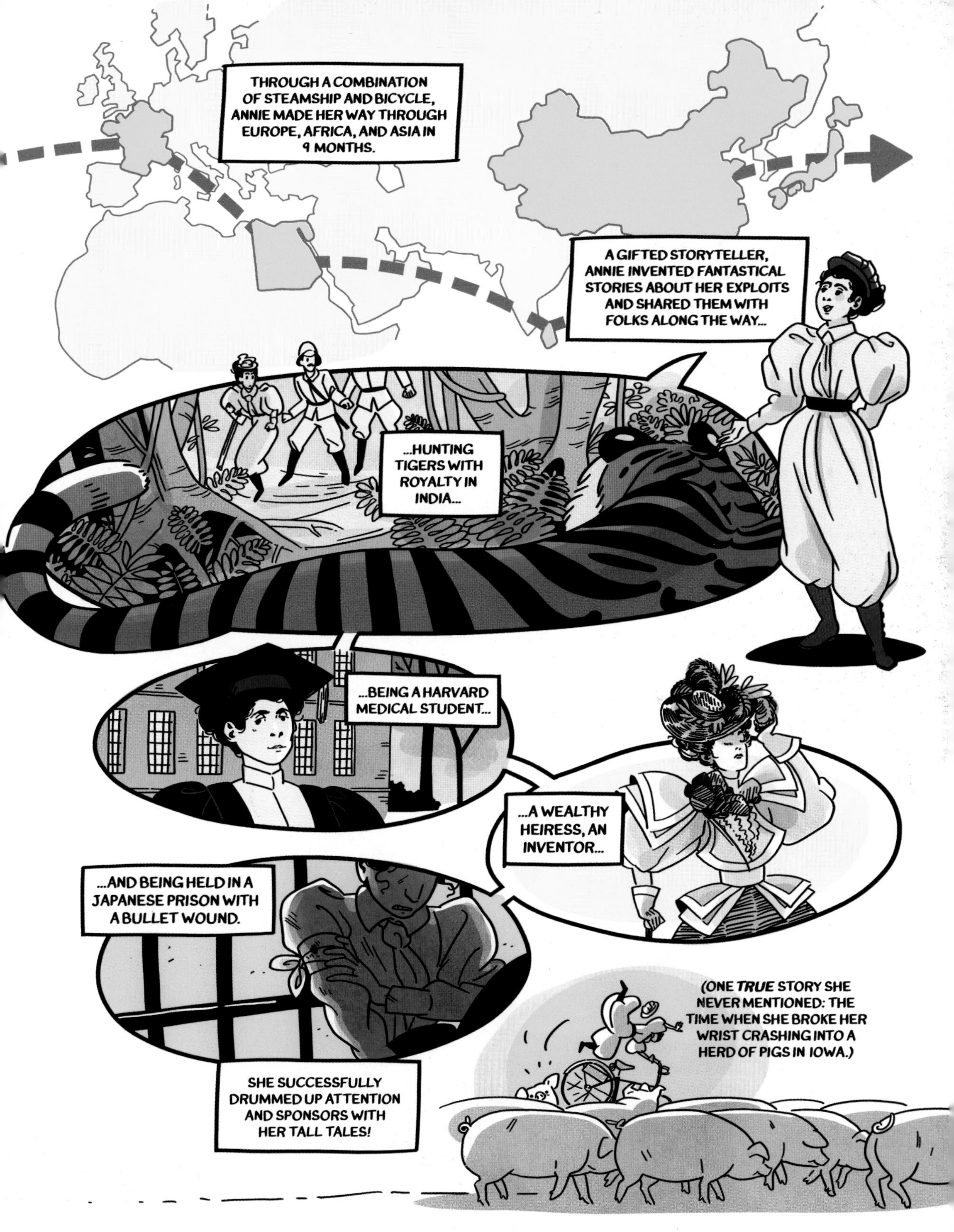
THROUGH A COMBINATION OF STEAMSHIP AND BICYCLE, ANNIE MADE HER WAY THROUGH EUROPE, AFRICA, AND ASIA IN 9 MONTHS.
A GIFTED STORYTELLER, ANNIE INVENTED FANTASTICAL STORIES ABOUT HER EXPLOITS AND SHARED THEM WITH FOLKS ALONG THE WAY...
...HUNTING TIGERS WITH ROYALTY IN INDIA...
...BEING A HARVARD MEDICAL STUDENT...
...A WEALTHY HEIRESS, AN INVENTOR...
...AND BEING HELD IN A JAPANESE PRISON WITH A BULLET WOUND.
(ONE *TRUE* STORY SHE NEVER MENTIONED: THE TIME WHEN SHE BROKE HER WRIST CRASHING INTO A HERD OF PIGS IN IOWA.)
SHE SUCCESSFULLY DRUMMED UP ATTENTION AND SPONSORS WITH HER TALL TALES!

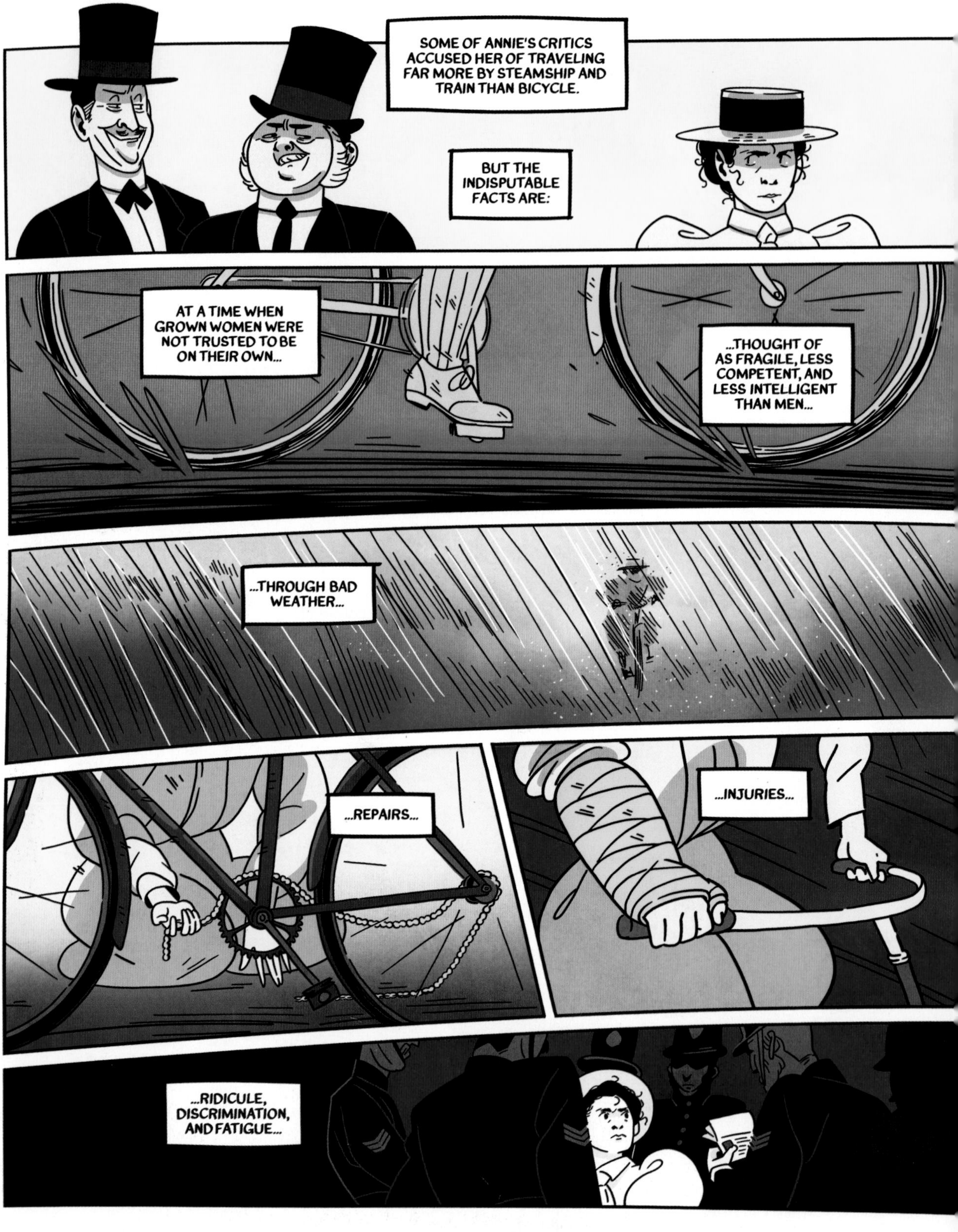
SOME OF ANNIE'S CRITICS ACCUSED HER OF TRAVELING FAR MORE BY STEAMSHIP AND TRAIN THAN BICYCLE.
BUT THE INDISPUTABLE FACTS ARE:
AT A TIME WHEN GROWN WOMEN WERE NOT TRUSTED TO BE ON THEIR OWN...
...THOUGHT OF AS FRAGILE, LESS COMPETENT, AND LESS INTELLIGENT THAN MEN...
...THROUGH BAD WEATHER...
...REPAIRS...
...INJURIES...
...RIDICULE, DISCRIMINATION, AND FATIGUE...

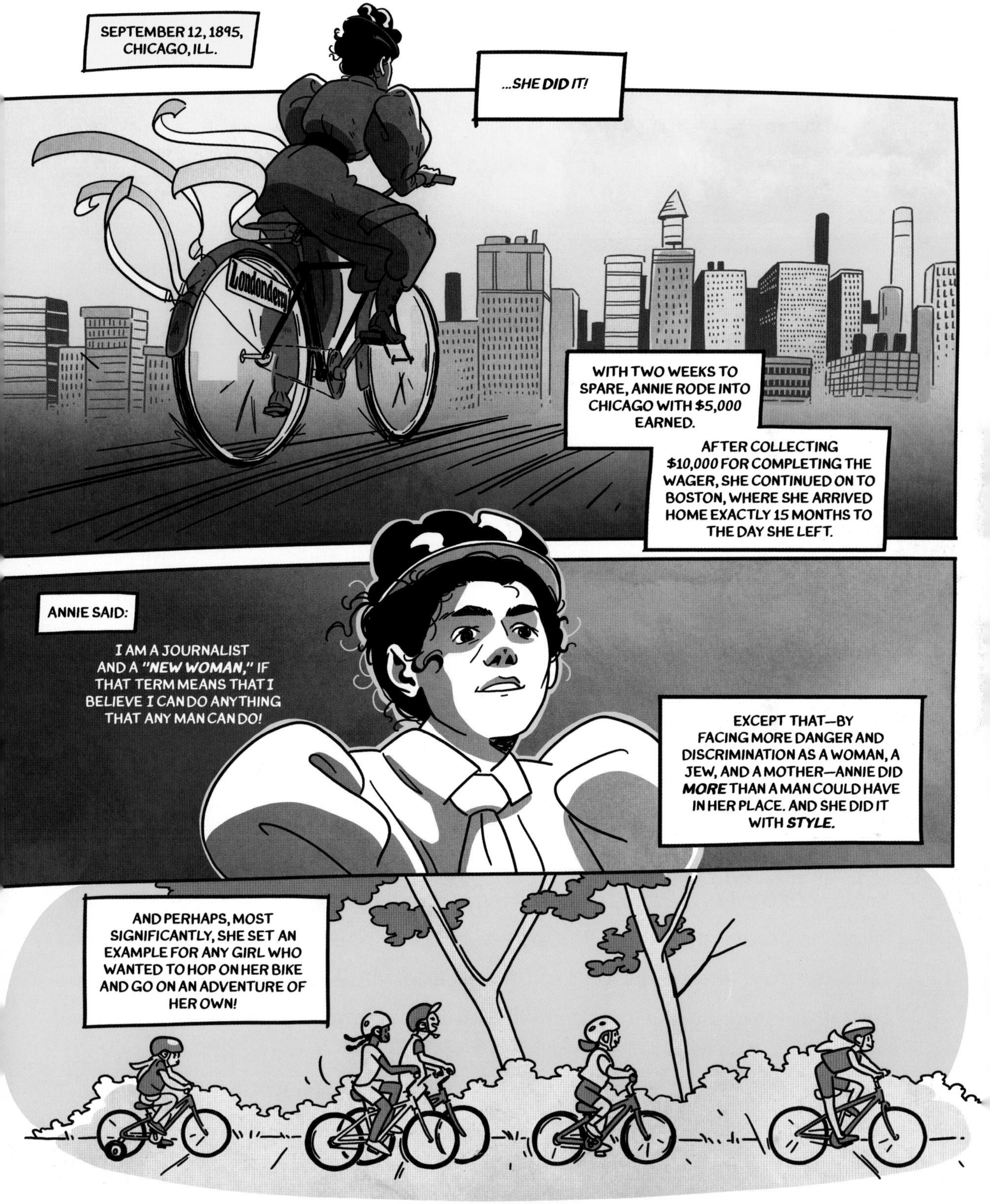
SEPTEMBER 12, 1895, CHICAGO, ILL.
...SHE *DID* IT!
Londonderry
WITH TWO WEEKS TO SPARE, ANNIE RODE INTO CHICAGO WITH $5,000 EARNED.
AFTER COLLECTING $10,000 FOR COMPLETING THE WAGER, SHE CONTINUED ON TO BOSTON, WHERE SHE ARRIVED HOME EXACTLY 15 MONTHS TO THE DAY SHE LEFT.
ANNIE SAID:
I AM A JOURNALIST AND A "*NEW WOMAN*," IF THAT TERM MEANS THAT I BELIEVE I CAN DO ANYTHING THAT ANY MAN CAN DO!
EXCEPT THAT—BY FACING MORE DANGER AND DISCRIMINATION AS A WOMAN, A JEW, AND A MOTHER—ANNIE DID *MORE* THAN A MAN COULD HAVE IN HER PLACE. AND SHE DID IT WITH *STYLE*.
AND PERHAPS, MOST SIGNIFICANTLY, SHE SET AN EXAMPLE FOR ANY GIRL WHO WANTED TO HOP ON HER BIKE AND GO ON AN ADVENTURE OF HER OWN!

The PRIMA Ballerina

• • • • •

MARIA TALLCHIEF
1925 ~ 2013

When Maria Tallchief danced, she looked as if she was floating across the stage. But as every ballerina knows, it takes strength and grit to make ballet look effortless, and Maria Tallchief had both. She was the first Native American woman to become a prima ballerina, and she wowed audiences. "A ballerina takes steps given to her and makes them her own," said Tallchief, and she did just that, beautifully, creating space for more dancers (of every background) to follow her lead.

MARIA AND ME

COUNT ALL THE THINGS YOU HAVE IN COMMON WITH MARIA TALLCHIEF.

- I love to dance.
- I like the spotlight.
- My legs are very strong.
- I try to always hold my head high.
- I will practice until I get it perfect.
- I want to see the whole world!
- And I want the world to see me.
- Music moves me.
- I also just love to wear tutus.
- I'm graceful.
- I'm free.

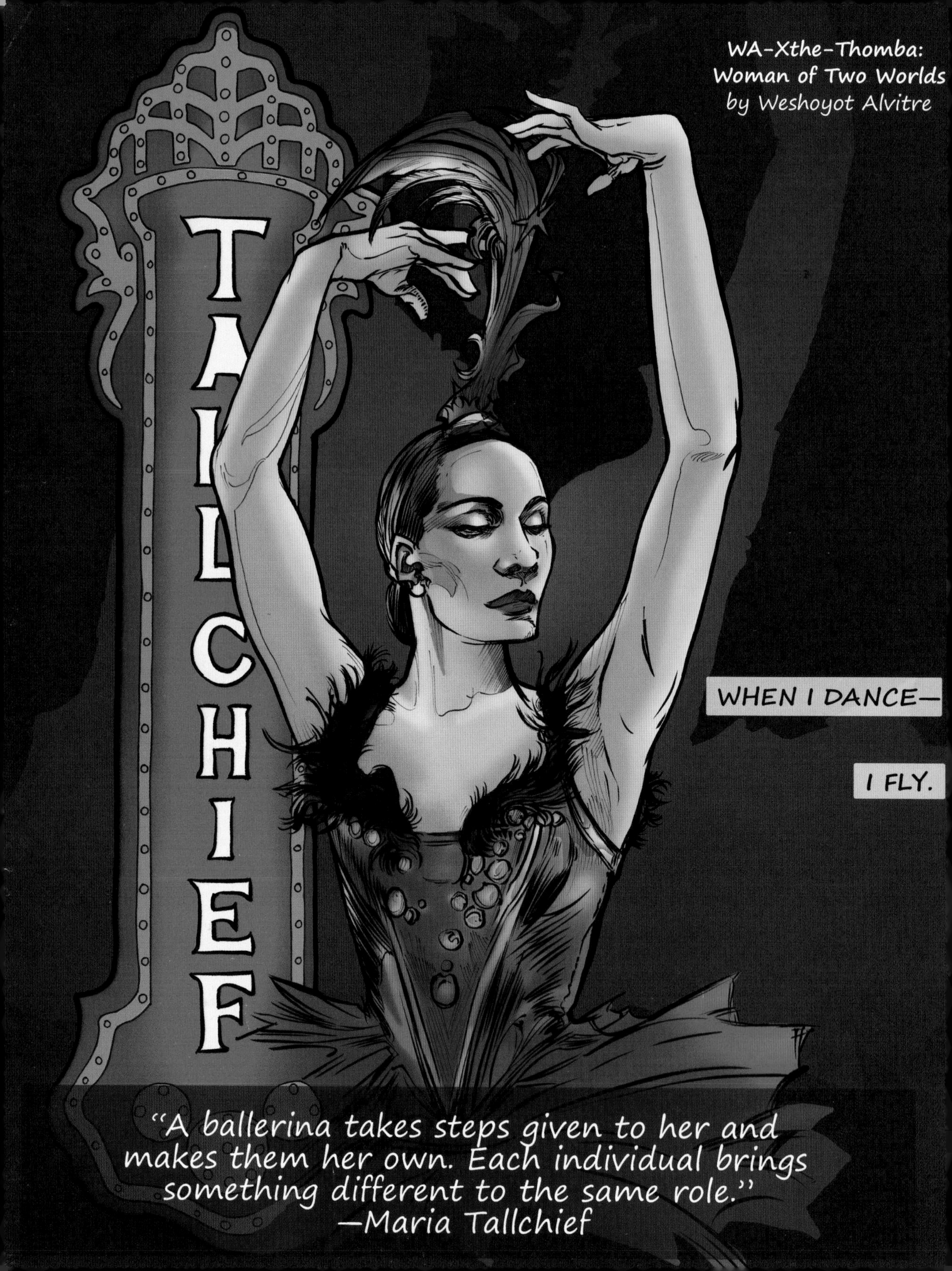
WA-Xthe-Thomba:
Woman of Two Worlds
by Weshoyot Alvitre
TALLCHIEF
WHEN I DANCE—
I FLY.
"A ballerina takes steps given to her and makes them her own. Each individual brings something different to the same role."
—Maria Tallchief

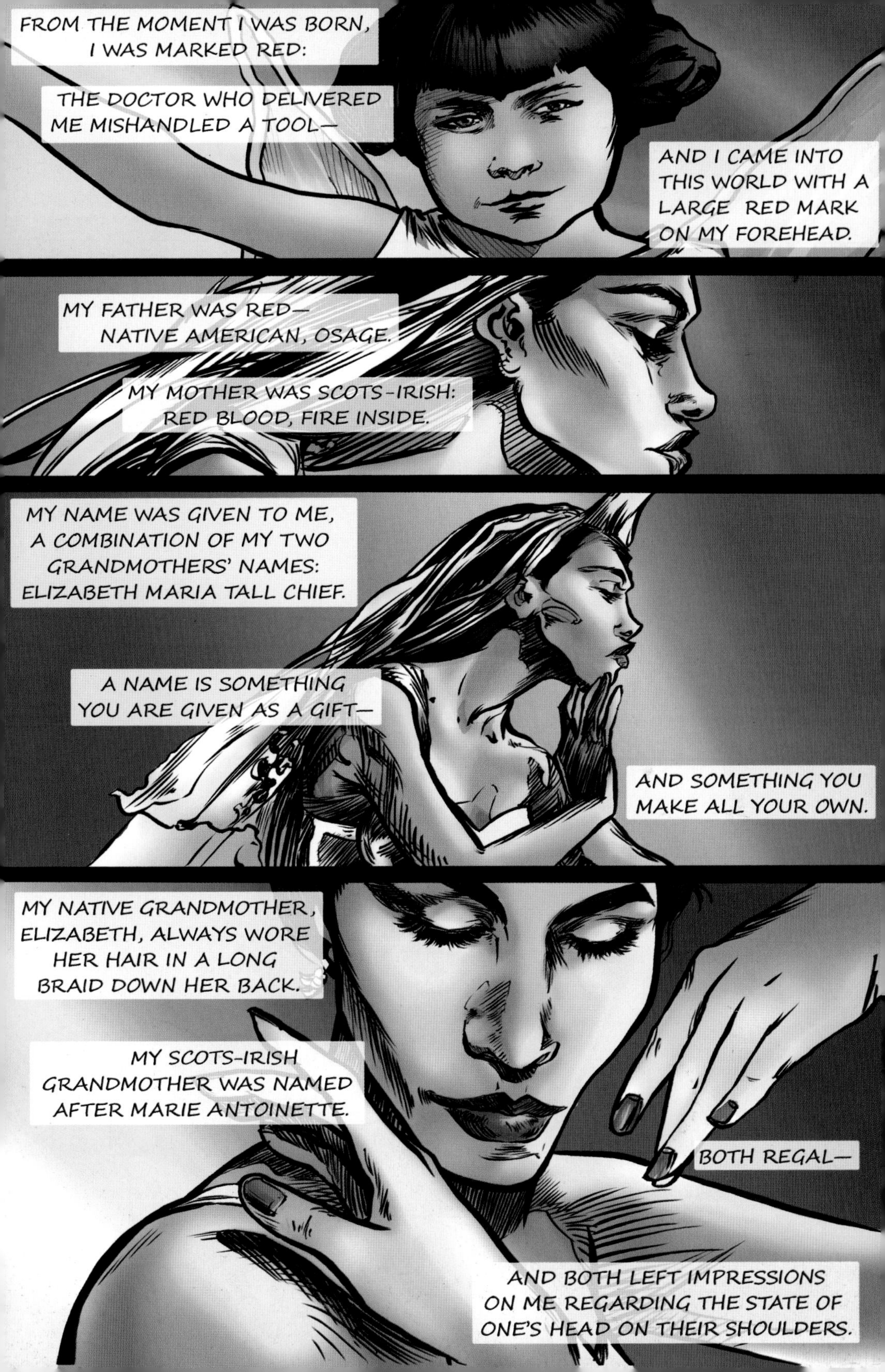
FROM THE MOMENT I WAS BORN, I WAS MARKED RED:
THE DOCTOR WHO DELIVERED ME MISHANDLED A TOOL—
AND I CAME INTO THIS WORLD WITH A LARGE RED MARK ON MY FOREHEAD.
MY FATHER WAS RED— NATIVE AMERICAN, OSAGE.
MY MOTHER WAS SCOTS-IRISH: RED BLOOD, FIRE INSIDE.
MY NAME WAS GIVEN TO ME, A COMBINATION OF MY TWO GRANDMOTHERS' NAMES: ELIZABETH MARIA TALL CHIEF.
A NAME IS SOMETHING YOU ARE GIVEN AS A GIFT—
AND SOMETHING YOU MAKE ALL YOUR OWN.
MY NATIVE GRANDMOTHER, ELIZABETH, ALWAYS WORE HER HAIR IN A LONG BRAID DOWN HER BACK.
MY SCOTS-IRISH GRANDMOTHER WAS NAMED AFTER MARIE ANTOINETTE.
BOTH REGAL—
AND BOTH LEFT IMPRESSIONS ON ME REGARDING THE STATE OF ONE'S HEAD ON THEIR SHOULDERS.

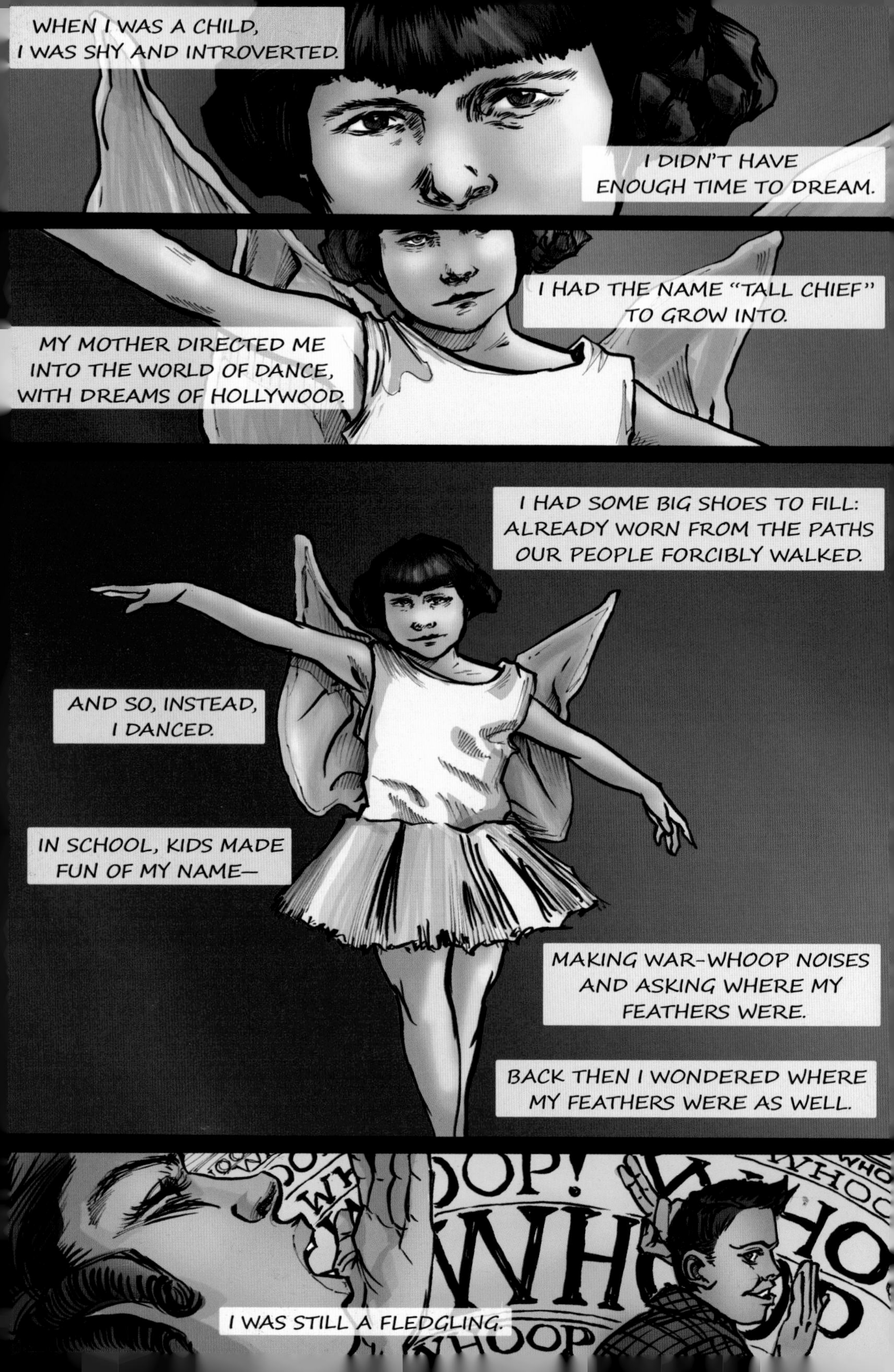
WHEN I WAS A CHILD, I WAS SHY AND INTROVERTED.
I DIDN'T HAVE ENOUGH TIME TO DREAM.
I HAD THE NAME "TALL CHIEF" TO GROW INTO.
MY MOTHER DIRECTED ME INTO THE WORLD OF DANCE, WITH DREAMS OF HOLLYWOOD.
I HAD SOME BIG SHOES TO FILL: ALREADY WORN FROM THE PATHS OUR PEOPLE FORCIBLY WALKED.
AND SO, INSTEAD, I DANCED.
IN SCHOOL, KIDS MADE FUN OF MY NAME—
MAKING WAR-WHOOP NOISES AND ASKING WHERE MY FEATHERS WERE.
BACK THEN I WONDERED WHERE MY FEATHERS WERE AS WELL.
WHOOP!
WHOOP
I WAS STILL A FLEDGLING.

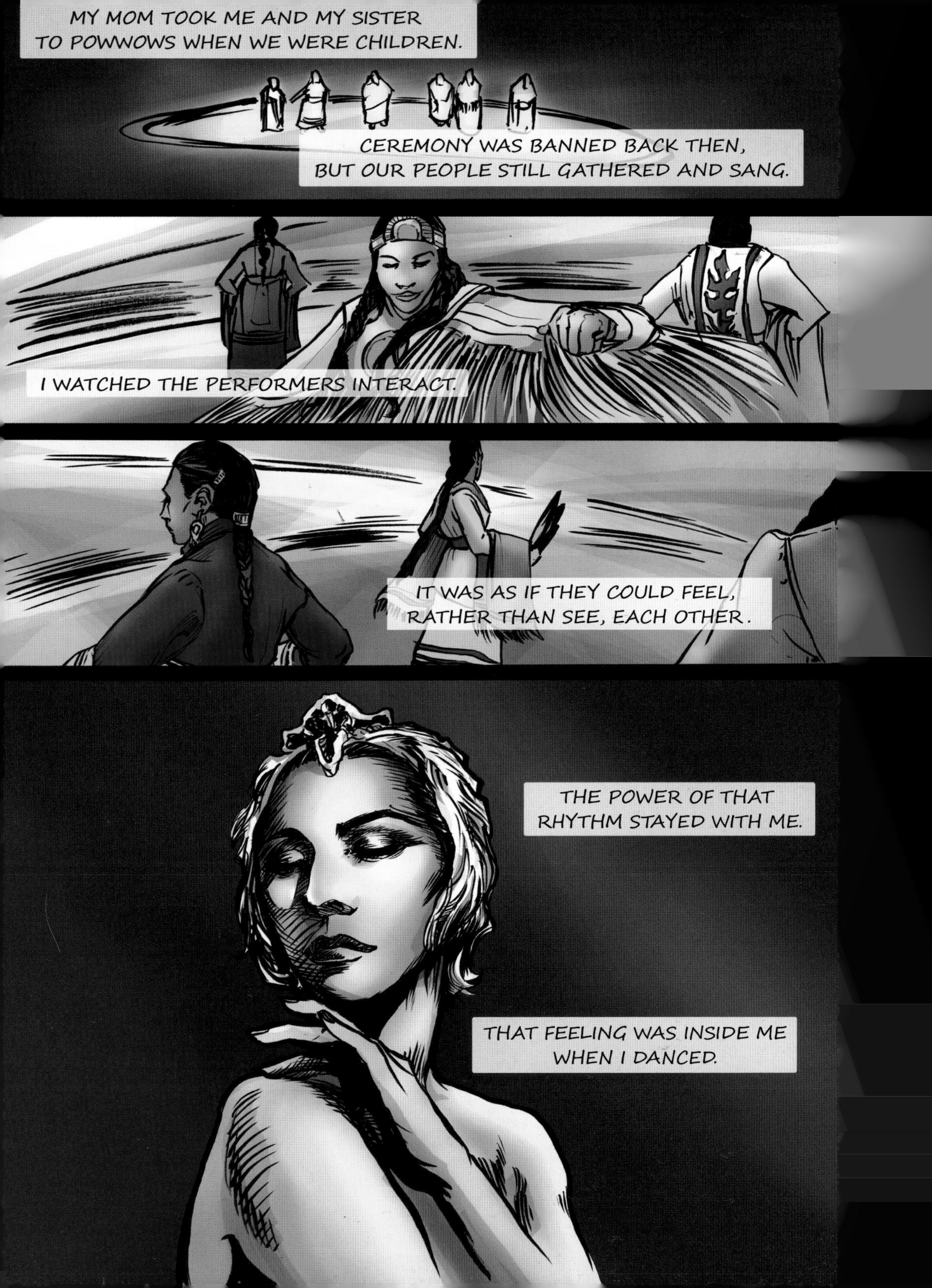
MY MOM TOOK ME AND MY SISTER TO POWWOWS WHEN WE WERE CHILDREN.
CEREMONY WAS BANNED BACK THEN, BUT OUR PEOPLE STILL GATHERED AND SANG.
I WATCHED THE PERFORMERS INTERACT.
IT WAS AS IF THEY COULD FEEL, RATHER THAN SEE, EACH OTHER.
THE POWER OF THAT RHYTHM STAYED WITH ME.
THAT FEELING WAS INSIDE ME WHEN I DANCED.

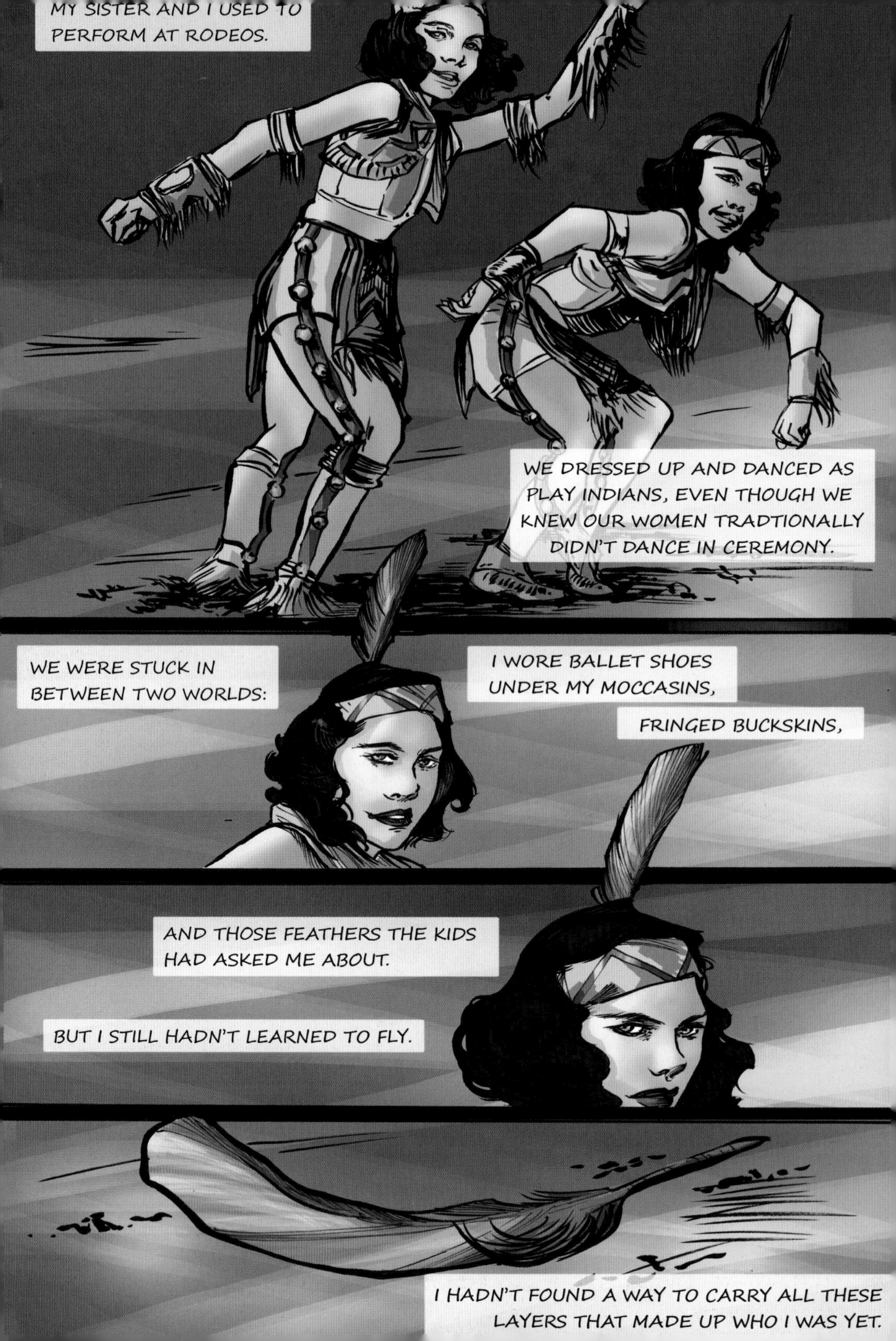
MY SISTER AND I USED TO PERFORM AT RODEOS.
WE DRESSED UP AND DANCED AS PLAY INDIANS, EVEN THOUGH WE KNEW OUR WOMEN TRADTIONALLY DIDN'T DANCE IN CEREMONY.
WE WERE STUCK IN BETWEEN TWO WORLDS:
I WORE BALLET SHOES UNDER MY MOCCASINS,
FRINGED BUCKSKINS,
AND THOSE FEATHERS THE KIDS HAD ASKED ME ABOUT.
BUT I STILL HADN'T LEARNED TO FLY.
I HADN'T FOUND A WAY TO CARRY ALL THESE LAYERS THAT MADE UP WHO I WAS YET.

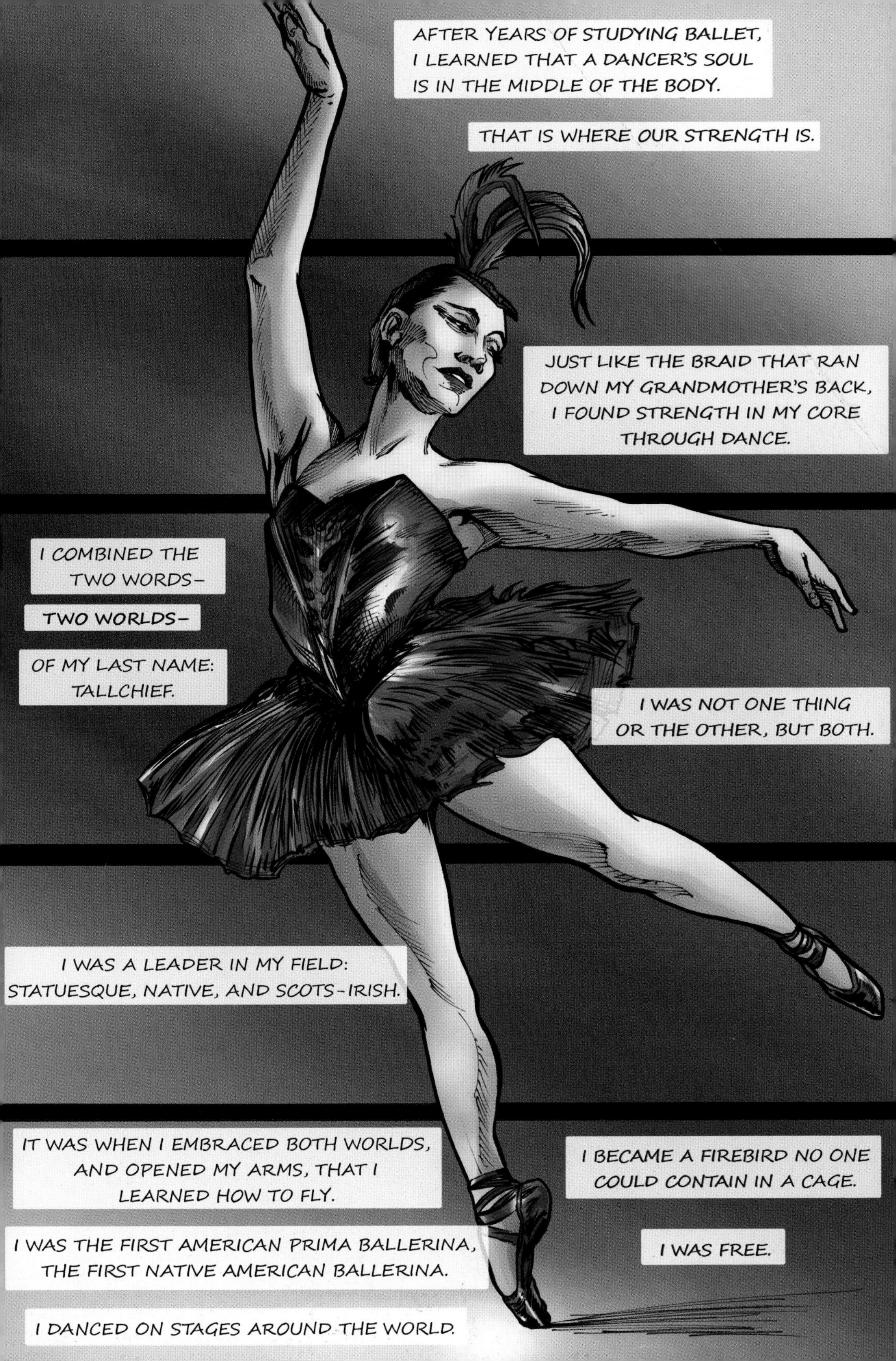
AFTER YEARS OF STUDYING BALLET, I LEARNED THAT A DANCER'S SOUL IS IN THE MIDDLE OF THE BODY.
THAT IS WHERE OUR STRENGTH IS.
JUST LIKE THE BRAID THAT RAN DOWN MY GRANDMOTHER'S BACK, I FOUND STRENGTH IN MY CORE THROUGH DANCE.
I COMBINED THE TWO WORDS—
TWO WORLDS—
OF MY LAST NAME: TALLCHIEF.
I WAS NOT ONE THING OR THE OTHER, BUT BOTH.
I WAS A LEADER IN MY FIELD: STATUESQUE, NATIVE, AND SCOTS-IRISH.
IT WAS WHEN I EMBRACED BOTH WORLDS, AND OPENED MY ARMS, THAT I LEARNED HOW TO FLY.
I WAS THE FIRST AMERICAN PRIMA BALLERINA, THE FIRST NATIVE AMERICAN BALLERINA.
I DANCED ON STAGES AROUND THE WORLD.
I BECAME A FIREBIRD NO ONE COULD CONTAIN IN A CAGE.
I WAS FREE.

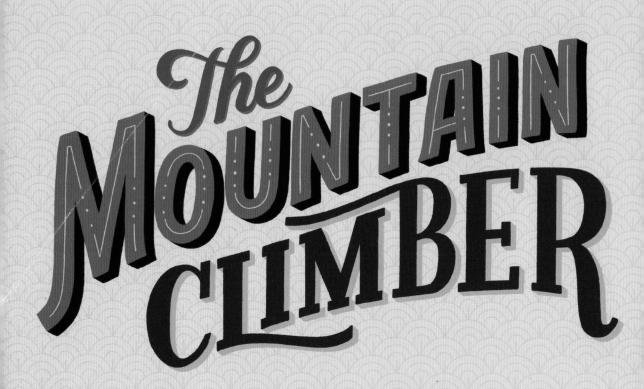

The MOUNTAIN CLIMBER

· · · · ·

JUNKO TABEI
1939~2016

Keep climbing. Every step you take brings you closer to your goal. That's the sort of determination that four-foot-nine-inch-tall mountain climber Junko Tabei brought to climb the 29,029-foot-tall Mt. Everest. Not even an avalanche could stop her from becoming the first woman ever to reach its peak, the highest in the world.

JUNKO AND ME

COUNT ALL THE THINGS YOU HAVE IN COMMON WITH JUNKO TABEI.

- I love being outside.
- I don't even mind the cold.
- I like starting clubs with my friends.
- I don't need to brag about what I can do—I just like to do it.
- I don't need an audience.
- I love to challenge myself.
- I am my own cheerleader.
- I'm independent.
- I'm lucky.
- I'm determined.

JUNKO TABEI
THE FIRST WOMAN on MT. EVEREST
How long have you been climbing?
My first time was when I was ten years old.
BY MARINAOMI

A teacher led us up a local mountain.

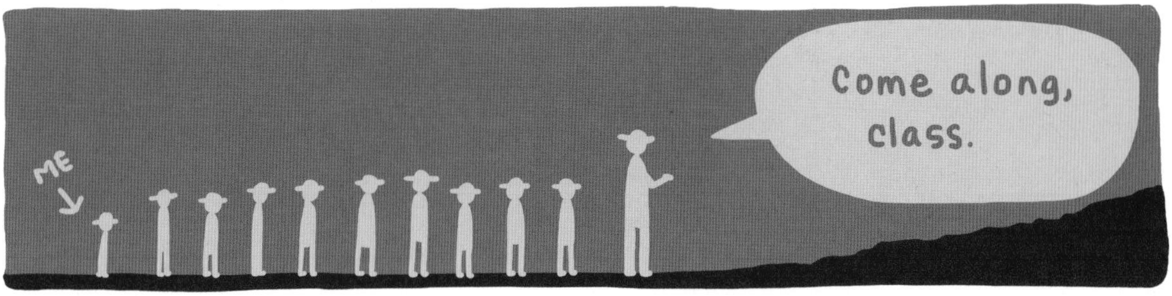
ME
Come along, class.

As we reached the top, I was shocked.

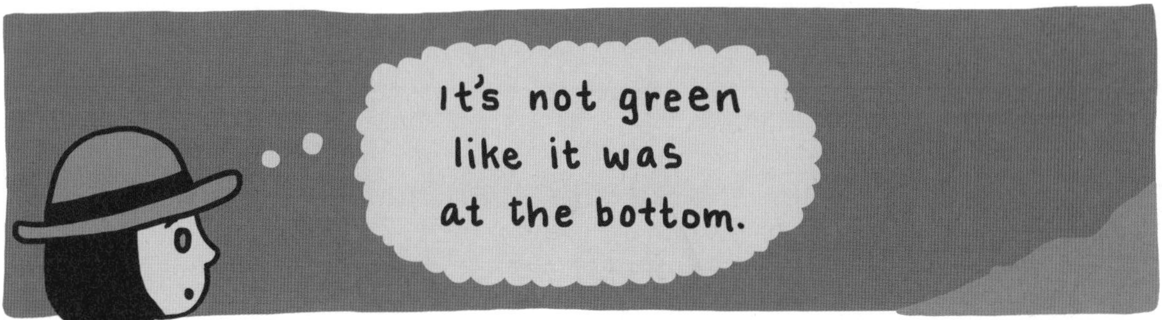
It's not green like it was at the bottom.

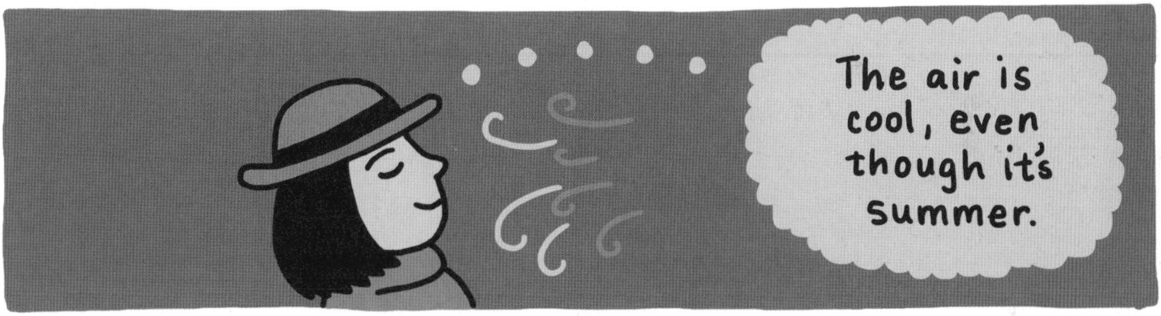
The air is cool, even though it's summer.

I loved everything about it, especially that it wasn't a competition.

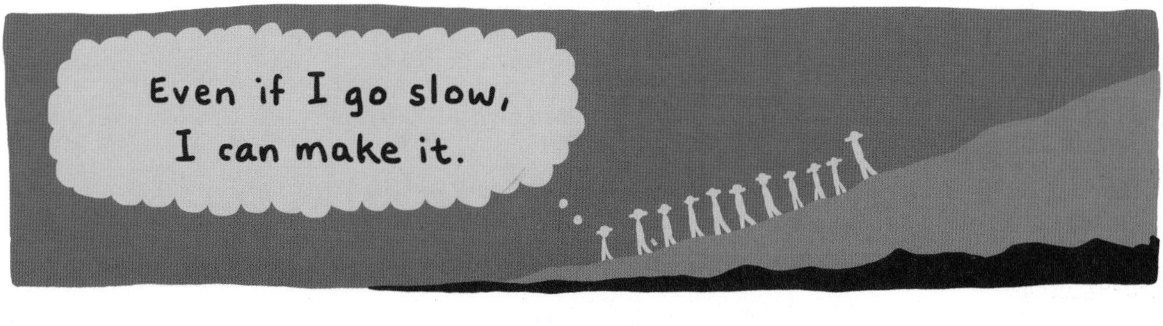
Even if I go slow, I can make it.

I didn't get to climb again for a long while.

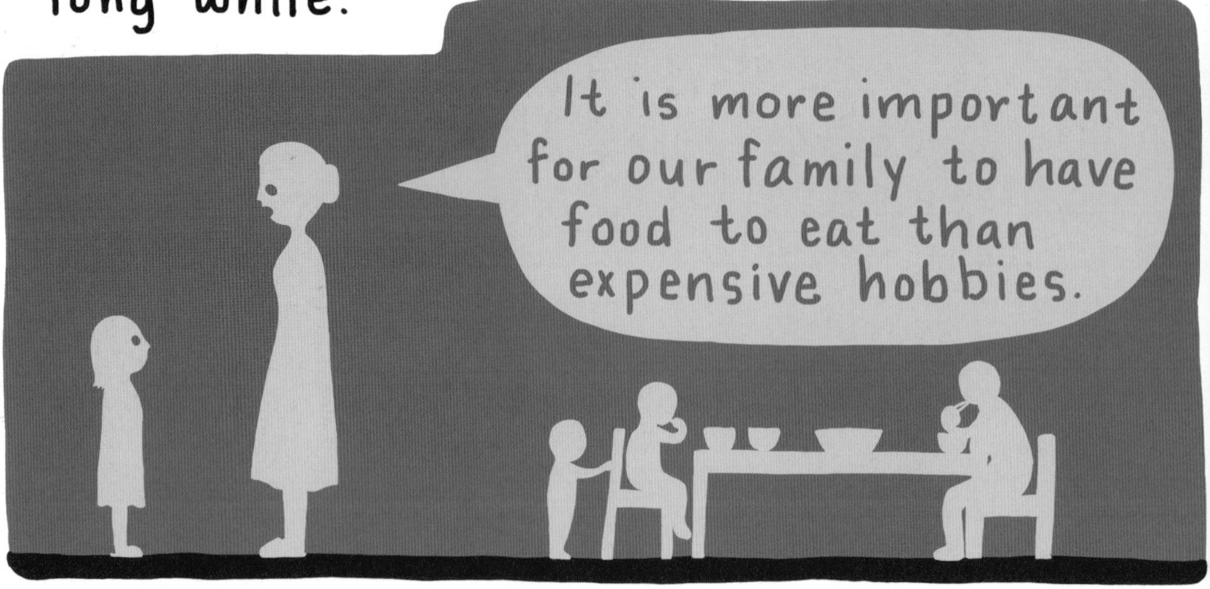
It is more important for our family to have food to eat than expensive hobbies.

In college, I joined a coed climbing group, but I had fantasies of being in an all-women group, even though no such thing existed.

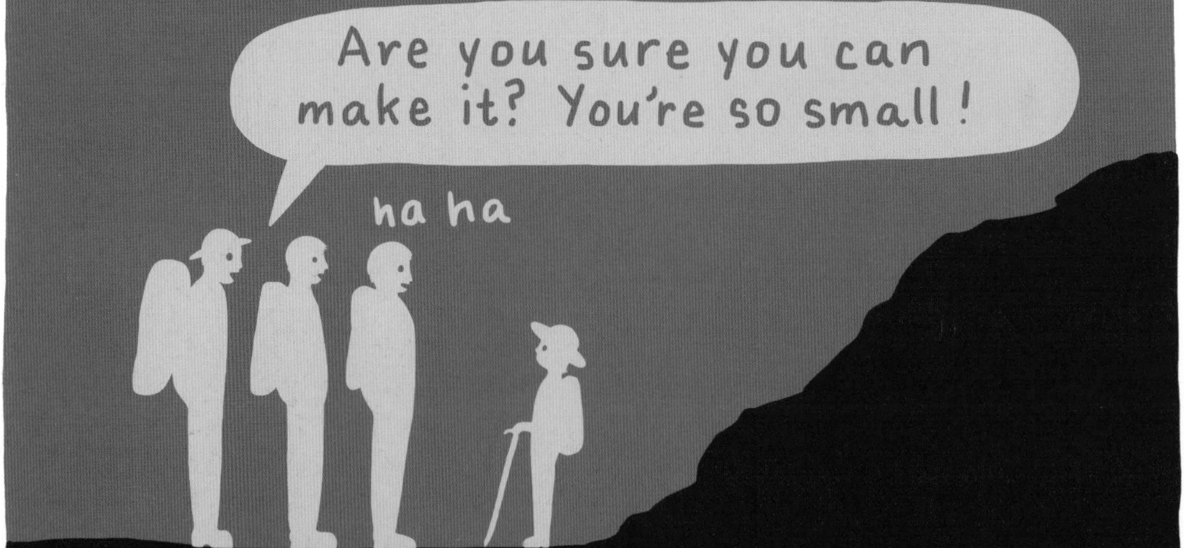
Are you sure you can make it? You're so small!
ha ha

I see! I'm glad you created this group, then.
Oh, here we are at Camp 2. We're close to the summit now.

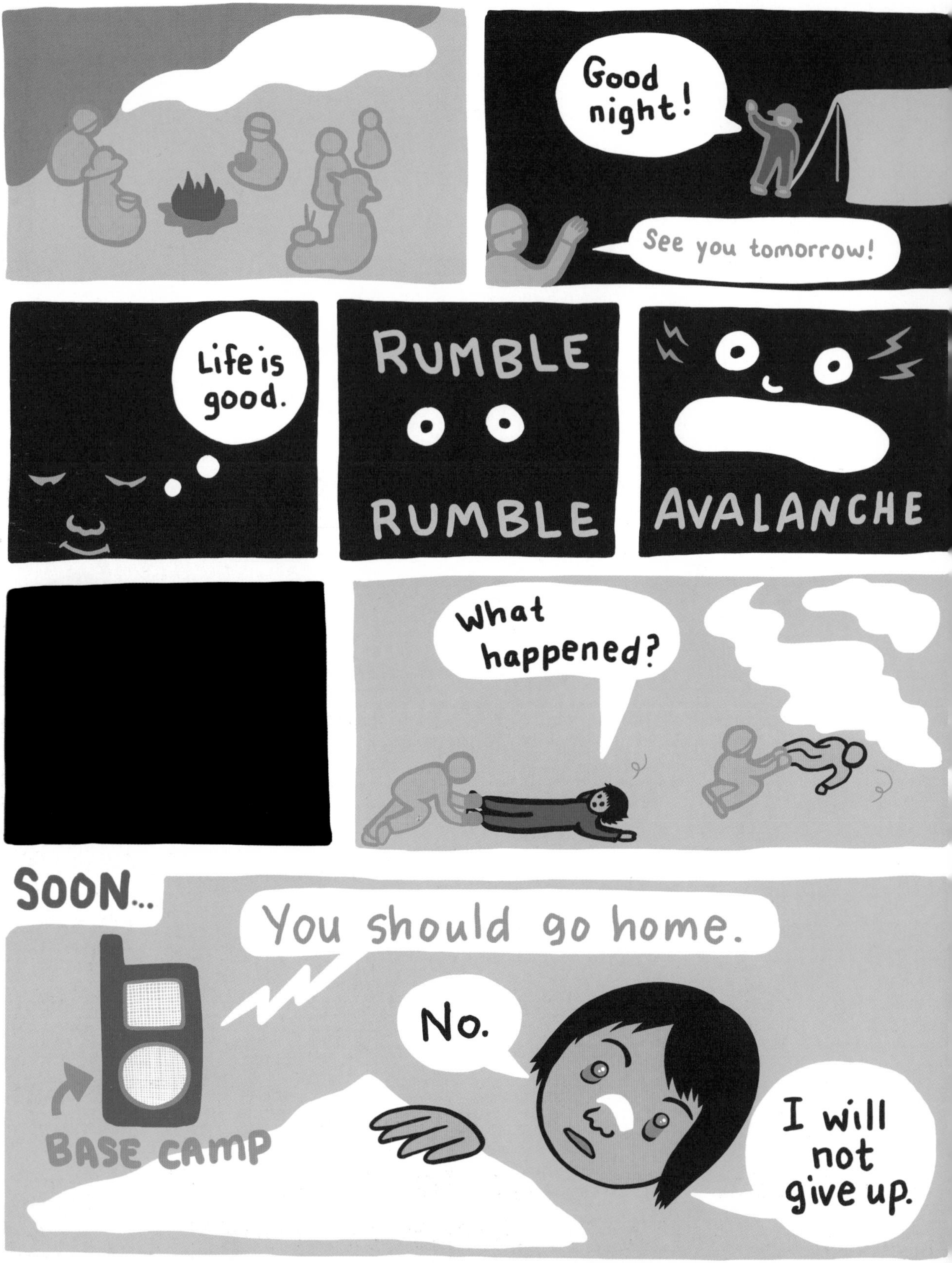
Good night!
See you tomorrow!
Life is good.
RUMBLE
RUMBLE
AVALANCHE
What happened?
SOON...
You should go home.
BASE CAMP
No.
I will not give up.

TWELVE DAYS LATER...

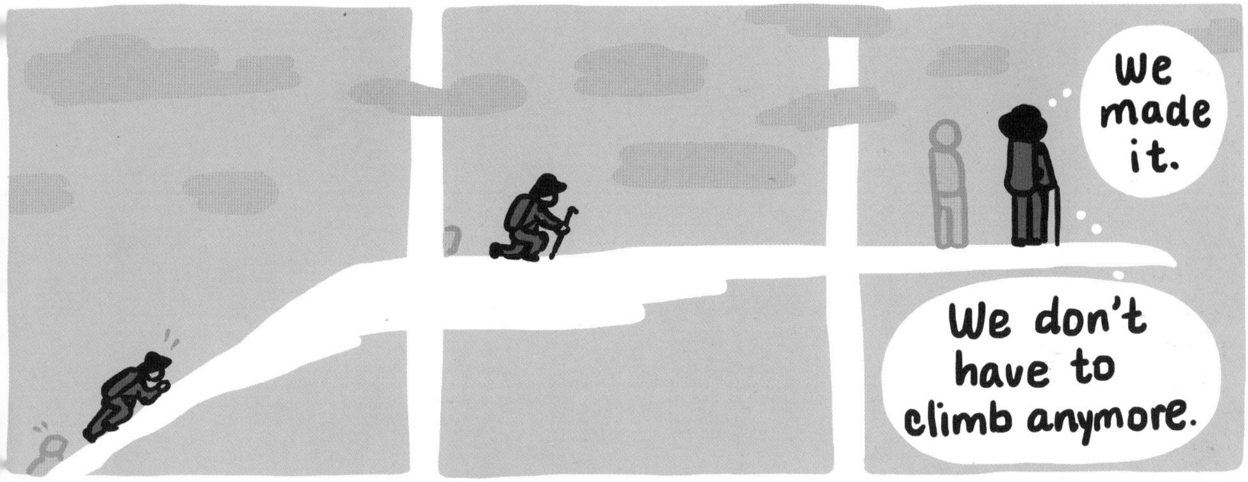

We made it.
We don't have to climb anymore.

JUNKO TABEI WAS THE FIRST WOMAN TO EVER REACH THE SUMMIT OF MT. EVEREST, THE HIGHEST MOUNTAIN IN THE WORLD.

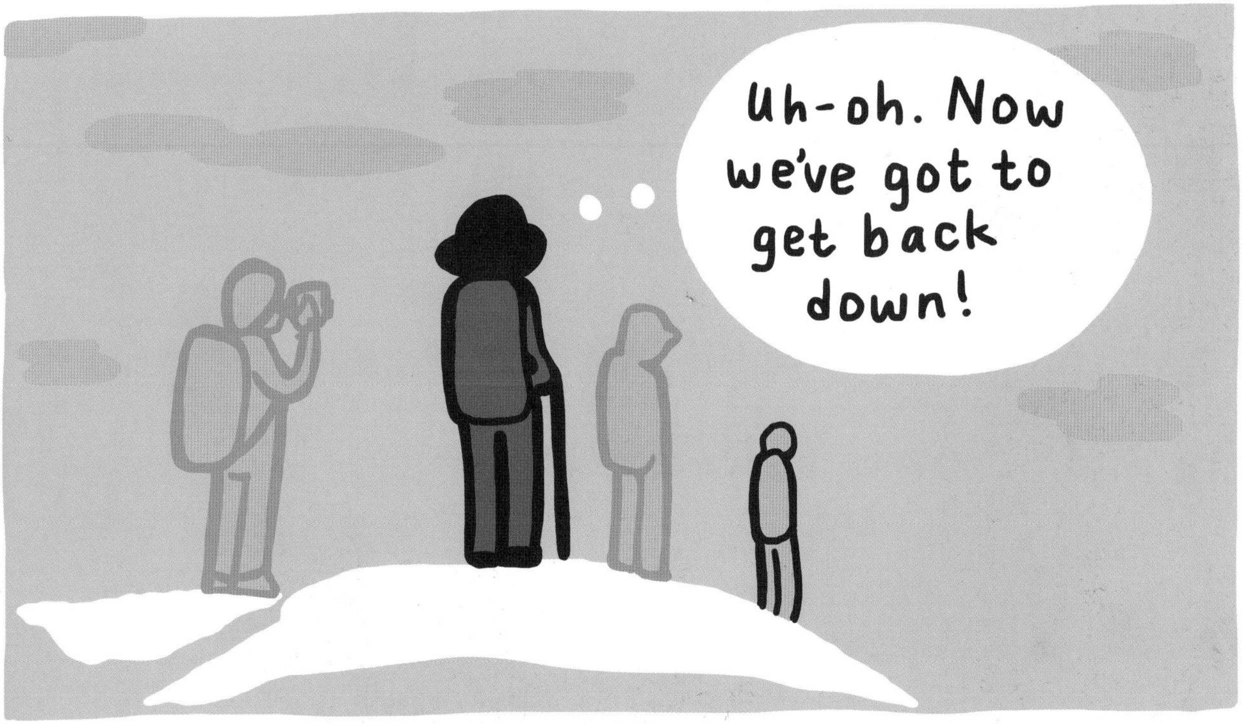

Uh-oh. Now we've got to get back down!

SHE LATER WENT ON TO CLIMB THE HIGHEST PEAK ON EVERY CONTINENT.

THE END

Create

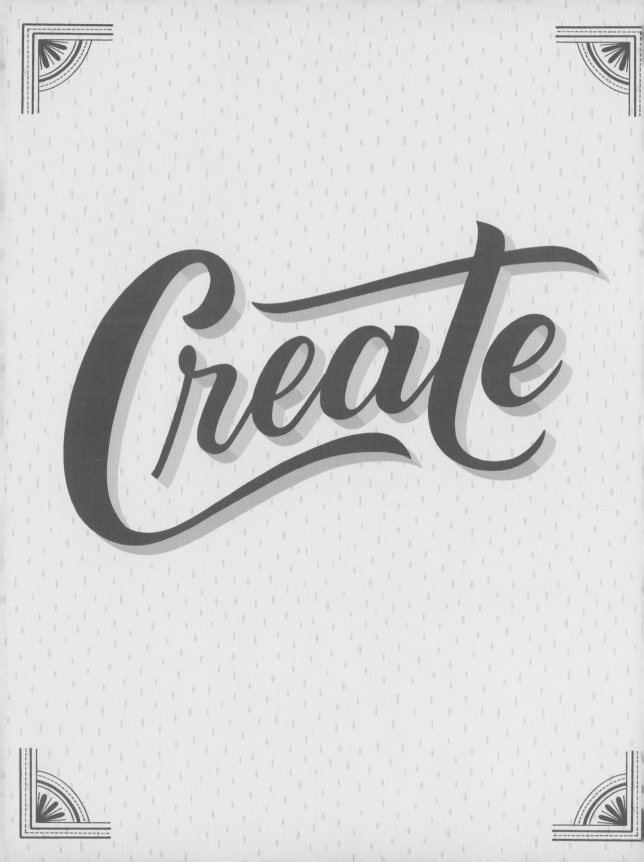

Art is an expression of who you are and how you feel at any given moment in time, so there is no wrong way to make it. One minute, you might feel like a silly, rhyming poem written in curly purple letters, and the next, you might feel like a pile of green, blue, and black paint, smeared thick onto a canvas. Great artists and makers, like the five in this chapter, use their tools to make us think and feel more deeply than we could have ever imagined. Their art, in all its forms, helps connect us to our hopes and fears, our sadness and joy, our dreams and each other, and their work makes the world a more beautiful place.

THE PASSIONATE PAINTER

· · · · ·

FRIDA KAHLO
1907 ~ 1954

Her life was full of hardship and pain, but Mexican painter Frida Kahlo channeled her sadness into beauty, proving that strength is not based on the size of one's muscles, but instead on the size of one's heart.

FRIDA AND ME

COUNT ALL THE THINGS YOU HAVE IN COMMON WITH FRIDA KAHLO.

- I like to paint with bright colors.
- I adore animals.
- I have an imaginary friend.
- Sometimes I daydream that I'm somewhere else.
- I dress however I please.
- I know that what makes me different makes me special.
- I love the people in my life fiercely.
- I want to add beauty to the world.
- I'm persistent.
- I'm resilient.

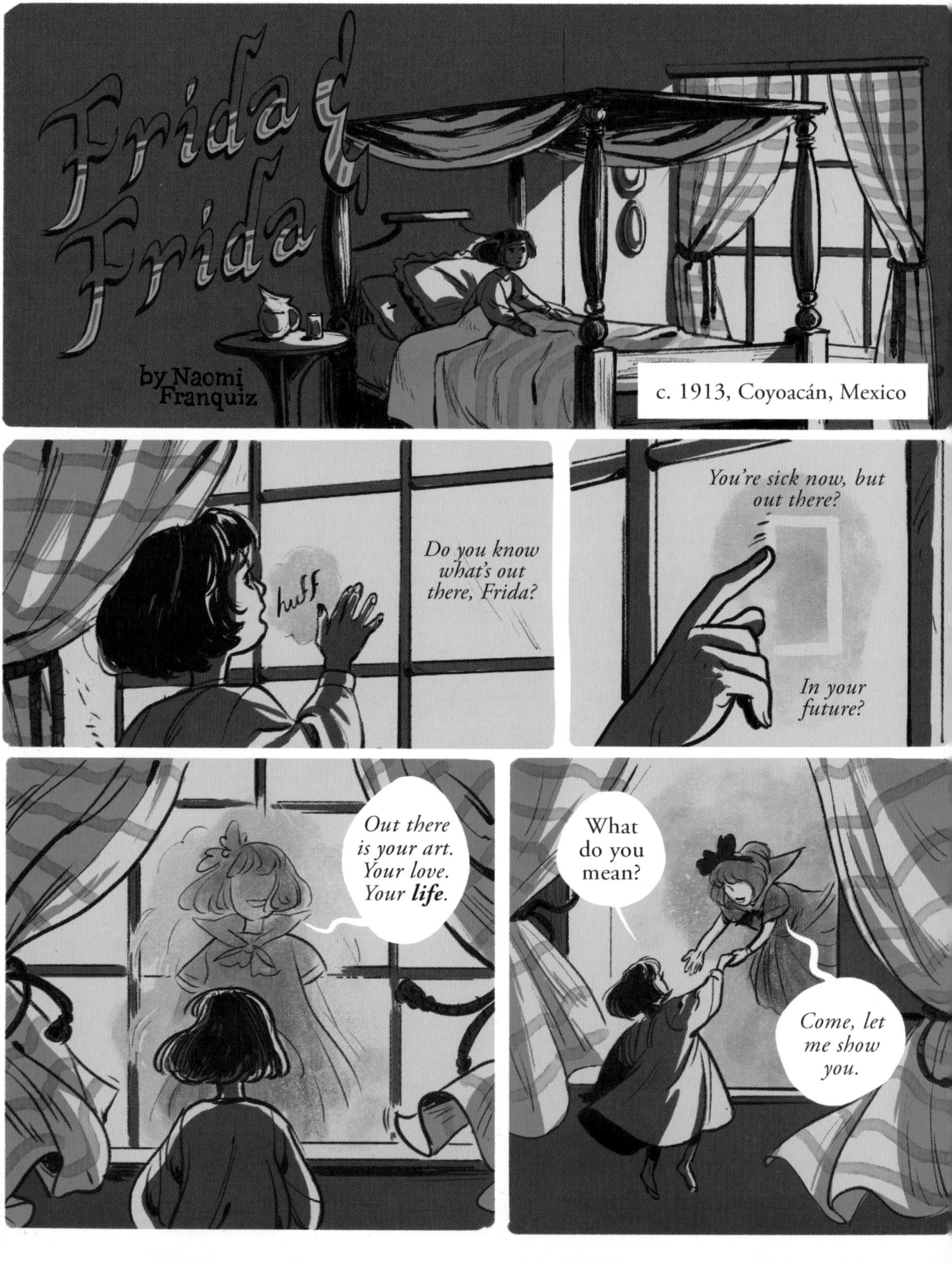

Frida & Frida
by Naomi Franquiz
c. 1913, Coyoacán, Mexico
huff
Do you know what's out there, Frida?
You're sick now, but out there?
In your future?
Out there is your art. Your love. Your life.
What do you mean?
Come, let me show you.

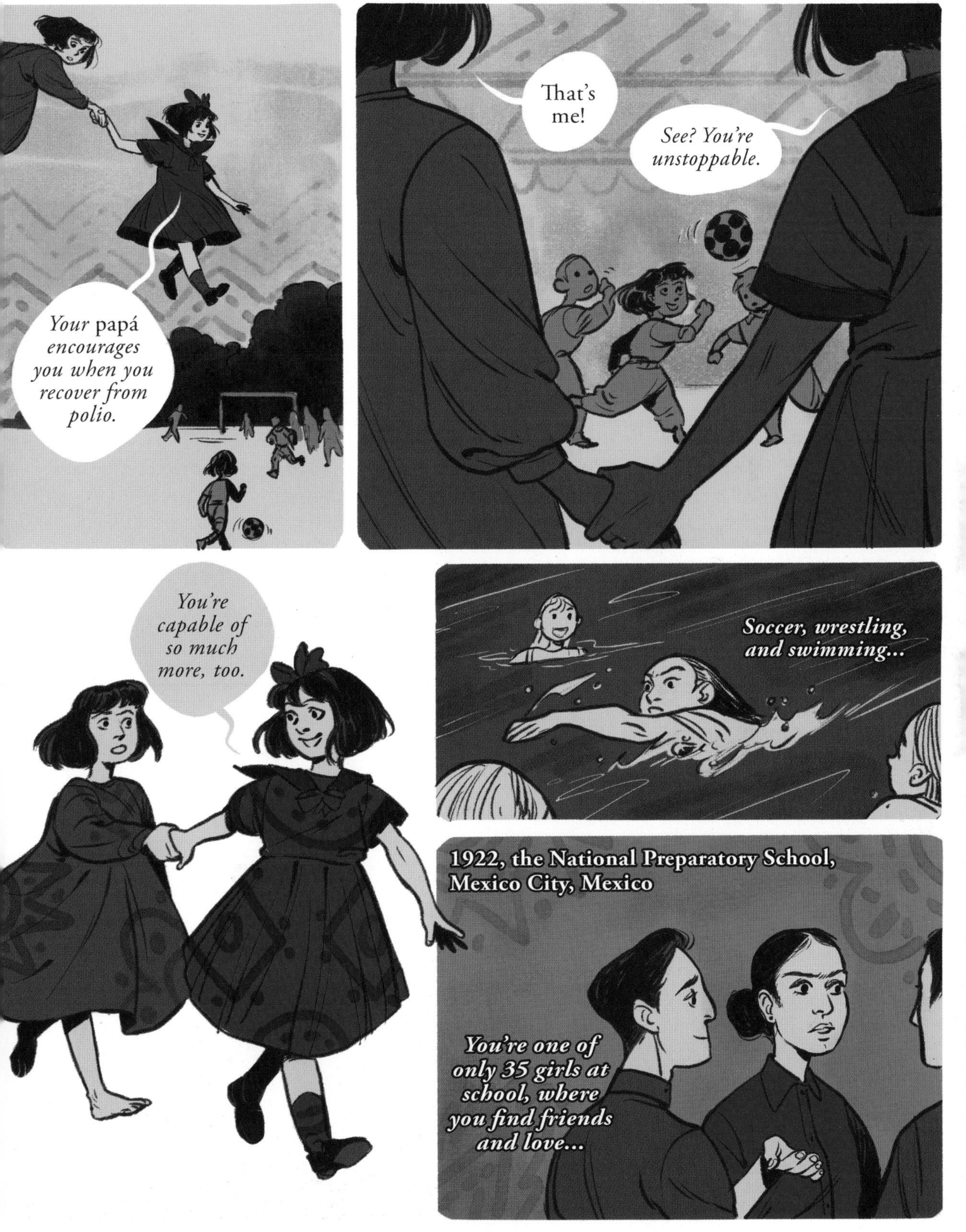
Your papá encourages you when you recover from polio.
That's me!
See? You're unstoppable.
You're capable of so much more, too.
Soccer, wrestling, and swimming...
1922, the National Preparatory School, Mexico City, Mexico
You're one of only 35 girls at school, where you find friends and love...

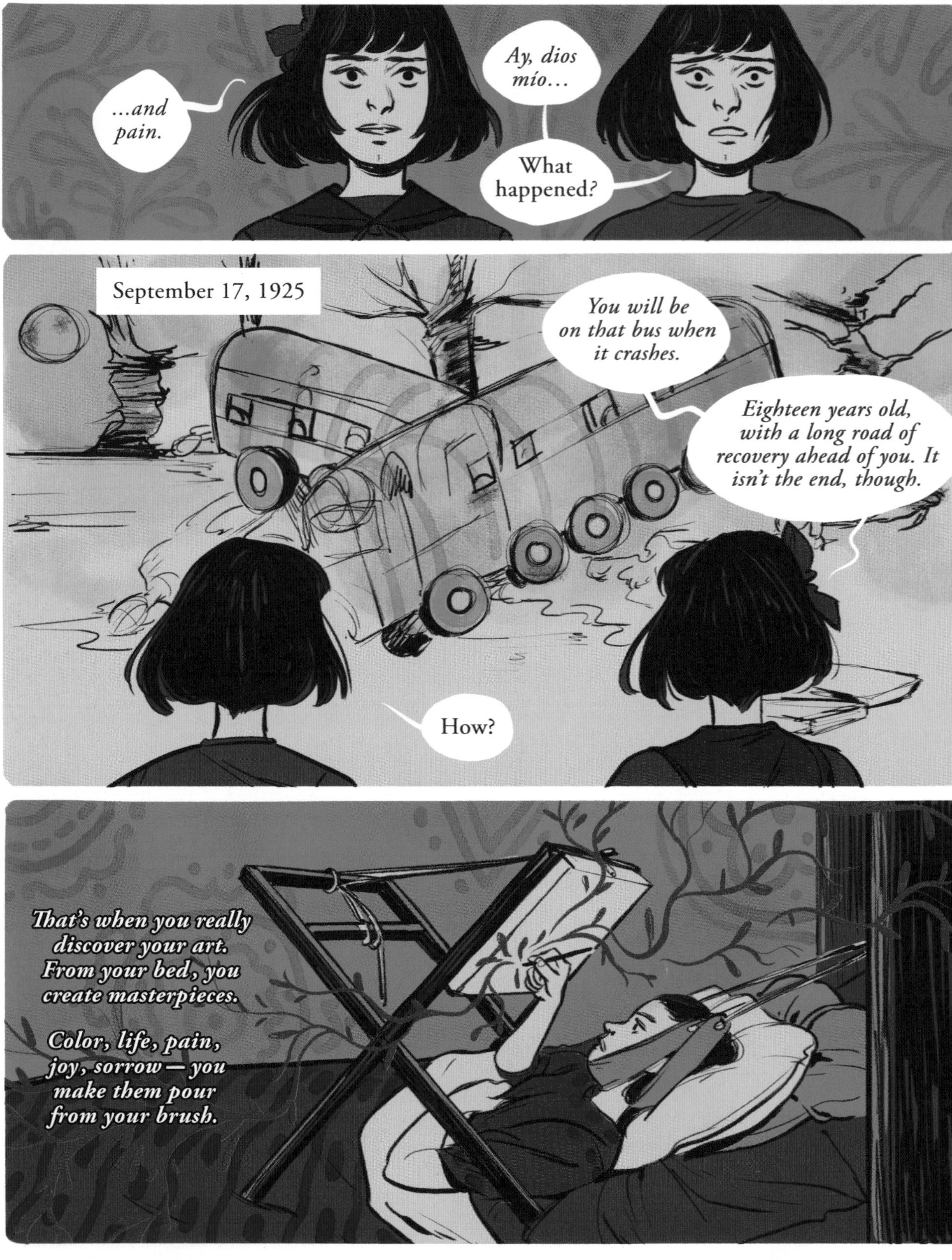
...and pain.
Ay, dios mío...
What happened?
September 17, 1925
You will be on that bus when it crashes.
Eighteen years old, with a long road of recovery ahead of you. It isn't the end, though.
How?
That's when you really discover your art. From your bed, you create masterpieces.
Color, life, pain, joy, sorrow — you make them pour from your brush.

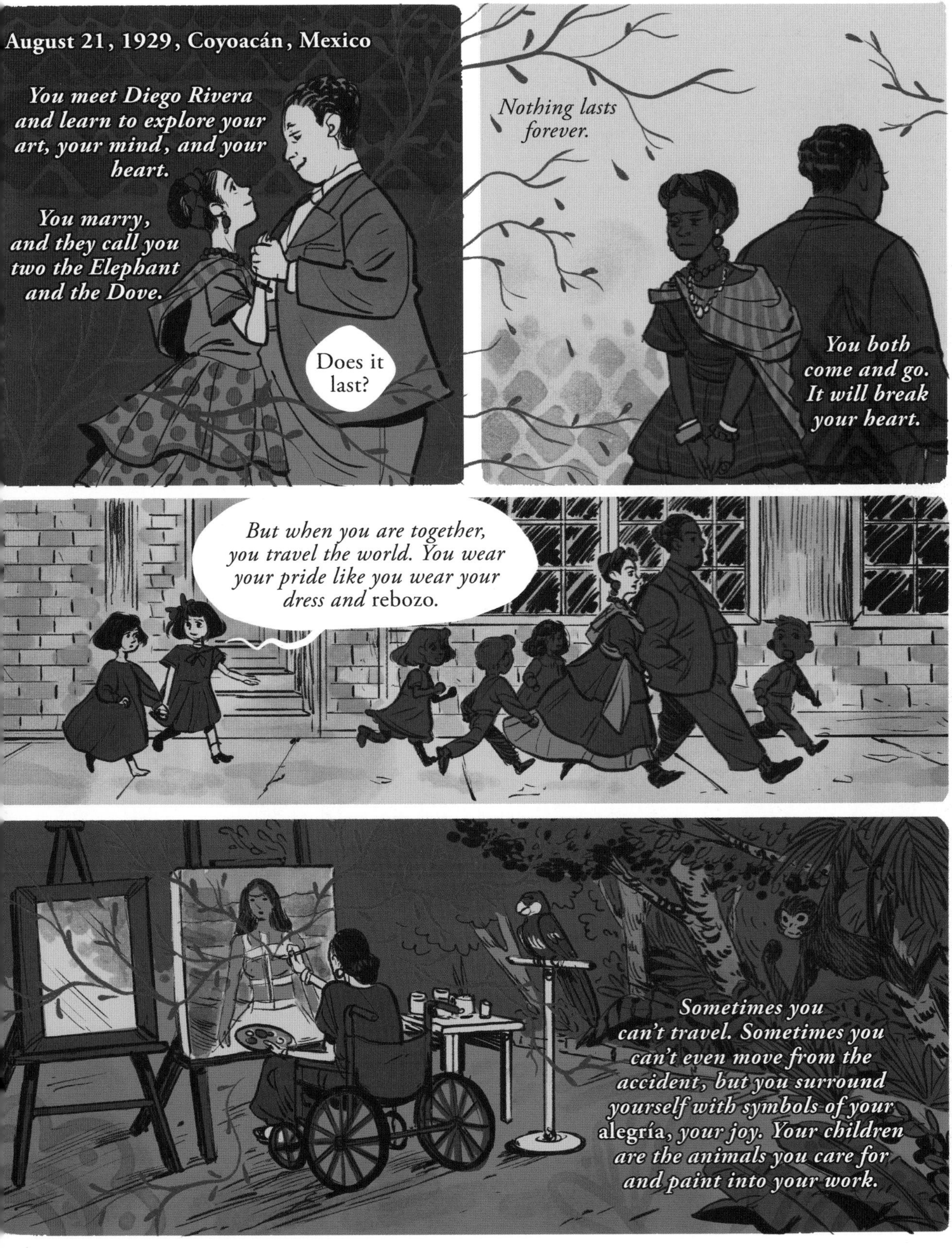
August 21, 1929, Coyoacán, Mexico
You meet Diego Rivera and learn to explore your art, your mind, and your heart.
You marry, and they call you two the Elephant and the Dove.
Does it last?
Nothing lasts forever.
You both come and go. It will break your heart.
But when you are together, you travel the world. You wear your pride like you wear your dress and rebozo.
Sometimes you can't travel. Sometimes you can't even move from the accident, but you surround yourself with symbols of your alegría, your joy. Your children are the animals you care for and paint into your work.

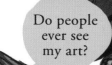

Do people ever see my art?

Do I get to share any of this pain and joy?

Of course.

You have pain and healing in your future, but you see life in a way that people years from now will admire.

"I never paint dreams or nightmares. I paint my own reality."

Your art hangs in galleries around the world, both in your lifetime and years after you're gone.

One day, you will tell the world your truth.

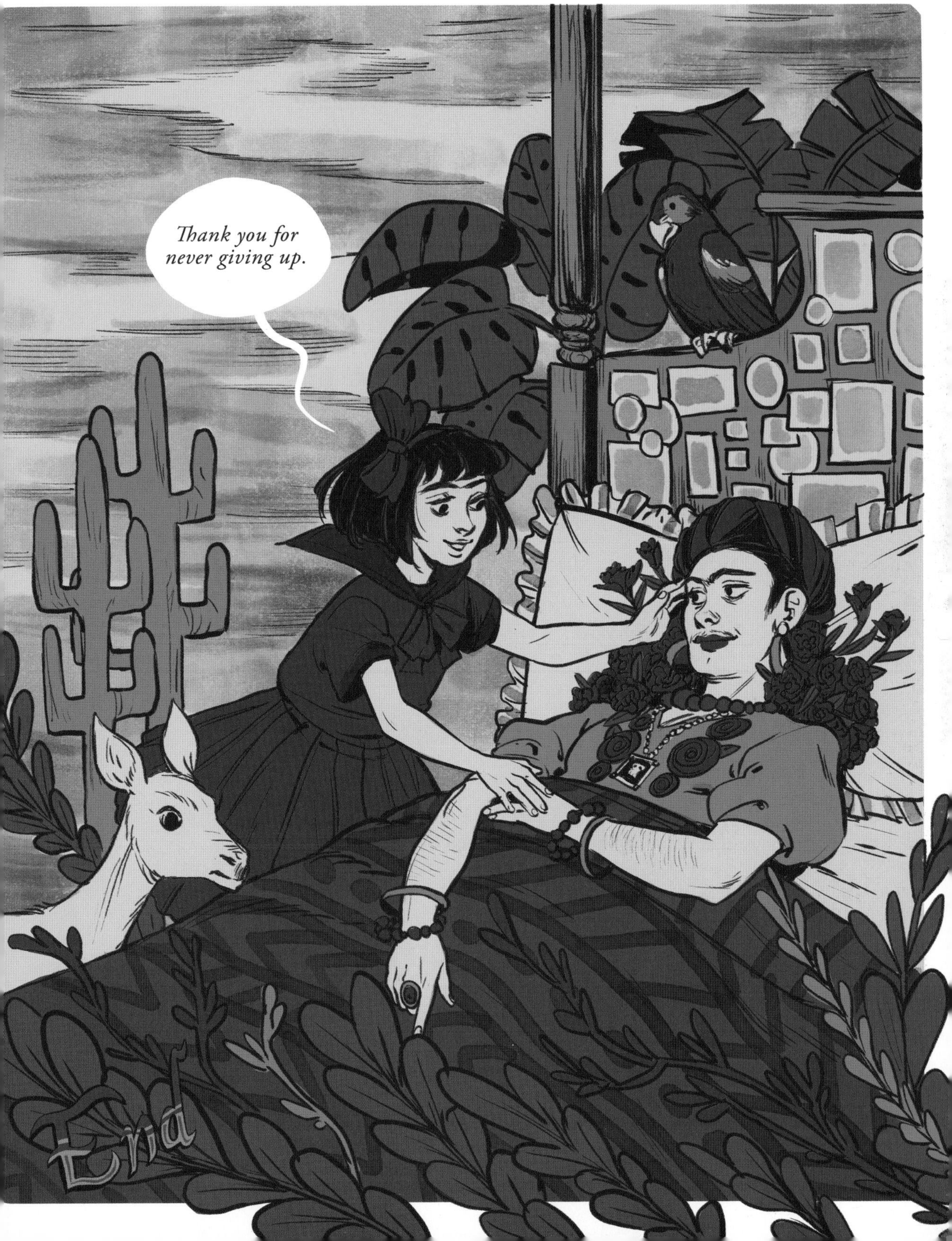
Thank you for never giving up.

The SINGING SPY

.....

JOSEPHINE BAKER
1906 ~ 1975

When singer and dancer Josephine Baker was given standing ovations at her performances, her audiences had no idea how much praise she truly deserved. Offstage, she was a secret spy who outwitted Nazis to help bring peace to the world.

JOSEPHINE AND ME

COUNT ALL THE THINGS YOU HAVE IN COMMON WITH JOSEPHINE BAKER.

- I like to dance.
- I sing all the time.
- Acting gives me a thrill.
- I like to go new places.
- I want to have a big family and lots of pets.
- Secrets are safe with me.
- I'm good at acting.
- I stand up for what's right.
- I'm bold.
- I'm fierce.

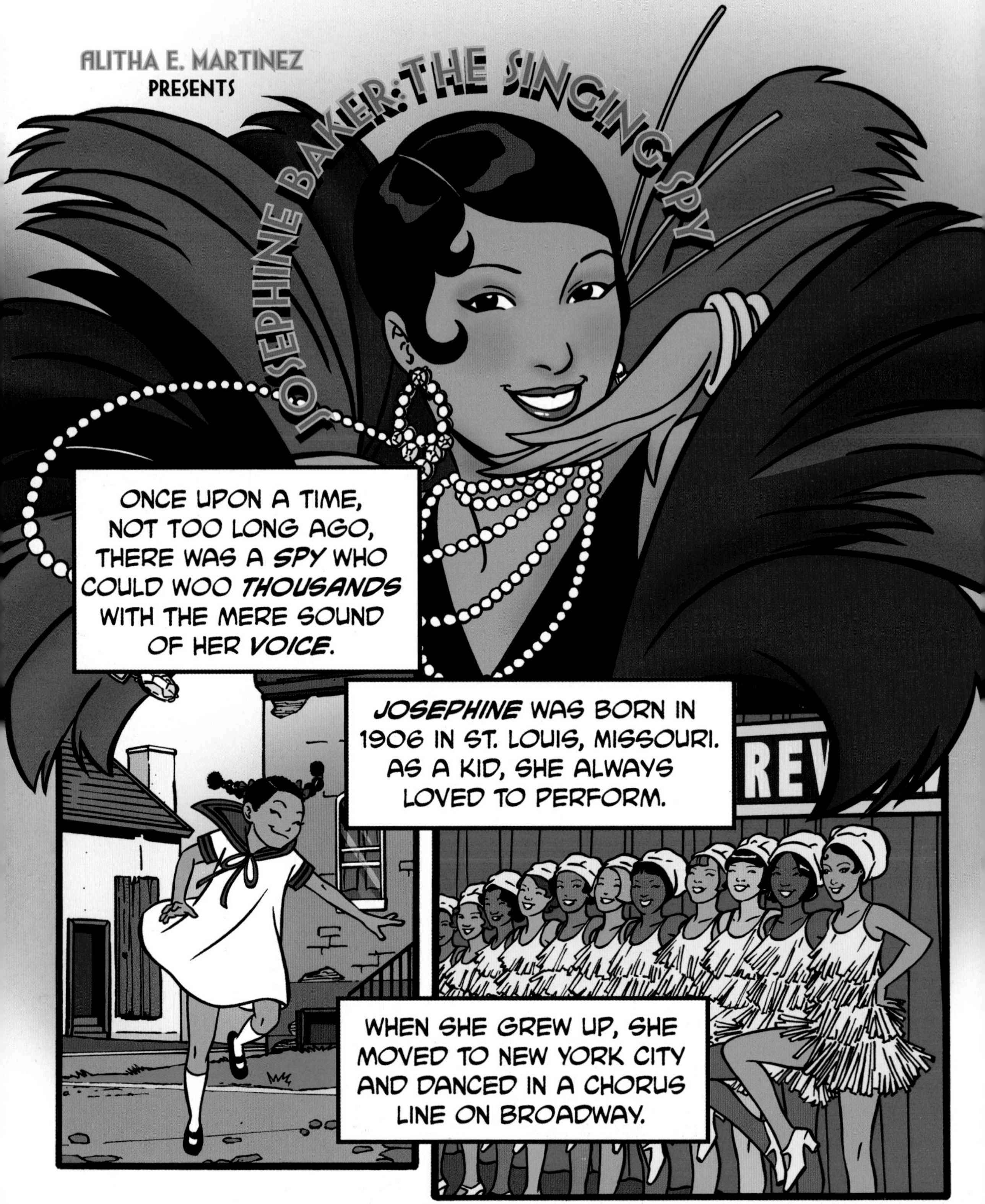
ALITHA E. MARTINEZ
PRESENTS
JOSEPHINE BAKER: THE SINGING SPY
ONCE UPON A TIME, NOT TOO LONG AGO, THERE WAS A *SPY* WHO COULD WOO ***THOUSANDS*** WITH THE MERE SOUND OF HER *VOICE*.
JOSEPHINE WAS BORN IN 1906 IN ST. LOUIS, MISSOURI. AS A KID, SHE ALWAYS LOVED TO PERFORM.
REV
WHEN SHE GREW UP, SHE MOVED TO NEW YORK CITY AND DANCED IN A CHORUS LINE ON BROADWAY.

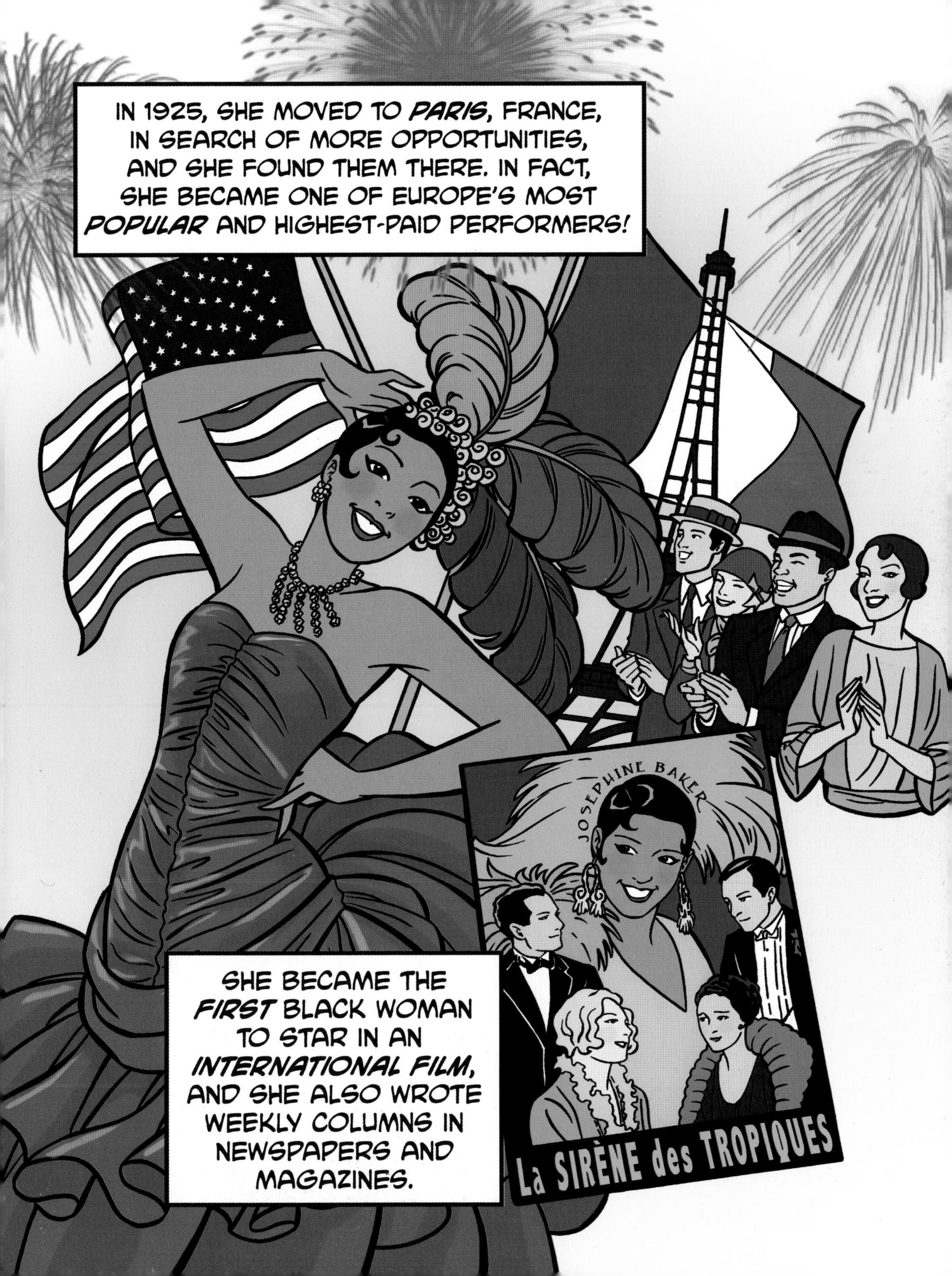
IN 1925, SHE MOVED TO *PARIS*, FRANCE, IN SEARCH OF MORE OPPORTUNITIES, AND SHE FOUND THEM THERE. IN FACT, SHE BECAME ONE OF EUROPE'S MOST *POPULAR* AND HIGHEST-PAID PERFORMERS!
JOSEPHINE BAKER
SHE BECAME THE *FIRST* BLACK WOMAN TO STAR IN AN *INTERNATIONAL FILM*, AND SHE ALSO WROTE WEEKLY COLUMNS IN NEWSPAPERS AND MAGAZINES.
La SIRÈNE des TROPIQUES

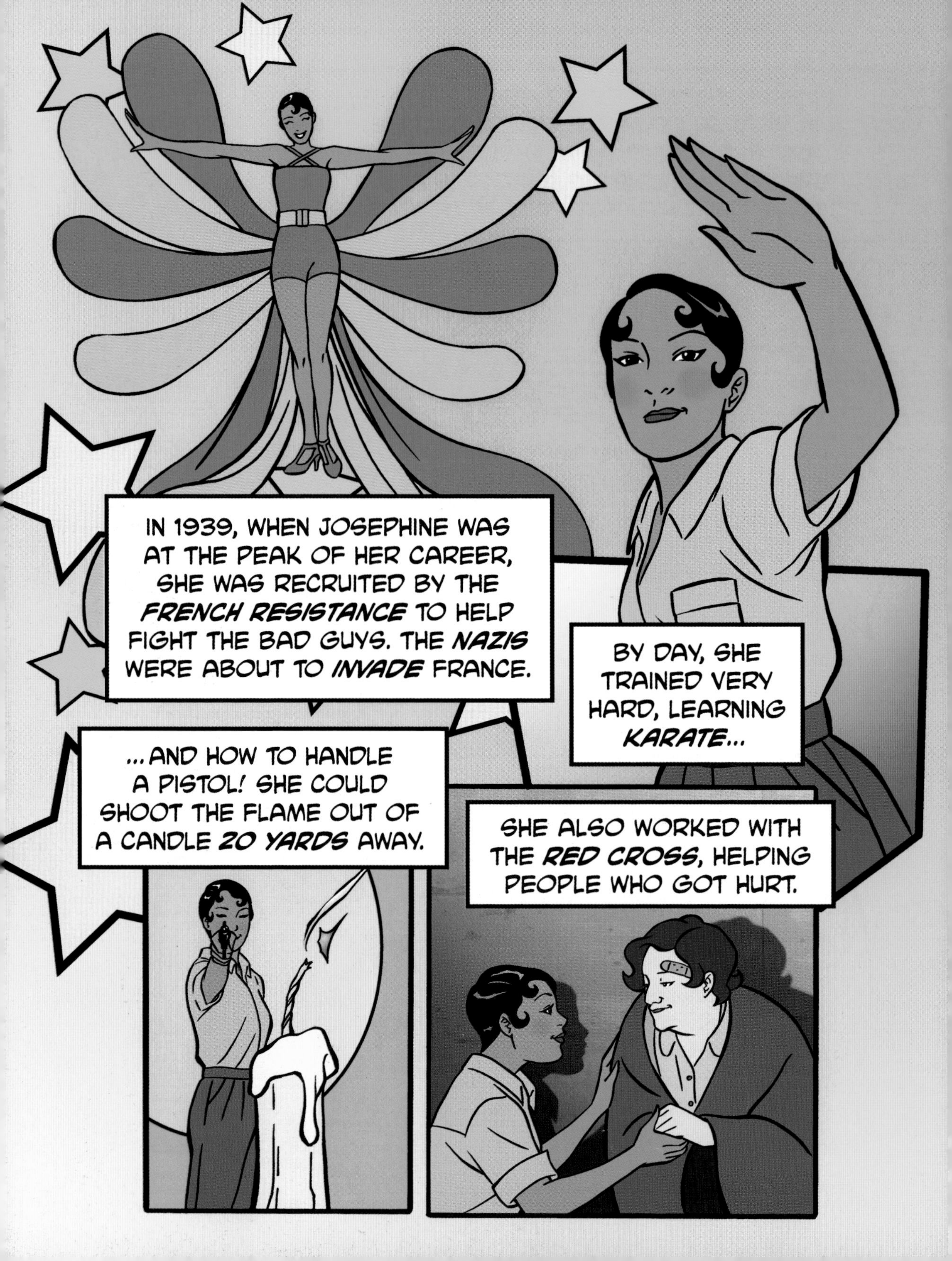

IN 1939, WHEN JOSEPHINE WAS AT THE PEAK OF HER CAREER, SHE WAS RECRUITED BY THE *FRENCH RESISTANCE* TO HELP FIGHT THE BAD GUYS. THE *NAZIS* WERE ABOUT TO *INVADE* FRANCE.
BY DAY, SHE TRAINED VERY HARD, LEARNING *KARATE*...
...AND HOW TO HANDLE A PISTOL! SHE COULD SHOOT THE FLAME OUT OF A CANDLE *20 YARDS* AWAY.
SHE ALSO WORKED WITH THE *RED CROSS*, HELPING PEOPLE WHO GOT HURT.

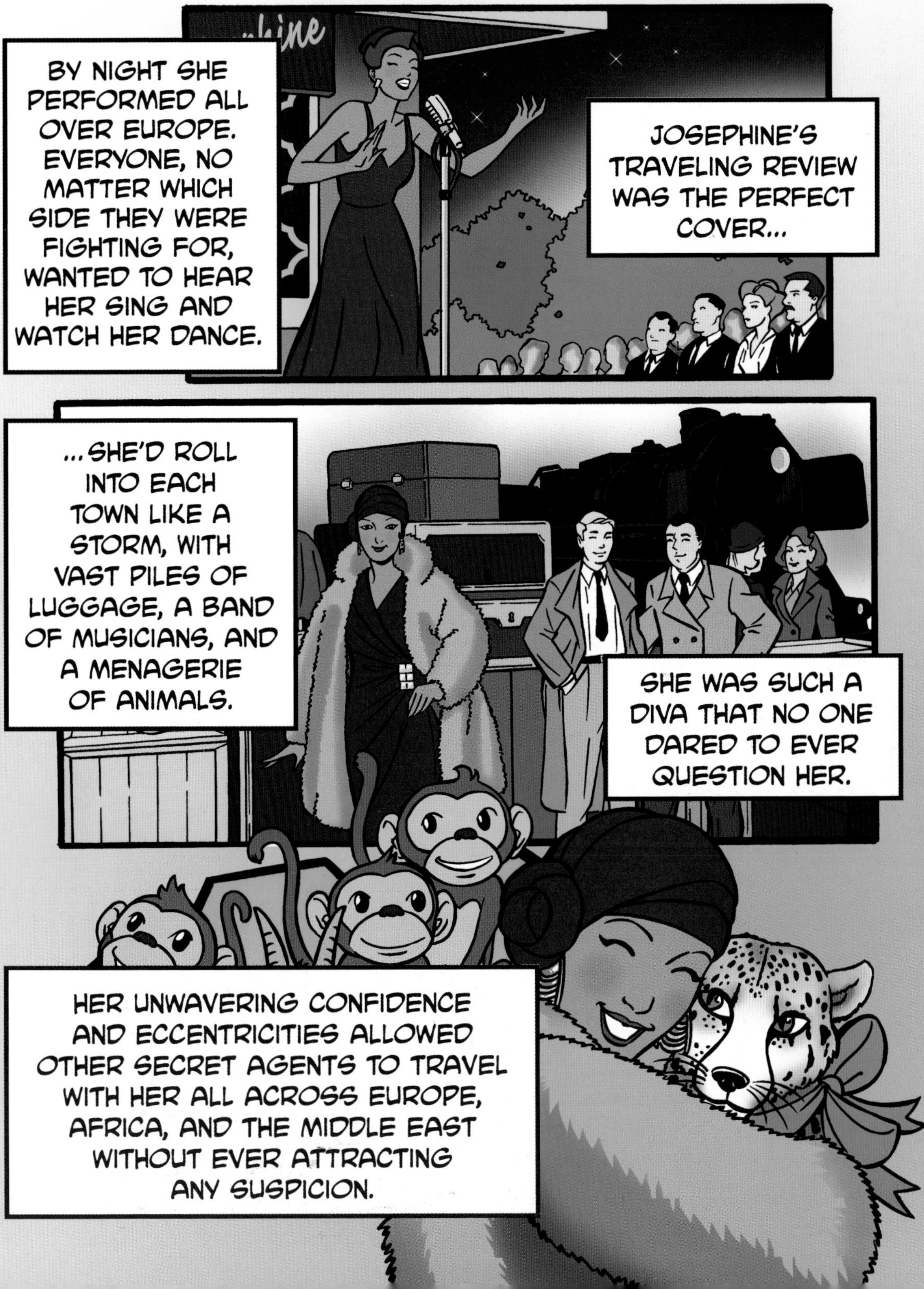

BY NIGHT SHE PERFORMED ALL OVER EUROPE. EVERYONE, NO MATTER WHICH SIDE THEY WERE FIGHTING FOR, WANTED TO HEAR HER SING AND WATCH HER DANCE.
JOSEPHINE'S TRAVELING REVIEW WAS THE PERFECT COVER...
...SHE'D ROLL INTO EACH TOWN LIKE A STORM, WITH VAST PILES OF LUGGAGE, A BAND OF MUSICIANS, AND A MENAGERIE OF ANIMALS.
SHE WAS SUCH A DIVA THAT NO ONE DARED TO EVER QUESTION HER.
HER UNWAVERING CONFIDENCE AND ECCENTRICITIES ALLOWED OTHER SECRET AGENTS TO TRAVEL WITH HER ALL ACROSS EUROPE, AFRICA, AND THE MIDDLE EAST WITHOUT EVER ATTRACTING ANY SUSPICION.

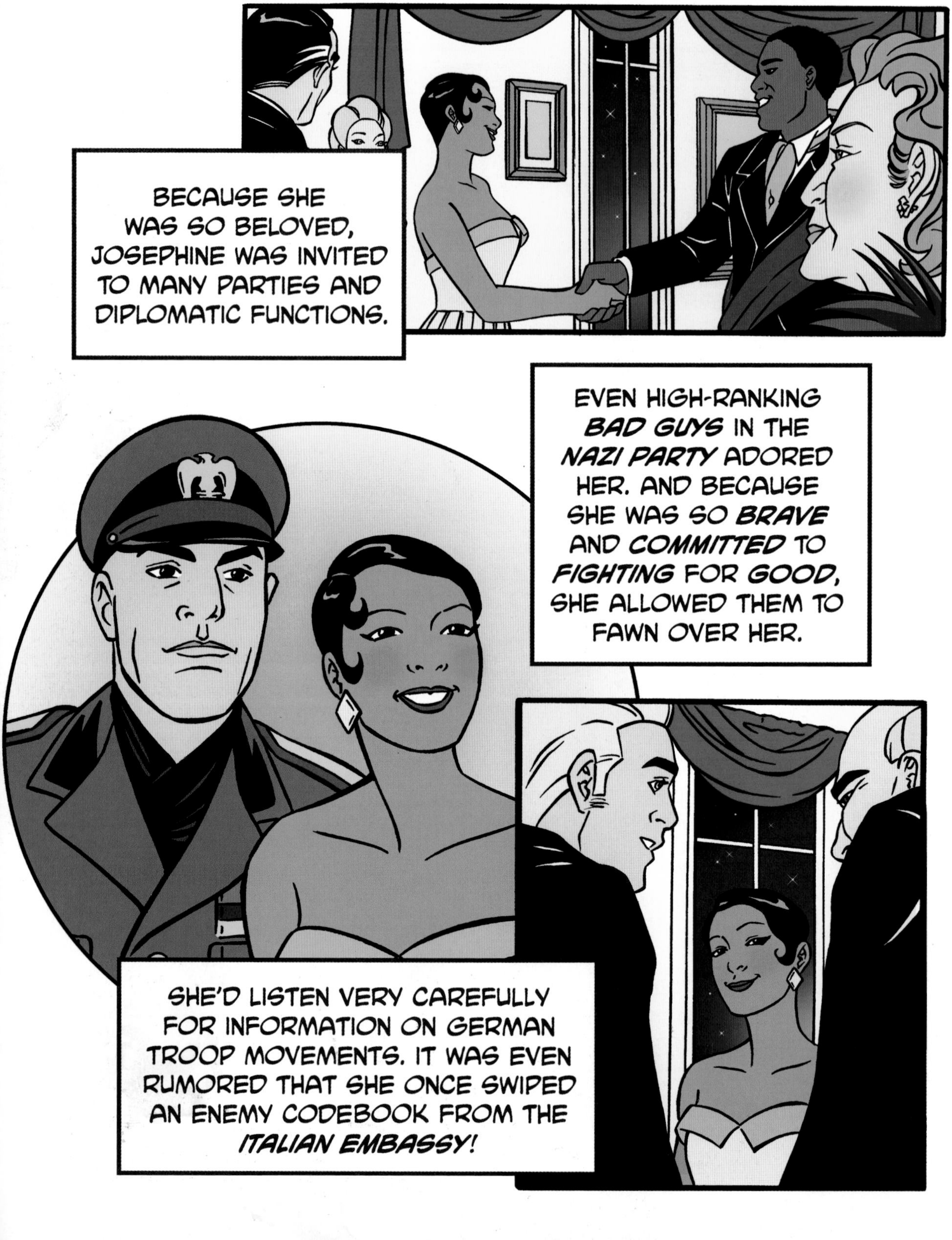
BECAUSE SHE WAS SO BELOVED, JOSEPHINE WAS INVITED TO MANY PARTIES AND DIPLOMATIC FUNCTIONS.
EVEN HIGH-RANKING *BAD GUYS* IN THE *NAZI PARTY* ADORED HER. AND BECAUSE SHE WAS SO *BRAVE* AND *COMMITTED* TO *FIGHTING* FOR *GOOD*, SHE ALLOWED THEM TO FAWN OVER HER.
SHE'D LISTEN VERY CAREFULLY FOR INFORMATION ON GERMAN TROOP MOVEMENTS. IT WAS EVEN RUMORED THAT SHE ONCE SWIPED AN ENEMY CODEBOOK FROM THE *ITALIAN EMBASSY*!

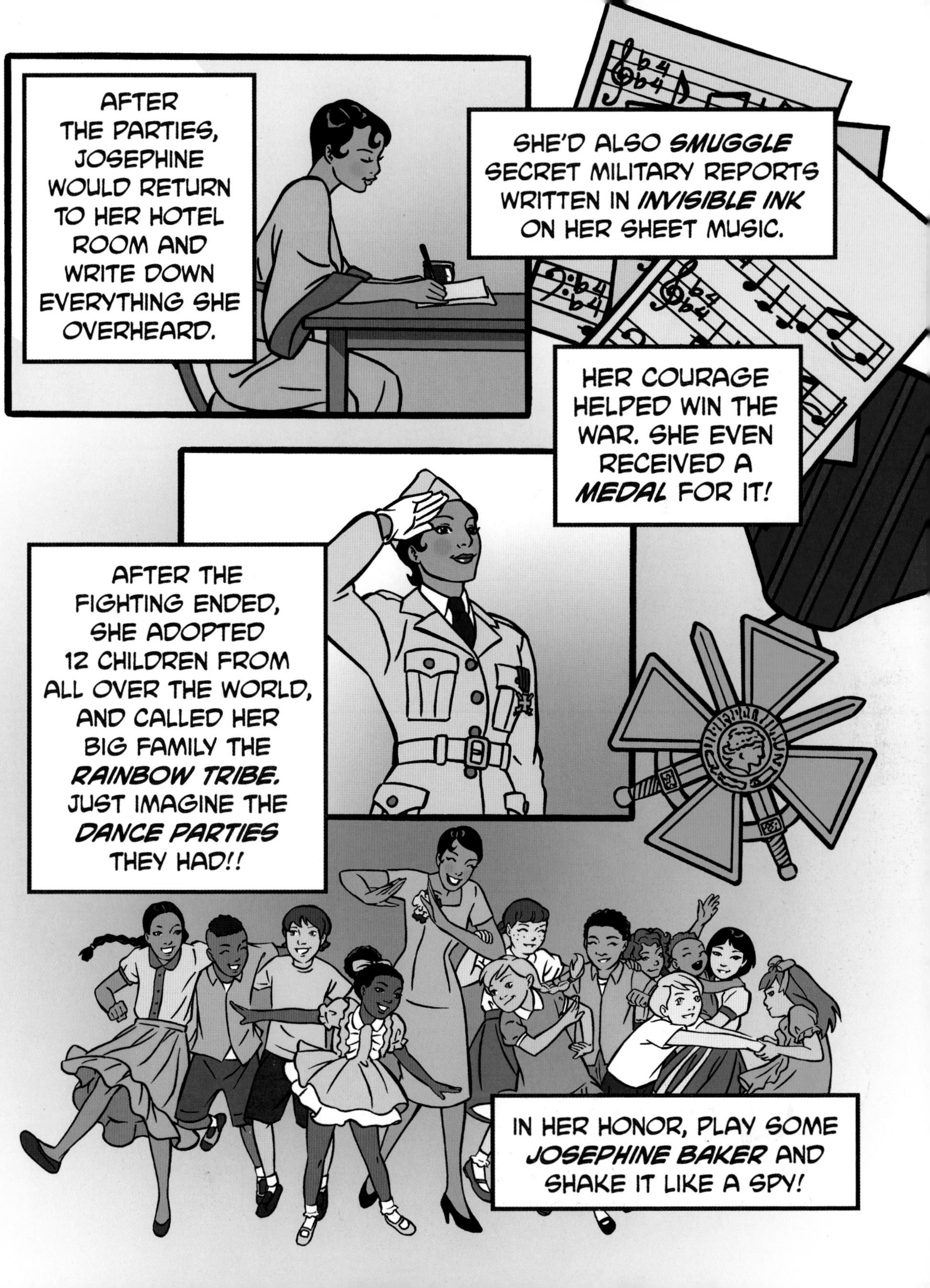

AFTER THE PARTIES, JOSEPHINE WOULD RETURN TO HER HOTEL ROOM AND WRITE DOWN EVERYTHING SHE OVERHEARD.
SHE'D ALSO *SMUGGLE* SECRET MILITARY REPORTS WRITTEN IN *INVISIBLE INK* ON HER SHEET MUSIC.
HER COURAGE HELPED WIN THE WAR. SHE EVEN RECEIVED A *MEDAL* FOR IT!
AFTER THE FIGHTING ENDED, SHE ADOPTED 12 CHILDREN FROM ALL OVER THE WORLD, AND CALLED HER BIG FAMILY THE *RAINBOW TRIBE.* JUST IMAGINE THE *DANCE PARTIES* THEY HAD!!
IN HER HONOR, PLAY SOME *JOSEPHINE BAKER* AND SHAKE IT LIKE A SPY!

THE Storyteller

• • • • •

MARY SHELLEY
1797~1851

On a dark and stormy night in 1816, Mary Shelley told a story unlike one anyone had ever heard before. It was so magnificently horrifying that she forever changed the way we think of monsters—and ourselves.

MARY AND ME

COUNT ALL THE THINGS YOU HAVE IN COMMON WITH MARY SHELLEY.

- I love to make up stories.
- Spooky things thrill me.
- My dreams are so vivid, and I remember lots of them.
- I like to think about why people behave as they do.
- I keep a diary.
- I have a lot of friends who are creative, just like me.
- Sometimes when I try to write, nothing comes.
- Sometimes my stories practically tell themselves.
- I'm thoughtful.
- I'm expressive.

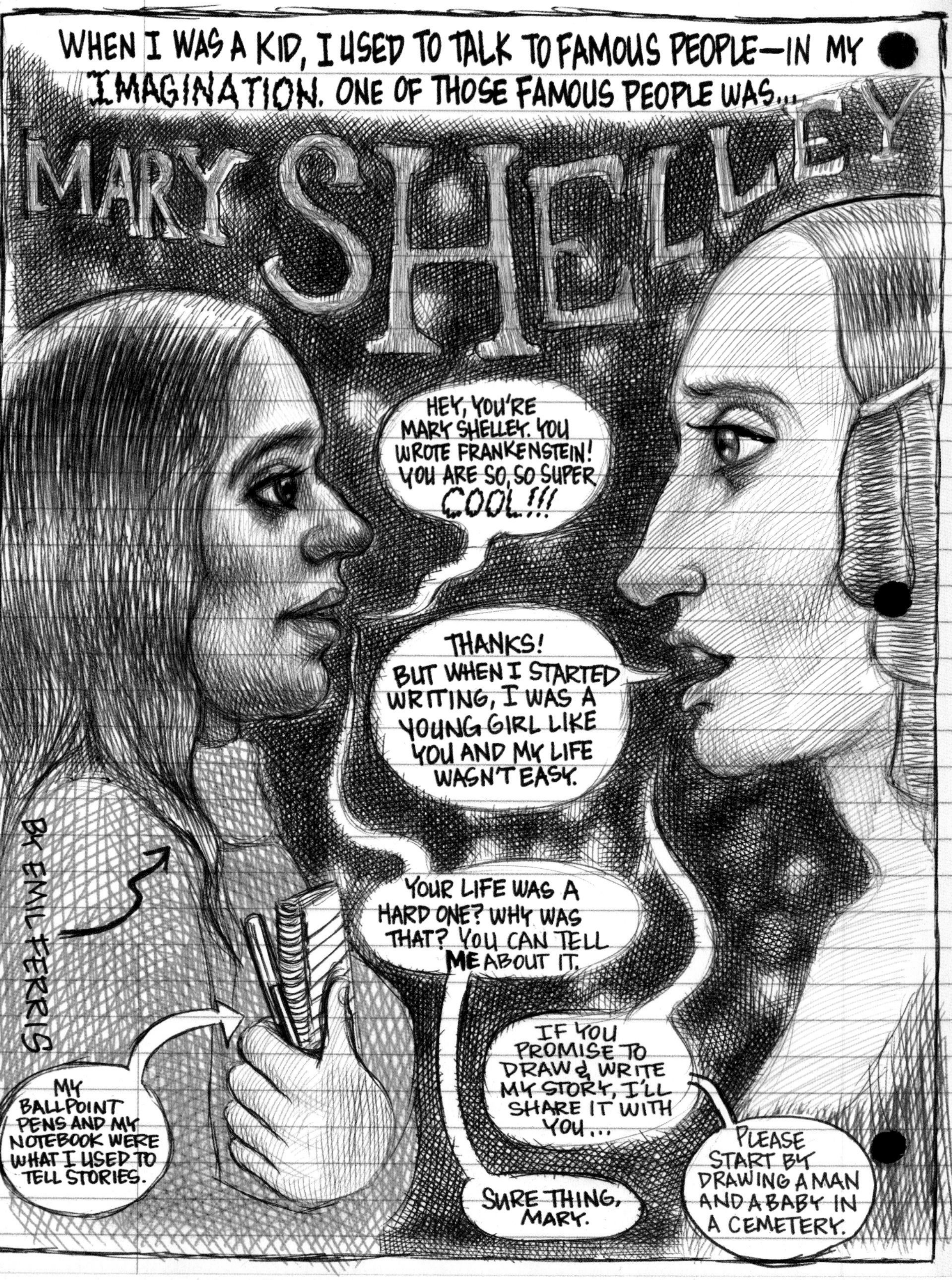

WHEN I WAS A KID, I USED TO TALK TO FAMOUS PEOPLE—IN MY IMAGINATION. ONE OF THOSE FAMOUS PEOPLE WAS...
MARY SHELLEY
HEY, YOU'RE MARY SHELLEY. YOU WROTE FRANKENSTEIN! YOU ARE SO, SO SUPER COOL!!!
THANKS! BUT WHEN I STARTED WRITING, I WAS A YOUNG GIRL LIKE YOU AND MY LIFE WASN'T EASY.
YOUR LIFE WAS A HARD ONE? WHY WAS THAT? YOU CAN TELL ME ABOUT IT.
IF YOU PROMISE TO DRAW & WRITE MY STORY, I'LL SHARE IT WITH YOU...
SURE THING, MARY.
PLEASE START BY DRAWING A MAN AND A BABY IN A CEMETERY.
BY EMIL FERRIS
MY BALLPOINT PENS AND MY NOTEBOOK WERE WHAT I USED TO TELL STORIES.

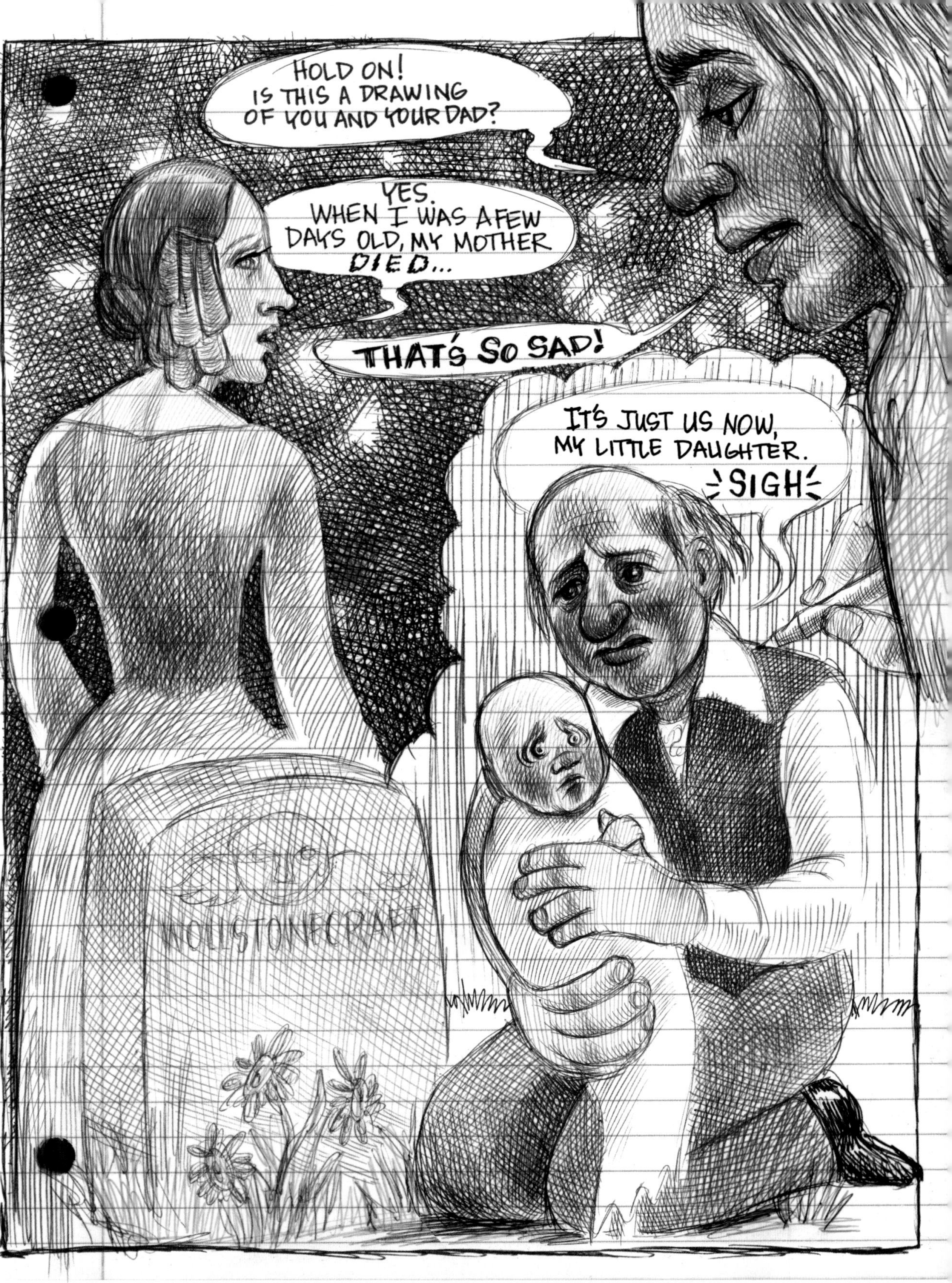
HOLD ON! IS THIS A DRAWING OF YOU AND YOUR DAD?
YES. WHEN I WAS A FEW DAYS OLD, MY MOTHER DIED...
THAT'S SO SAD!
IT'S JUST US NOW, MY LITTLE DAUGHTER.
SIGH
WOLLSTONECRAFT

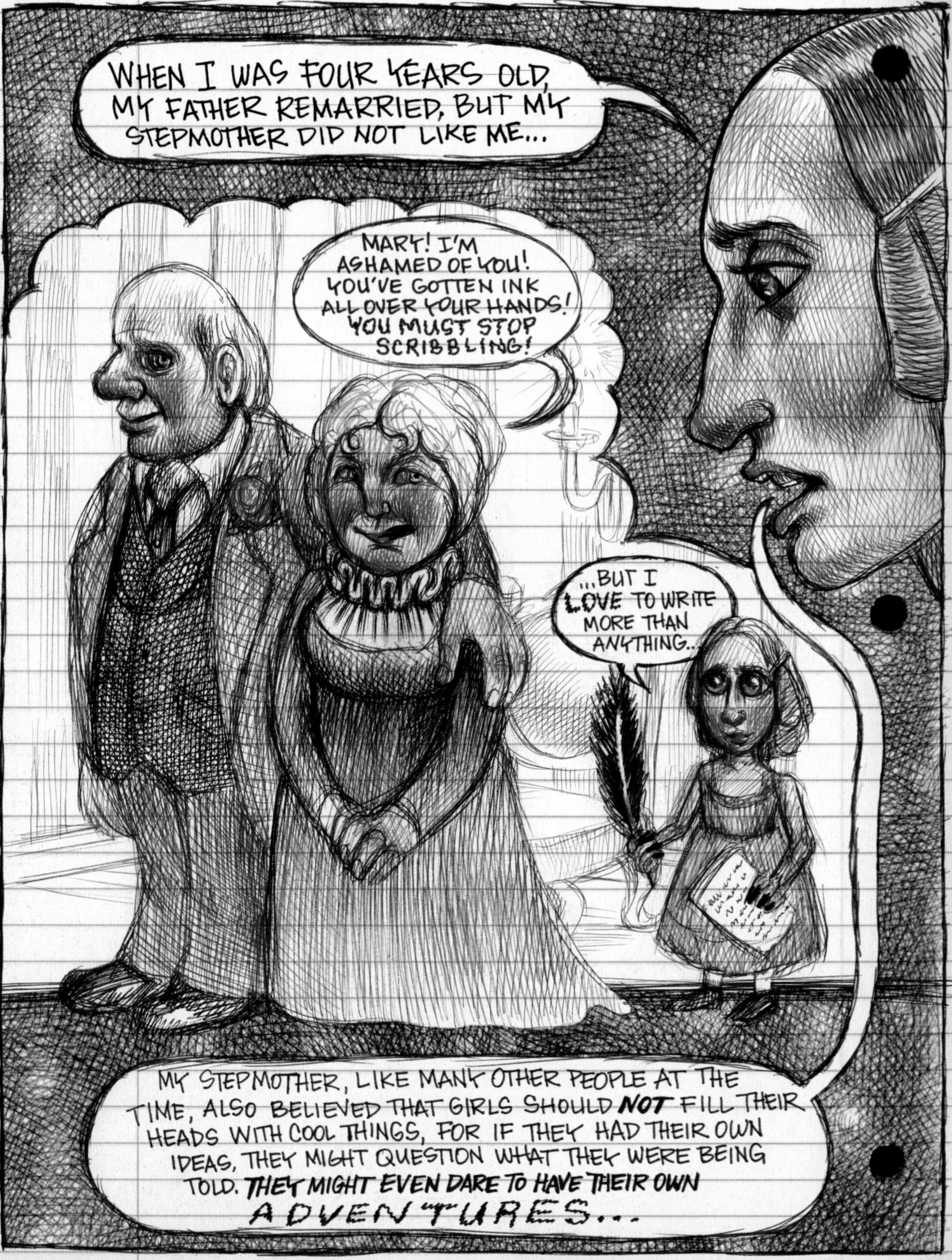
WHEN I WAS FOUR YEARS OLD, MY FATHER REMARRIED, BUT MY STEPMOTHER DID NOT LIKE ME...
MARY! I'M ASHAMED OF YOU! YOU'VE GOTTEN INK ALL OVER YOUR HANDS! YOU MUST STOP SCRIBBLING!
...BUT I LOVE TO WRITE MORE THAN ANYTHING...
MY STEPMOTHER, LIKE MANY OTHER PEOPLE AT THE TIME, ALSO BELIEVED THAT GIRLS SHOULD NOT FILL THEIR HEADS WITH COOL THINGS, FOR IF THEY HAD THEIR OWN IDEAS, THEY MIGHT QUESTION WHAT THEY WERE BEING TOLD. THEY MIGHT EVEN DARE TO HAVE THEIR OWN ADVENTURES...

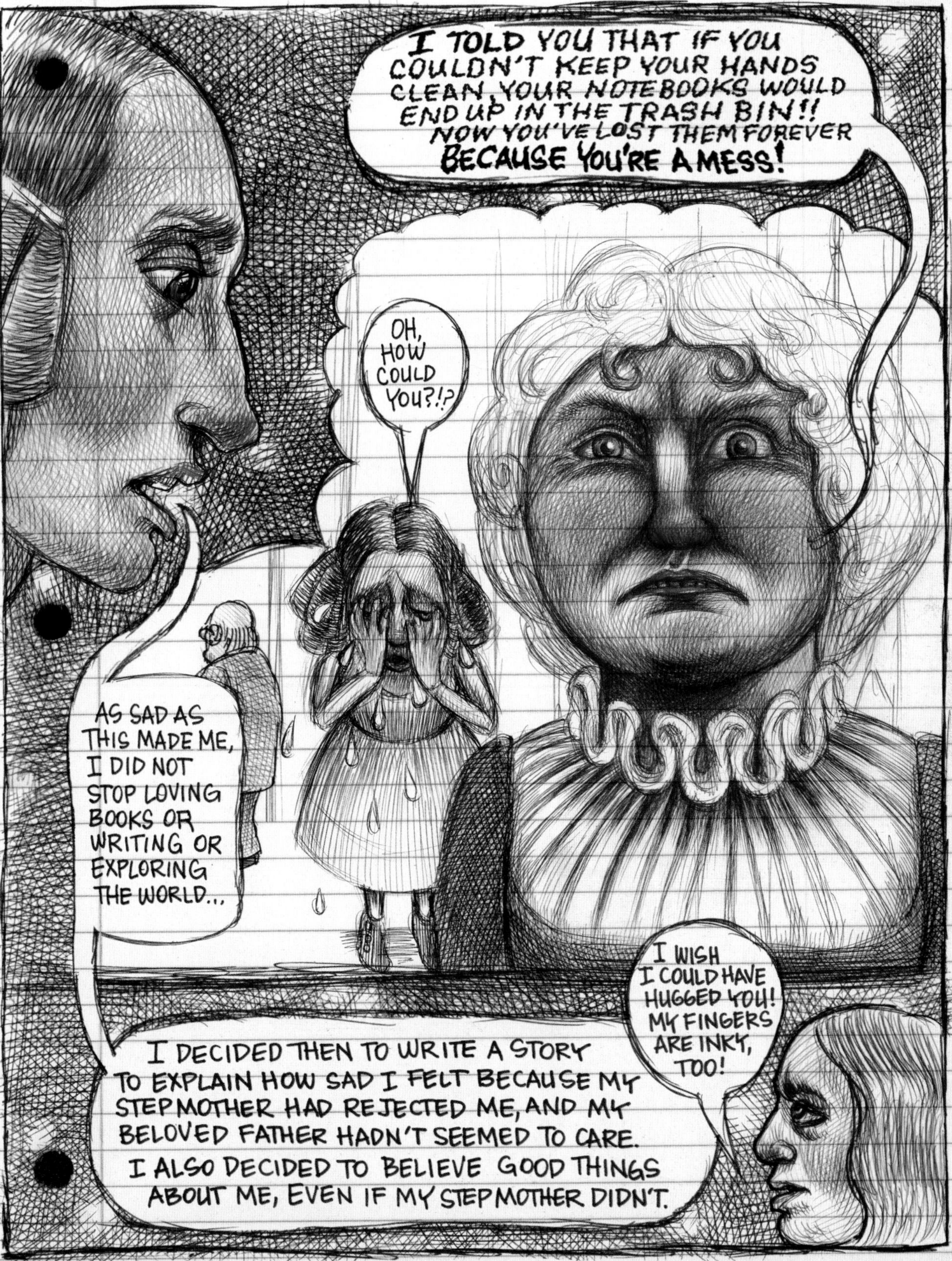
I TOLD YOU THAT IF YOU COULDN'T KEEP YOUR HANDS CLEAN, YOUR NOTEBOOKS WOULD END UP IN THE TRASH BIN!! NOW YOU'VE LOST THEM FOREVER BECAUSE YOU'RE A MESS!
OH, HOW COULD YOU?!?
AS SAD AS THIS MADE ME, I DID NOT STOP LOVING BOOKS OR WRITING OR EXPLORING THE WORLD...
I DECIDED THEN TO WRITE A STORY TO EXPLAIN HOW SAD I FELT BECAUSE MY STEPMOTHER HAD REJECTED ME, AND MY BELOVED FATHER HADN'T SEEMED TO CARE. I ALSO DECIDED TO BELIEVE GOOD THINGS ABOUT ME, EVEN IF MY STEPMOTHER DIDN'T.
I WISH I COULD HAVE HUGGED YOU! MY FINGERS ARE INKY, TOO!

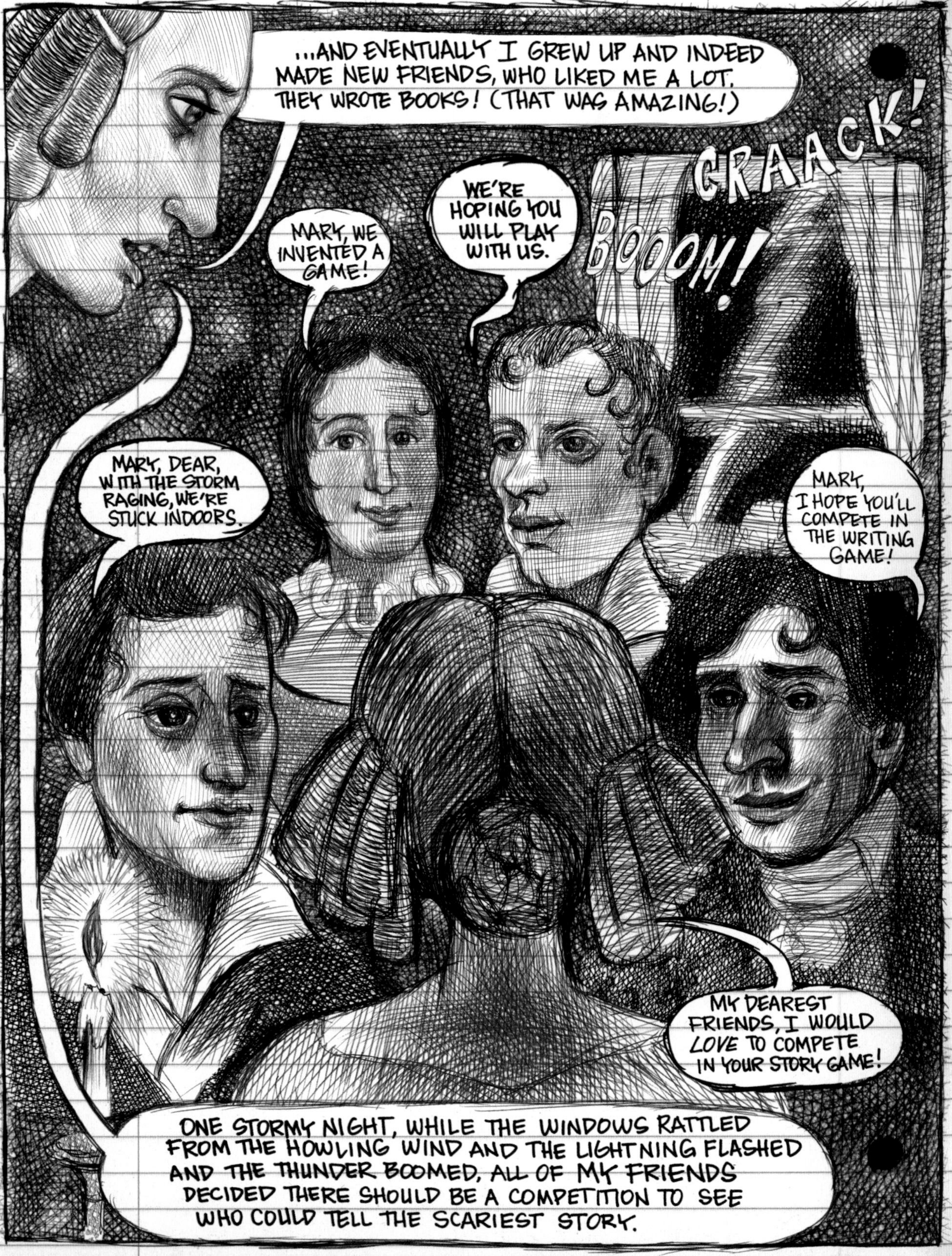
...AND EVENTUALLY I GREW UP AND INDEED MADE NEW FRIENDS, WHO LIKED ME A LOT. THEY WROTE BOOKS! (THAT WAS AMAZING!)
CRAACK!
BOOOM!
MARY, WE INVENTED A GAME!
WE'RE HOPING YOU WILL PLAY WITH US.
MARY, DEAR, WITH THE STORM RAGING, WE'RE STUCK INDOORS.
MARY, I HOPE YOU'LL COMPETE IN THE WRITING GAME!
MY DEAREST FRIENDS, I WOULD *LOVE* TO COMPETE IN YOUR STORY GAME!
ONE STORMY NIGHT, WHILE THE WINDOWS RATTLED FROM THE HOWLING WIND AND THE LIGHTNING FLASHED AND THE THUNDER BOOMED, ALL OF MY FRIENDS DECIDED THERE SHOULD BE A COMPETITION TO SEE WHO COULD TELL THE SCARIEST STORY.

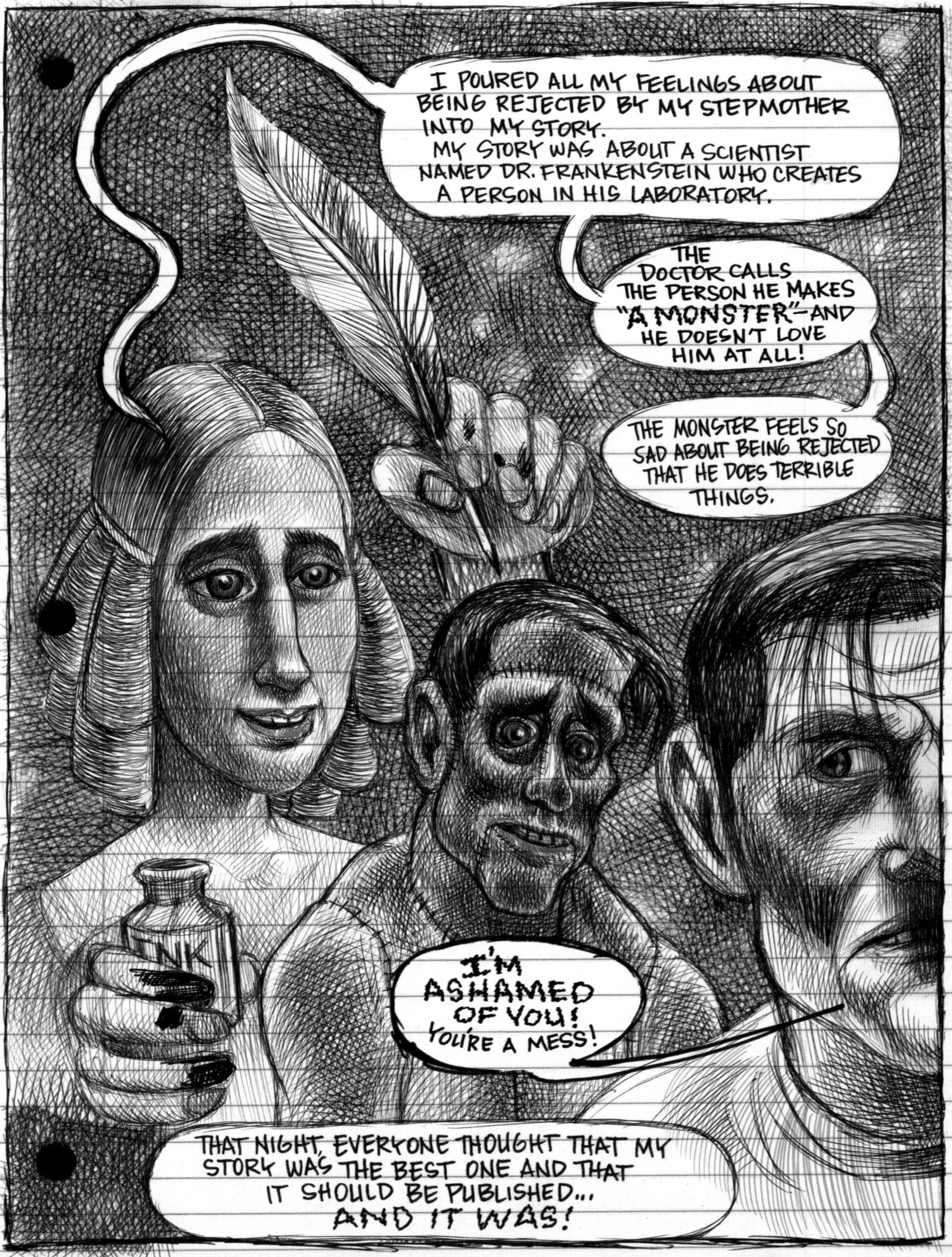
I POURED ALL MY FEELINGS ABOUT BEING REJECTED BY MY STEPMOTHER INTO MY STORY. MY STORY WAS ABOUT A SCIENTIST NAMED DR. FRANKENSTEIN WHO CREATES A PERSON IN HIS LABORATORY.
THE DOCTOR CALLS THE PERSON HE MAKES "A MONSTER"—AND HE DOESN'T LOVE HIM AT ALL!
THE MONSTER FEELS SO SAD ABOUT BEING REJECTED THAT HE DOES TERRIBLE THINGS.
INK
I'M ASHAMED OF YOU! YOU'RE A MESS!
THAT NIGHT, EVERYONE THOUGHT THAT MY STORY WAS THE BEST ONE AND THAT IT SHOULD BE PUBLISHED... AND IT WAS!

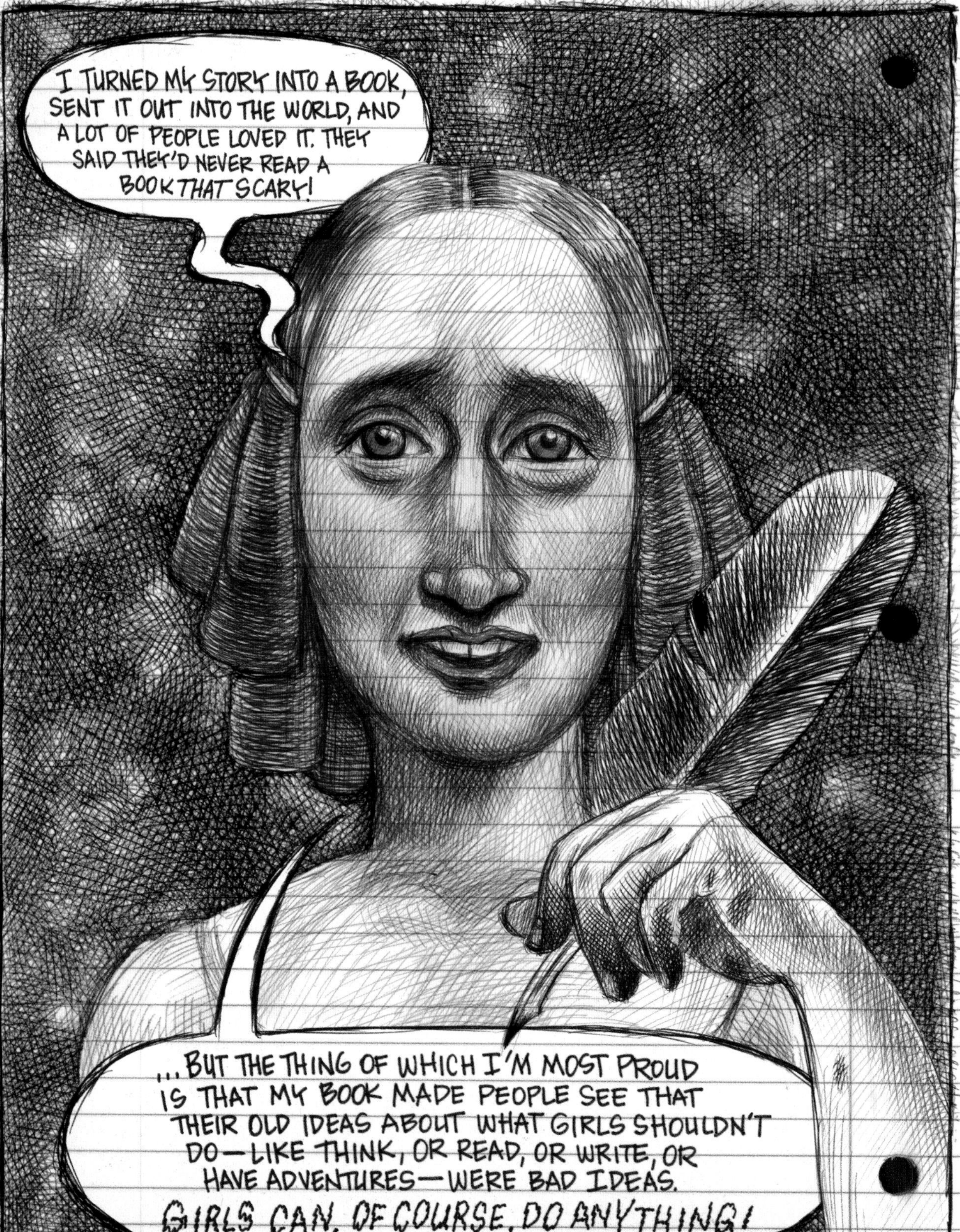
I TURNED MY STORY INTO A BOOK, SENT IT OUT INTO THE WORLD, AND A LOT OF PEOPLE LOVED IT. THEY SAID THEY'D NEVER READ A BOOK THAT SCARY!
...BUT THE THING OF WHICH I'M MOST PROUD IS THAT MY BOOK MADE PEOPLE SEE THAT THEIR OLD IDEAS ABOUT WHAT GIRLS SHOULDN'T DO—LIKE THINK, OR READ, OR WRITE, OR HAVE ADVENTURES—WERE BAD IDEAS. GIRLS CAN, OF COURSE, DO ANYTHING!

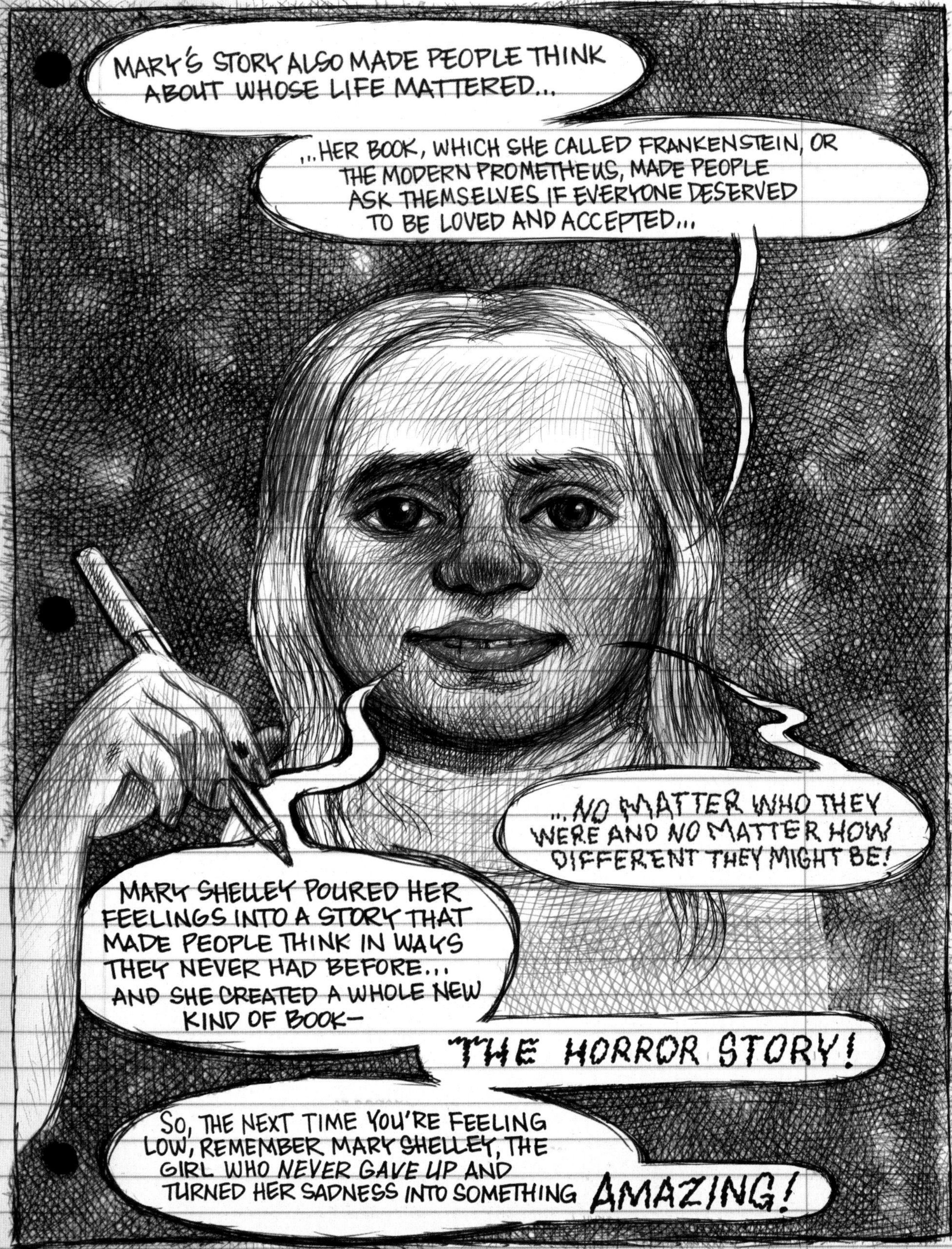
MARY'S STORY ALSO MADE PEOPLE THINK ABOUT WHOSE LIFE MATTERED...
...HER BOOK, WHICH SHE CALLED FRANKENSTEIN, OR THE MODERN PROMETHEUS, MADE PEOPLE ASK THEMSELVES IF EVERYONE DESERVED TO BE LOVED AND ACCEPTED...
...NO MATTER WHO THEY WERE AND NO MATTER HOW DIFFERENT THEY MIGHT BE!
MARY SHELLEY POURED HER FEELINGS INTO A STORY THAT MADE PEOPLE THINK IN WAYS THEY NEVER HAD BEFORE... AND SHE CREATED A WHOLE NEW KIND OF BOOK—
THE HORROR STORY!
SO, THE NEXT TIME YOU'RE FEELING LOW, REMEMBER MARY SHELLEY, THE GIRL WHO NEVER GAVE UP AND TURNED HER SADNESS INTO SOMETHING AMAZING!

THE LOVABLE CHEF

· · · · ·

JULIA CHILD
1912~2004

She was equal parts chef and teacher, but the lessons Julia Child taught us extended far beyond the kitchen. She showed us how to embrace the unfamiliar, laugh off our goofs, and enjoy every delicious moment of our lives.

JULIA AND ME

COUNT ALL THE THINGS YOU HAVE IN COMMON WITH JULIA CHILD.

- I love to cook.
- I love to eat.
- I'm willing to try almost anything once.
- When I discover something new, I try to learn everything I can about it.
- I like to share what I learn with others.
- My mistakes inspire me to keep learning.
- I defy other people's expectations of me.
- I can laugh at myself.
- I'm mindful.
- I'm joyful.

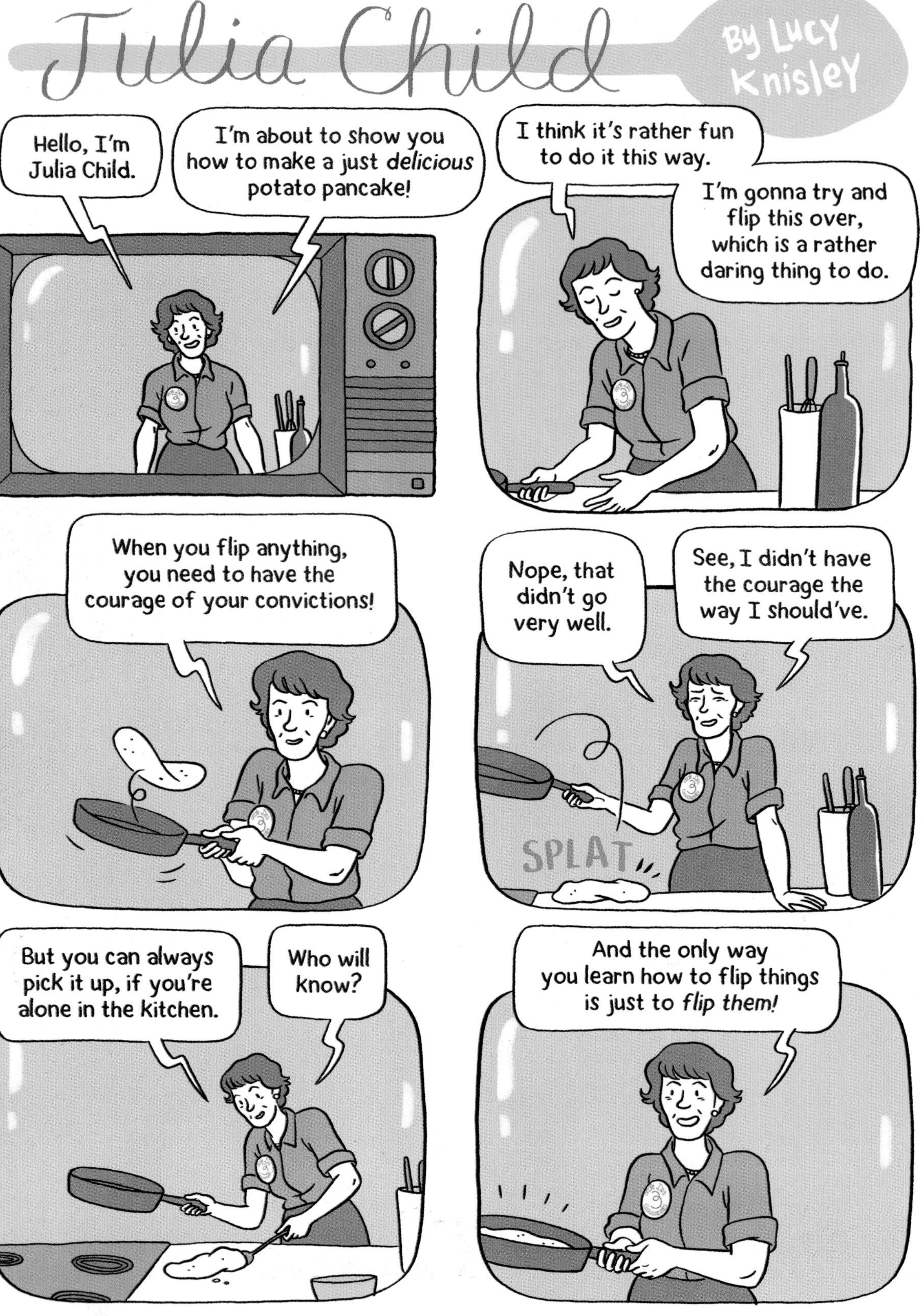
Julia Child
By Lucy Knisley
Hello, I'm Julia Child.
I'm about to show you how to make a just *delicious* potato pancake!
I think it's rather fun to do it this way.
I'm gonna try and flip this over, which is a rather daring thing to do.
When you flip anything, you need to have the courage of your convictions!
Nope, that didn't go very well.
See, I didn't have the courage the way I should've.
SPLAT
But you can always pick it up, if you're alone in the kitchen.
Who will know?
And the only way you learn how to flip things is just to *flip them!*

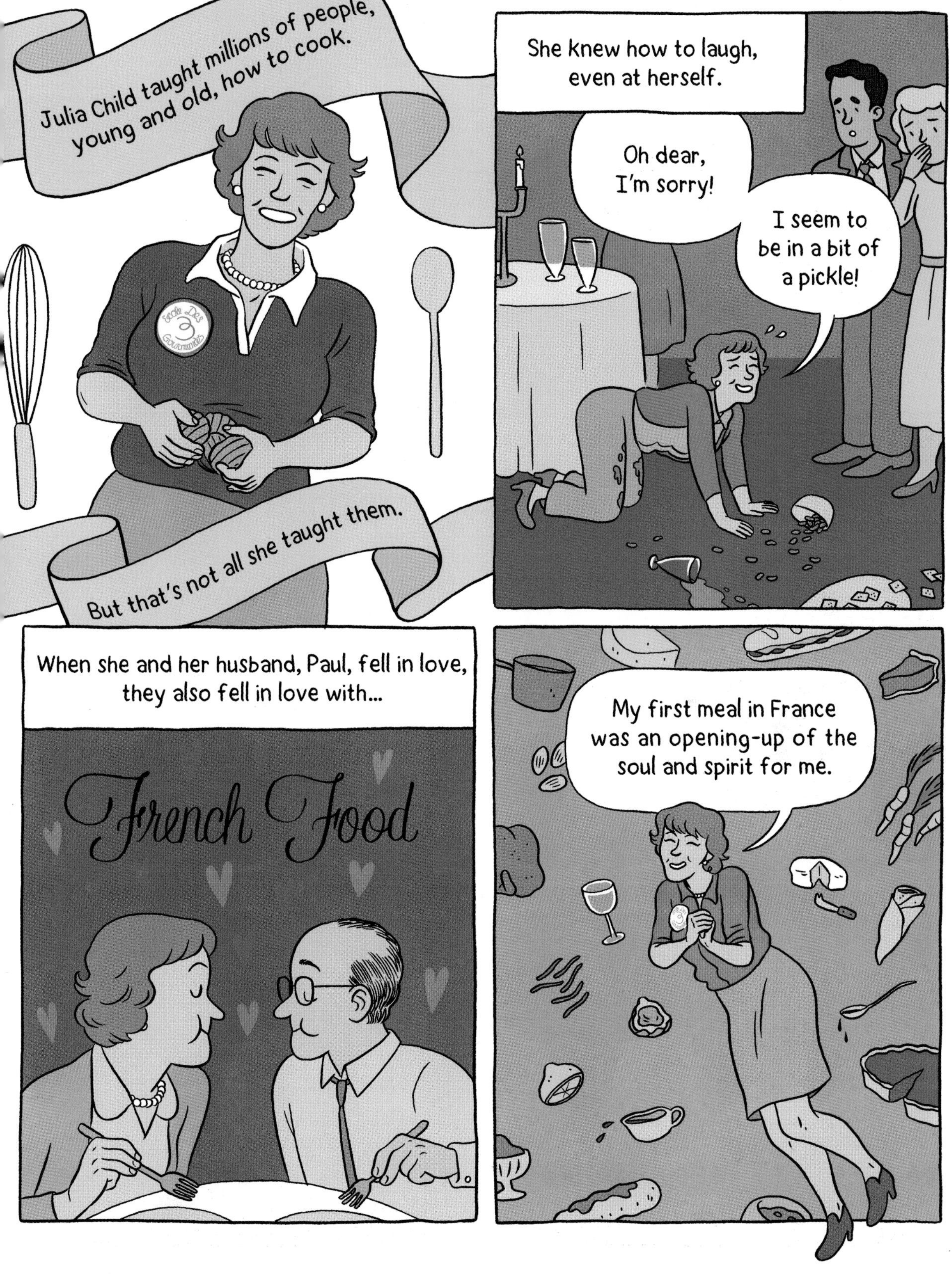
Julia Child taught millions of people, young and old, how to cook.
École Des Gourmandes
But that's not all she taught them.
She knew how to laugh, even at herself.
Oh dear, I'm sorry!
I seem to be in a bit of a pickle!
When she and her husband, Paul, fell in love, they also fell in love with...
French Food
My first meal in France was an opening-up of the soul and spirit for me.

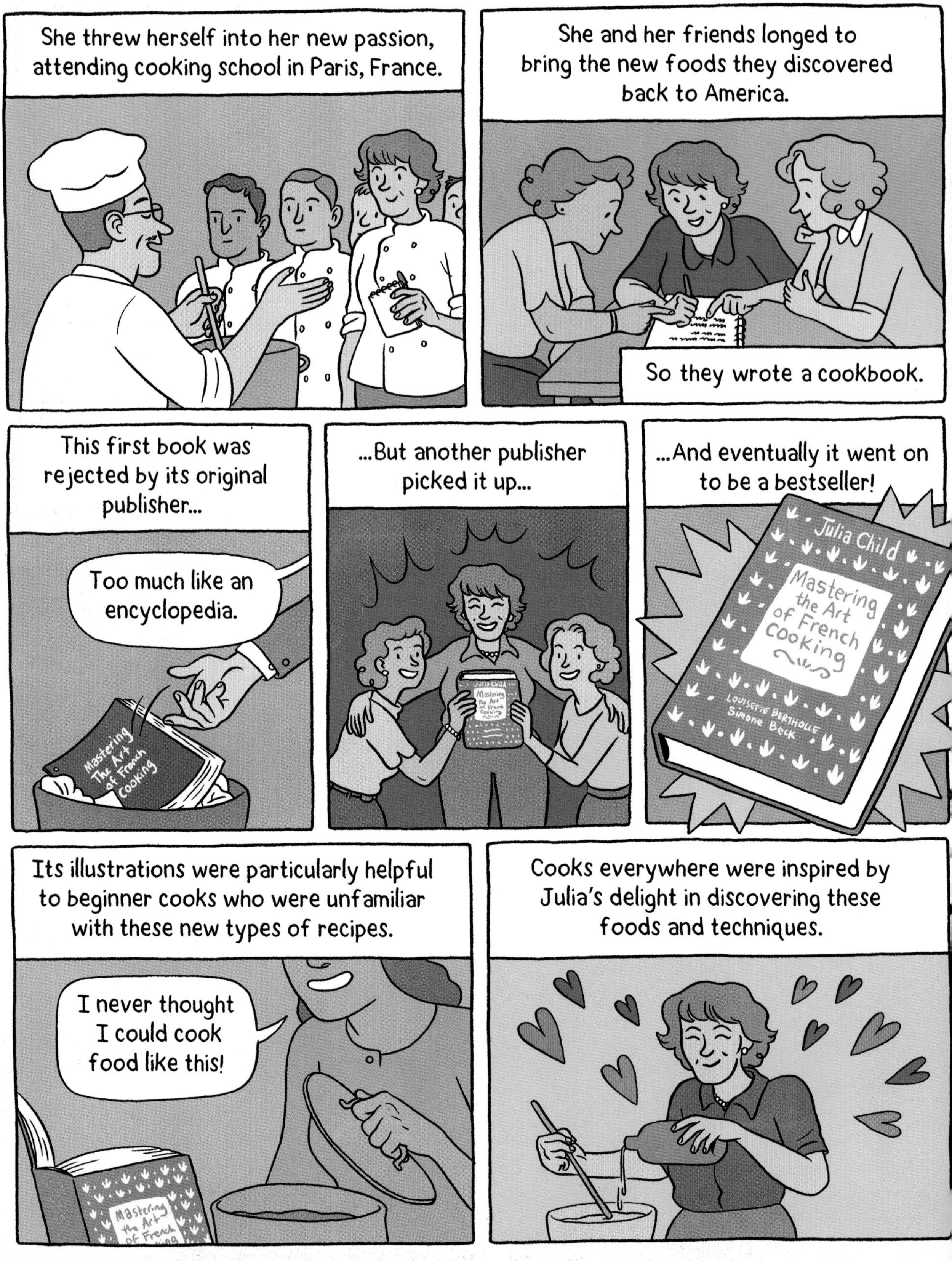
She threw herself into her new passion, attending cooking school in Paris, France.
She and her friends longed to bring the new foods they discovered back to America.
So they wrote a cookbook.
This first book was rejected by its original publisher...
Too much like an encyclopedia.
Mastering The Art of French Cooking
...But another publisher picked it up...
...And eventually it went on to be a bestseller!
Julia Child
Mastering the Art of French Cooking
Louisette Bertholle
Simone Beck
Its illustrations were particularly helpful to beginner cooks who were unfamiliar with these new types of recipes.
I never thought I could cook food like this!
Cooks everywhere were inspired by Julia's delight in discovering these foods and techniques.

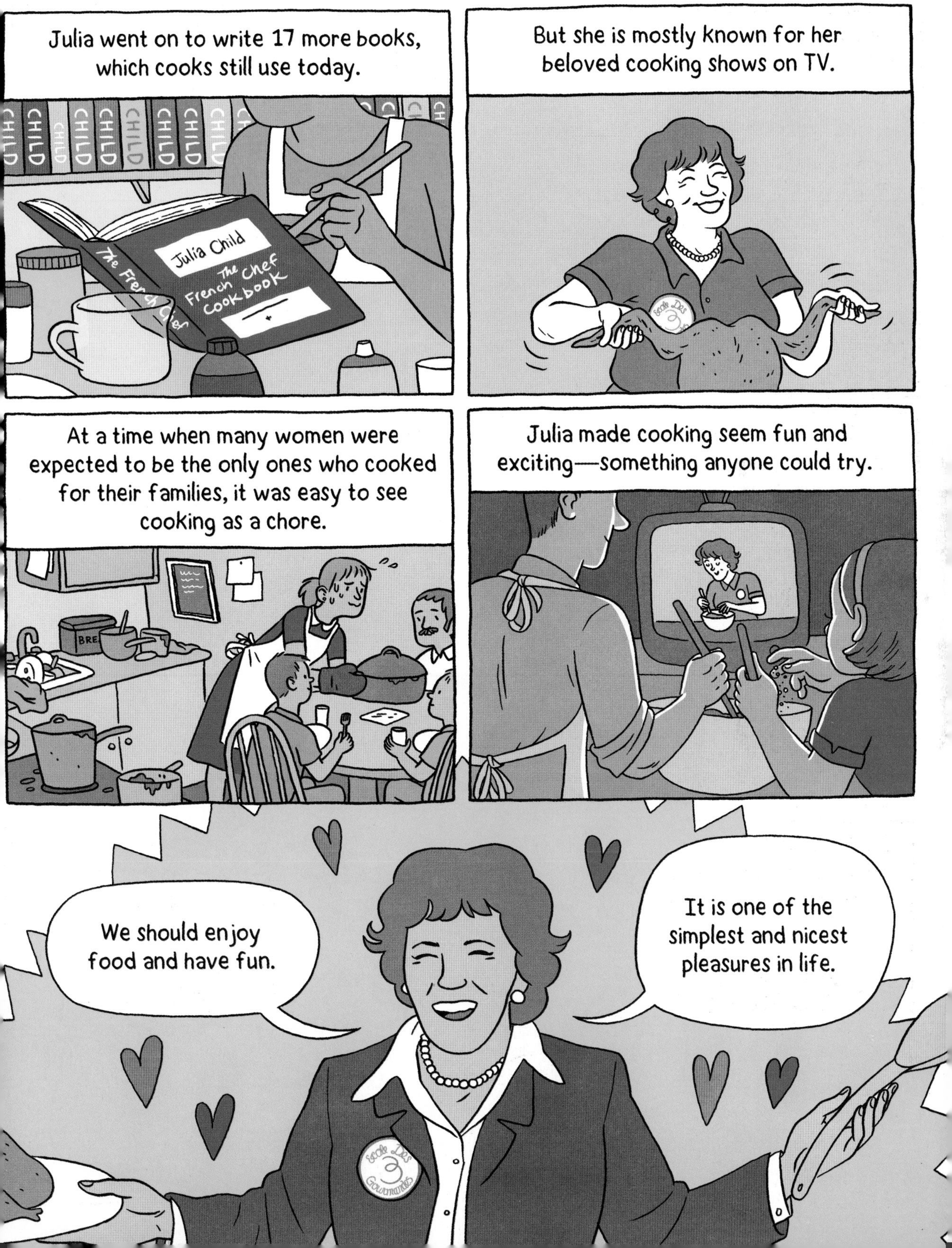
Julia went on to write 17 more books, which cooks still use today.
CHILD CHILD CHILD CHILD CHILD CHILD CHILD CHILD CHILD
Julia Child
The French Chef Cookbook
The French Chef
But she is mostly known for her beloved cooking shows on TV.
At a time when many women were expected to be the only ones who cooked for their families, it was easy to see cooking as a chore.
BRE
Julia made cooking seem fun and exciting—something anyone could try.
We should enjoy food and have fun.
It is one of the simplest and nicest pleasures in life.
Ecole Des Gourmandes

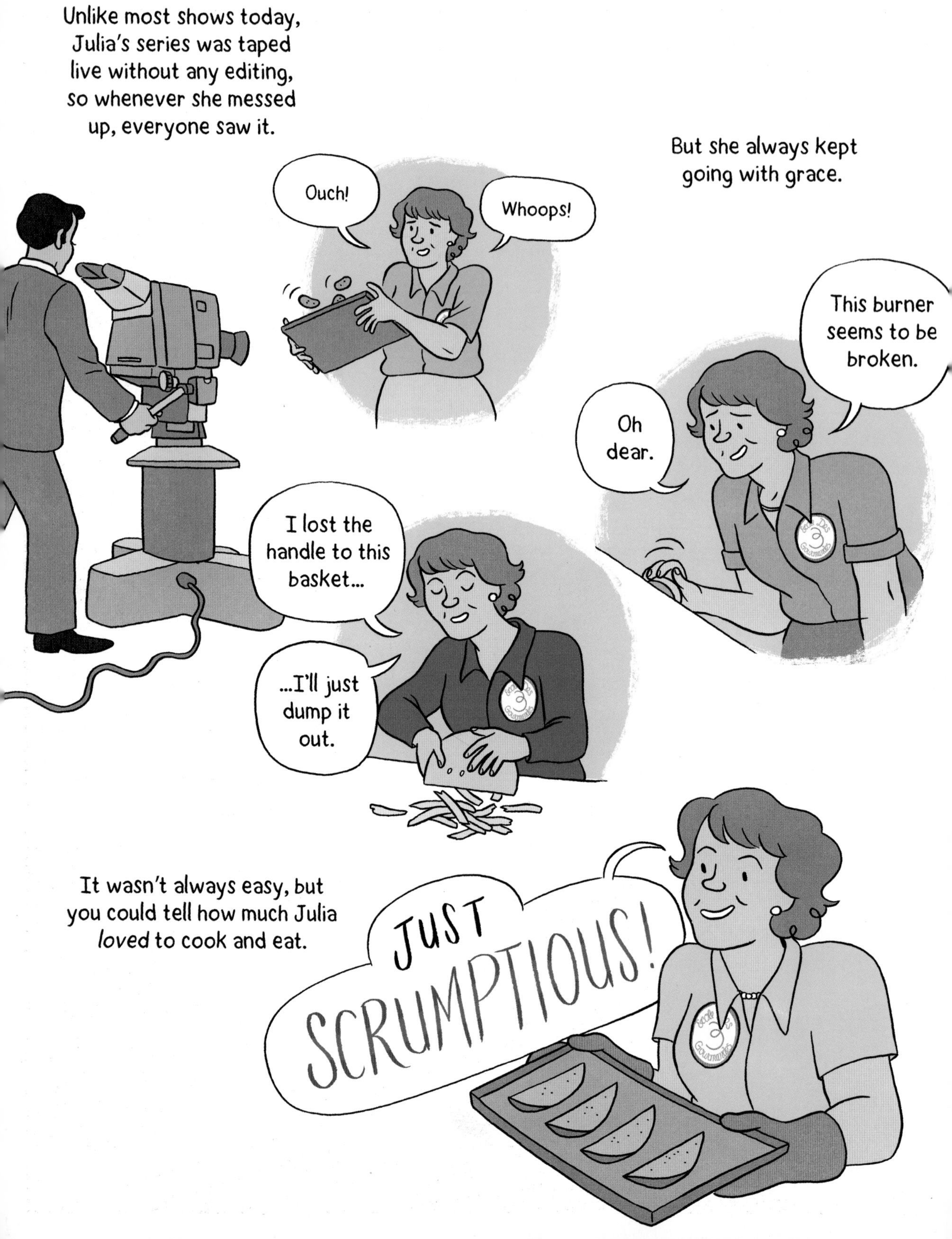
Unlike most shows today, Julia's series was taped live without any editing, so whenever she messed up, everyone saw it.
Ouch!
Whoops!
But she always kept going with grace.
This burner seems to be broken.
Oh dear.
I lost the handle to this basket...
...I'll just dump it out.
It wasn't always easy, but you could tell how much Julia *loved* to cook and eat.
JUST SCRUMPTIOUS!

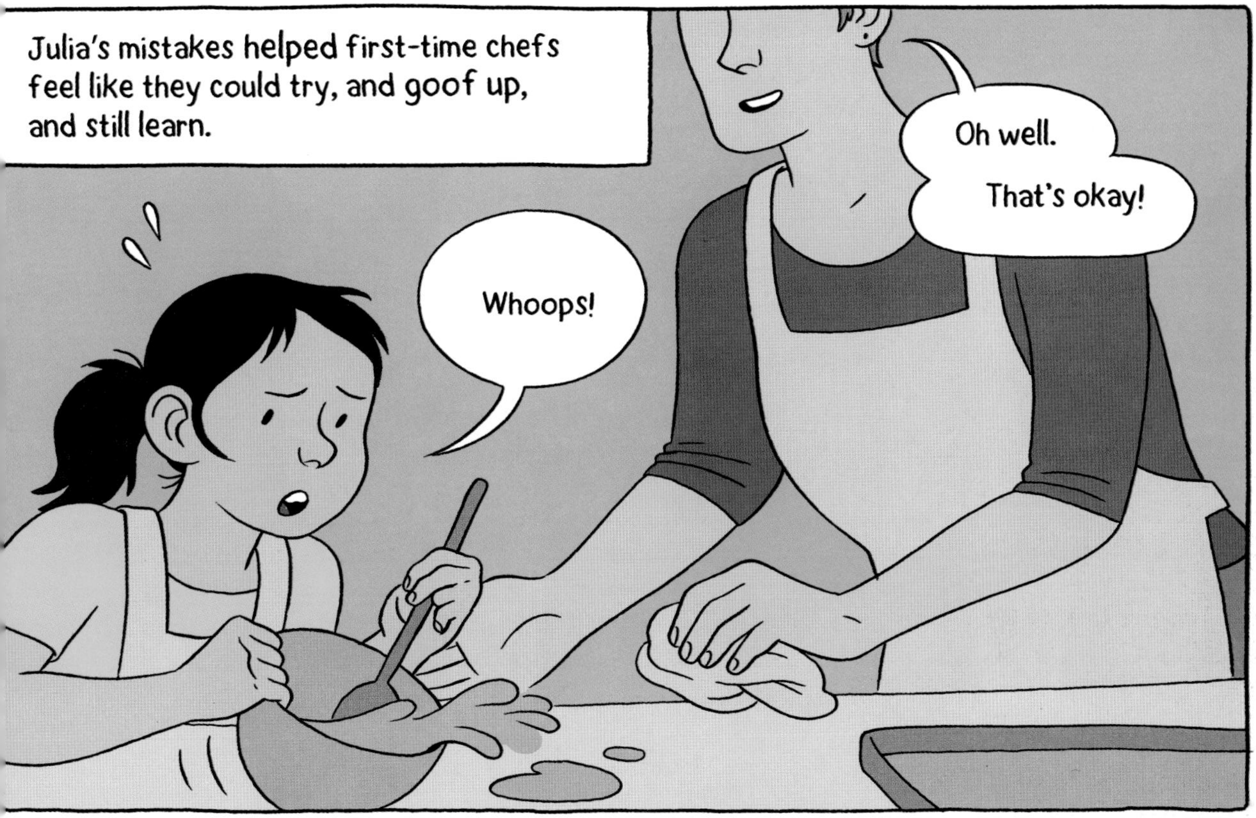
Julia's mistakes helped first-time chefs feel like they could try, and goof up, and still learn.
Oh well.
That's okay!
Whoops!

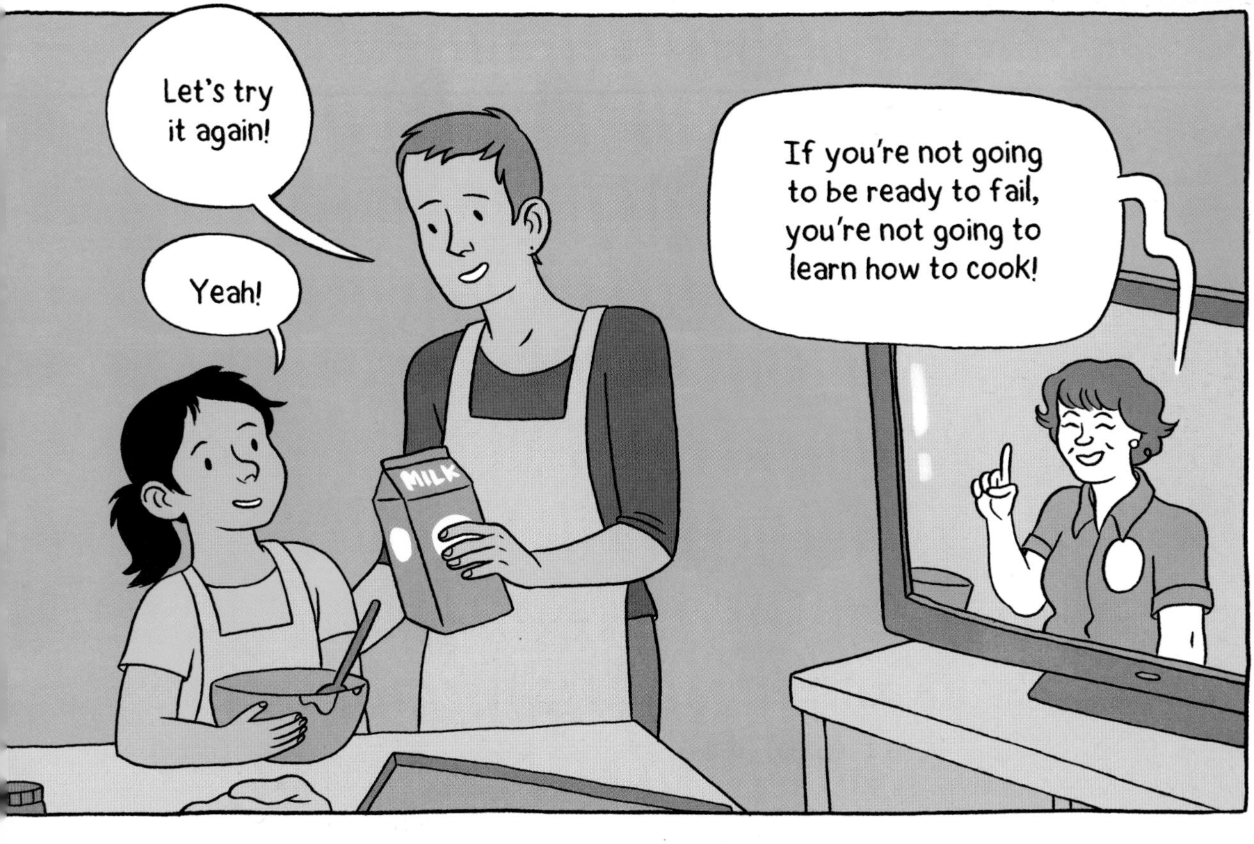
Let's try it again!
Yeah!
If you're not going to be ready to fail, you're not going to learn how to cook!
MILK

THE SOULFUL POET

......

MAYA ANGELOU

1928 ~ 2014

As a child, Maya Angelou stopped speaking for many years, fearful of the power of her voice after a terrible trauma frightened her into silence. Her love of poetry inspired her to speak out again, and once she did, she never stopped. As a poet, writer, and activist, she inspired us all to be our most phenomenal selves.

MAYA AND ME

COUNT ALL THE THINGS YOU HAVE IN COMMON WITH MAYA ANGELOU.

- I love to write.
- You'll rarely find me without a book in my hand.
- I like to try to make words rhyme.
- I'm pretty quiet until I have something to say.
- I'm curious to see what it's like to live in a different country.
- I don't want to choose one job—I want to do lots of different things.
- I believe all people should be treated equally.
- I know that what I have to say is important.
- I'm creative.
- I'm powerful.

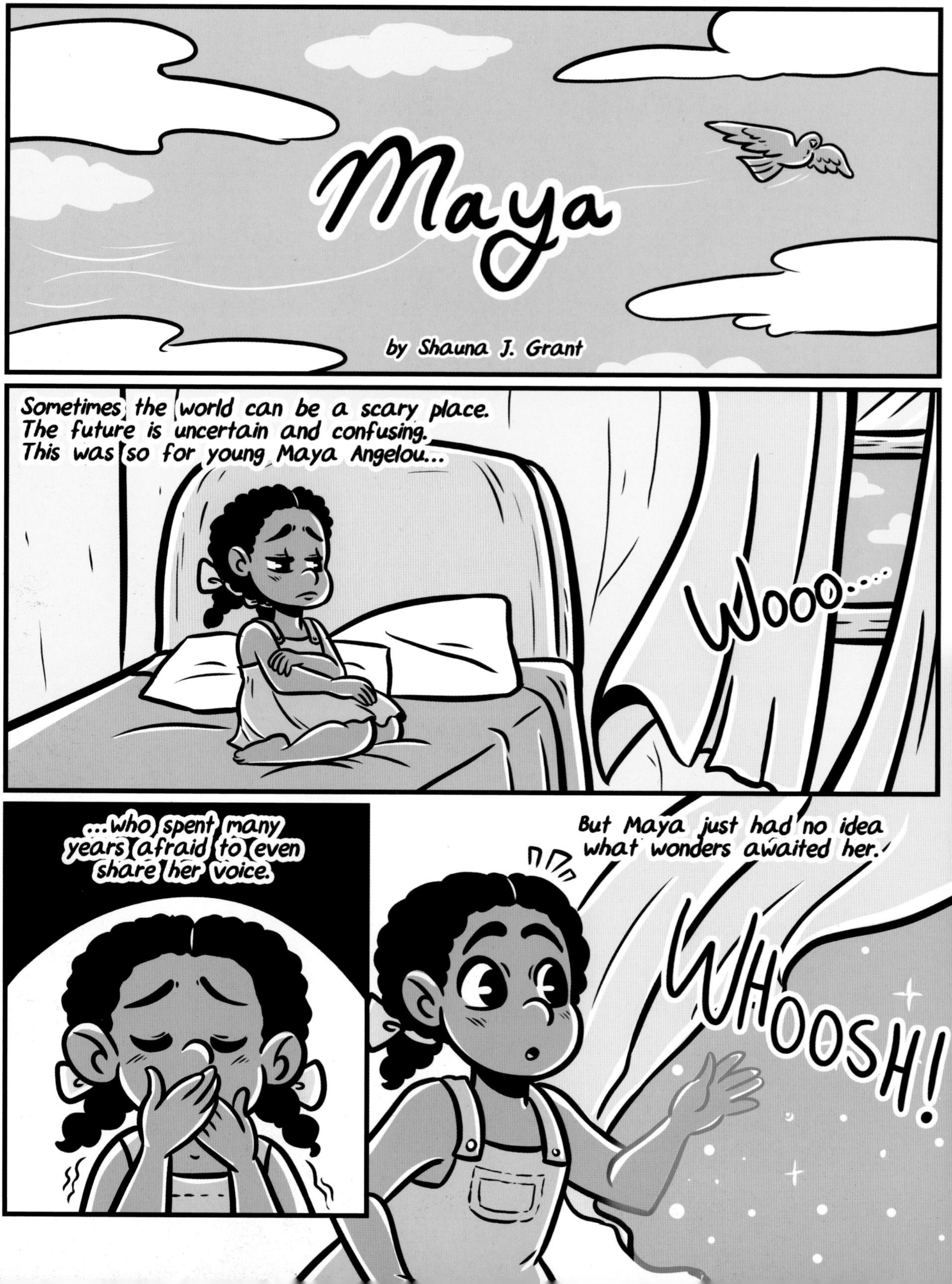
Maya
by Shauna J. Grant
Sometimes the world can be a scary place. The future is uncertain and confusing. This was so for young Maya Angelou...
Wooo....
...who spent many years afraid to even share her voice.
But Maya just had no idea what wonders awaited her.
WHOOSH!

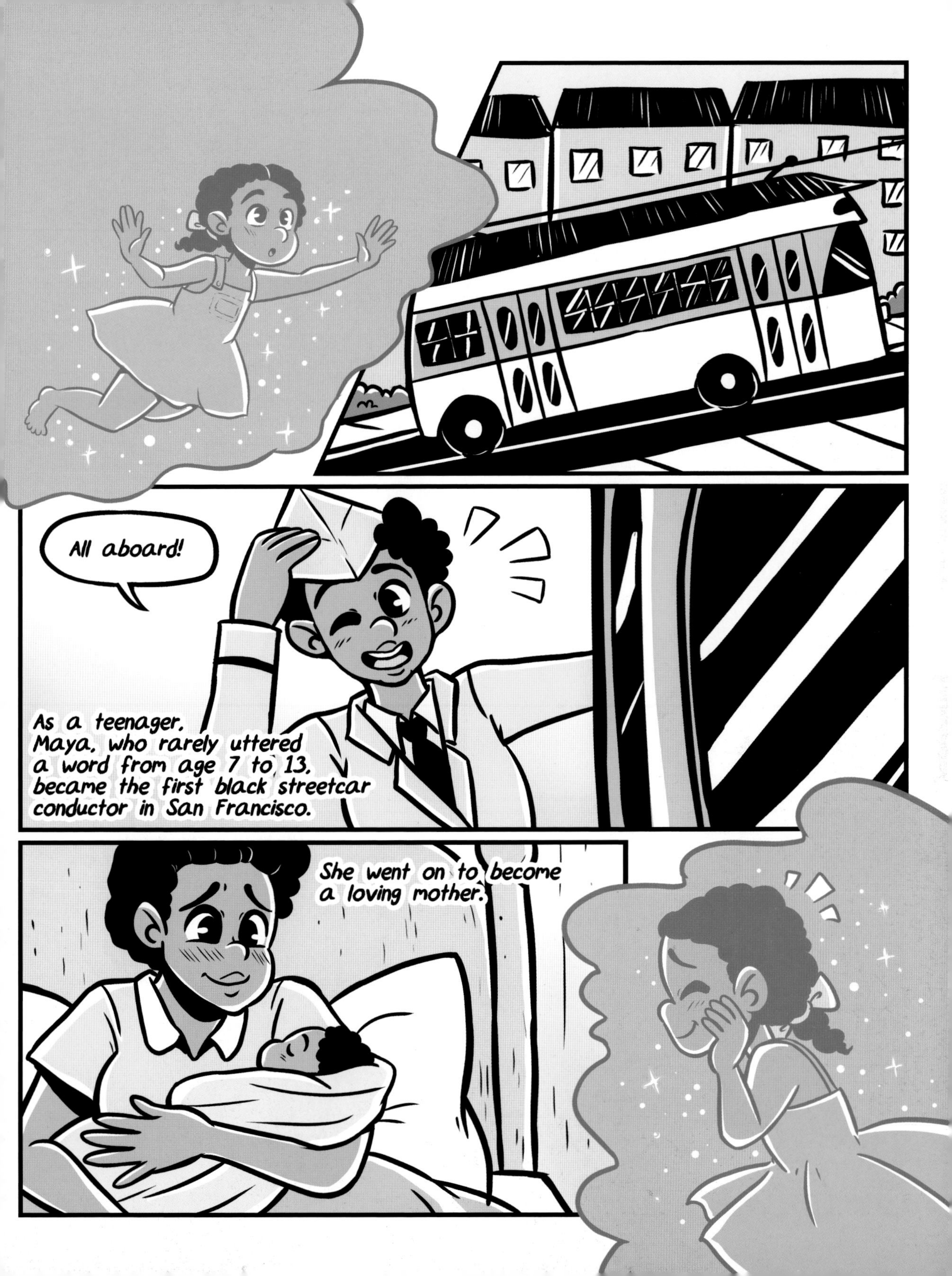
All aboard!
As a teenager, Maya, who rarely uttered a word from age 7 to 13, became the first black streetcar conductor in San Francisco.
She went on to become a loving mother.

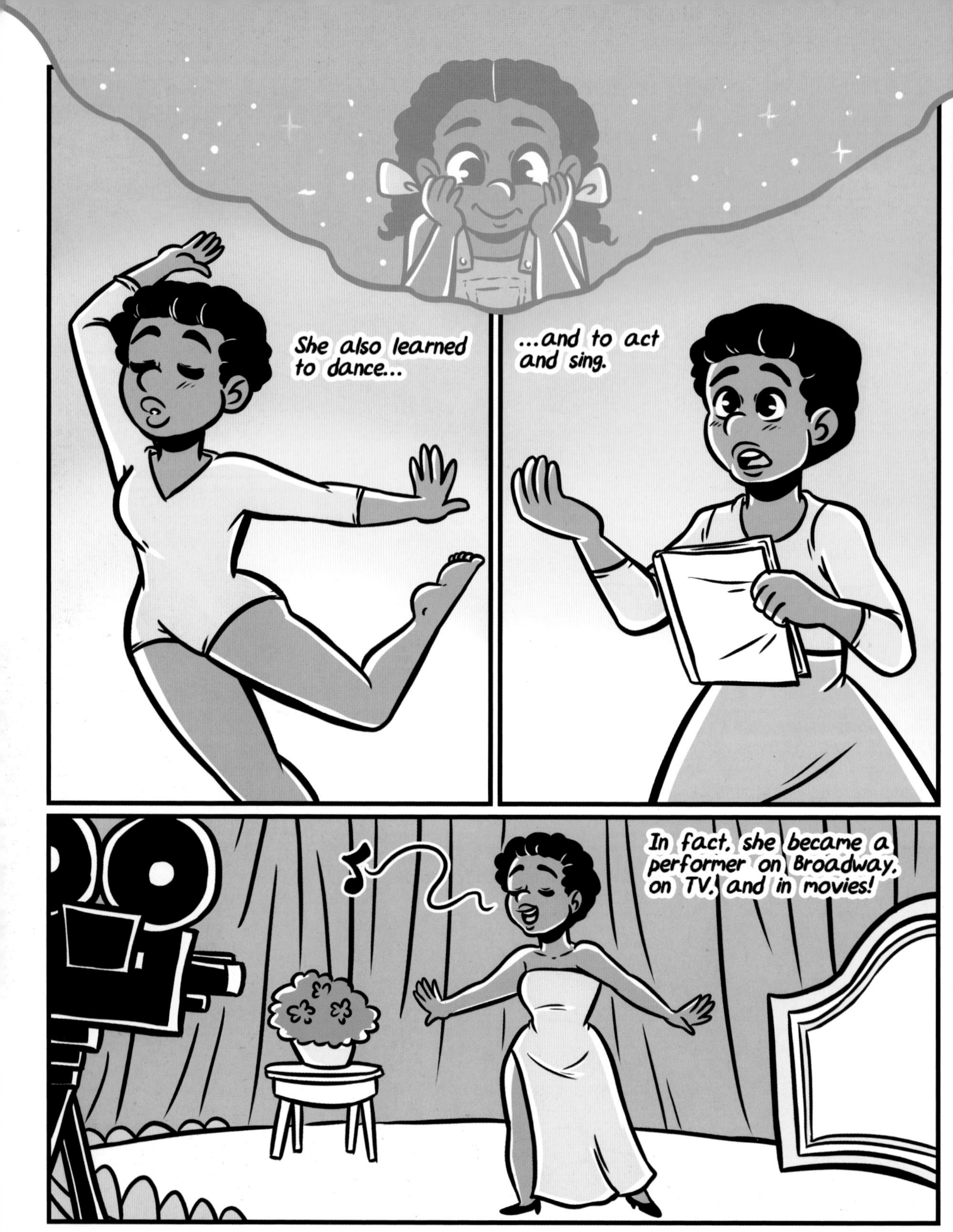
She also learned to dance...
...and to act and sing.
In fact, she became a performer on Broadway, on TV, and in movies!

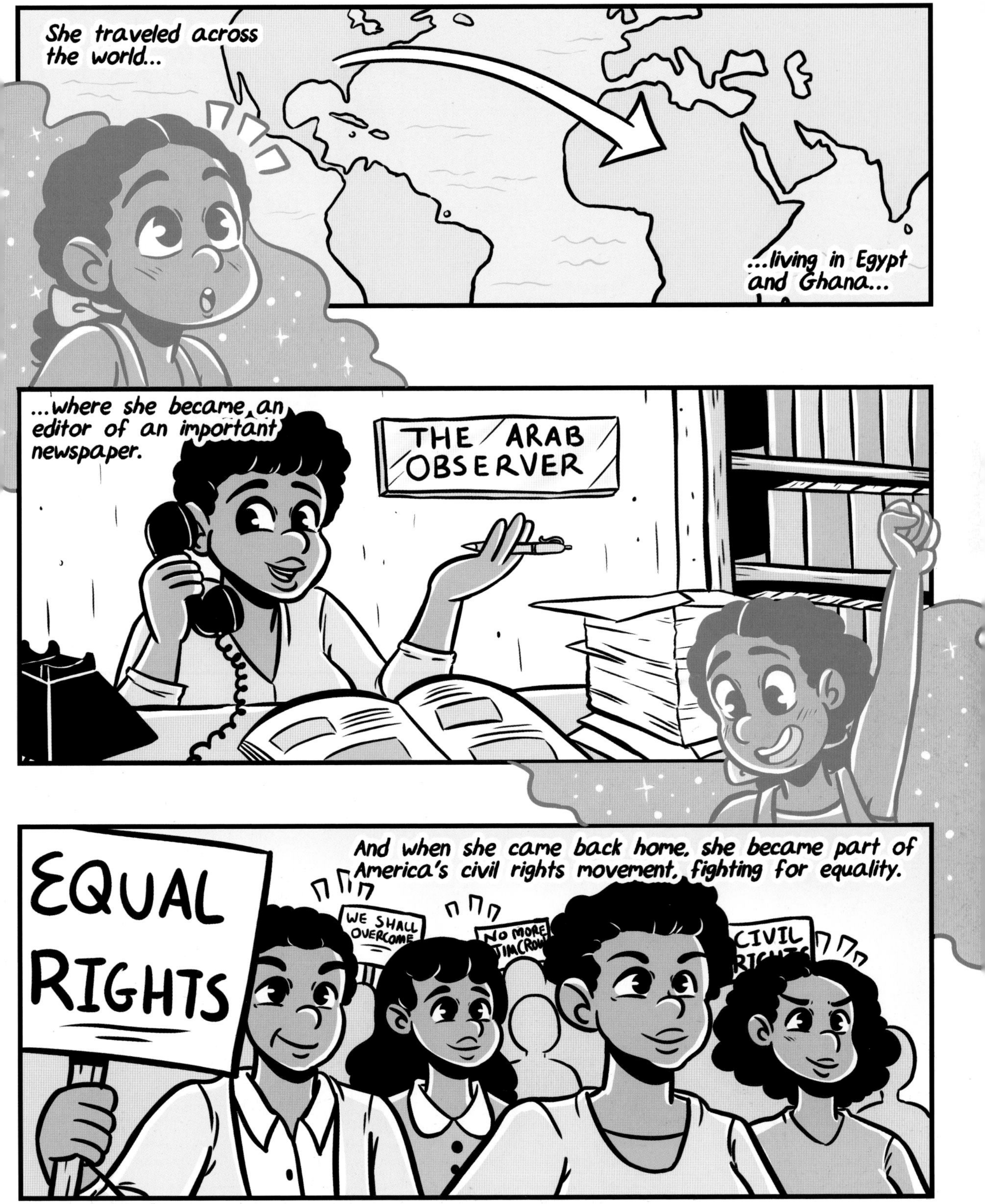
She traveled across the world...
...living in Egypt and Ghana...
...where she became an editor of an important newspaper.
THE ARAB OBSERVER
And when she came back home, she became part of America's civil rights movement, fighting for equality.
EQUAL RIGHTS
WE SHALL OVERCOME
NO MORE JIMCROW
CIVIL

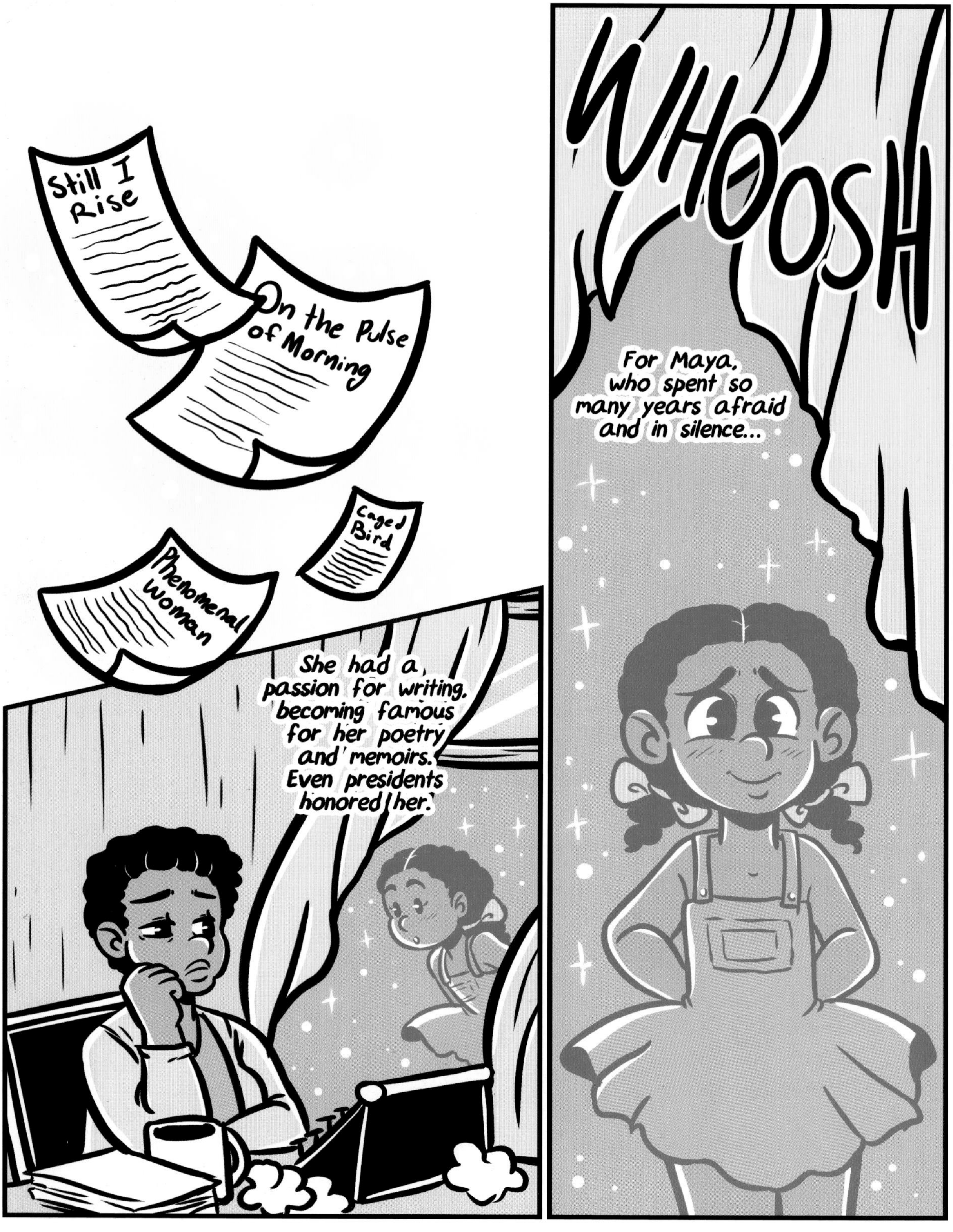
Still I Rise
On the Pulse of Morning
Caged Bird
Phenomenal Woman
She had a passion for writing, becoming famous for her poetry and memoirs. Even presidents honored her.
WHOOSH
For Maya, who spent so many years afraid and in silence...

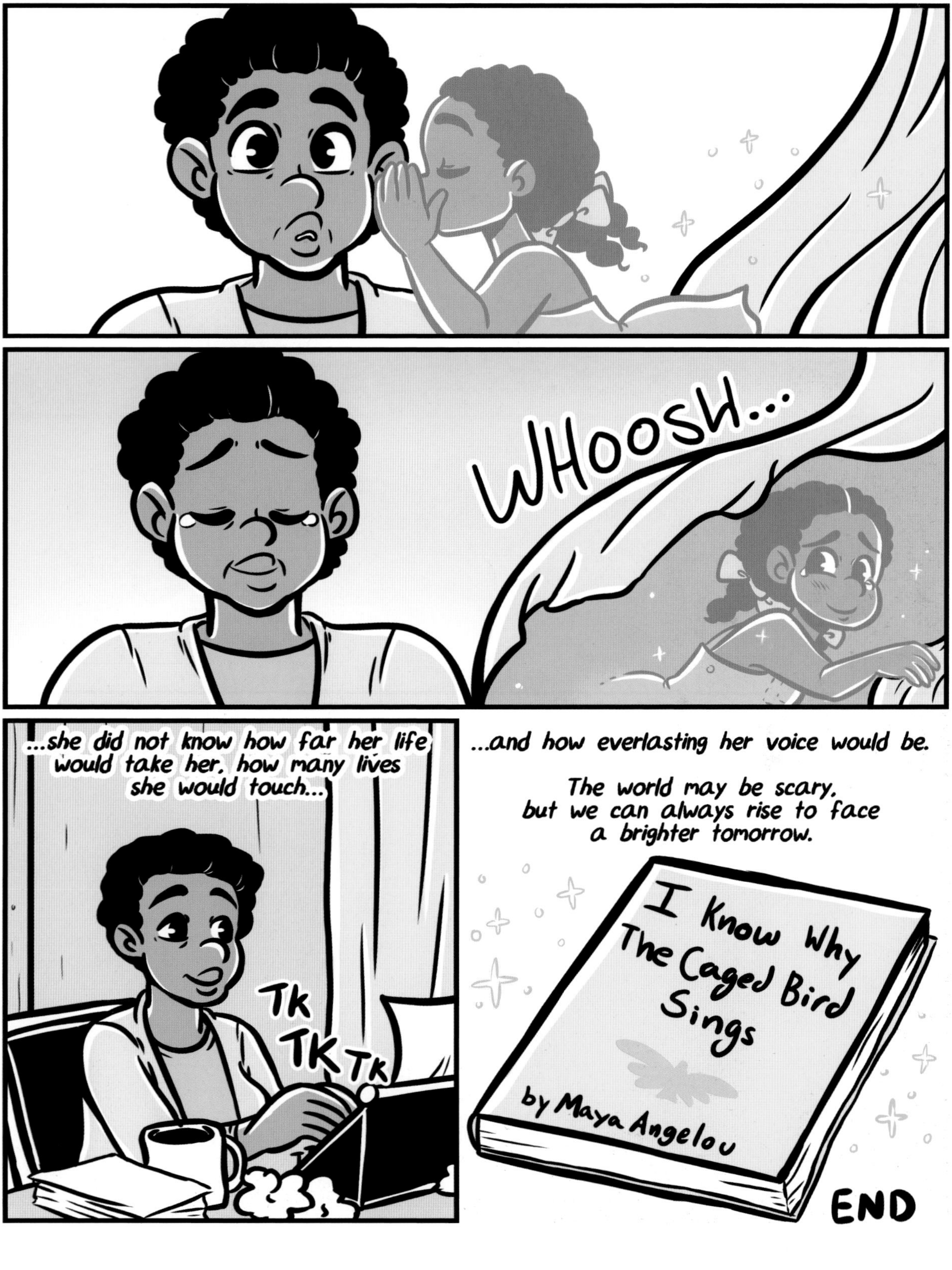
WHOOSH...
...she did not know how far her life would take her, how many lives she would touch...
TK
TK TK
...and how everlasting her voice would be.
The world may be scary, but we can always rise to face a brighter tomorrow.
I Know Why The Caged Bird Sings
by Maya Angelou
END

RALLY

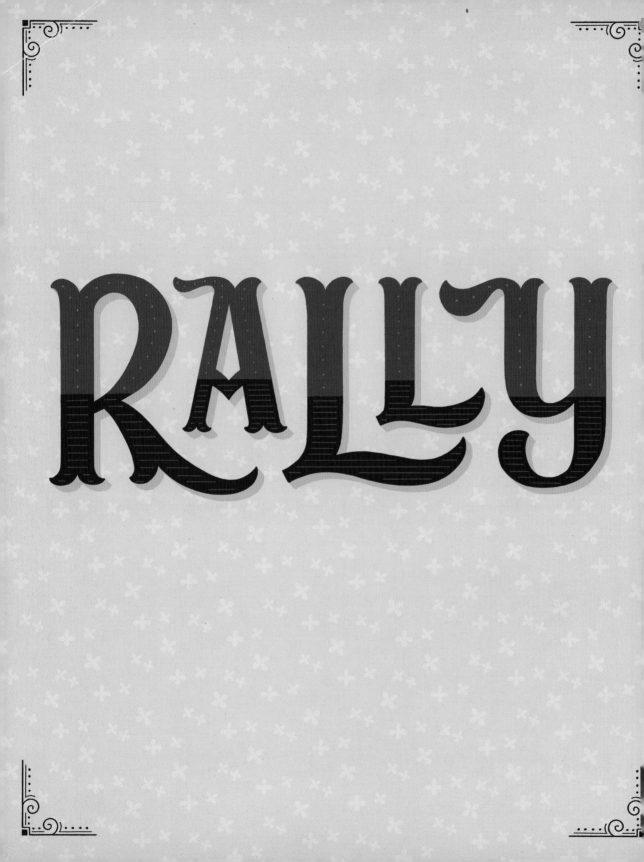

The world doesn't usually change unless people who see something unfair decide to change it themselves. Standing up for what's right, especially if you're the first (or only) one to do it, requires great courage, clarity, and determination. The five activist-heroes in this chapter all risked their careers, reputations, and, in some cases, even their lives, to make the world a better, fairer place for us all. *Your* voice matters just as much as theirs. To make a difference, all you have to do is start to use it.

THE DARING DETECTIVE

·····

KATE WARNE
1833 ~ 1868

She was as bold as she was brave. After Kate Warne, considered America's first female detective, uncovered details about a plot to kill president-elect Abraham Lincoln before his inauguration, she personally led his middle-of-the-night escape on a train, forever changing the course of our nation.

KATE AND ME

COUNT ALL THE THINGS YOU HAVE IN COMMON WITH KATE WARNE.

- I enjoy solving mysteries.
- I'm good at pretending.
- I can talk to people even when I feel shy.
- I pay attention to everything around me.
- My parents say I have great hearing!
- People are often surprised about how strong I am.
- If someone needs help I can help them.
- Even danger doesn't scare me.
- I'm shrewd.
- I'm courageous.

Photo is believed to be Kate Warne, in disguise as a Union soldier

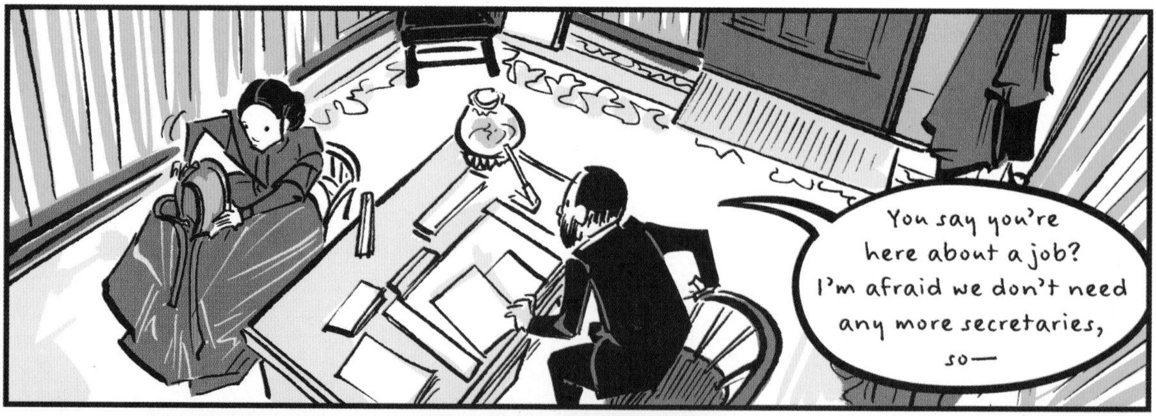
You say you're here about a job? I'm afraid we don't need any more secretaries, so—

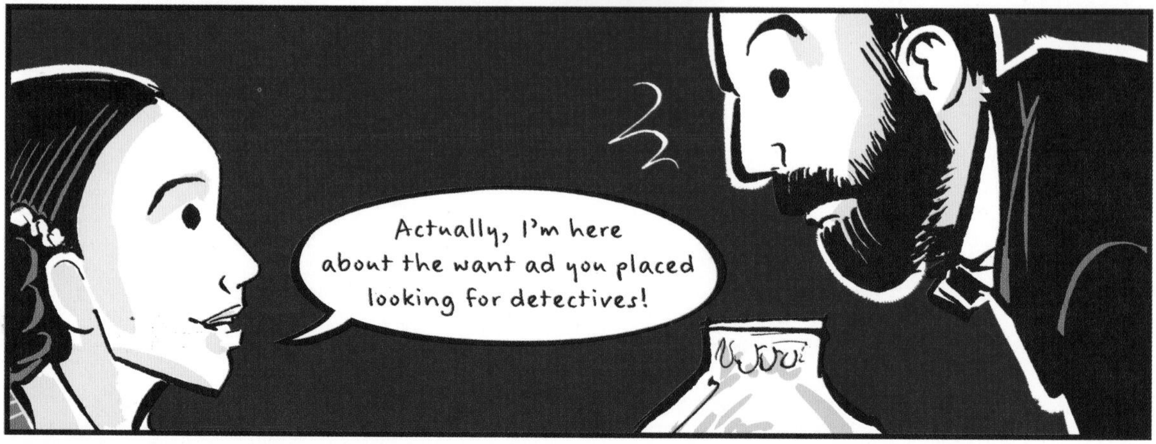
Actually, I'm here about the want ad you placed looking for detectives!

KATE WARNE

How the United States' First Female Detective Saved Abraham Lincoln's Life

by Molly Brooks

Very little is known about Kate Warne's life before the day in 1856 that she walked into the Chicago office of the now-legendary Pinkerton National Detective Agency and talked Allan Pinkerton into hiring her as the first female detective—not only in his company, but in the *country*.

She was 23 years old, and a widow, and *very* determined.

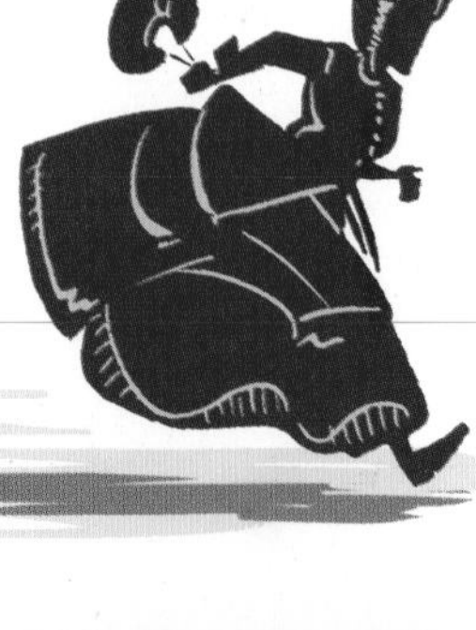

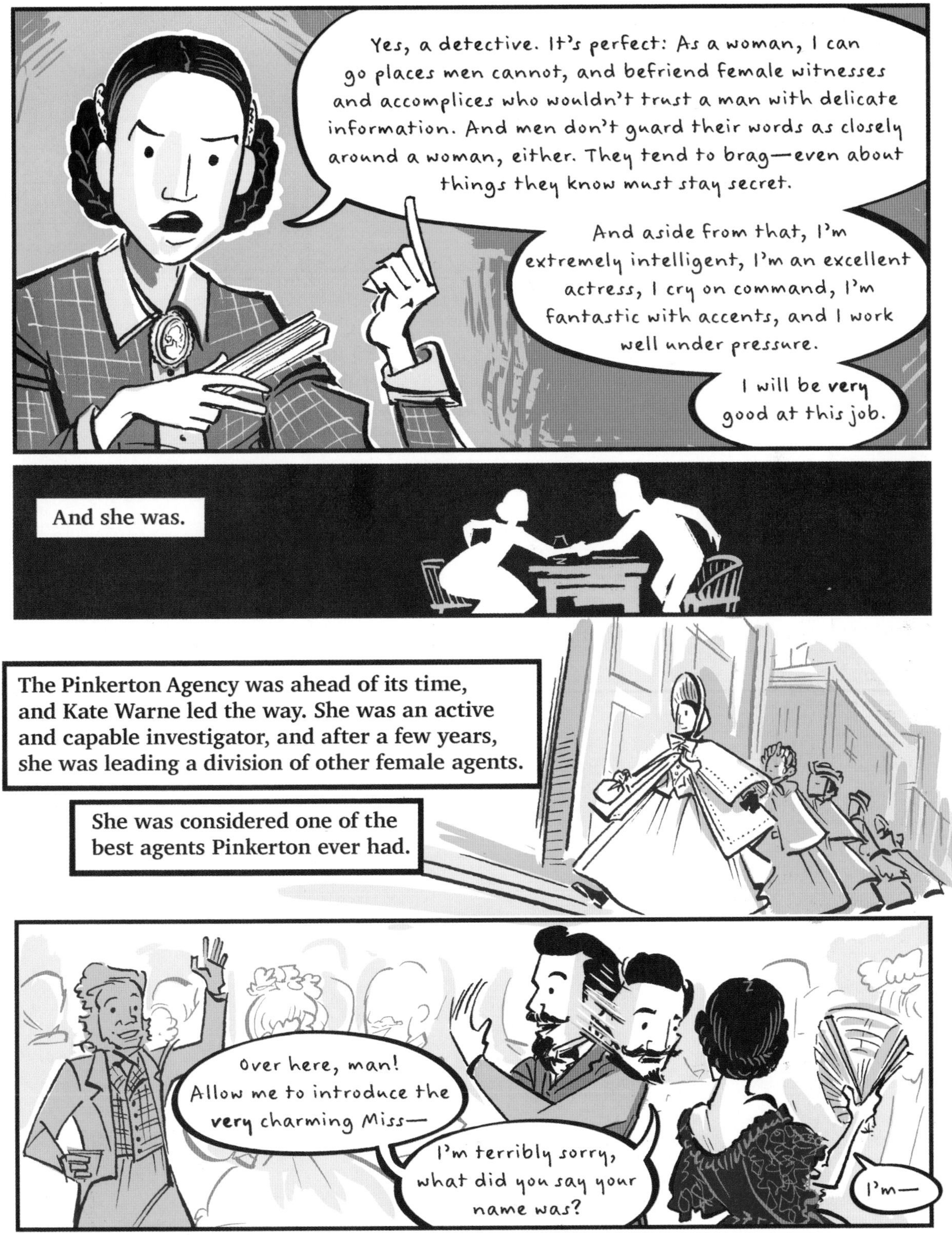

Yes, a detective. It's perfect: As a woman, I can go places men cannot, and befriend female witnesses and accomplices who wouldn't trust a man with delicate information. And men don't guard their words as closely around a woman, either. They tend to brag—even about things they know must stay secret.
And aside from that, I'm extremely intelligent, I'm an excellent actress, I cry on command, I'm fantastic with accents, and I work well under pressure.
I will be **very** good at this job.
And she was.
The Pinkerton Agency was ahead of its time, and Kate Warne led the way. She was an active and capable investigator, and after a few years, she was leading a division of other female agents.
She was considered one of the best agents Pinkerton ever had.
Over here, man! Allow me to introduce the **very** charming Miss—
I'm terribly sorry, what did you say your name was?
I'm—

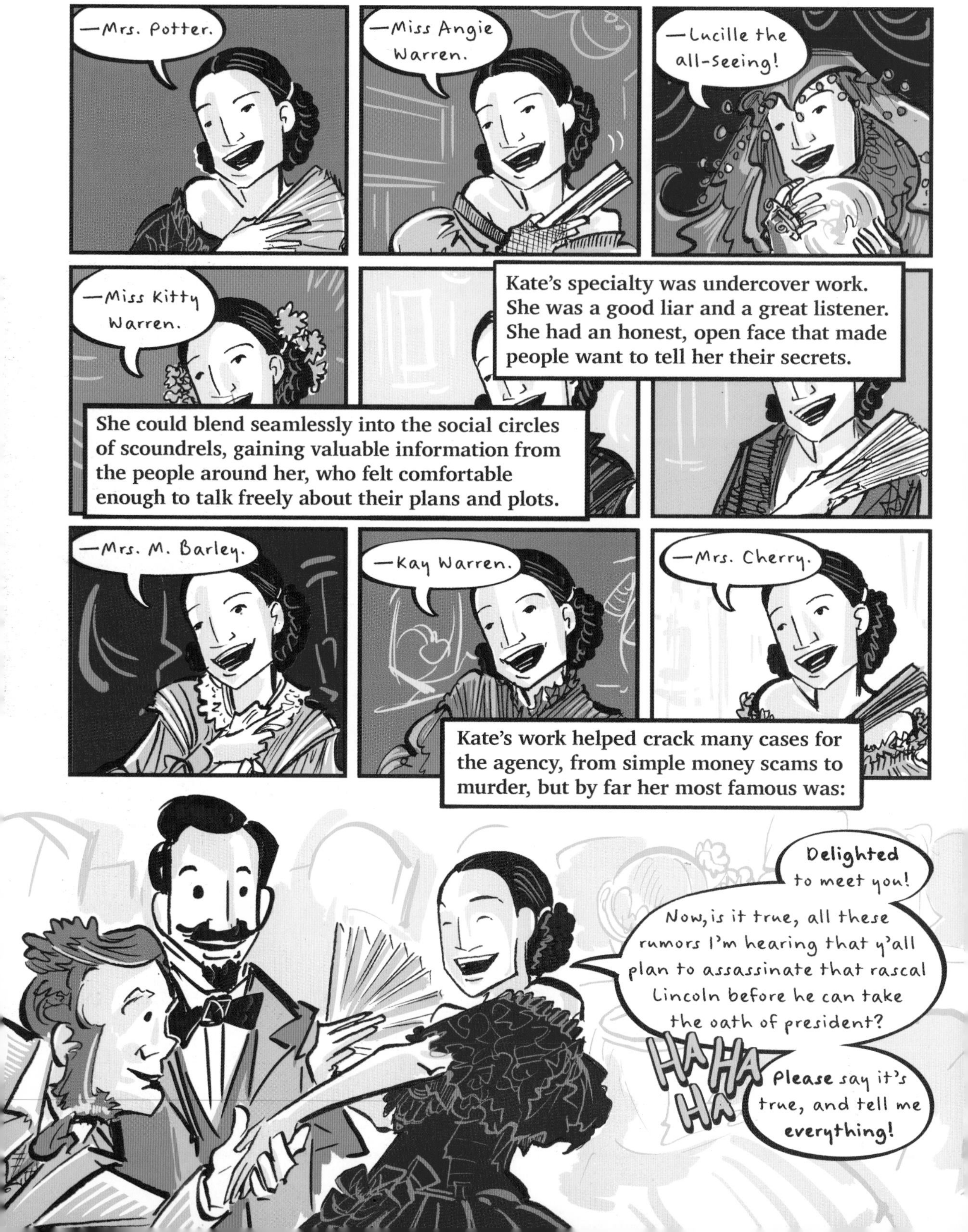
—Mrs. Potter.
—Miss Angie Warren.
—Lucille the all-seeing!
—Miss Kitty Warren.
Kate's specialty was undercover work. She was a good liar and a great listener. She had an honest, open face that made people want to tell her their secrets.
She could blend seamlessly into the social circles of scoundrels, gaining valuable information from the people around her, who felt comfortable enough to talk freely about their plans and plots.
—Mrs. M. Barley.
—Kay Warren.
—Mrs. Cherry.
Kate's work helped crack many cases for the agency, from simple money scams to murder, but by far her most famous was:
Delighted to meet you!
Now, is it true, all these rumors I'm hearing that y'all plan to assassinate that rascal Lincoln before he can take the oath of president?
HA HA HA
Please say it's true, and tell me everything!

THE BALTIMORE PLOT

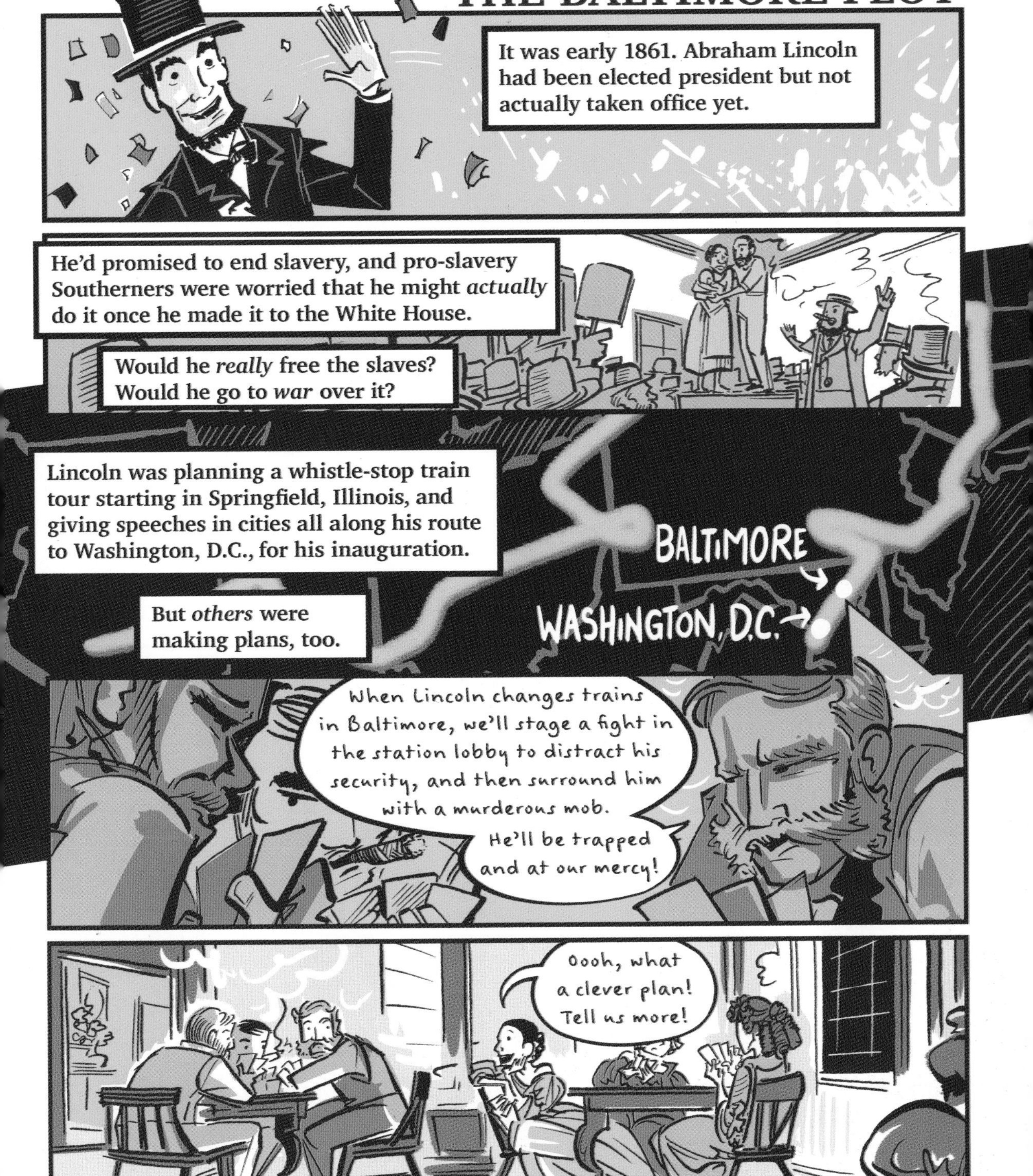
It was early 1861. Abraham Lincoln had been elected president but not actually taken office yet.
He'd promised to end slavery, and pro-slavery Southerners were worried that he might *actually* do it once he made it to the White House.
Would he *really* free the slaves? Would he go to *war* over it?
Lincoln was planning a whistle-stop train tour starting in Springfield, Illinois, and giving speeches in cities all along his route to Washington, D.C., for his inauguration.
BALTIMORE
WASHINGTON, D.C.
But *others* were making plans, too.
When Lincoln changes trains in Baltimore, we'll stage a fight in the station lobby to distract his security, and then surround him with a murderous mob.
He'll be trapped and at our mercy!
Oooh, what a clever plan! Tell us more!

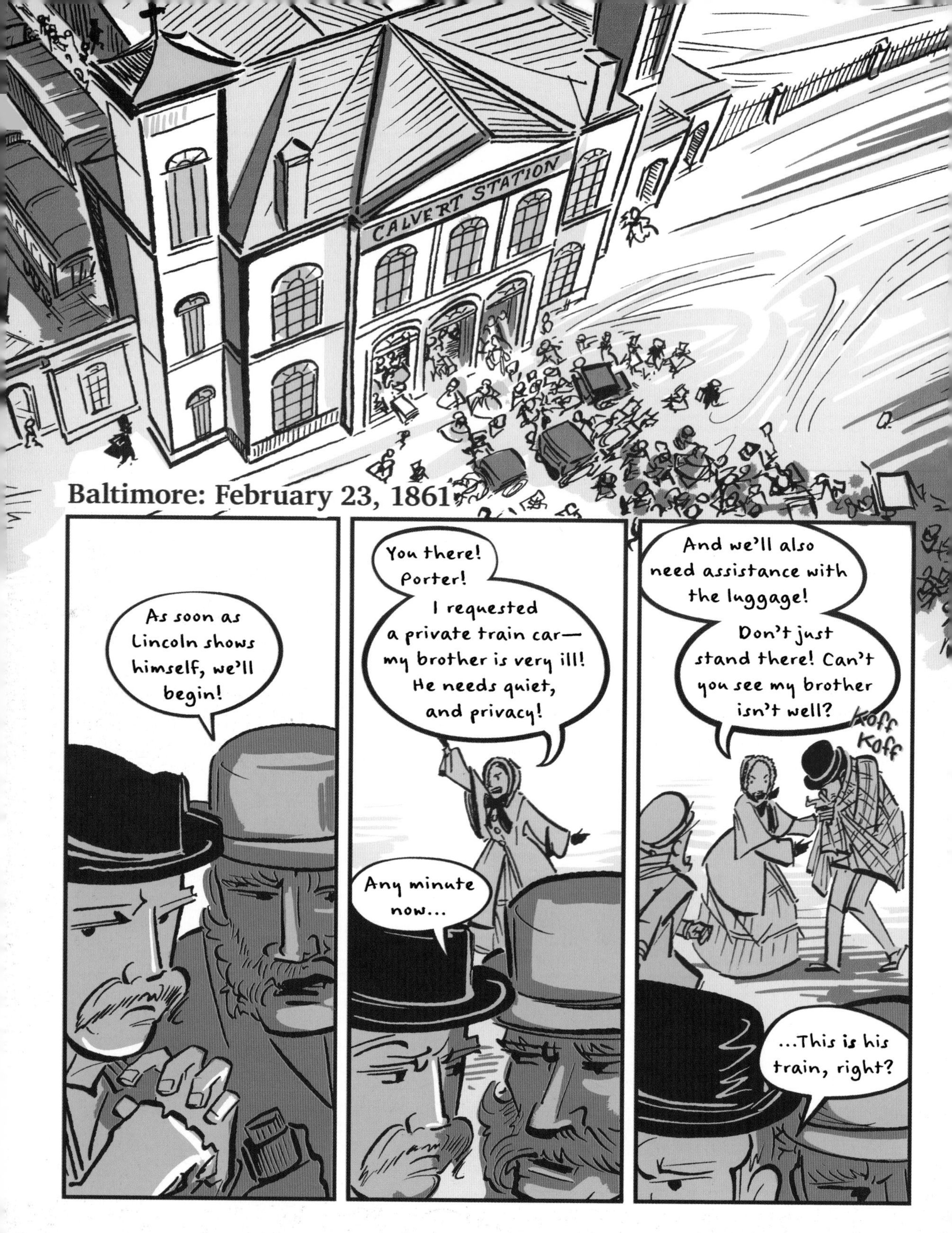
CALVERT STATION
Baltimore: February 23, 1861
As soon as Lincoln shows himself, we'll begin!
You there! Porter!
I requested a private train car— my brother is very ill! He needs quiet, and privacy!
Any minute now...
And we'll also need assistance with the luggage!
Don't just stand there! Can't you see my brother isn't well?
KOFF KOFF
...This is his train, right?

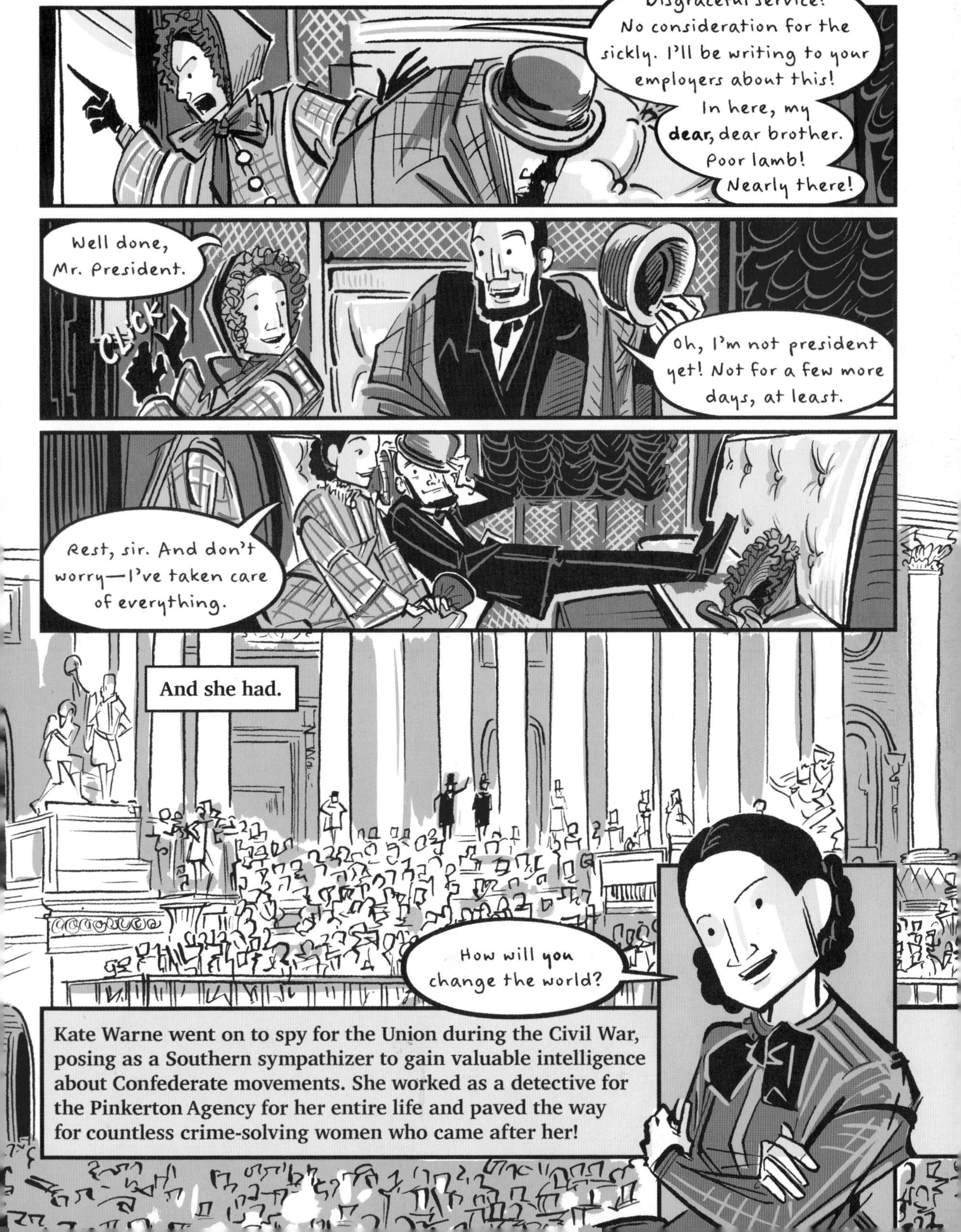
Disgraceful service! No consideration for the sickly. I'll be writing to your employers about this!
In here, my **dear,** dear brother. Poor lamb! Nearly there!
Well done, Mr. President.
CLICK
Oh, I'm not president yet! Not for a few more days, at least.
Rest, sir. And don't worry—I've taken care of everything.
And she had.
How will **you** change the world?
Kate Warne went on to spy for the Union during the Civil War, posing as a Southern sympathizer to gain valuable intelligence about Confederate movements. She worked as a detective for the Pinkerton Agency for her entire life and paved the way for countless crime-solving women who came after her!

THE UNDERCOVER REPORTER

· · · · ·

NELLIE BLY

1864 ~ 1922

She didn't just report the news. Nellie Bly lived it. As a pioneer investigative journalist, she went undercover in some very scary places to report firsthand on what it was like for the people inside. She gave voice to those who didn't have one, and her writing changed lives—and minds.

NELLIE AND ME

COUNT ALL THE THINGS YOU HAVE IN COMMON WITH NELLIE BLY.

- I have a lot to say.
- I like to tell spectacular but real stories.
- I like to investigate things.
- I expect people to be honest.
- I'm not shy about calling out dishonesty.
- I can fill notebooks with my discoveries.
- I want to see my writing published around the world.
- I won't take no for an answer.
- I'm ambitious.
- I'm devoted to the truth.

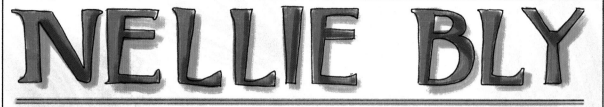

NELLIE BLY

INTREPID REPORTER

By Jackie Roche

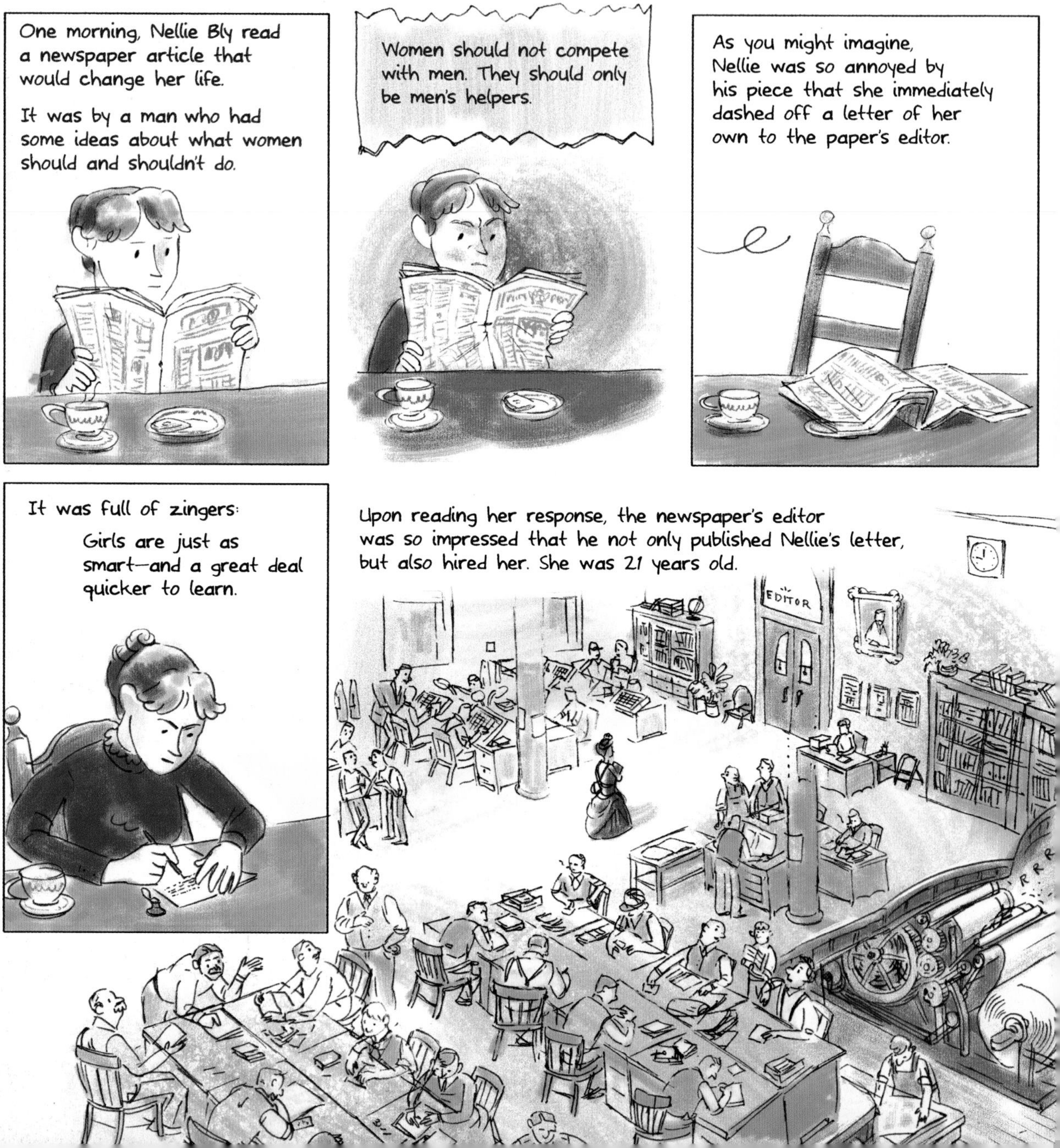

One morning, Nellie Bly read a newspaper article that would change her life.
It was by a man who had some ideas about what women should and shouldn't do.
Women should not compete with men. They should only be men's helpers.
As you might imagine, Nellie was so annoyed by his piece that she immediately dashed off a letter of her own to the paper's editor.
It was full of zingers:
Girls are just as smart—and a great deal quicker to learn.
Upon reading her response, the newspaper's editor was so impressed that he not only published Nellie's letter, but also hired her. She was 21 years old.
EDITOR
RRR

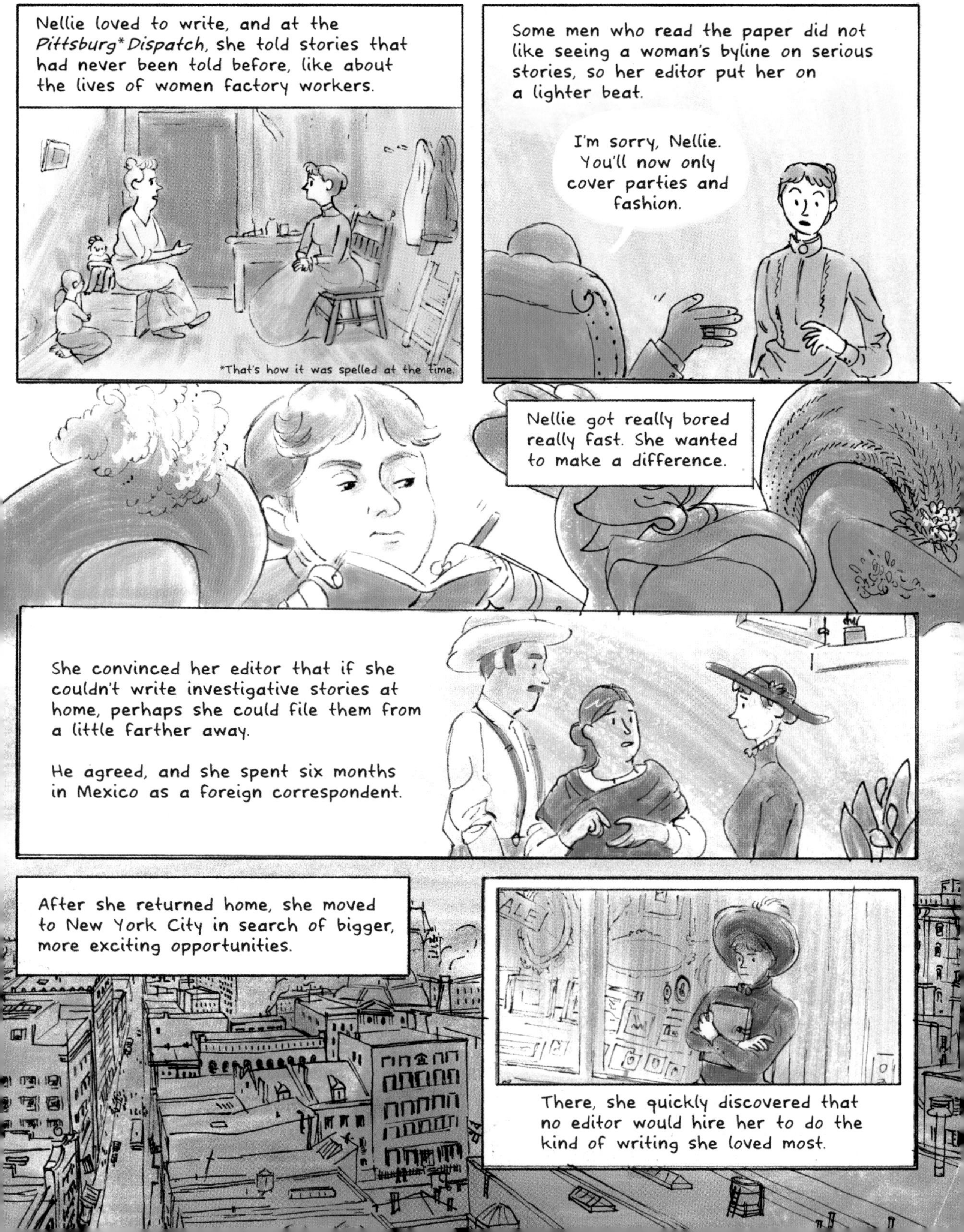
Nellie loved to write, and at the *Pittsburg* Dispatch*, she told stories that had never been told before, like about the lives of women factory workers.
*That's how it was spelled at the time.
Some men who read the paper did not like seeing a woman's byline on serious stories, so her editor put her on a lighter beat.
I'm sorry, Nellie. You'll now only cover parties and fashion.
Nellie got really bored really fast. She wanted to make a difference.
She convinced her editor that if she couldn't write investigative stories at home, perhaps she could file them from a little farther away.
He agreed, and she spent six months in Mexico as a foreign correspondent.
After she returned home, she moved to New York City in search of bigger, more exciting opportunities.
There, she quickly discovered that no editor would hire her to do the kind of writing she loved most.

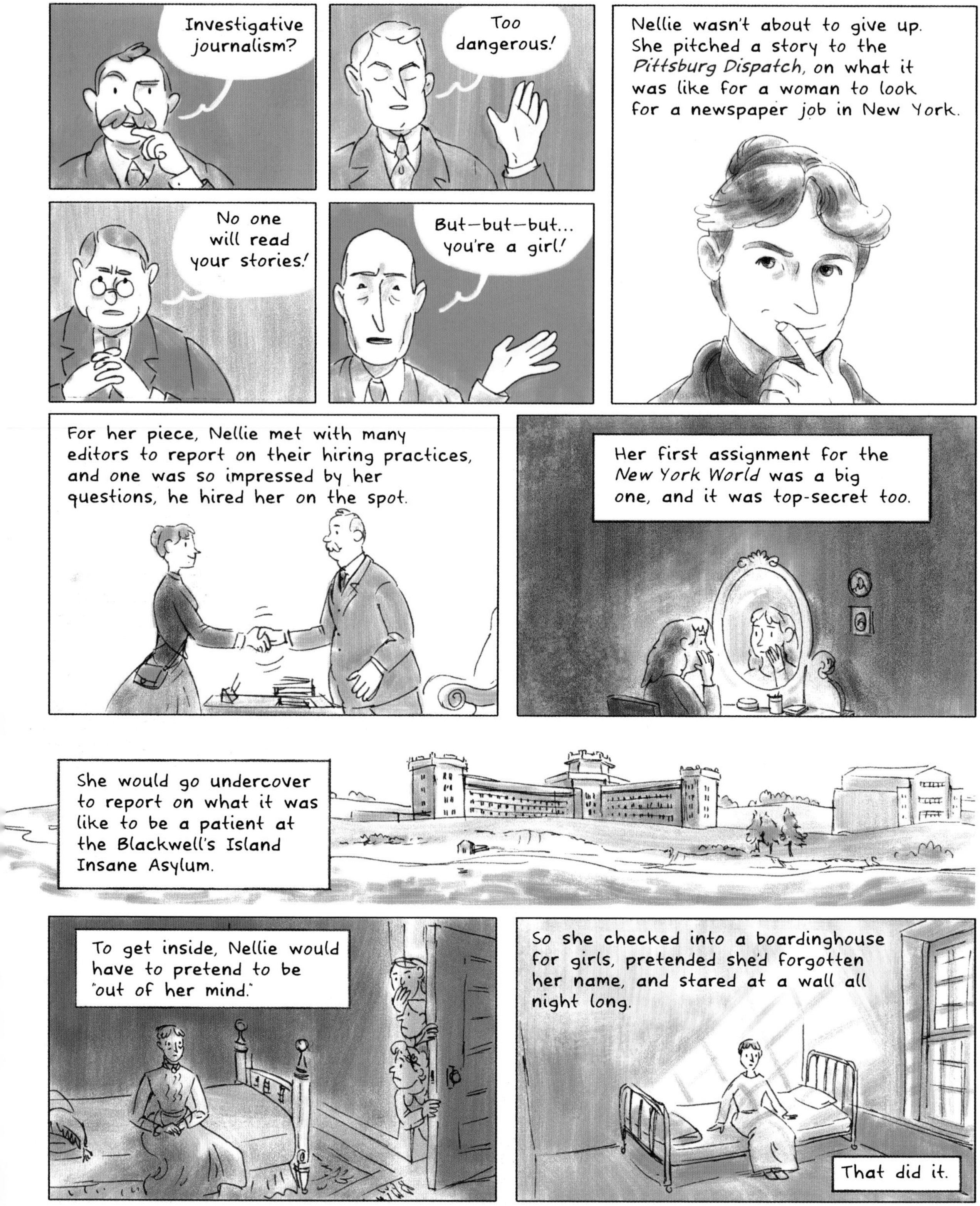
Investigative journalism?
Too dangerous!
Nellie wasn't about to give up. She pitched a story to the *Pittsburg Dispatch*, on what it was like for a woman to look for a newspaper job in New York.
No one will read your stories!
But—but—but... you're a girl!
For her piece, Nellie met with many editors to report on their hiring practices, and one was so impressed by her questions, he hired her on the spot.
Her first assignment for the *New York World* was a big one, and it was top-secret too.
She would go undercover to report on what it was like to be a patient at the Blackwell's Island Insane Asylum.
To get inside, Nellie would have to pretend to be "out of her mind."
So she checked into a boardinghouse for girls, pretended she'd forgotten her name, and stared at a wall all night long.
That did it.

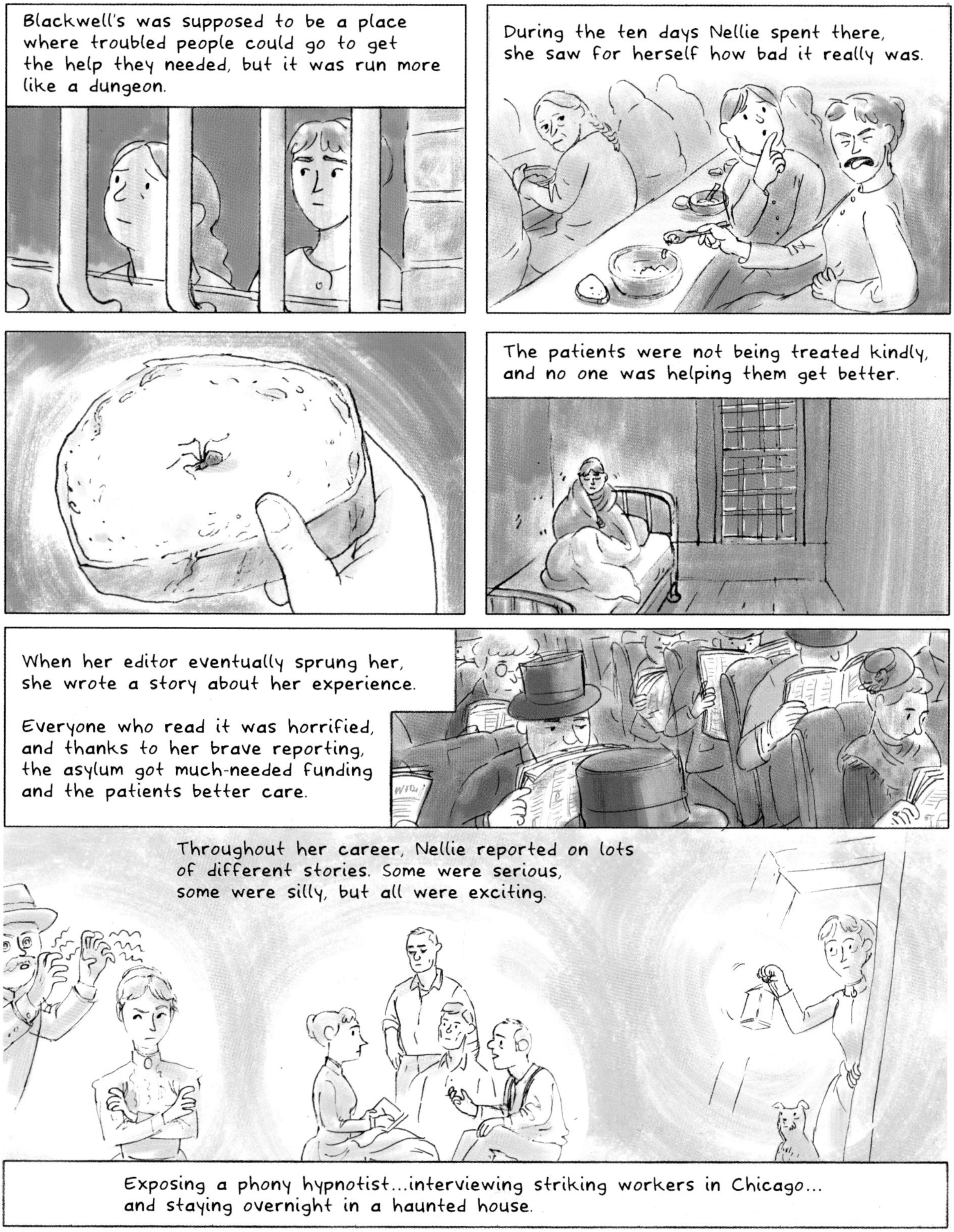
Blackwell's was supposed to be a place where troubled people could go to get the help they needed, but it was run more like a dungeon.
During the ten days Nellie spent there, she saw for herself how bad it really was.
The patients were not being treated kindly, and no one was helping them get better.
When her editor eventually sprung her, she wrote a story about her experience.
Everyone who read it was horrified, and thanks to her brave reporting, the asylum got much-needed funding and the patients better care.
Throughout her career, Nellie reported on lots of different stories. Some were serious, some were silly, but all were exciting.
Exposing a phony hypnotist...interviewing striking workers in Chicago... and staying overnight in a haunted house.

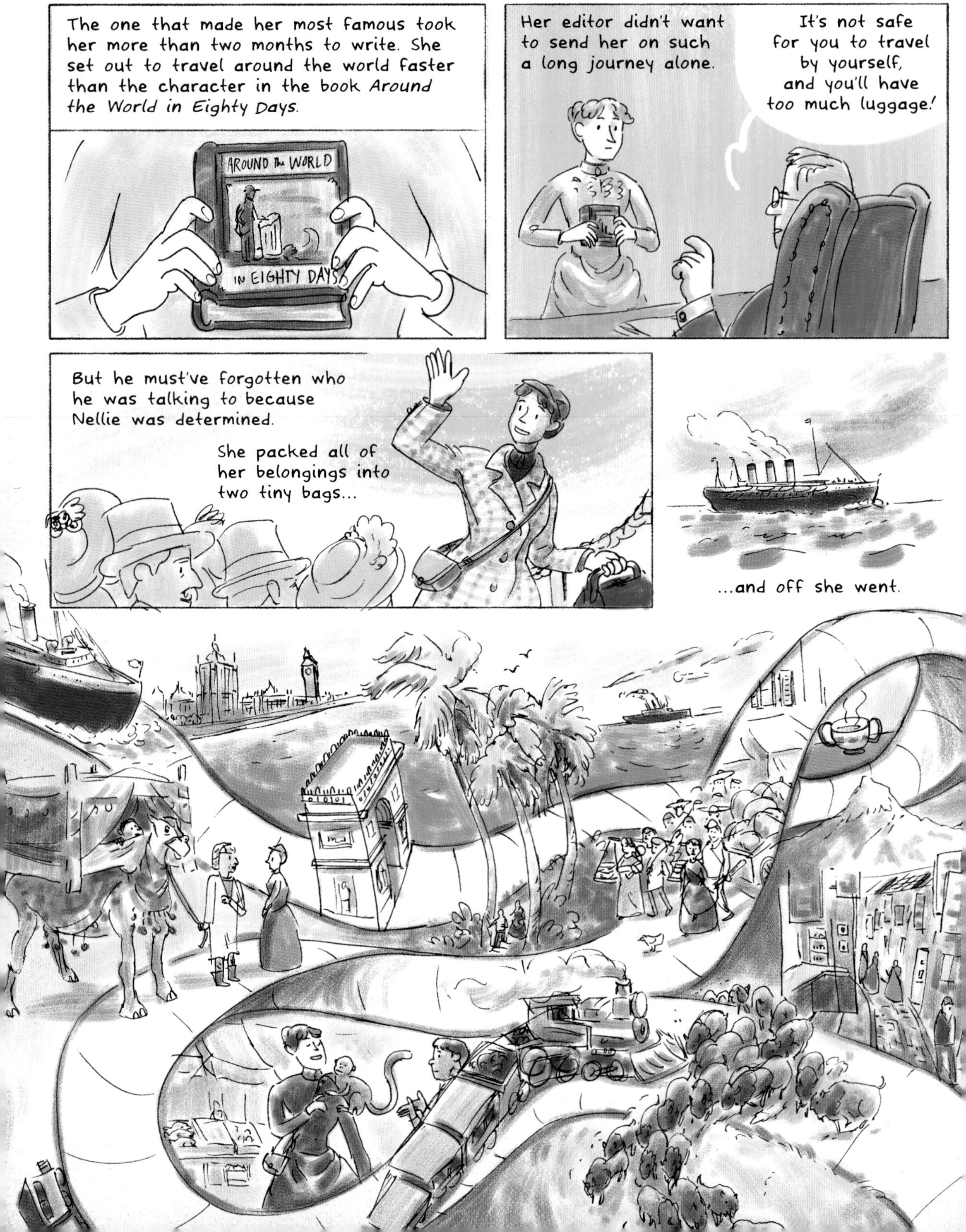
The one that made her most famous took her more than two months to write. She set out to travel around the world faster than the character in the book *Around the World in Eighty Days*.
AROUND THE WORLD IN EIGHTY DAYS
Her editor didn't want to send her on such a long journey alone.
It's not safe for you to travel by yourself, and you'll have too much luggage!
But he must've forgotten who he was talking to because Nellie was determined.
She packed all of her belongings into two tiny bags...
...and off she went.

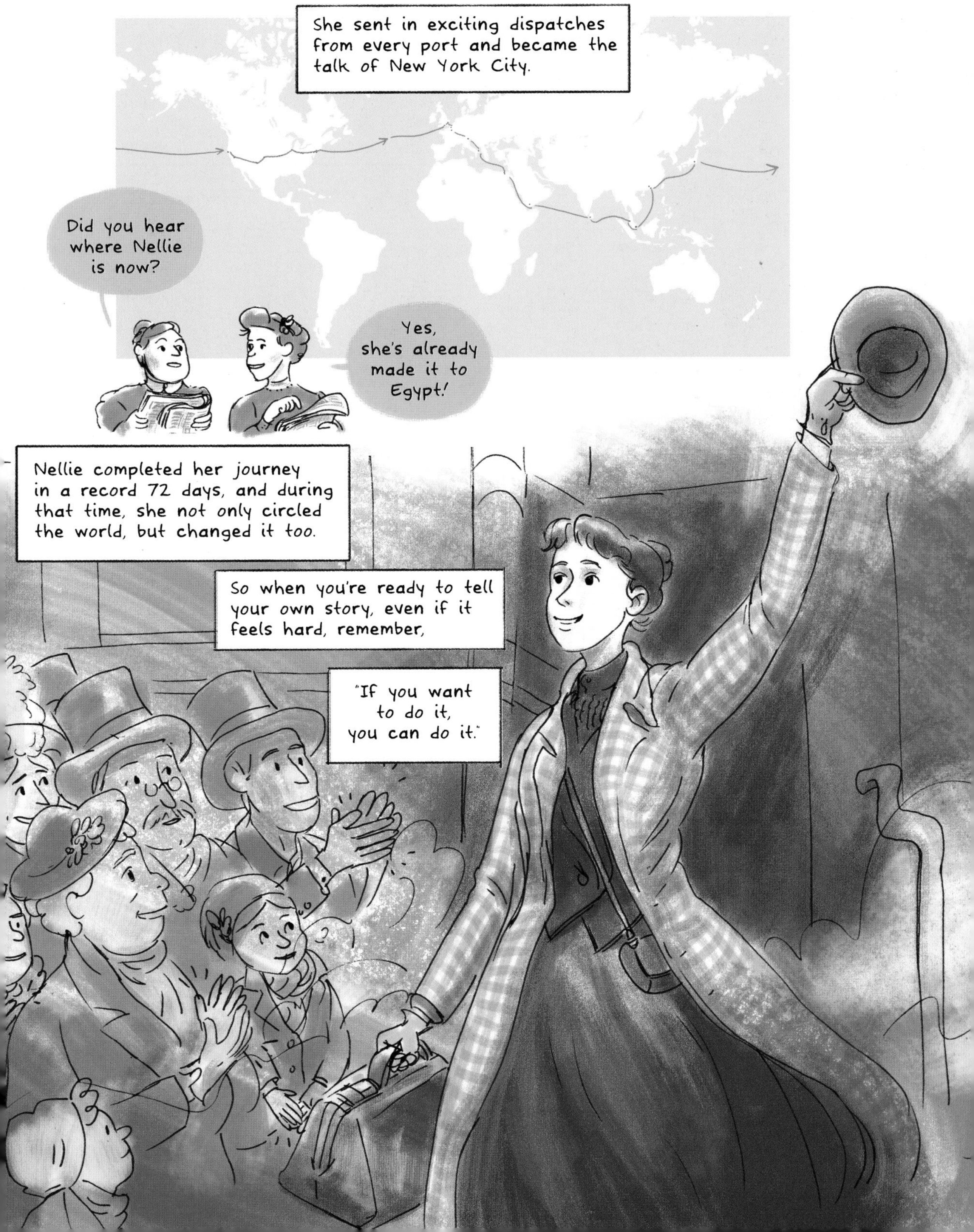
She sent in exciting dispatches from every port and became the talk of New York City.
Did you hear where Nellie is now?
Yes, she's already made it to Egypt!
Nellie completed her journey in a record 72 days, and during that time, she not only circled the world, but changed it too.
So when you're ready to tell your own story, even if it feels hard, remember,
"If you want to do it, you can do it."

THE JUSTICE WARRIOR

· · · · ·

ELEANOR ROOSEVELT
1884 ~ 1962

She was supposed to stay quiet. That's how First Ladies always behaved, at least until she came along. When her husband, Franklin Delano Roosevelt, was elected president, Eleanor Roosevelt used her new platform to speak out for women's rights, civil rights, and human rights. She inspired not only the nation but the world, and even today, her words of wisdom still remind us of the just way forward.

ELEANOR AND ME

COUNT ALL THE THINGS YOU HAVE IN COMMON WITH ELEANOR ROOSEVELT.

- People expect me to be quiet, but I have a lot to say.
- I prefer to say what I want.
- I like to get my ideas out there.
- I want to write things people will read.
- If someone in my family is sick, I help care for them.
- When I see something I know is wrong, I try to fix it.
- I want better things for myself and everyone else too.
- When people feel down, I encourage them.
- I'm witty.
- I'm wise.

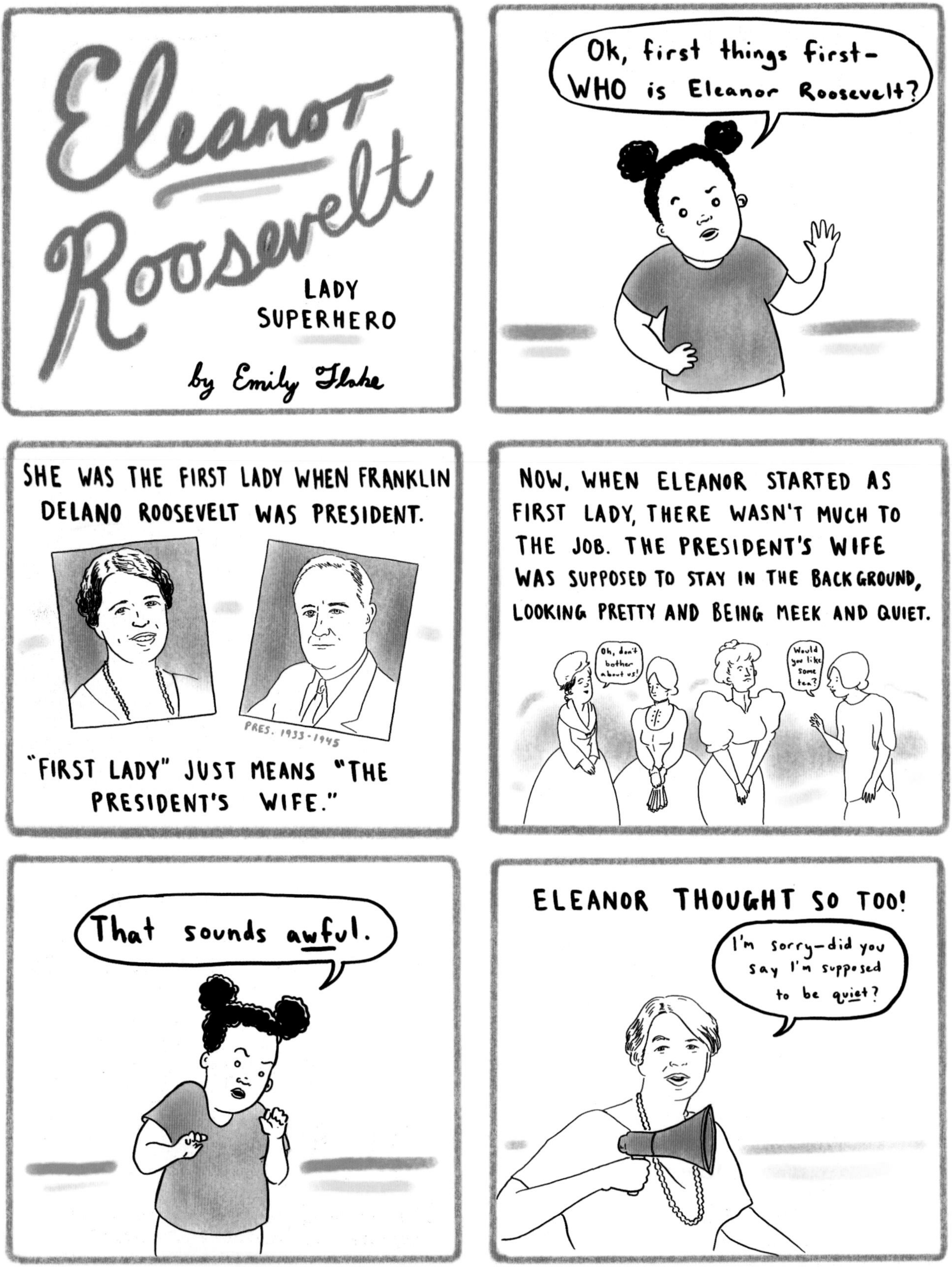
Eleanor Roosevelt
LADY SUPERHERO
by Emily Flake
Ok, first things first— WHO is Eleanor Roosevelt?
SHE WAS THE FIRST LADY WHEN FRANKLIN DELANO ROOSEVELT WAS PRESIDENT.
PRES. 1933–1945
"FIRST LADY" JUST MEANS "THE PRESIDENT'S WIFE."
NOW, WHEN ELEANOR STARTED AS FIRST LADY, THERE WASN'T MUCH TO THE JOB. THE PRESIDENT'S WIFE WAS SUPPOSED TO STAY IN THE BACKGROUND, LOOKING PRETTY AND BEING MEEK AND QUIET.
Oh, don't bother about us!
Would you like some tea?
That sounds awful.
ELEANOR THOUGHT SO TOO!
I'm sorry—did you say I'm supposed to be quiet?

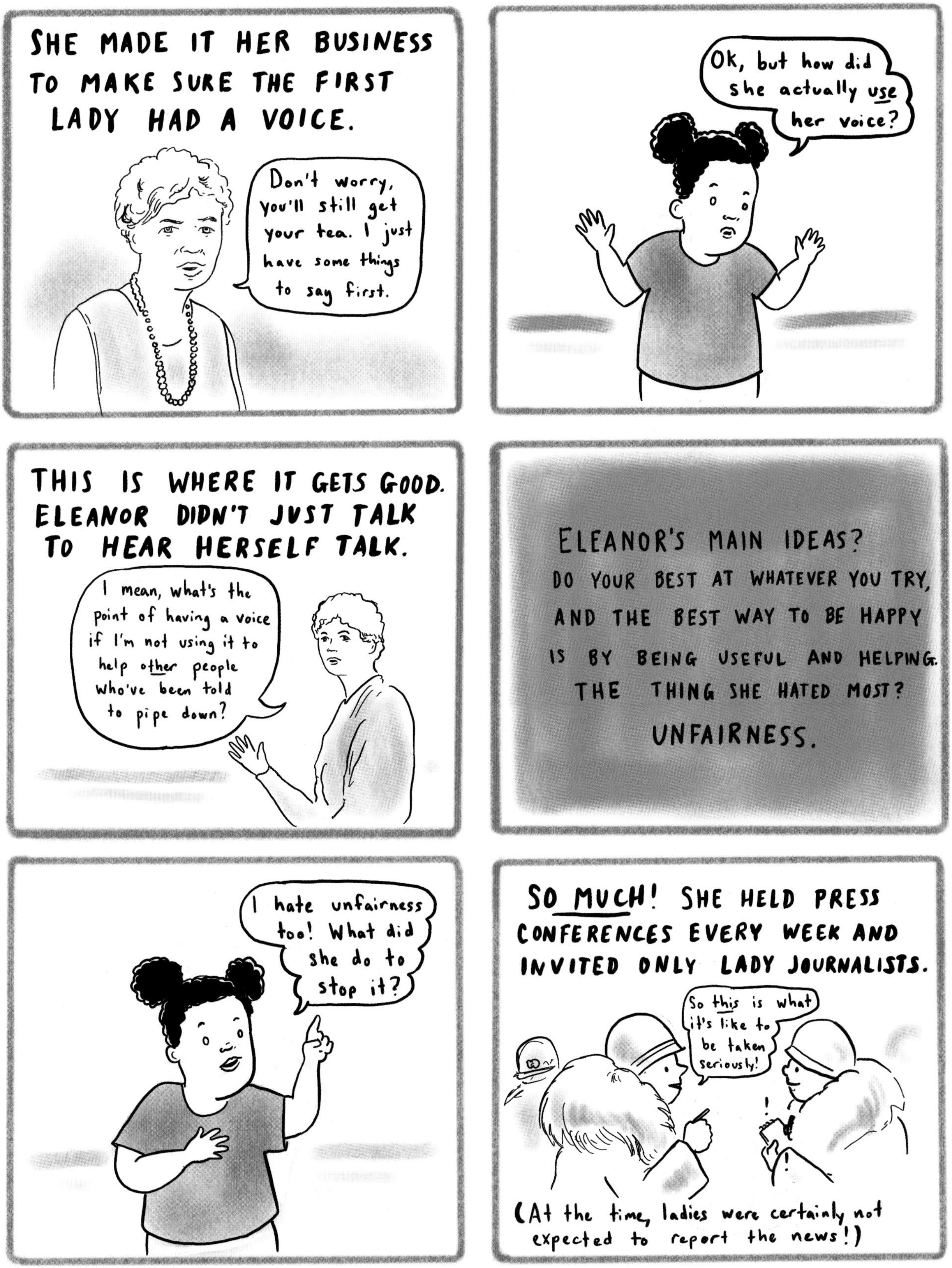
SHE MADE IT HER BUSINESS TO MAKE SURE THE FIRST LADY HAD A VOICE.
Don't worry, you'll still get your tea. I just have some things to say first.
Ok, but how did she actually use her voice?
THIS IS WHERE IT GETS GOOD. ELEANOR DIDN'T JUST TALK TO HEAR HERSELF TALK.
I mean, what's the point of having a voice if I'm not using it to help other people who've been told to pipe down?
ELEANOR'S MAIN IDEAS? DO YOUR BEST AT WHATEVER YOU TRY, AND THE BEST WAY TO BE HAPPY IS BY BEING USEFUL AND HELPING. THE THING SHE HATED MOST? UNFAIRNESS.
I hate unfairness too! What did she do to stop it?
SO MUCH! SHE HELD PRESS CONFERENCES EVERY WEEK AND INVITED ONLY LADY JOURNALISTS.
So this is what it's like to be taken seriously!
!
!
(At the time, ladies were certainly not expected to report the news!)

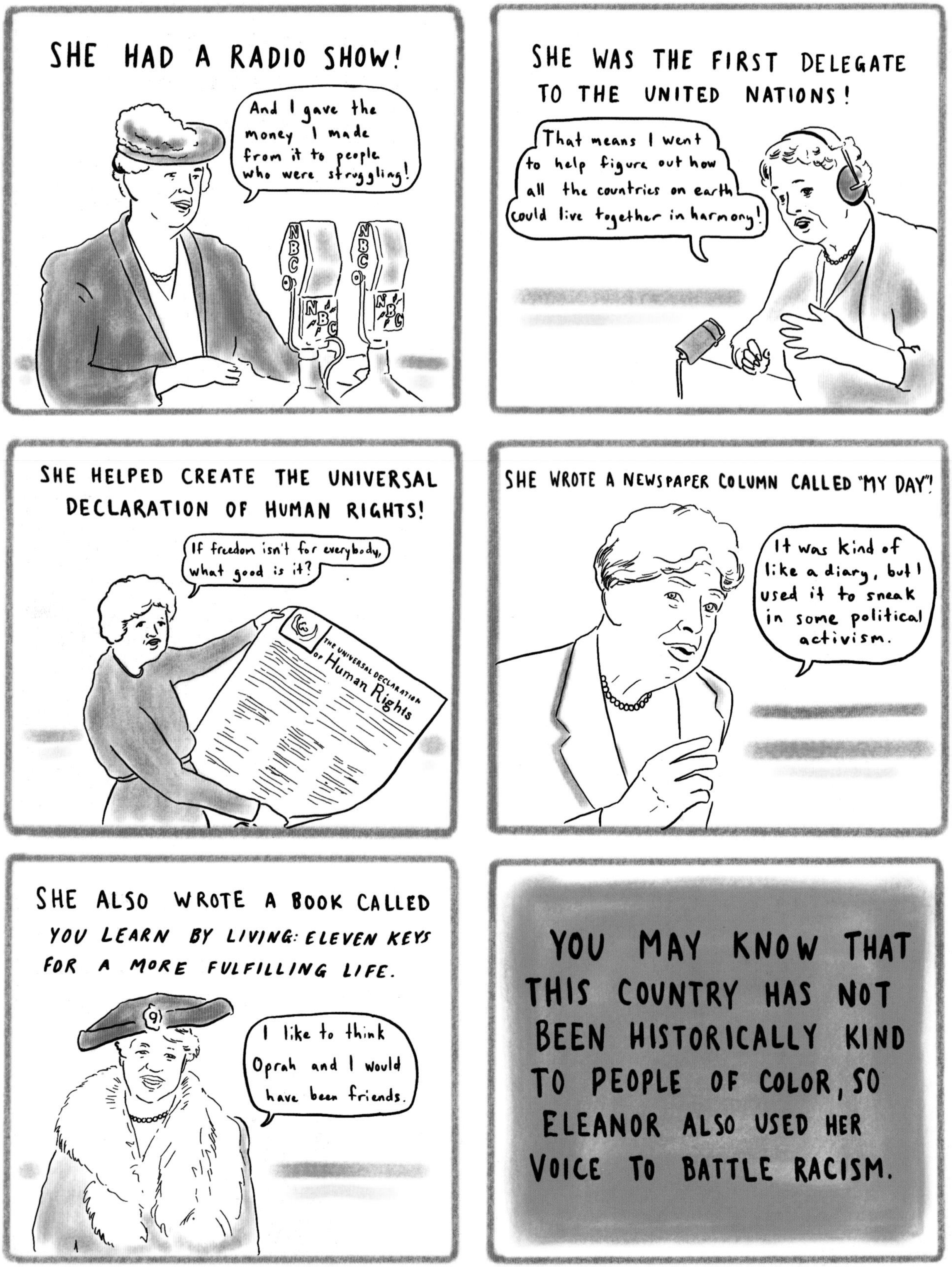
SHE HAD A RADIO SHOW!
And I gave the money I made from it to people who were struggling!
NBC
SHE WAS THE FIRST DELEGATE TO THE UNITED NATIONS!
That means I went to help figure out how all the countries on earth could live together in harmony!
SHE HELPED CREATE THE UNIVERSAL DECLARATION OF HUMAN RIGHTS!
If freedom isn't for everybody, what good is it?
THE UNIVERSAL DECLARATION OF Human Rights
SHE WROTE A NEWSPAPER COLUMN CALLED "MY DAY"!
It was kind of like a diary, but I used it to sneak in some political activism.
SHE ALSO WROTE A BOOK CALLED *YOU LEARN BY LIVING: ELEVEN KEYS FOR A MORE FULFILLING LIFE.*
I like to think Oprah and I would have been friends.
YOU MAY KNOW THAT THIS COUNTRY HAS NOT BEEN HISTORICALLY KIND TO PEOPLE OF COLOR, SO ELEANOR ALSO USED HER VOICE TO BATTLE RACISM.

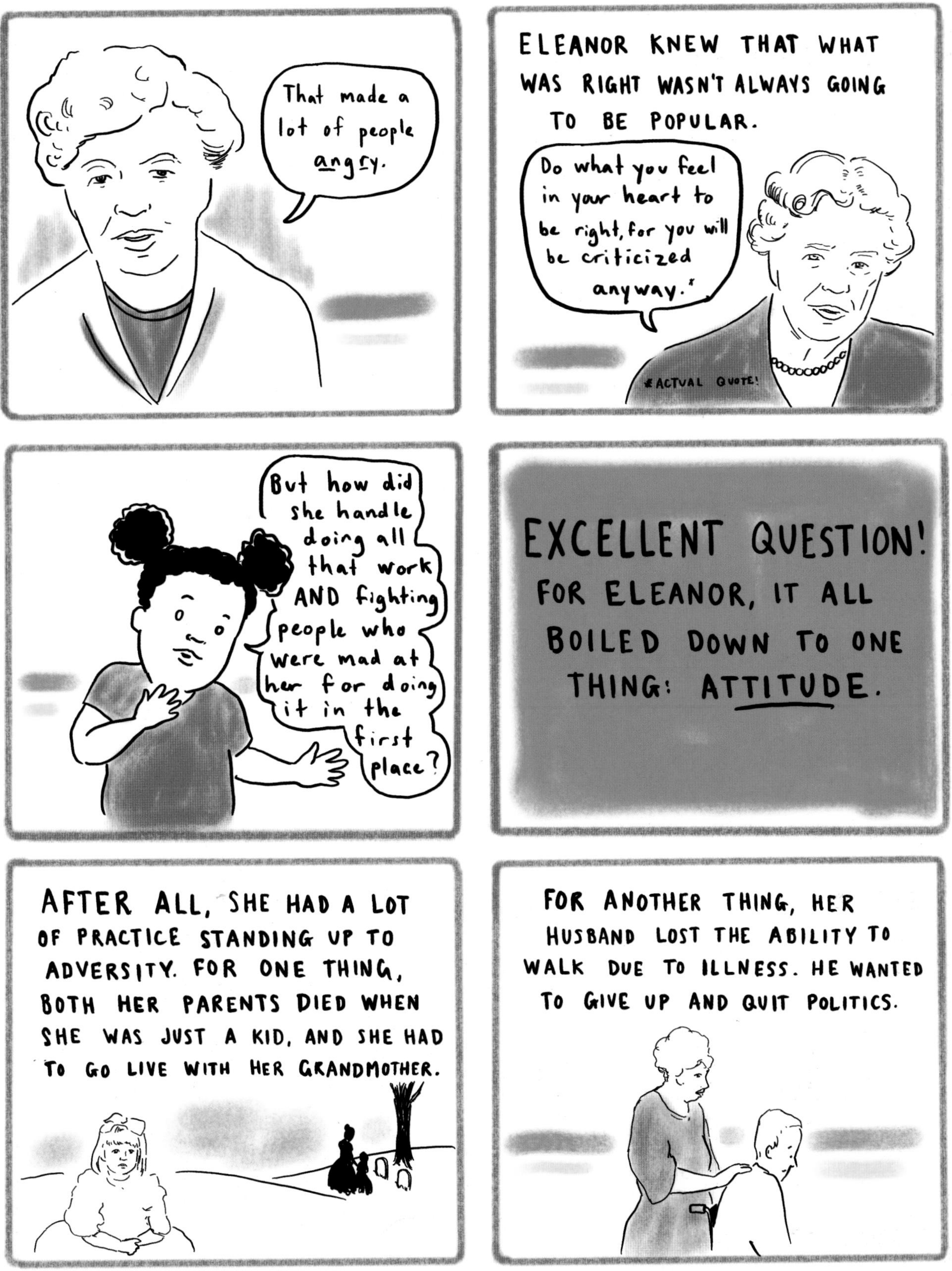

That made a lot of people angry.
ELEANOR KNEW THAT WHAT WAS RIGHT WASN'T ALWAYS GOING TO BE POPULAR.
Do what you feel in your heart to be right, for you will be criticized anyway.*
*ACTUAL QUOTE!
But how did she handle doing all that work AND fighting people who were mad at her for doing it in the first place?
EXCELLENT QUESTION!
FOR ELEANOR, IT ALL BOILED DOWN TO ONE THING: ATTITUDE.
AFTER ALL, SHE HAD A LOT OF PRACTICE STANDING UP TO ADVERSITY. FOR ONE THING, BOTH HER PARENTS DIED WHEN SHE WAS JUST A KID, AND SHE HAD TO GO LIVE WITH HER GRANDMOTHER.
FOR ANOTHER THING, HER HUSBAND LOST THE ABILITY TO WALK DUE TO ILLNESS. HE WANTED TO GIVE UP AND QUIT POLITICS.

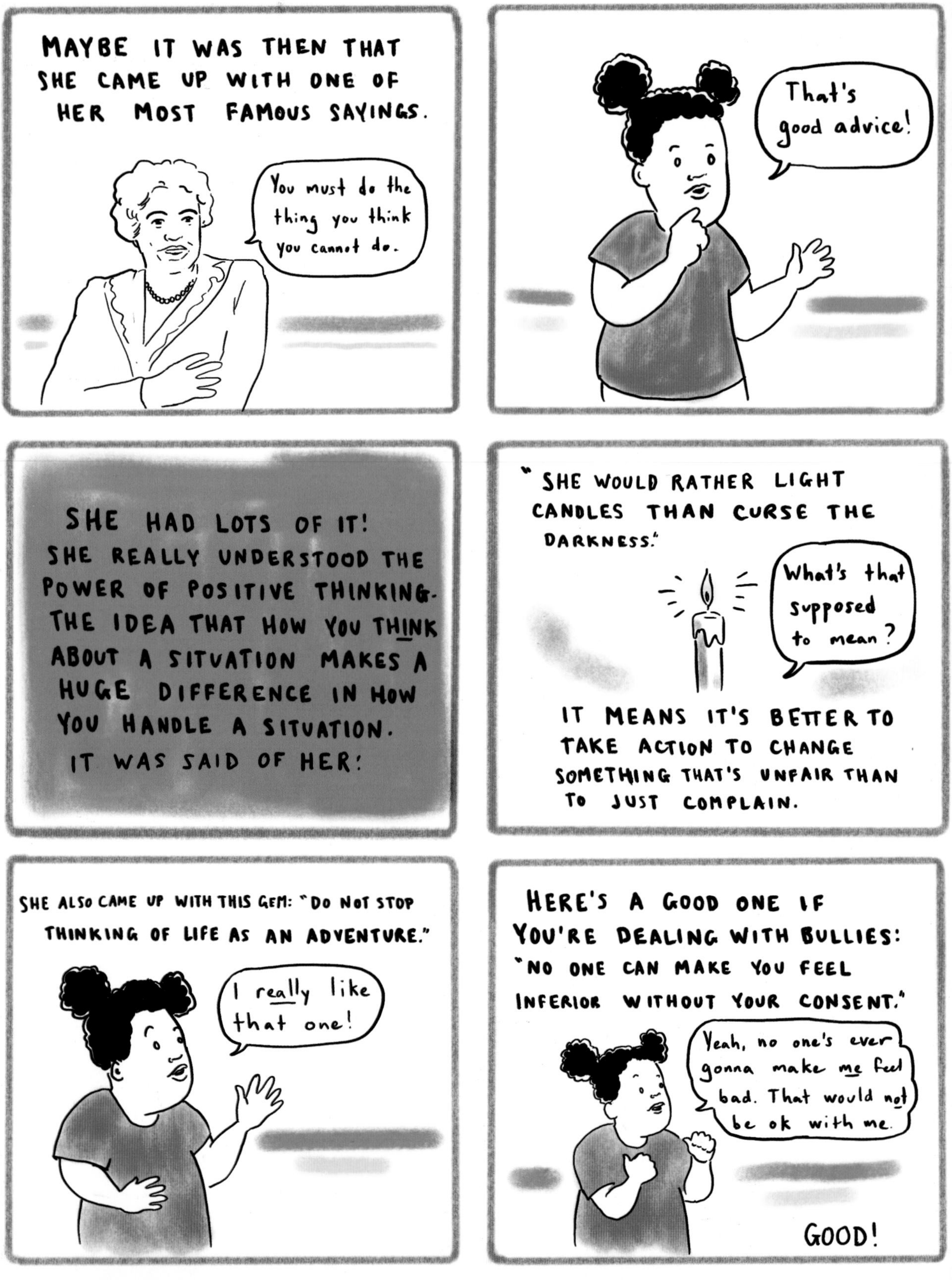
MAYBE IT WAS THEN THAT SHE CAME UP WITH ONE OF HER MOST FAMOUS SAYINGS.
You must do the thing you think you cannot do.
That's good advice!
SHE HAD LOTS OF IT! SHE REALLY UNDERSTOOD THE POWER OF POSITIVE THINKING. THE IDEA THAT HOW YOU THINK ABOUT A SITUATION MAKES A HUGE DIFFERENCE IN HOW YOU HANDLE A SITUATION. IT WAS SAID OF HER:
"SHE WOULD RATHER LIGHT CANDLES THAN CURSE THE DARKNESS."
What's that supposed to mean?
IT MEANS IT'S BETTER TO TAKE ACTION TO CHANGE SOMETHING THAT'S UNFAIR THAN TO JUST COMPLAIN.
SHE ALSO CAME UP WITH THIS GEM: "DO NOT STOP THINKING OF LIFE AS AN ADVENTURE."
I really like that one!
HERE'S A GOOD ONE IF YOU'RE DEALING WITH BULLIES: "NO ONE CAN MAKE YOU FEEL INFERIOR WITHOUT YOUR CONSENT."
Yeah, no one's ever gonna make me feel bad. That would not be ok with me.
GOOD!

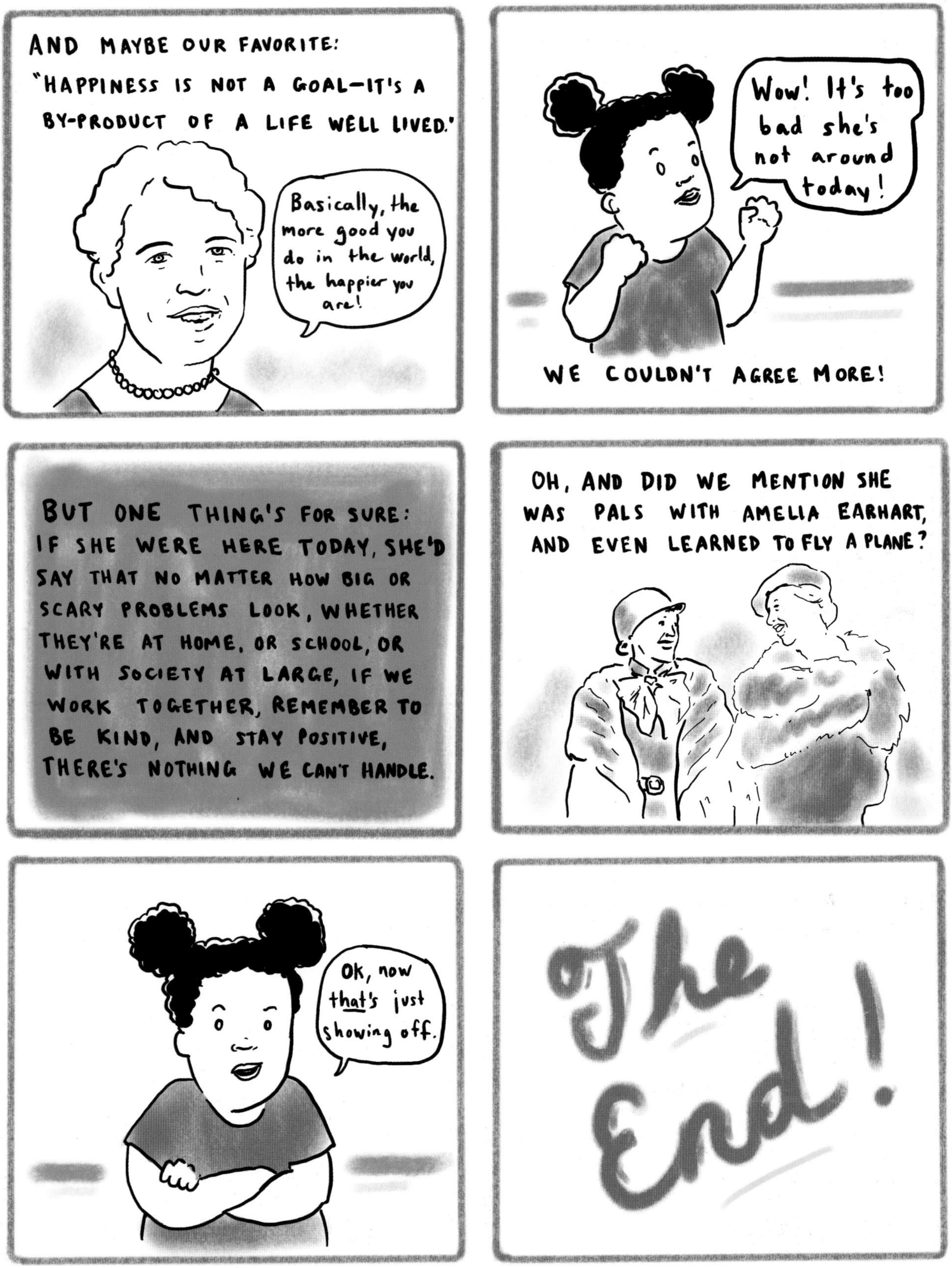

AND MAYBE OUR FAVORITE:
"HAPPINESS IS NOT A GOAL—IT'S A BY-PRODUCT OF A LIFE WELL LIVED."
Basically, the more good you do in the world, the happier you are!
Wow! It's too bad she's not around today!
WE COULDN'T AGREE MORE!
BUT ONE THING'S FOR SURE: IF SHE WERE HERE TODAY, SHE'D SAY THAT NO MATTER HOW BIG OR SCARY PROBLEMS LOOK, WHETHER THEY'RE AT HOME, OR SCHOOL, OR WITH SOCIETY AT LARGE, IF WE WORK TOGETHER, REMEMBER TO BE KIND, AND STAY POSITIVE, THERE'S NOTHING WE CAN'T HANDLE.
OH, AND DID WE MENTION SHE WAS PALS WITH AMELIA EARHART, AND EVEN LEARNED TO FLY A PLANE?
Ok, now that's just showing off.
The End!

THE CIVIL RIGHTS HERO

• • • • •

ROSA PARKS
1913 ~ 2005

She was just one woman on one bus in one city in Alabama, and yet Rosa Parks's refusal to give up her seat to a white passenger eventually led to the end of racial segregation in America. Big change often starts with one small but righteous act.

ROSA AND ME

COUNT ALL THE THINGS YOU HAVE IN COMMON WITH ROSA PARKS.

- Because I'm small, people sometimes underestimate me.
- I know how important I am.
- People think I'm quiet—but I'm not.
- When I talk, people listen.
- I think all people should be treated fairly.
- I know that every action has consequences.
- I do not allow myself to be diminished.
- When they go low, I go high.
- I also like to sew! And make things fit together the right way.
- I'm a leader.

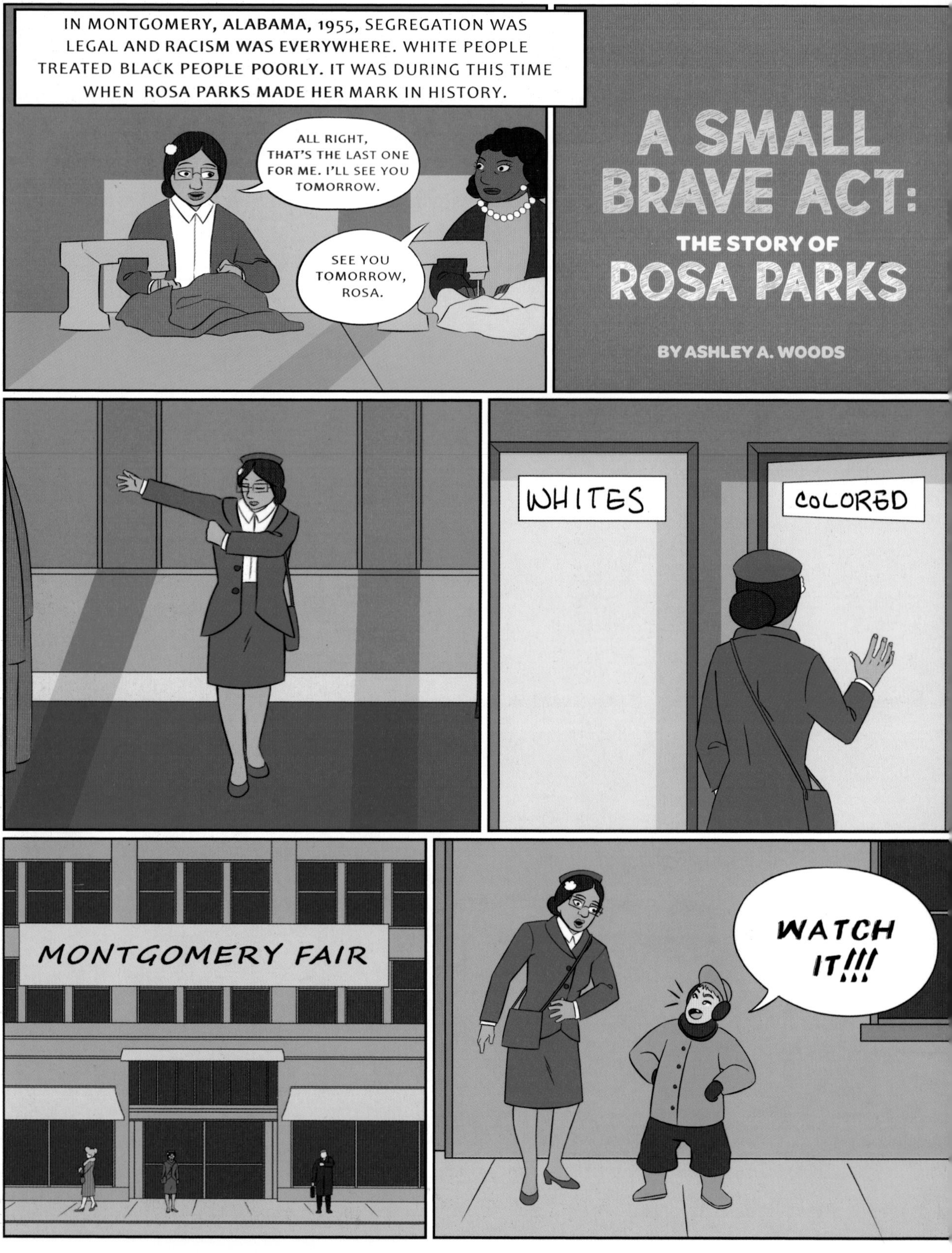
IN MONTGOMERY, ALABAMA, 1955, SEGREGATION WAS LEGAL AND RACISM WAS EVERYWHERE. WHITE PEOPLE TREATED BLACK PEOPLE POORLY. IT WAS DURING THIS TIME WHEN ROSA PARKS MADE HER MARK IN HISTORY.
ALL RIGHT, THAT'S THE LAST ONE FOR ME. I'LL SEE YOU TOMORROW.
SEE YOU TOMORROW, ROSA.
A SMALL BRAVE ACT:
THE STORY OF
ROSA PARKS
BY ASHLEY A. WOODS
WHITES
COLORED
MONTGOMERY FAIR
WATCH IT!!!

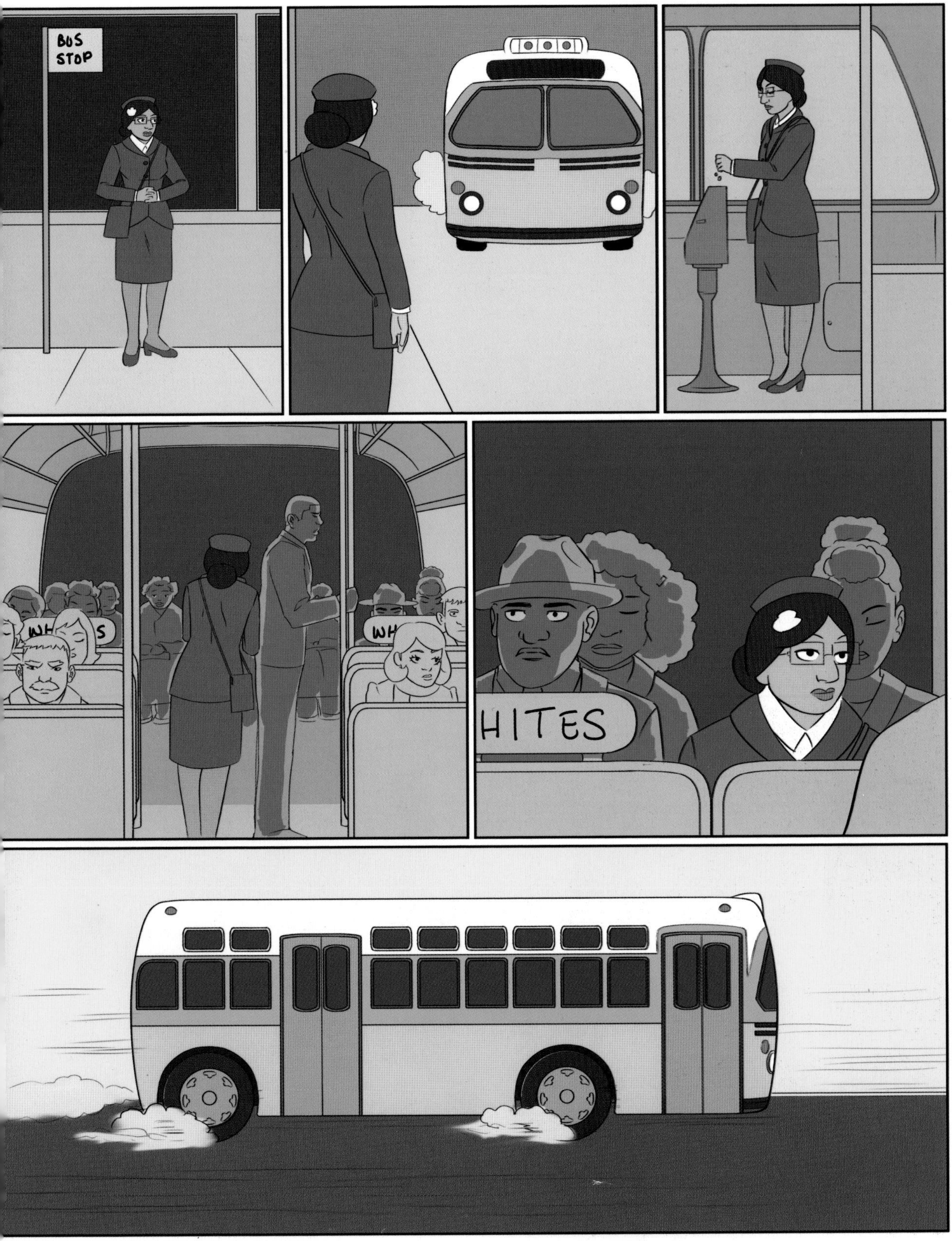
BUS
STOP
HITES

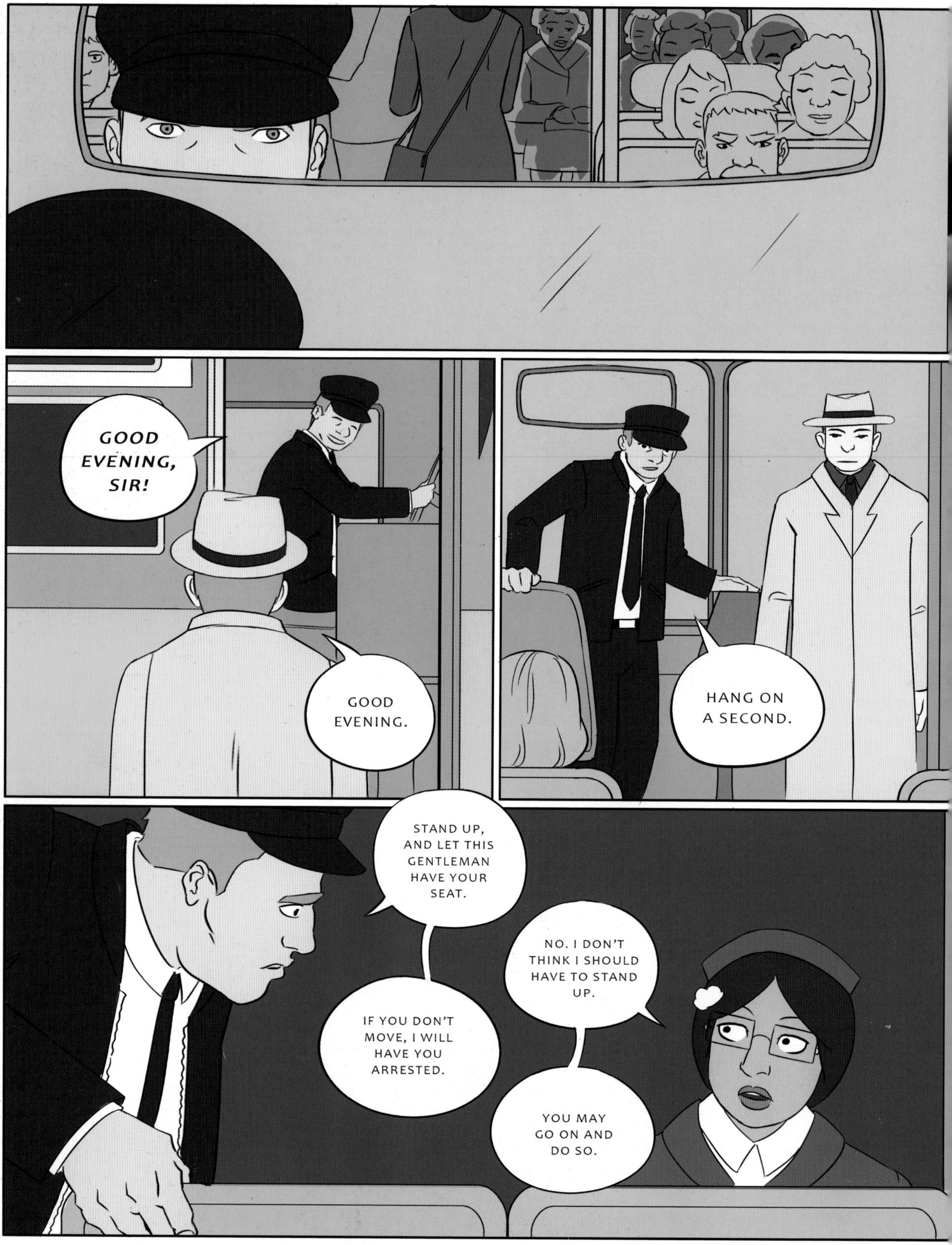
GOOD EVENING, SIR!
GOOD EVENING.
HANG ON A SECOND.
STAND UP, AND LET THIS GENTLEMAN HAVE YOUR SEAT.
IF YOU DON'T MOVE, I WILL HAVE YOU ARRESTED.
NO. I DON'T THINK I SHOULD HAVE TO STAND UP.
YOU MAY GO ON AND DO SO.

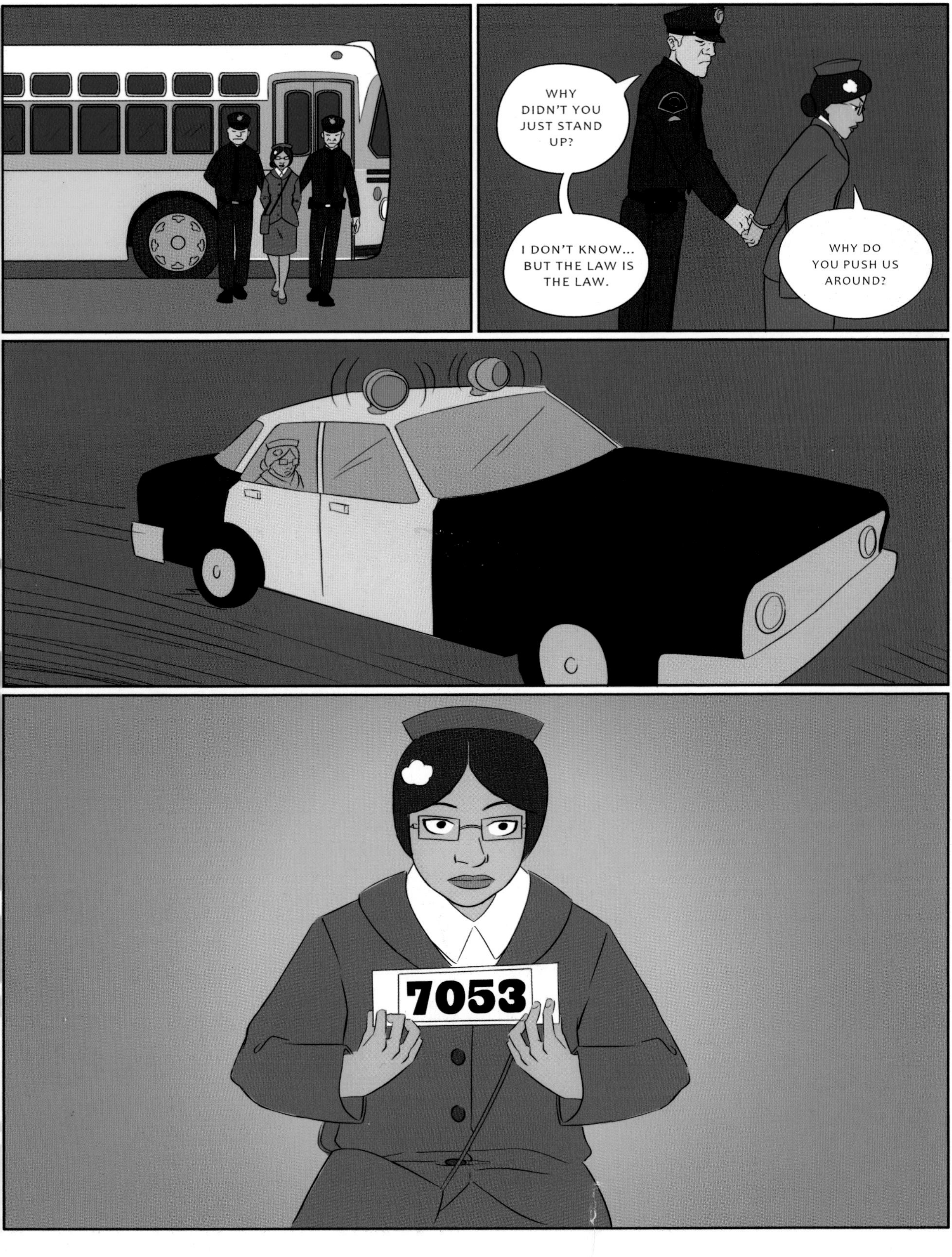
WHY DIDN'T YOU JUST STAND UP?
I DON'T KNOW... BUT THE LAW IS THE LAW.
WHY DO YOU PUSH US AROUND?
7053

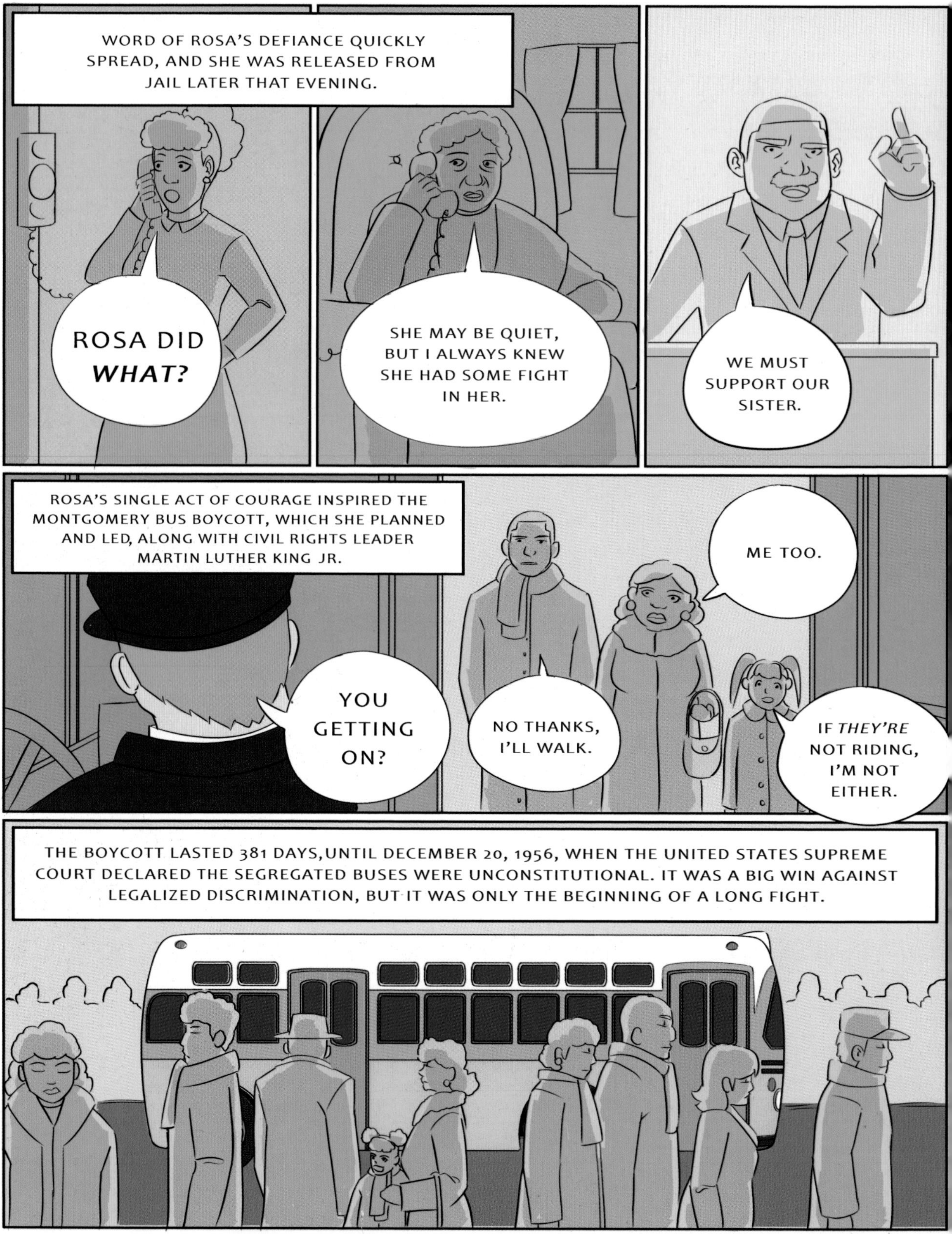
WORD OF ROSA'S DEFIANCE QUICKLY SPREAD, AND SHE WAS RELEASED FROM JAIL LATER THAT EVENING.
ROSA DID *WHAT?*
SHE MAY BE QUIET, BUT I ALWAYS KNEW SHE HAD SOME FIGHT IN HER.
WE MUST SUPPORT OUR SISTER.
ROSA'S SINGLE ACT OF COURAGE INSPIRED THE MONTGOMERY BUS BOYCOTT, WHICH SHE PLANNED AND LED, ALONG WITH CIVIL RIGHTS LEADER MARTIN LUTHER KING JR.
YOU GETTING ON?
NO THANKS, I'LL WALK.
ME TOO.
IF *THEY'RE* NOT RIDING, I'M NOT EITHER.
THE BOYCOTT LASTED 381 DAYS, UNTIL DECEMBER 20, 1956, WHEN THE UNITED STATES SUPREME COURT DECLARED THE SEGREGATED BUSES WERE UNCONSTITUTIONAL. IT WAS A BIG WIN AGAINST LEGALIZED DISCRIMINATION, BUT IT WAS ONLY THE BEGINNING OF A LONG FIGHT.

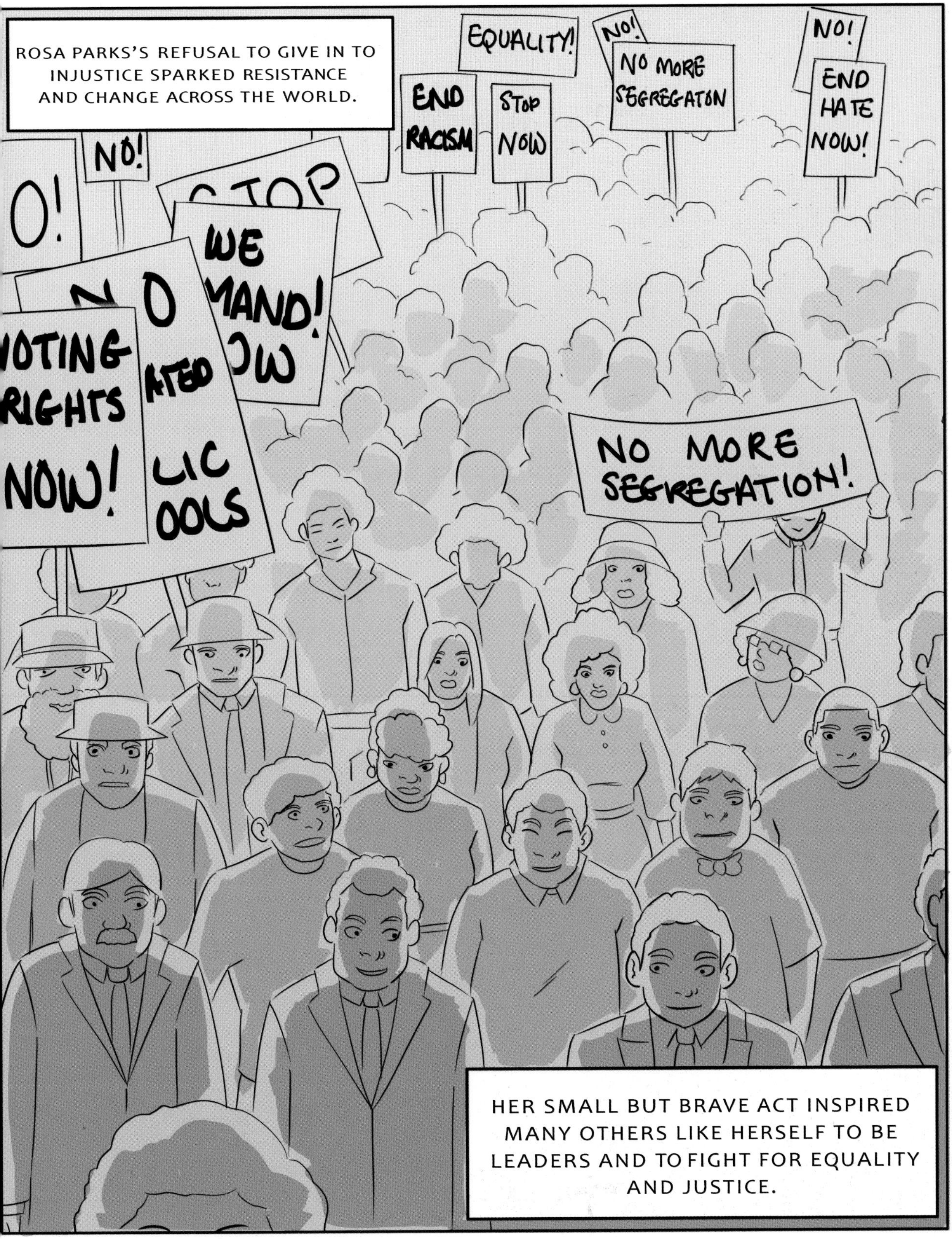
ROSA PARKS'S REFUSAL TO GIVE IN TO INJUSTICE SPARKED RESISTANCE AND CHANGE ACROSS THE WORLD.
EQUALITY!
NO!
NO MORE SEGREGATON
NO!
END HATE NOW!
END RACISM
STOP NOW
NO!
WE MAND! OW
NO MORE SEGREGATION!
HER SMALL BUT BRAVE ACT INSPIRED MANY OTHERS LIKE HERSELF TO BE LEADERS AND TO FIGHT FOR EQUALITY AND JUSTICE.

The RABBLE-Rouser

MOTHER JONES
1837 ～ 1930

Her real name was Mary, but everyone called her Mother, because she took care of the workers of the world as if they were her own children. Whenever and wherever they were treated unfairly, Mother Jones would show up and help them organize for better working conditions and pay. She knew our nation would succeed only if we all had a fighting chance.

MOTHER JONES AND ME

COUNT ALL THE THINGS YOU HAVE IN COMMON WITH MOTHER JONES.

- I stand up for what I believe in.
- I know how to get people's attention.
- I'm loud when I want to be.
- I'm good at giving speeches.
- You don't want to argue with me.
- I don't let disappointment stop me.
- I like to take care of other people.
- I want everyone to play fair.
- I'm relentless.
- I'm fiery.

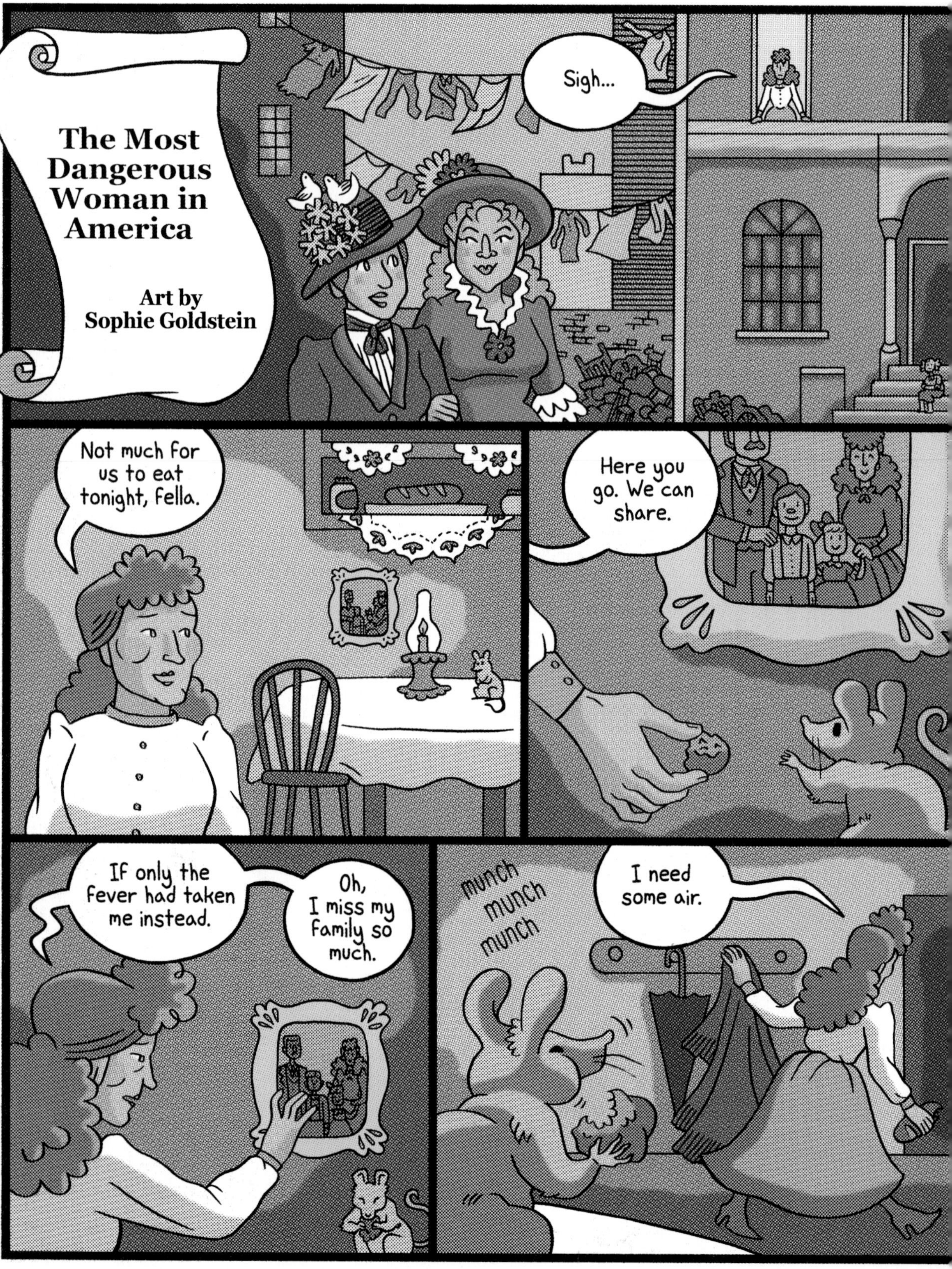
The Most Dangerous Woman in America
Art by Sophie Goldstein
Sigh...
Not much for us to eat tonight, fella.
Here you go. We can share.
If only the fever had taken me instead.
Oh, I miss my family so much.
munch munch munch
I need some air.

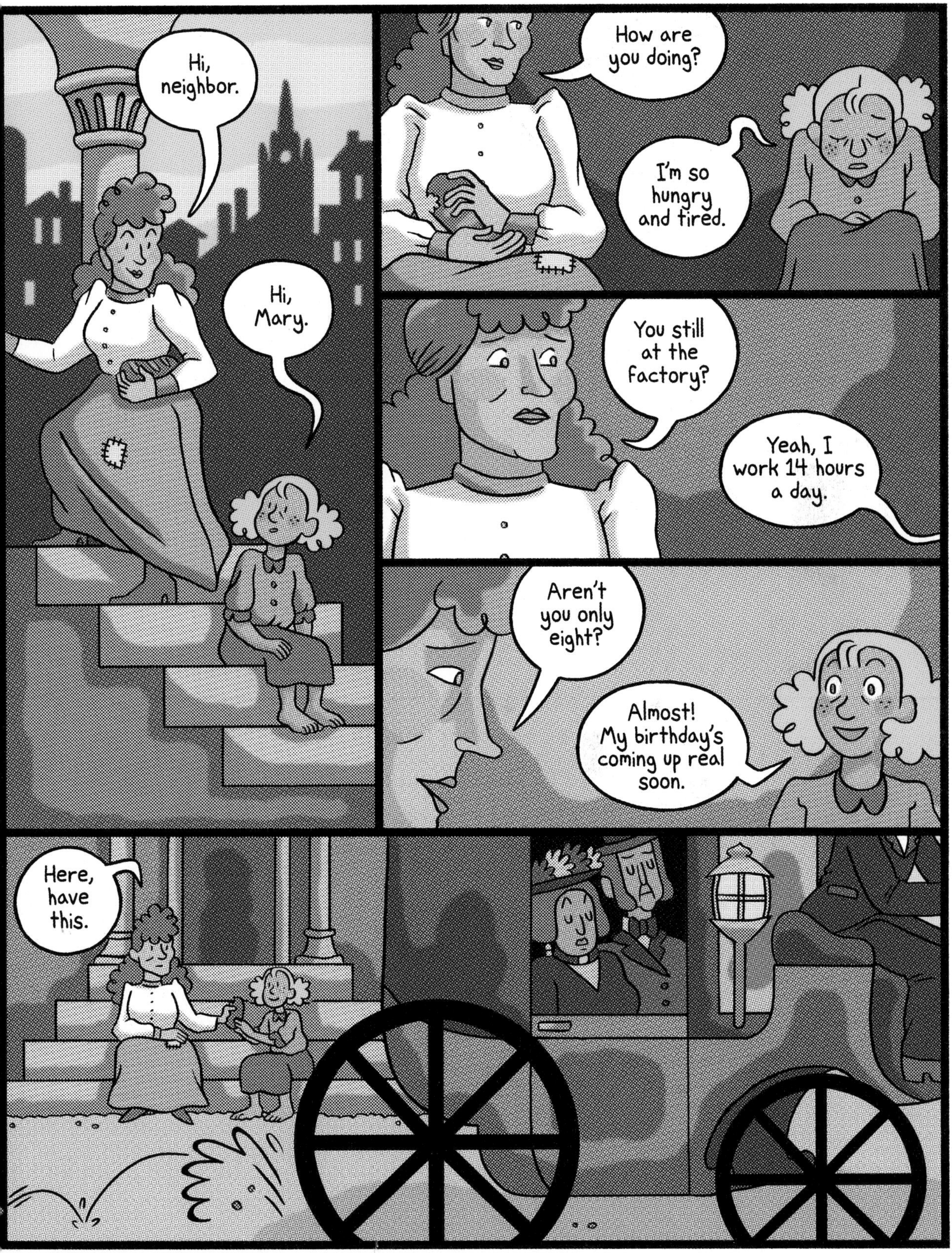
Hi, neighbor.
Hi, Mary.
How are you doing?
I'm so hungry and tired.
You still at the factory?
Yeah, I work 14 hours a day.
Aren't you only eight?
Almost! My birthday's coming up real soon.
Here, have this.

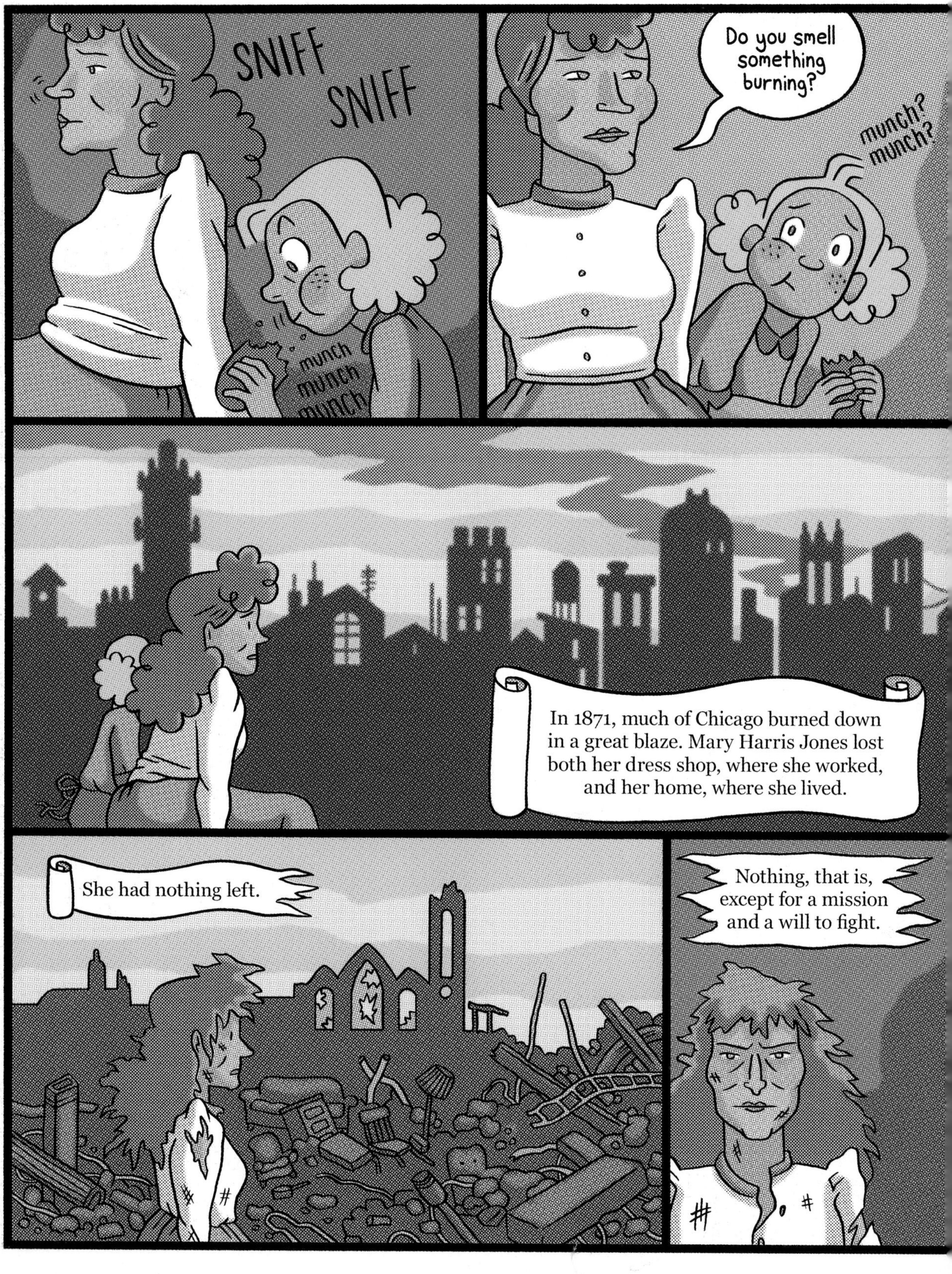
SNIFF SNIFF
munch munch munch
Do you smell something burning?
munch? munch?
In 1871, much of Chicago burned down in a great blaze. Mary Harris Jones lost both her dress shop, where she worked, and her home, where she lived.
She had nothing left.
Nothing, that is, except for a mission and a will to fight.

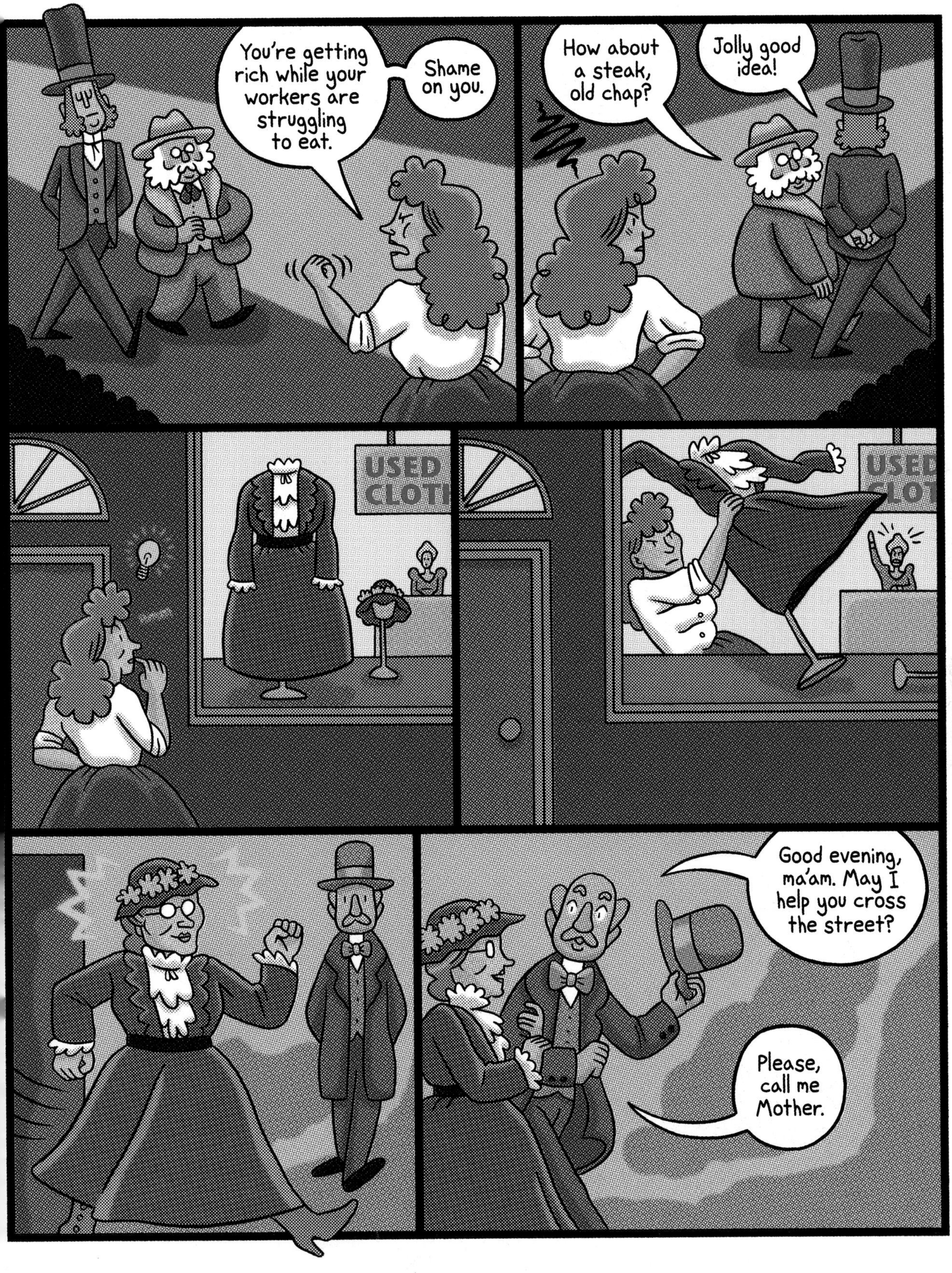
You're getting rich while your workers are struggling to eat.
Shame on you.
How about a steak, old chap?
Jolly good idea!
USED CLOTH
Good evening, ma'am. May I help you cross the street?
Please, call me Mother.

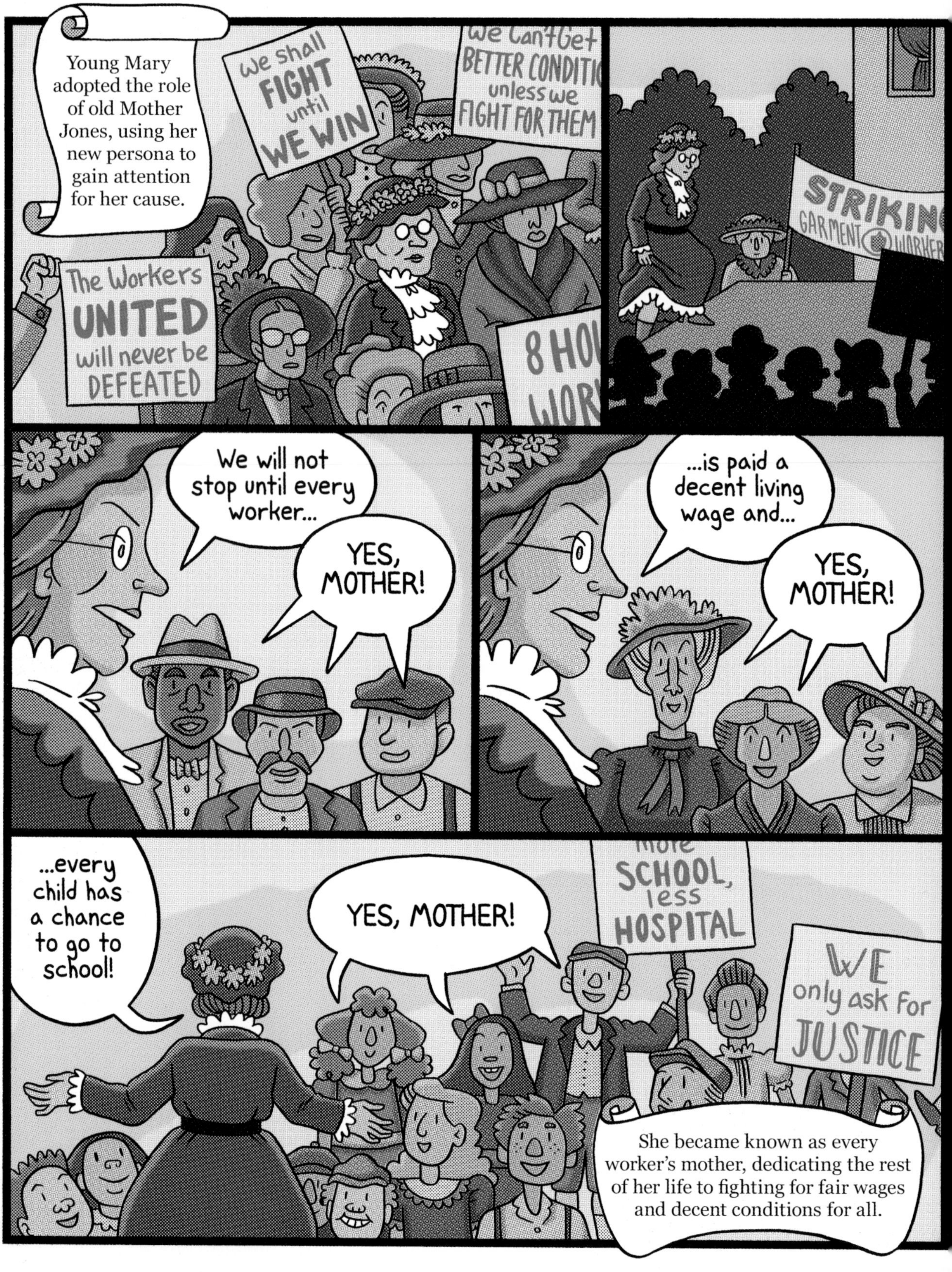

Young Mary adopted the role of old Mother Jones, using her new persona to gain attention for her cause.
We shall FIGHT until WE WIN
We Can't Get BETTER CONDITI unless we FIGHT FOR THEM
The Workers UNITED will never be DEFEATED
8 HOU WOR
STRIKIN GARMENT WORKER
We will not stop until every worker...
YES, MOTHER!
...is paid a decent living wage and...
YES, MOTHER!
...every child has a chance to go to school!
YES, MOTHER!
SCHOOL, less HOSPITAL
WE only ask for JUSTICE
She became known as every worker's mother, dedicating the rest of her life to fighting for fair wages and decent conditions for all.

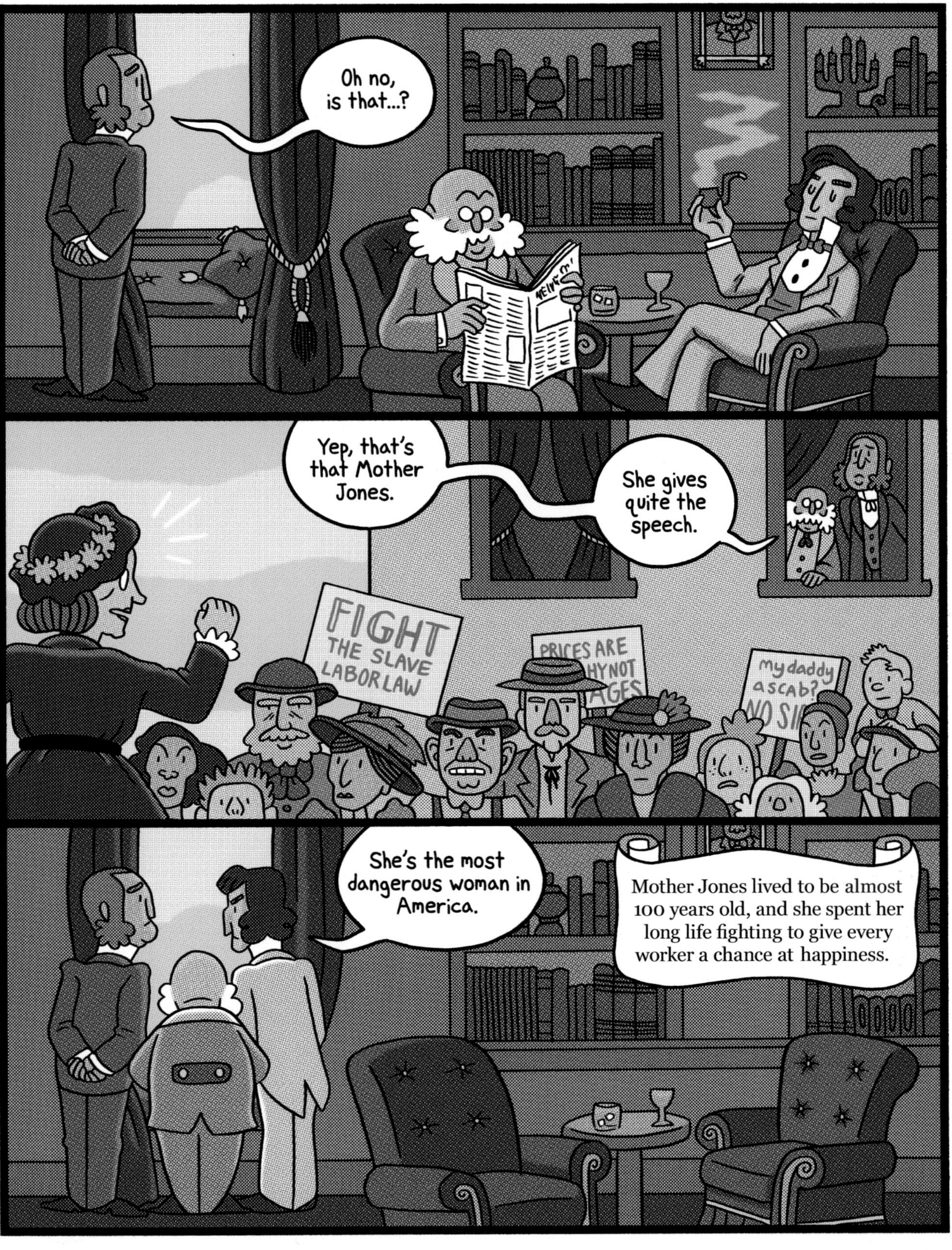

Oh no, is that...?
Yep, that's that Mother Jones.
She gives quite the speech.
FIGHT THE SLAVE LABOR LAW
PRICES ARE
my daddy a scab?
She's the most dangerous woman in America.
Mother Jones lived to be almost 100 years old, and she spent her long life fighting to give every worker a chance at happiness.

EXPLORE

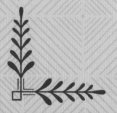

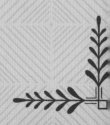

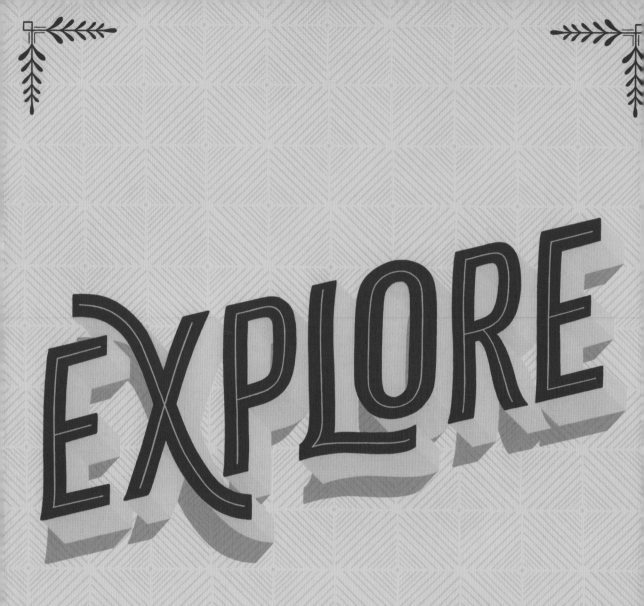

All the Noisemakers in this book are very brave, but the women in this chapter are brave in the way that you might most typically think of the word. They've not only faced frightening situations that would send others cowering, but they've actually sought them out *on purpose*, because they are adventurers by nature. They've done loop-the-loops in the sky, stood watch high in the mountains looking for forest fires, dived into dangerous waters to rescue others, and sailed around the world just for a chance to see beyond their own tiny towns. Let their courage and curiosity inspire you to seek out thrilling adventures and discover new worlds beyond the one you already know.

THE HIGH FLIER

• • • • •

BESSIE COLEMAN
1892 ~ 1926

As the first African American in history to earn a civilian pilot's license, Bessie Coleman is proof that if you dream big enough and work hard enough, the sky really is the limit.

BESSIE AND ME

COUNT ALL THE THINGS YOU HAVE IN COMMON WITH BESSIE COLEMAN.

- I like to fly in airplanes.
- Heights don't scare me.
- I can speak more than one language.
- When I get an idea in my head, I hang on tight to it.
- I won't take no for an answer.
- I enjoy putting on shows for other people.
- I sometimes imagine what it would be like to be a bird.
- I use my power to help other people.
- I persevere always.
- I'm daring.

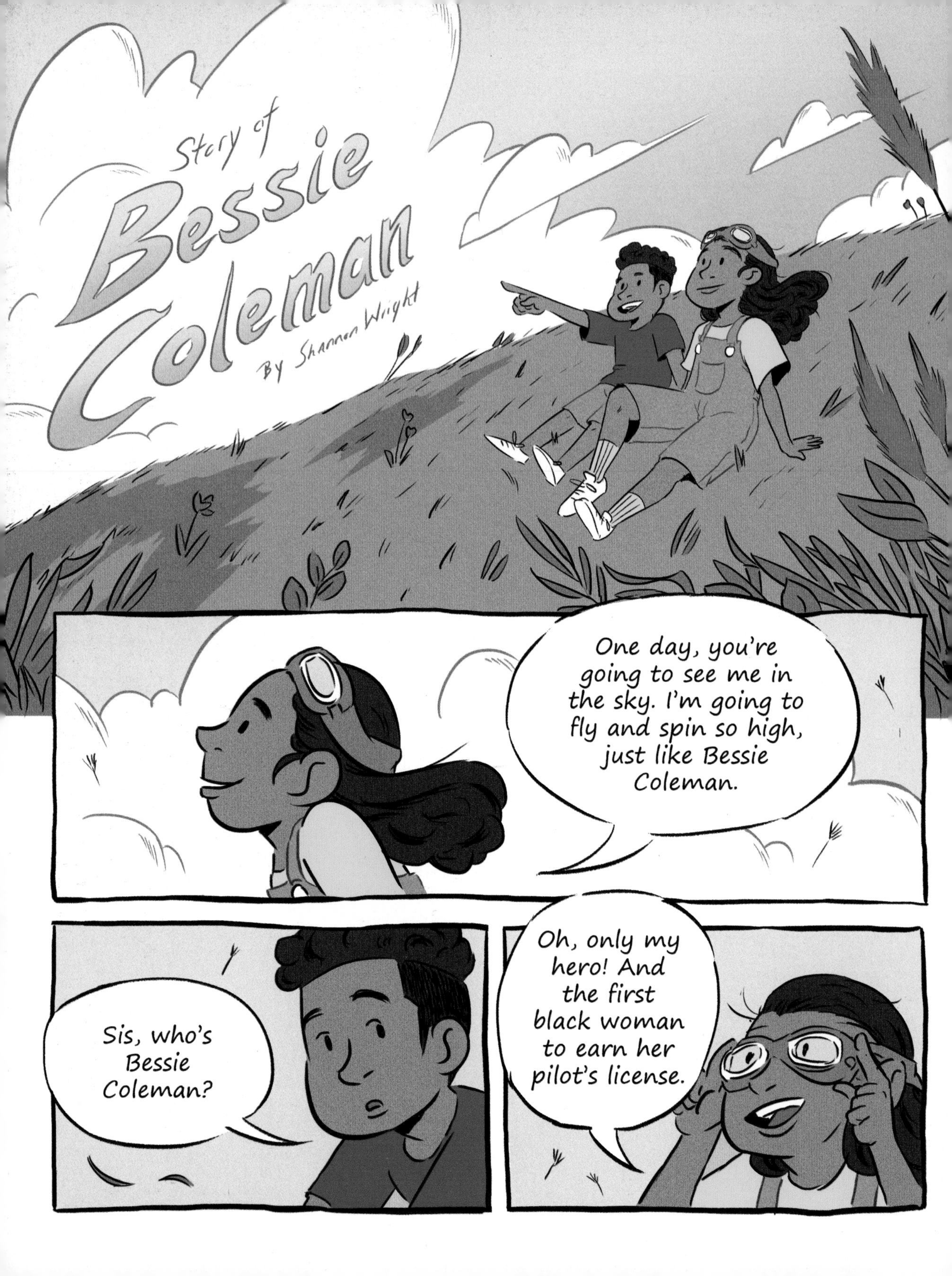
Story of
Bessie Coleman
By Shannon Wright
One day, you're going to see me in the sky. I'm going to fly and spin so high, just like Bessie Coleman.
Sis, who's Bessie Coleman?
Oh, only my hero! And the first black woman to earn her pilot's license.

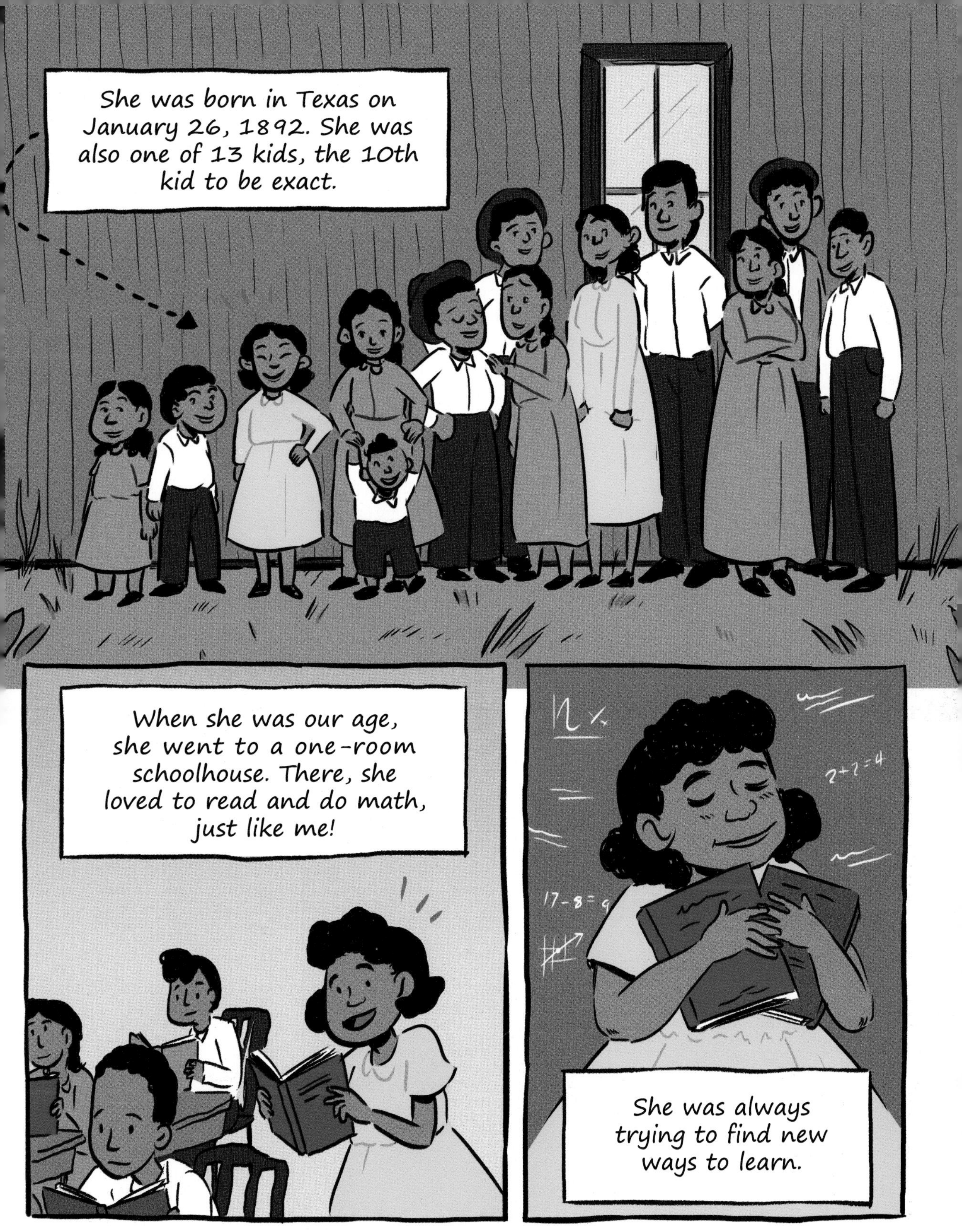
She was born in Texas on January 26, 1892. She was also one of 13 kids, the 10th kid to be exact.
When she was our age, she went to a one-room schoolhouse. There, she loved to read and do math, just like me!
2+2=4
She was always trying to find new ways to learn.

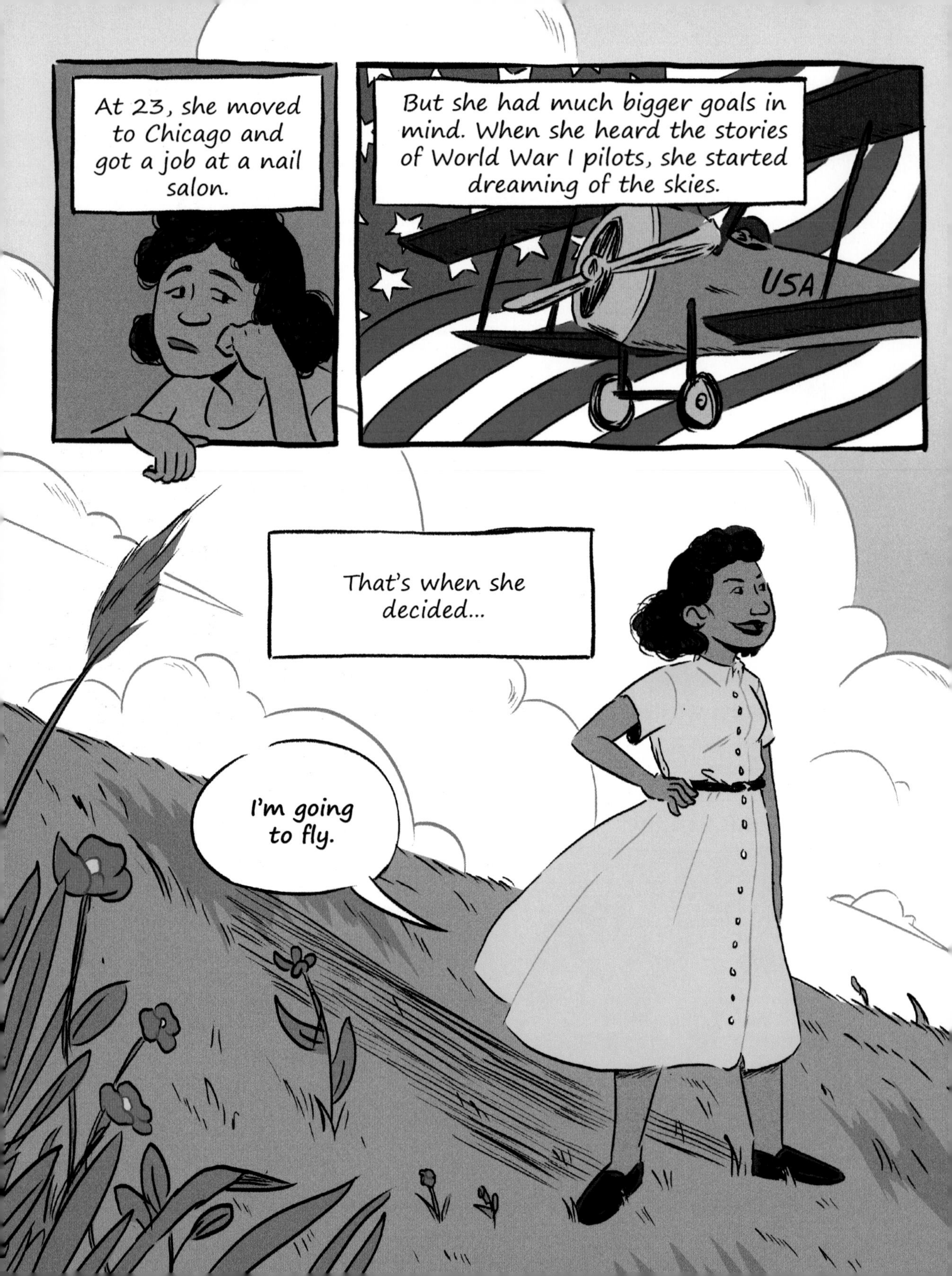
At 23, she moved to Chicago and got a job at a nail salon.
But she had much bigger goals in mind. When she heard the stories of World War I pilots, she started dreaming of the skies.
USA
That's when she decided...
I'm going to fly.

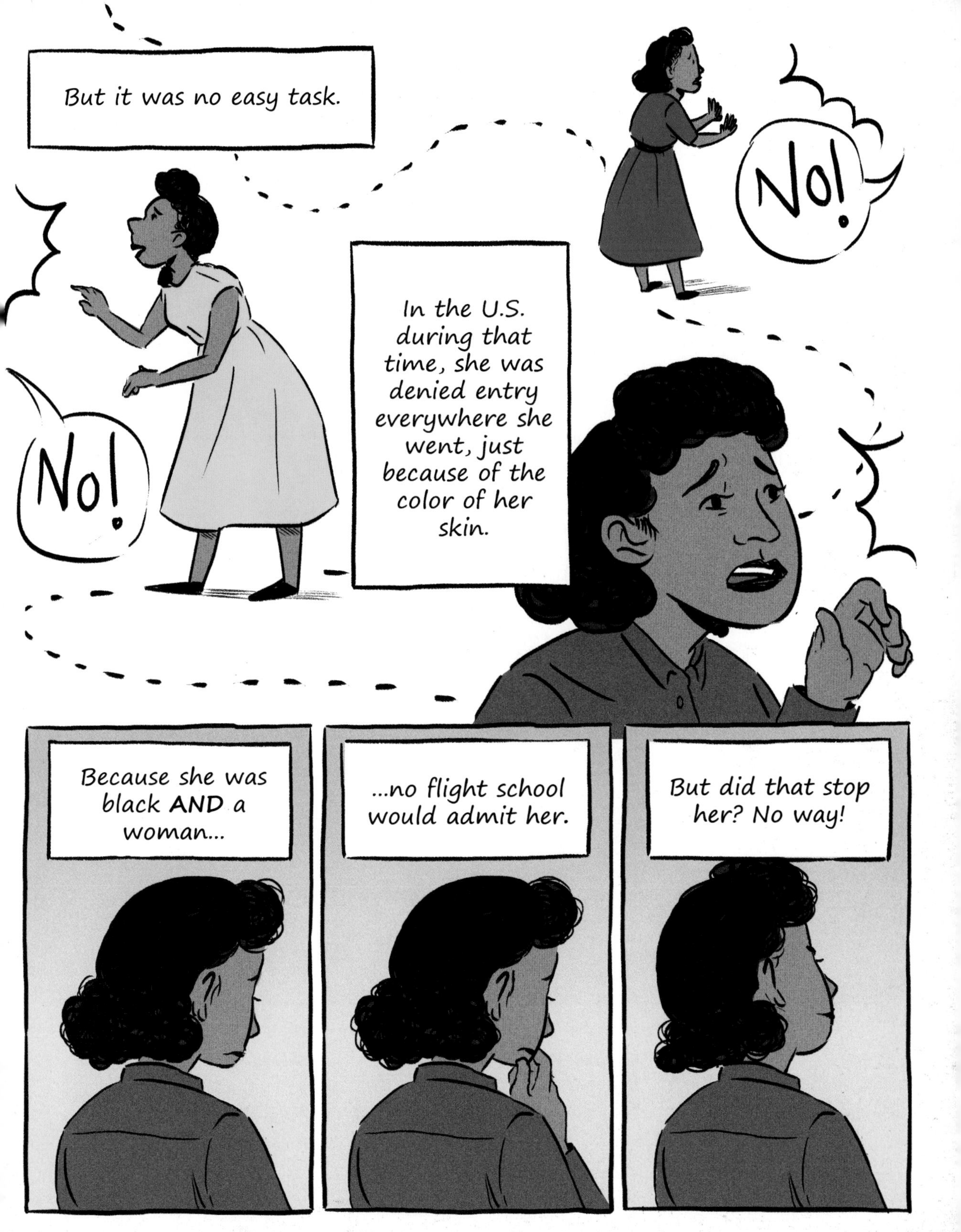

But it was no easy task.
No!
No!
In the U.S. during that time, she was denied entry everywhere she went, just because of the color of her skin.
Because she was black **AND** a woman...
...no flight school would admit her.
But did that stop her? No way!

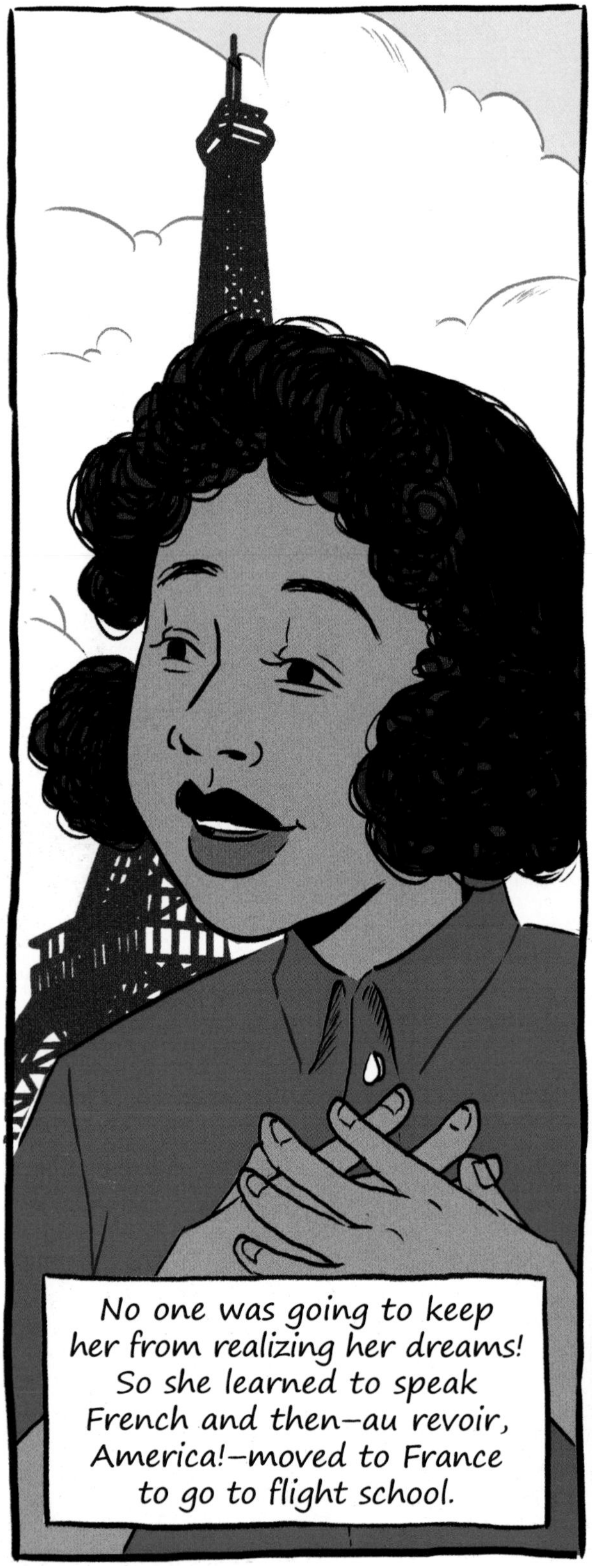
No one was going to keep her from realizing her dreams! So she learned to speak French and then—au revoir, America!—moved to France to go to flight school.

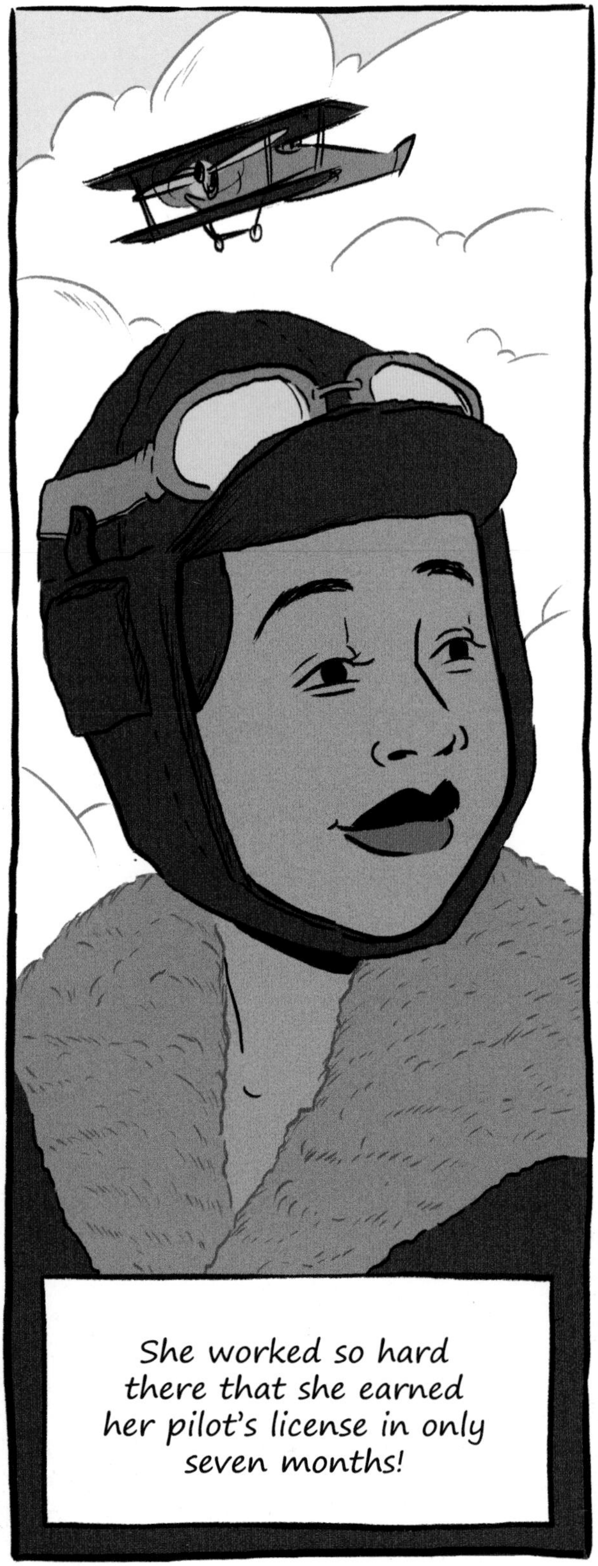
She worked so hard there that she earned her pilot's license in only seven months!

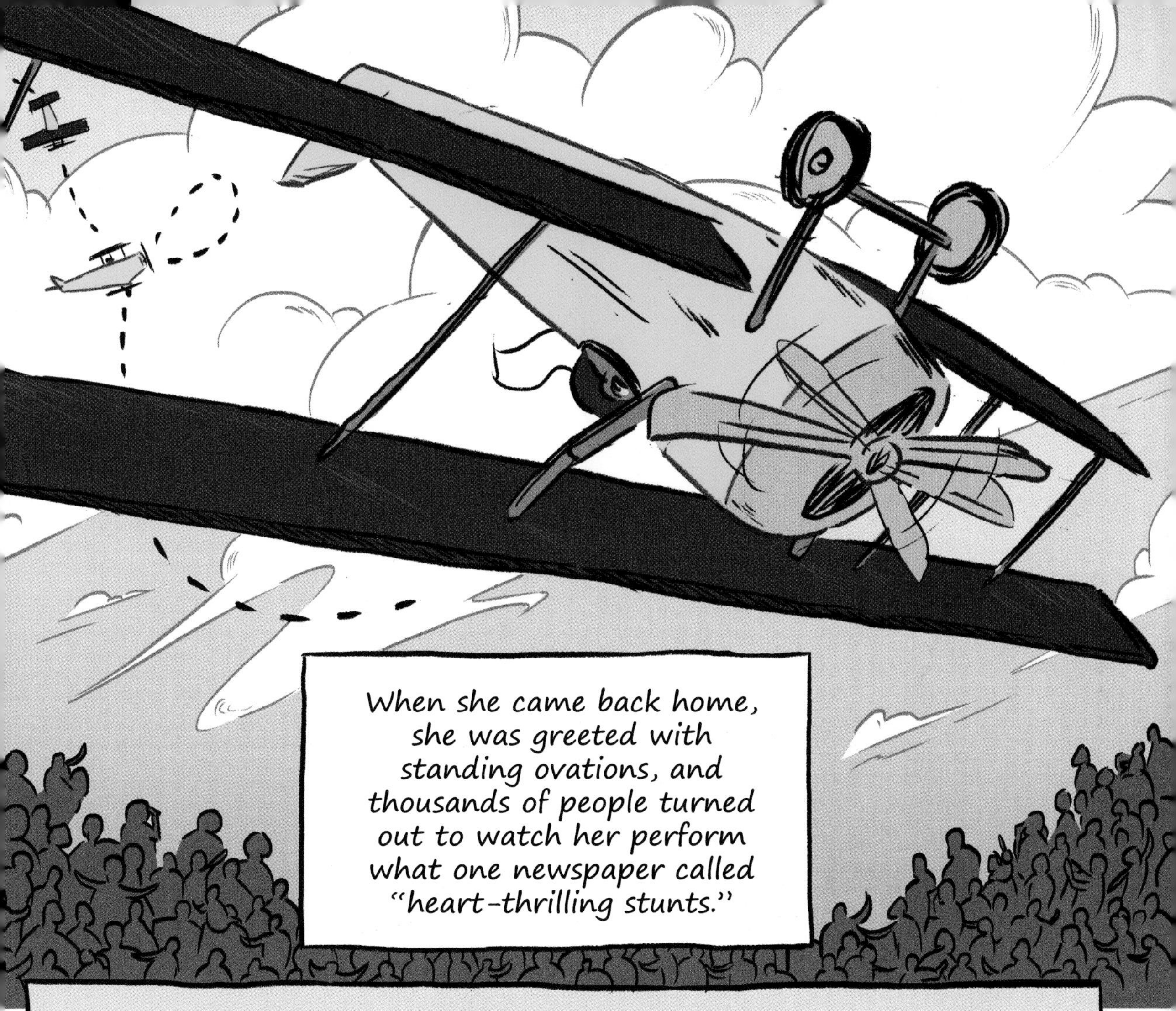
When she came back home, she was greeted with standing ovations, and thousands of people turned out to watch her perform what one newspaper called "heart-thrilling stunts."

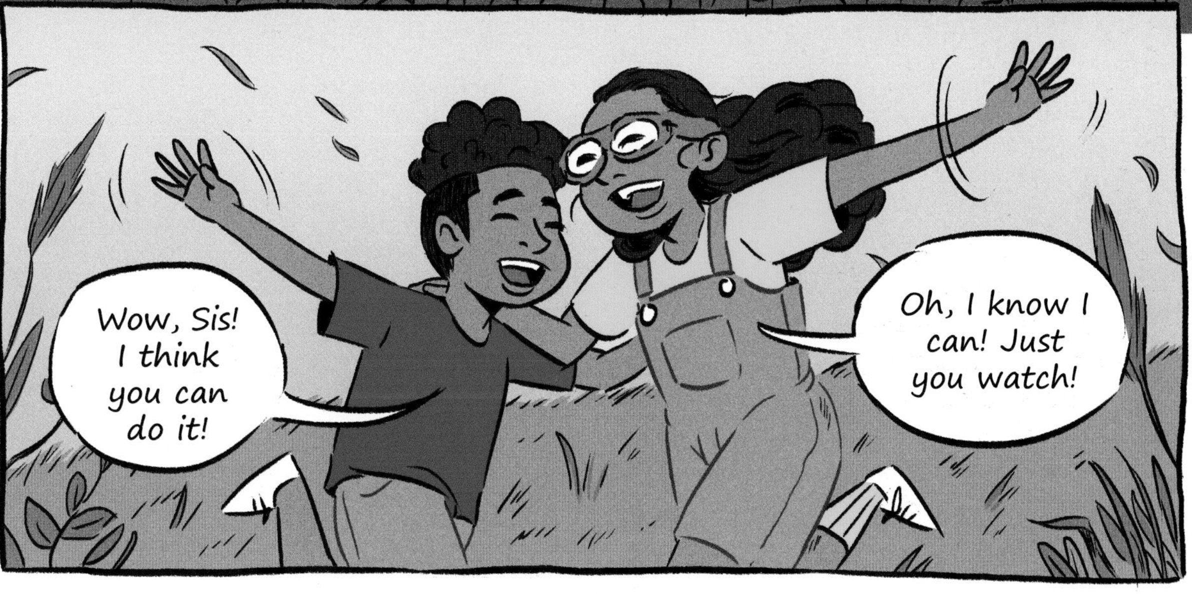
Wow, Sis! I think you can do it!
Oh, I know I can! Just you watch!

The FOREST PROTECTOR

· · · · ·

HALLIE DAGGETT
1878 ~ 1964

Would you like to sleep alone in a log cabin on top of a mountain where bears, coyotes, and wildcats roam? For Hallie Daggett, it was a dream come true. She was the first woman ever to be hired as a fire lookout for the United States Forest Service, and she faithfully kept her post for 14 years.

HALLIE AND ME

COUNT ALL THE THINGS YOU HAVE IN COMMON WITH HALLIE DAGGETT.

- I enjoy walking in the woods.
- Animals just seem to like me.
- When I'm by myself, I feel happy, not lonely.
- I go after what I want, even if no one has done it before.
- People have doubted me—and I've proved them wrong.
- I can spot trouble a mile away.
- I can make my own fun and don't need lots of stuff.
- I always prefer to be outside than inside.
- I'm attentive.
- I'm content.

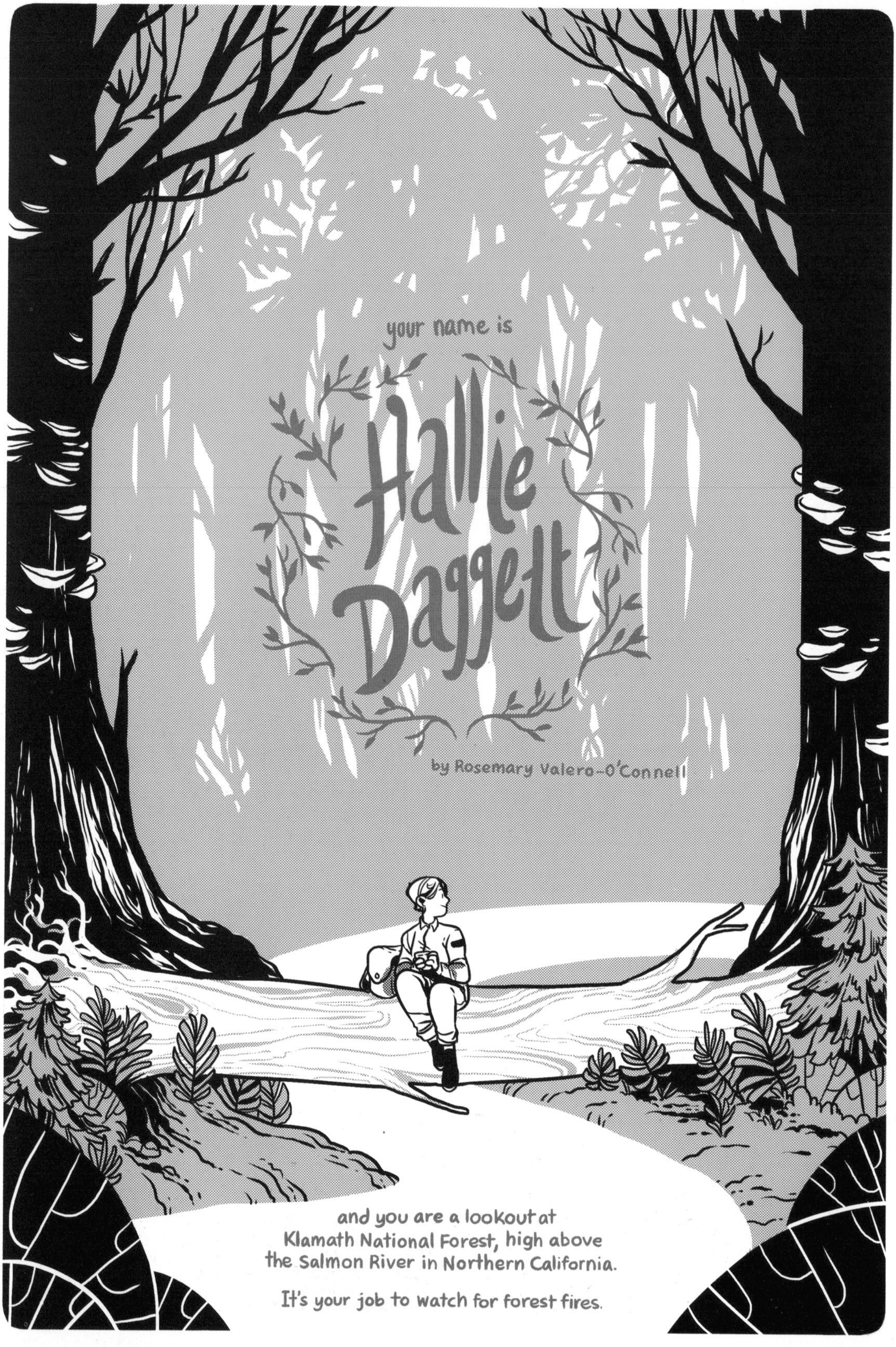

your name is
Hallie Daggett
by Rosemary Valero-O'Connell
and you are a lookout at
Klamath National Forest, high above
the Salmon River in Northern California.
It's your job to watch for forest fires.

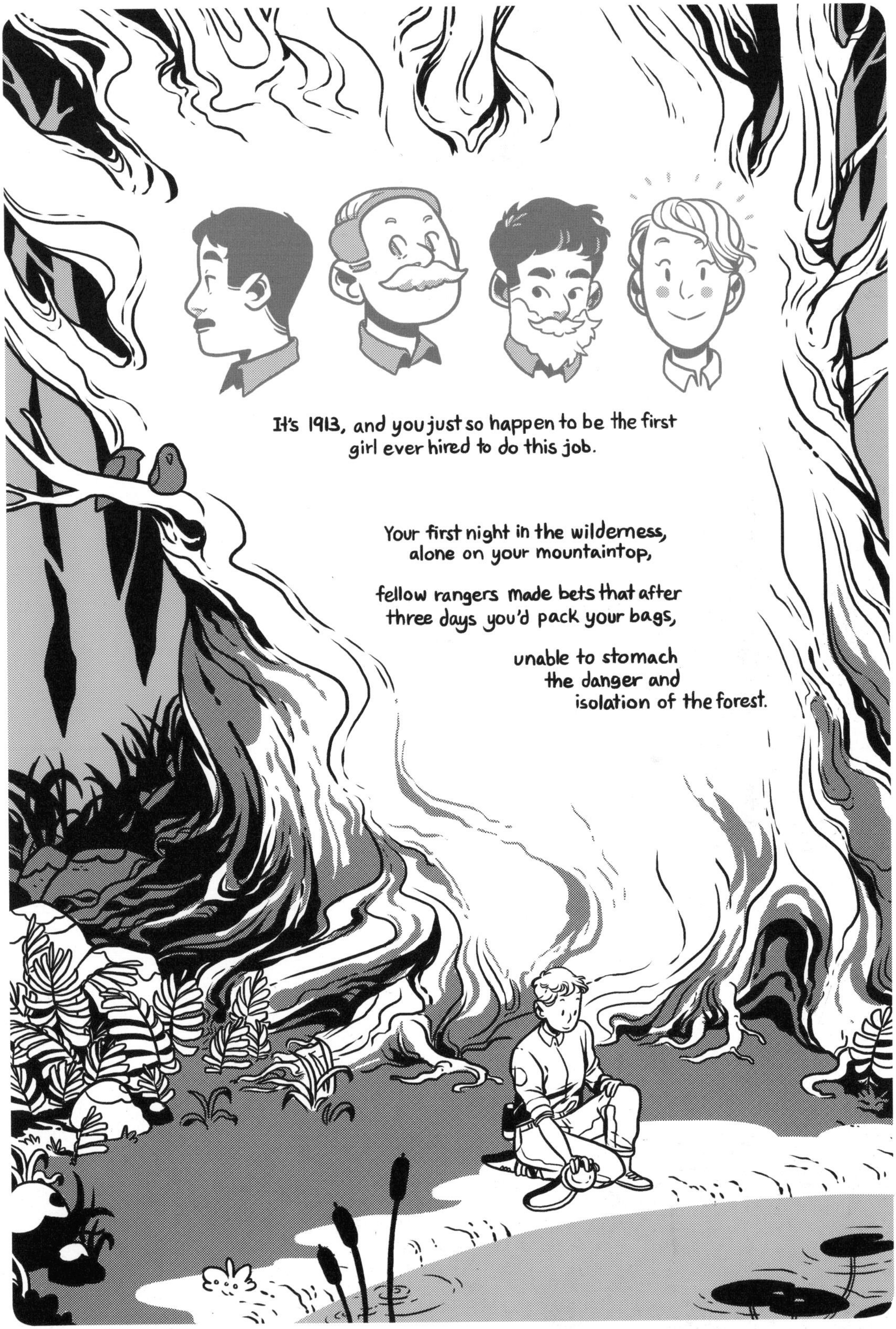
It's 1913, and you just so happen to be the first girl ever hired to do this job.
Your first night in the wilderness, alone on your mountaintop,
fellow rangers made bets that after three days you'd pack your bags,
unable to stomach the danger and isolation of the forest.

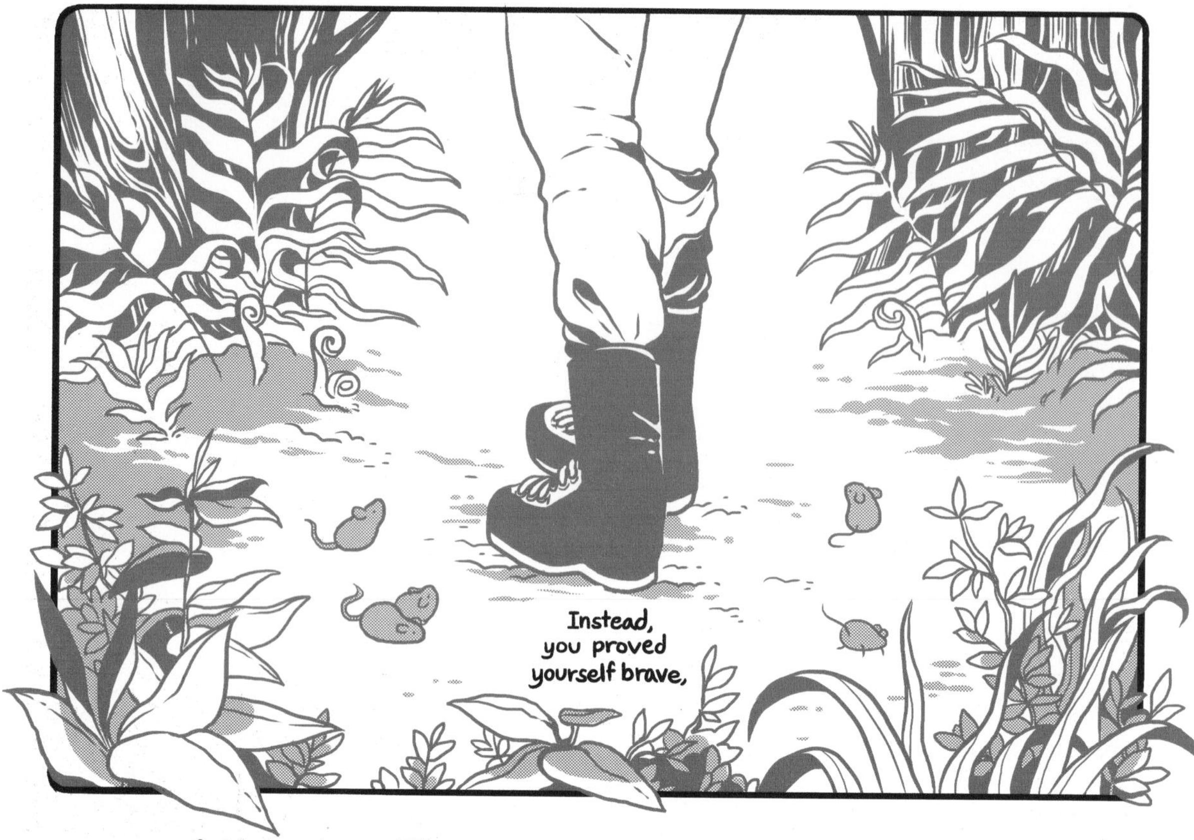
Instead, you proved yourself brave,

unafraid of any bear, wildfire, or electrical storm your new home might send your way.

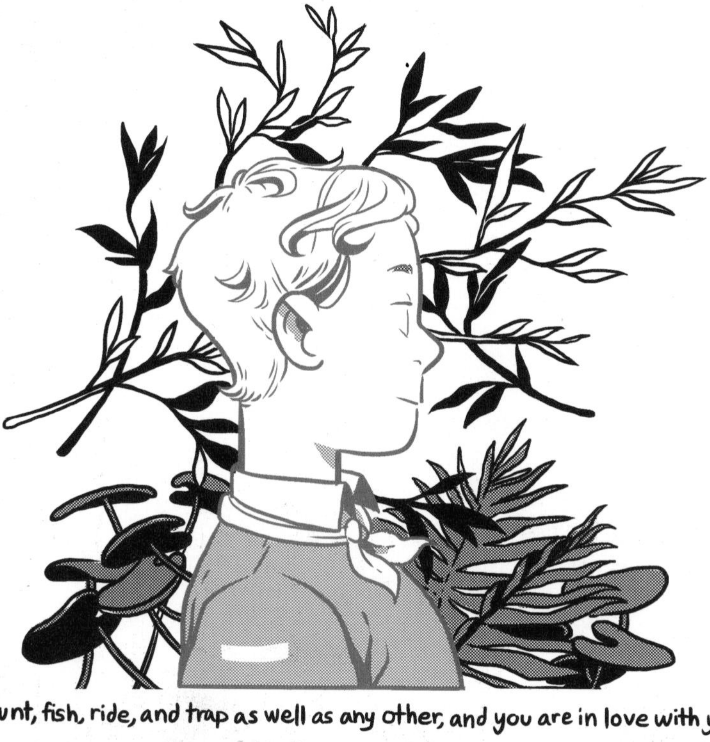

You can hunt, fish, ride, and trap as well as any other, and you are in love with your work.

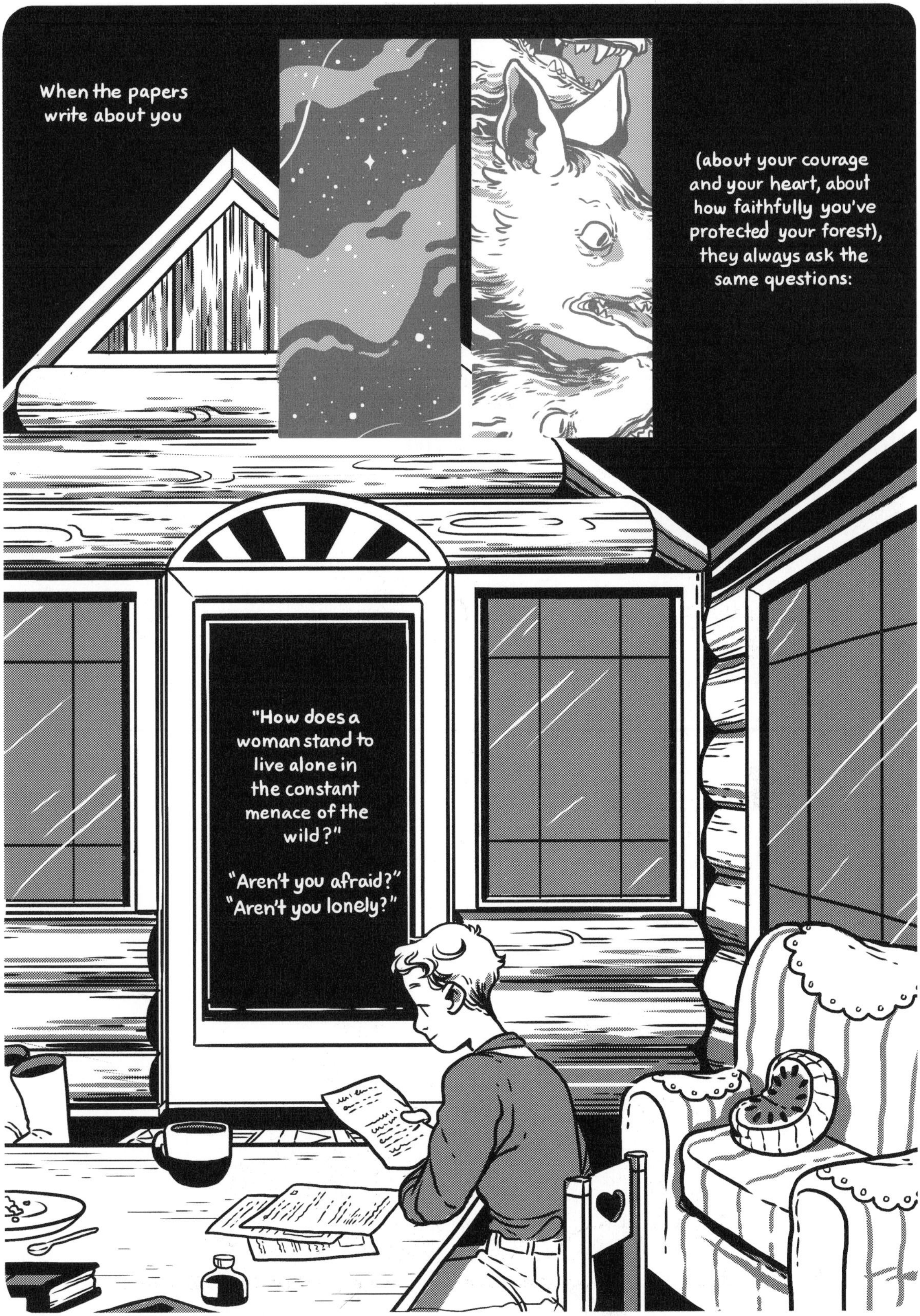
When the papers write about you
(about your courage and your heart, about how faithfully you've protected your forest), they always ask the same questions:
"How does a woman stand to live alone in the constant menace of the wild?"
"Aren't you afraid?"
"Aren't you lonely?"

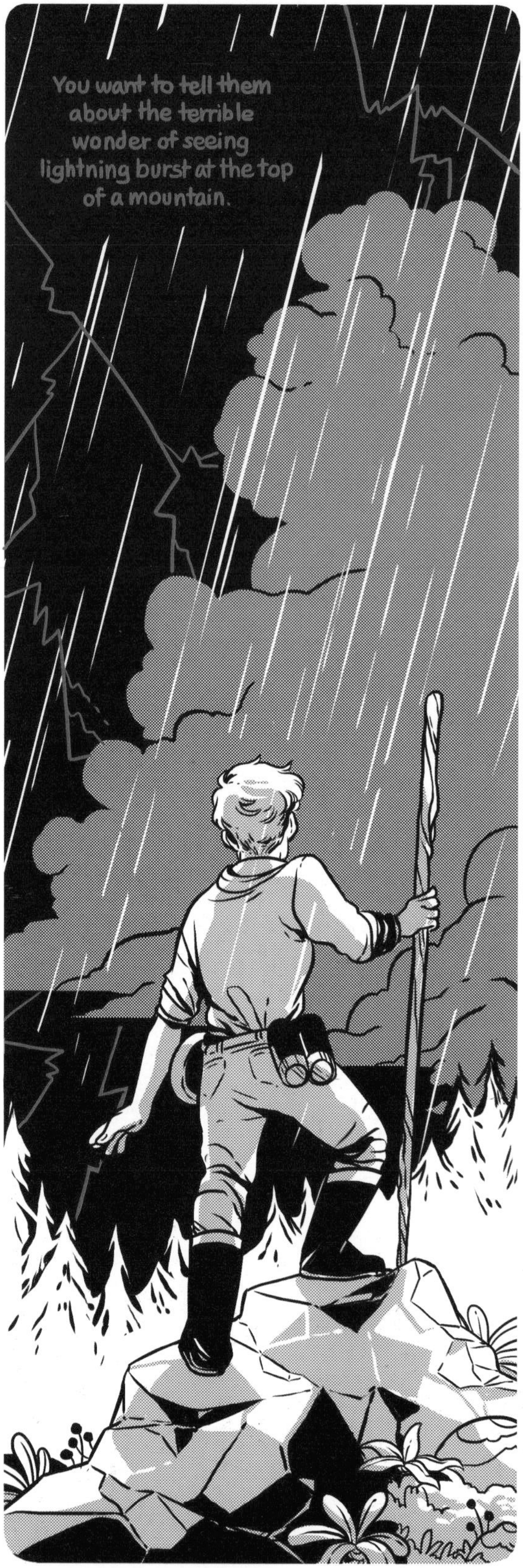
You want to tell them about the terrible wonder of seeing lightning burst at the top of a mountain.

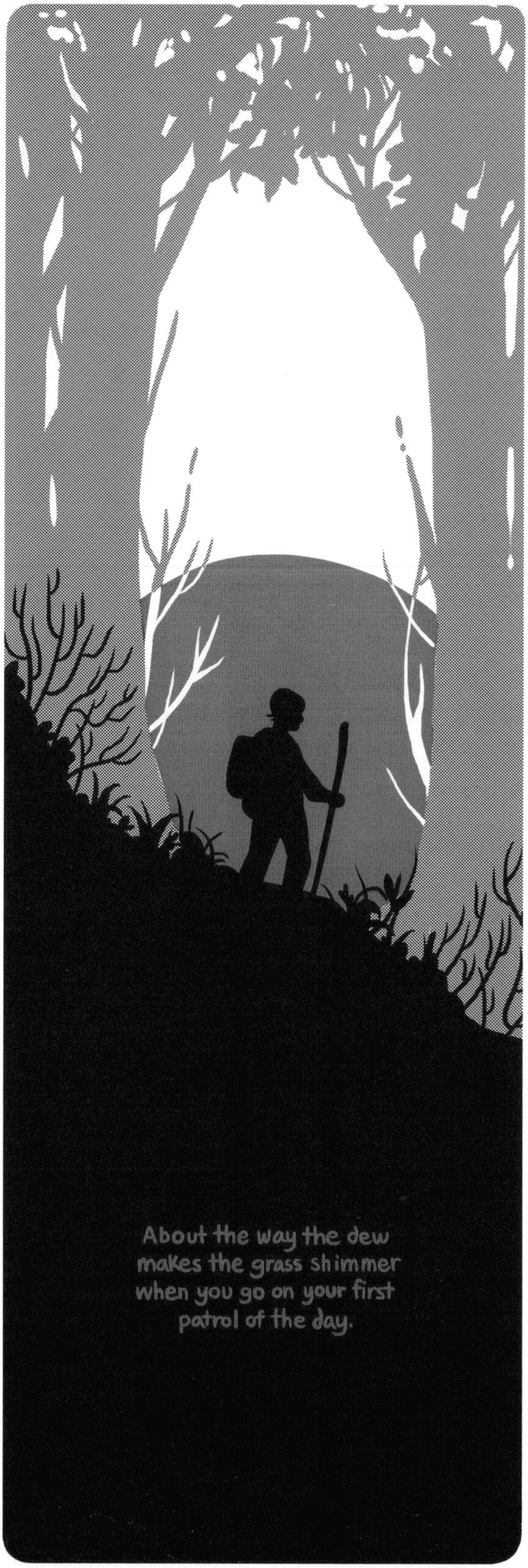
About the way the dew makes the grass shimmer when you go on your first patrol of the day.

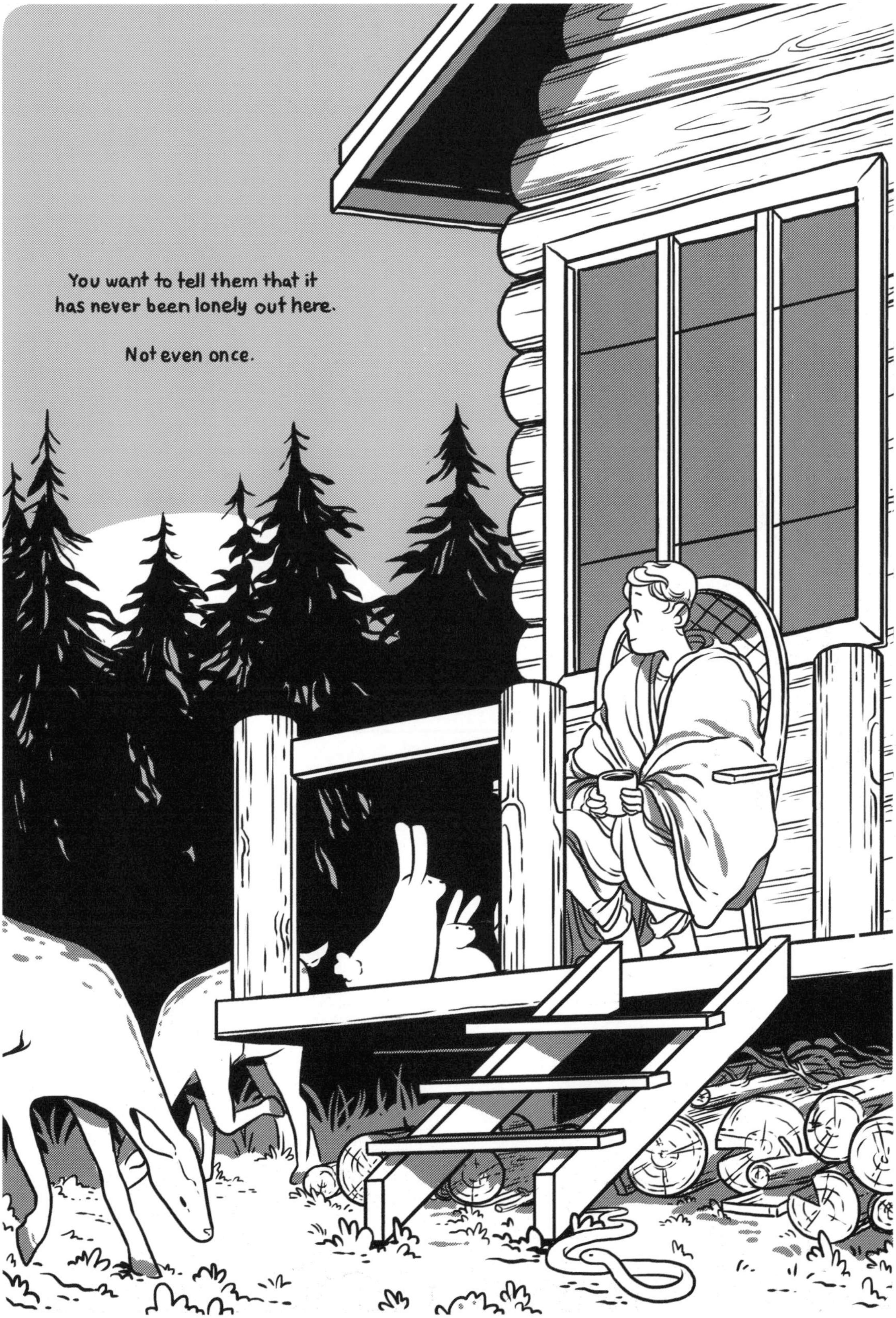
You want to tell them that it has never been lonely out here.
Not even once.

THE LIGHTHOUSE KEEPER

• • • • •

IDA LEWIS
1842 ~ 1911

Lighthouse keeper Ida Lewis kept watch over the sea, and she never hesitated to risk her own life to rescue someone else's. If a sailor needed help—no matter how big the waves, icy the waters, or stormy the night—she'd row out in her little boat and pull them to safety. That's why she was once known as "the bravest woman in America."

IDA AND ME

COUNT ALL THE THINGS YOU HAVE IN COMMON WITH IDA LEWIS.

- I love the ocean.
- I've row-row-rowed a boat.
- I like to swim.
- I help take care of my siblings.
- I'm a good helper to my parents too.
- I like to stick to a schedule.
- I prefer to avoid crowds—I'd rather be on my own.
- People can count on me.
- I'm responsible.
- I'm brave.

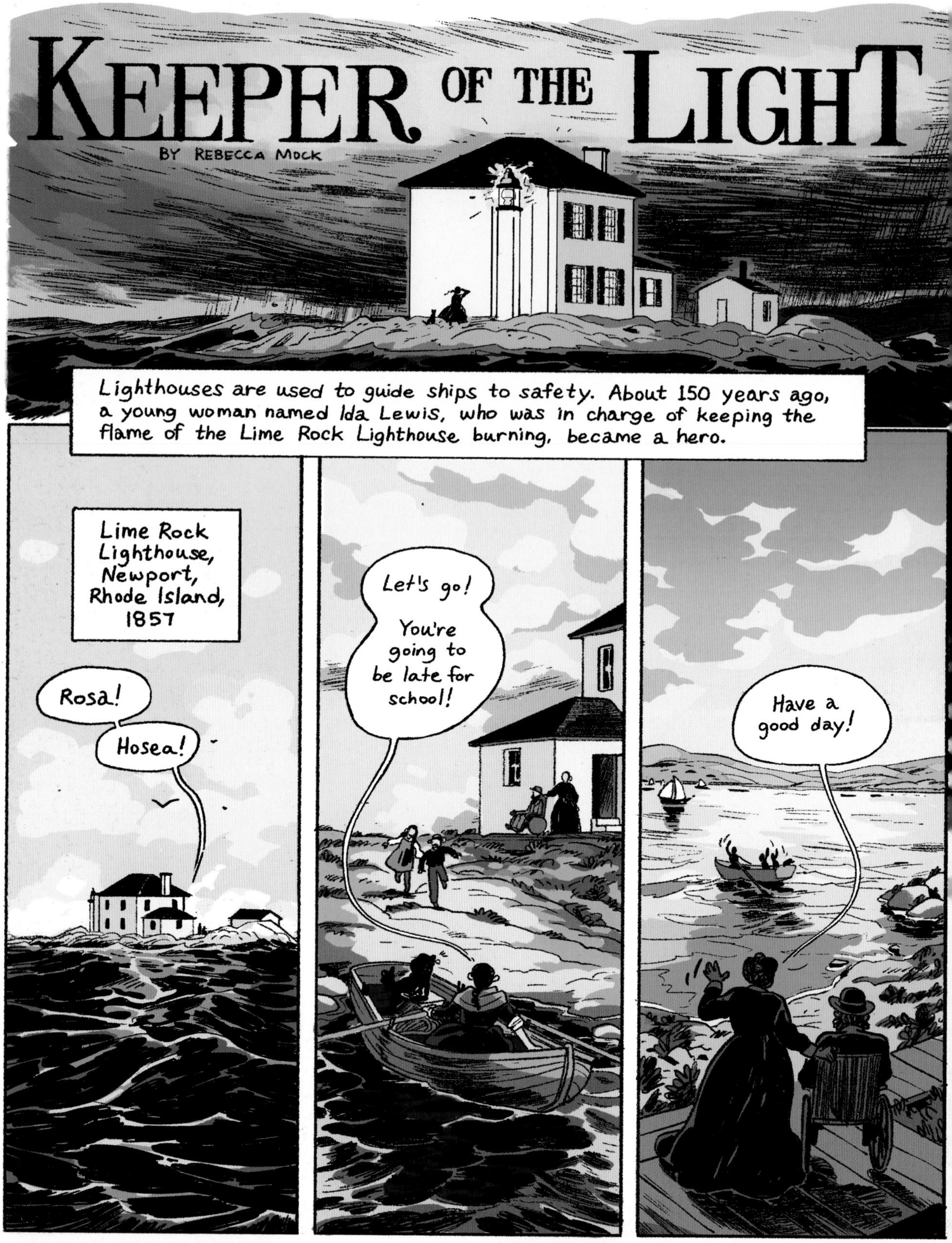

KEEPER OF THE LIGHT
BY REBECCA MOCK
Lighthouses are used to guide ships to safety. About 150 years ago, a young woman named Ida Lewis, who was in charge of keeping the flame of the Lime Rock Lighthouse burning, became a hero.
Lime Rock Lighthouse, Newport, Rhode Island, 1857
Rosa!
Hosea!
Let's go!
You're going to be late for school!
Have a good day!

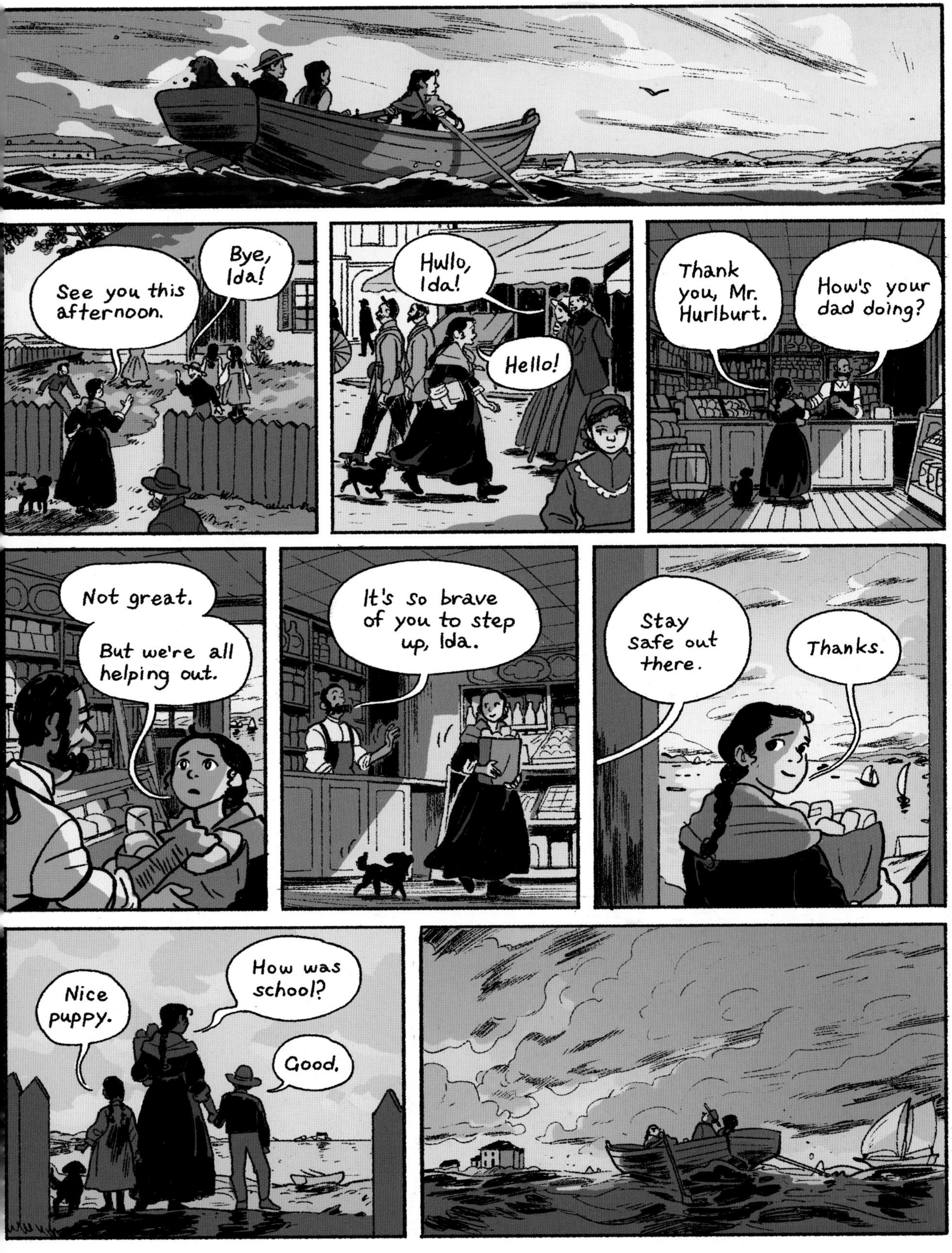
See you this afternoon.
Bye, Ida!
Hullo, Ida!
Hello!
Thank you, Mr. Hurlburt.
How's your dad doing?
Not great.
But we're all helping out.
It's so brave of you to step up, Ida.
Stay safe out there.
Thanks.
Nice puppy.
How was school?
Good.

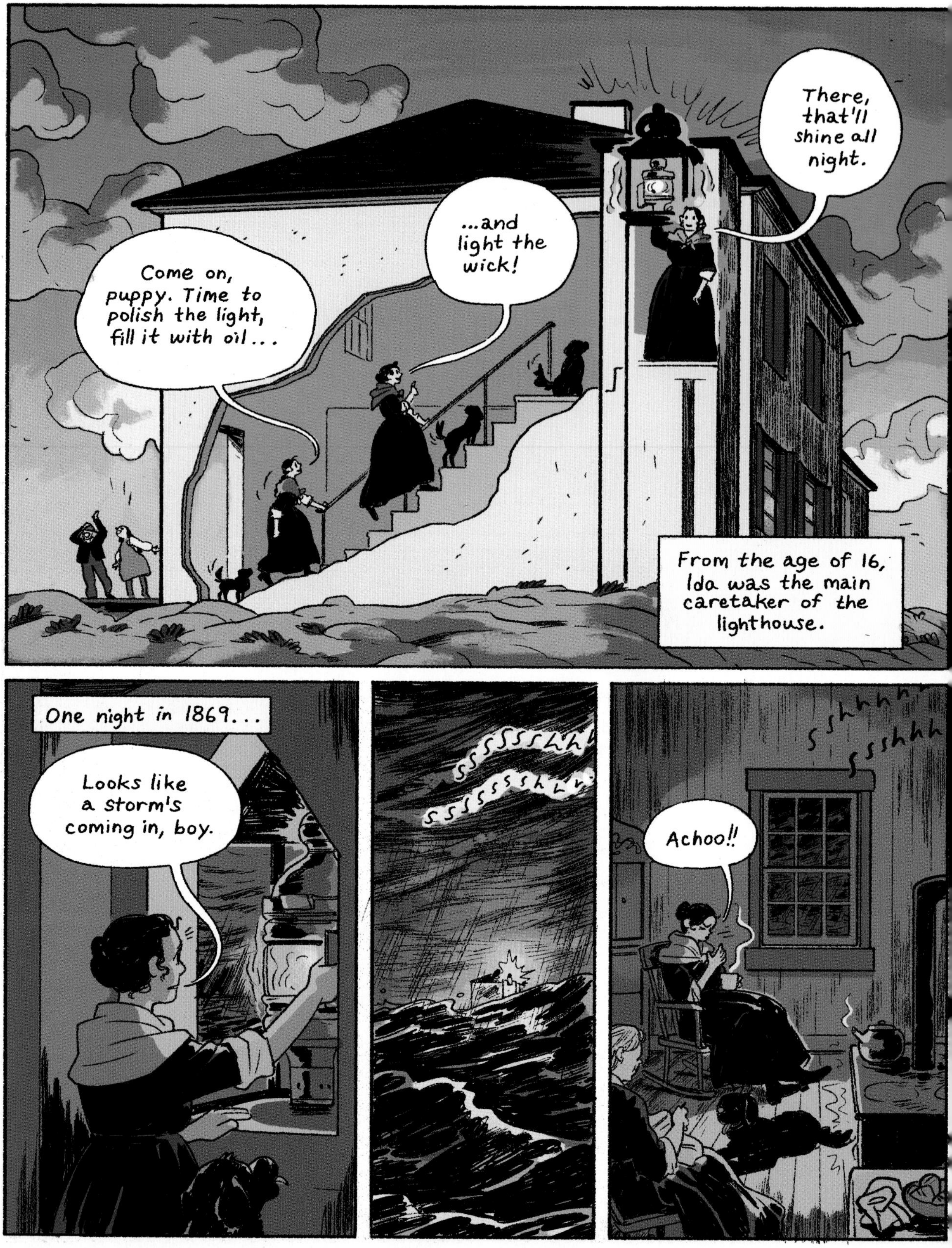
Come on, puppy. Time to polish the light, fill it with oil...
...and light the wick!
There, that'll shine all night.
From the age of 16, Ida was the main caretaker of the lighthouse.
One night in 1869...
Looks like a storm's coming in, boy.
Achoo!!

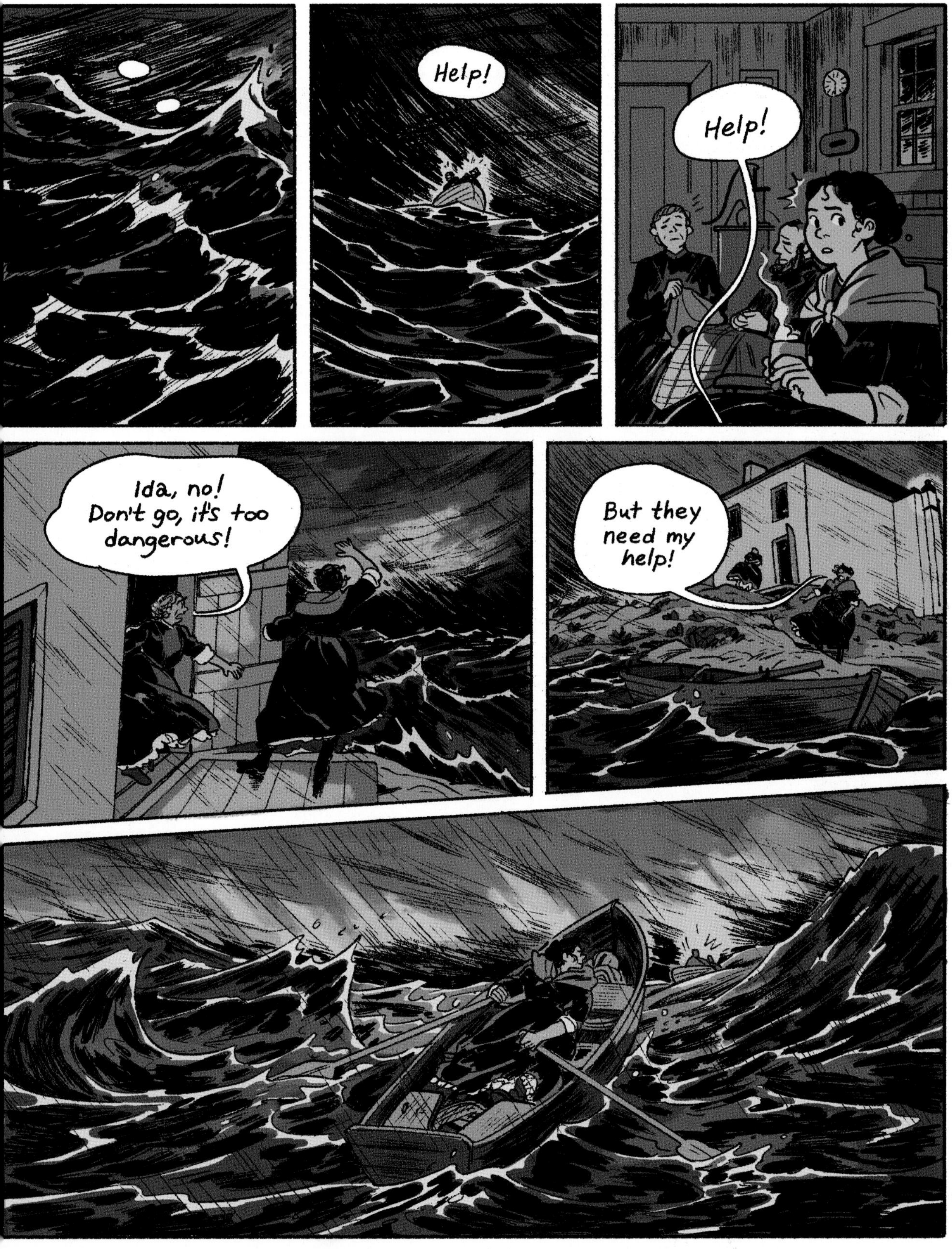
Help!
Help!
Ida, no! Don't go, it's too dangerous!
But they need my help!

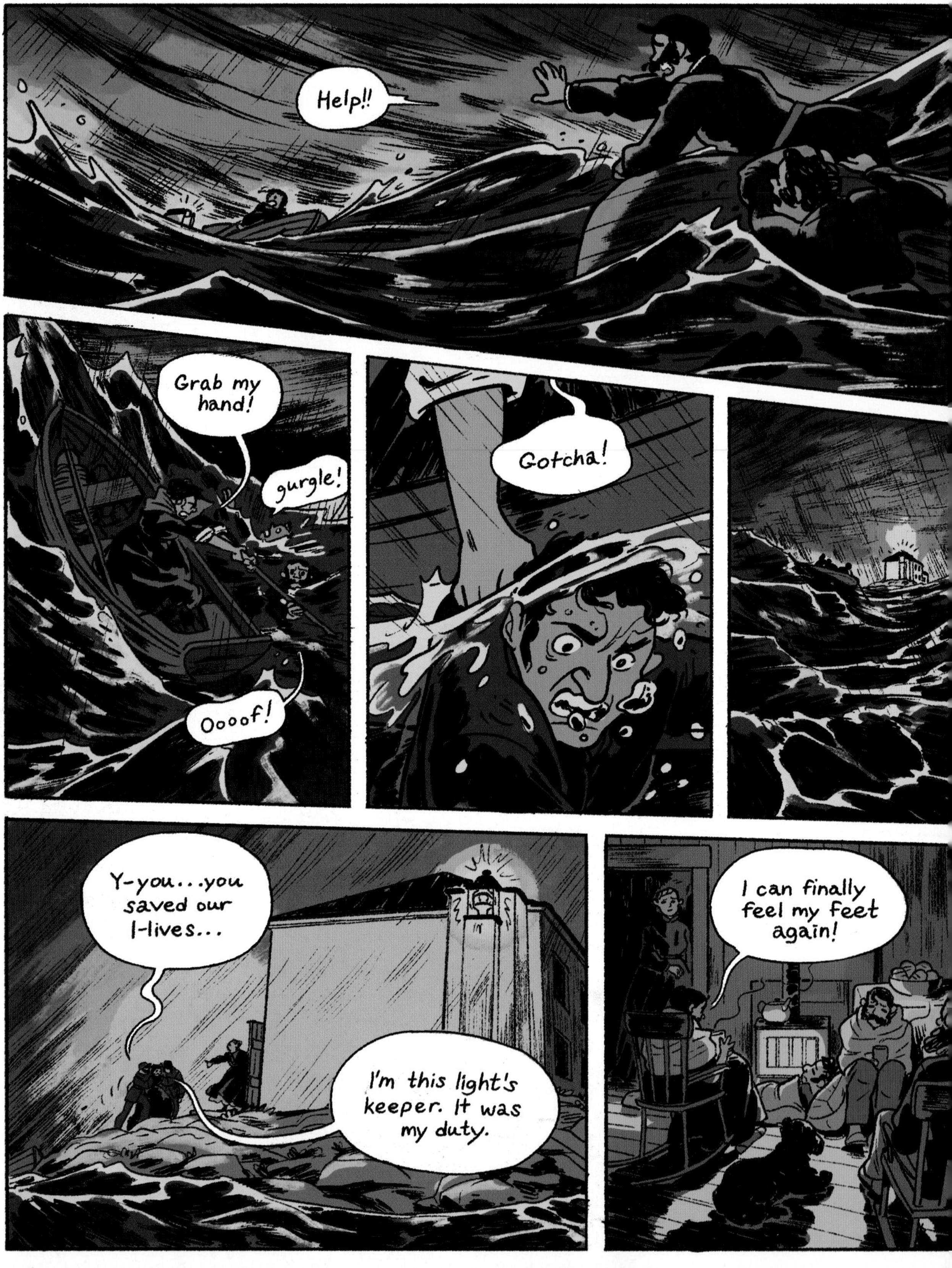
Help!!
Grab my hand!
gurgle!
Oooof!
Gotcha!
Y-you...you saved our l-lives...
I'm this light's keeper. It was my duty.
I can finally feel my feet again!

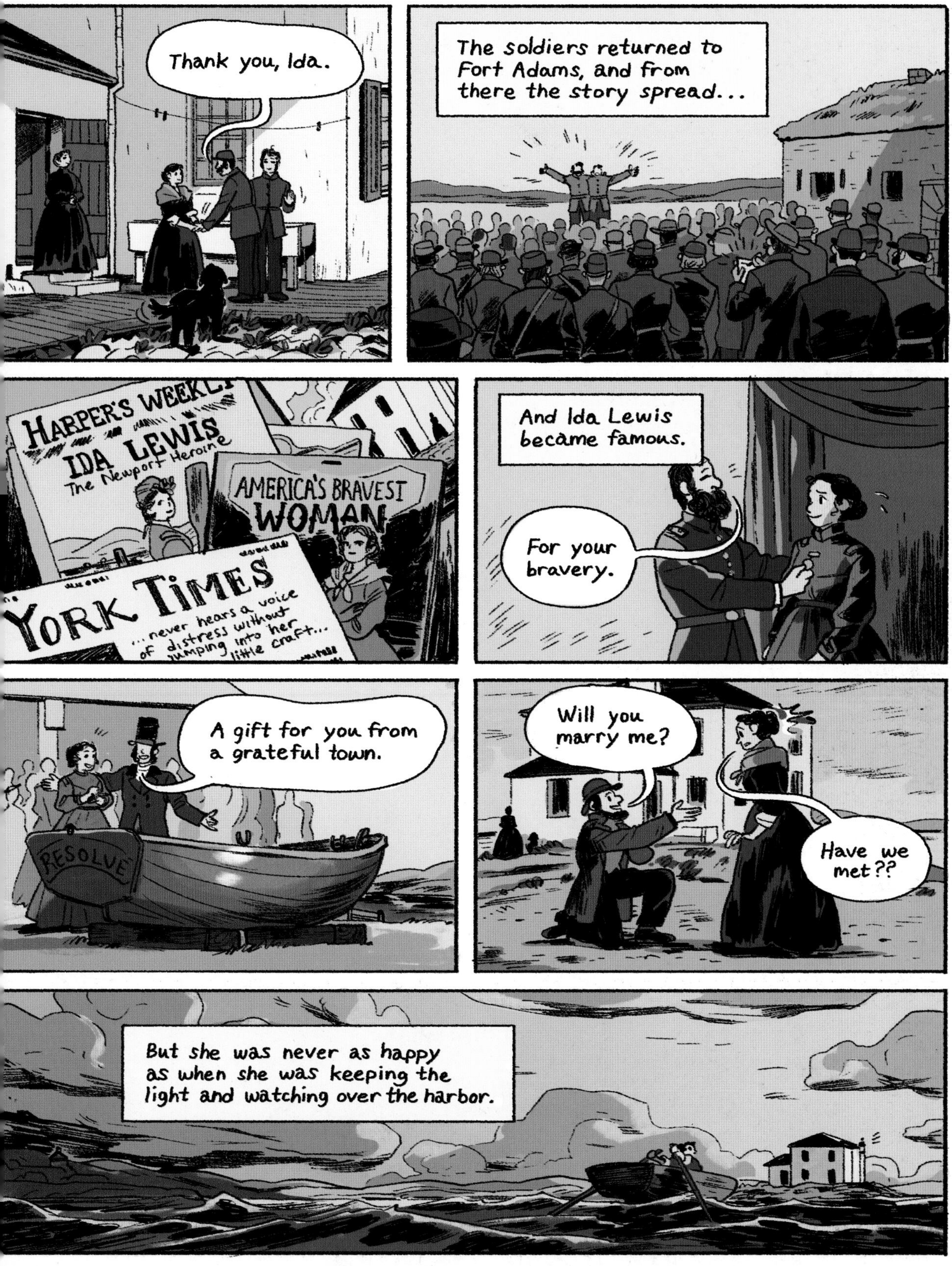

Thank you, Ida.
The soldiers returned to Fort Adams, and from there the story spread...
HARPER'S WEEKLY
IDA LEWIS
The Newport Heroine
AMERICA'S BRAVEST WOMAN
YORK TIMES
...never hears a voice of distress without jumping into her little craft...
And Ida Lewis became famous.
For your bravery.
A gift for you from a grateful town.
RESOLVE
Will you marry me?
Have we met??
But she was never as happy as when she was keeping the light and watching over the harbor.

THE *World* EXPLORER

· · · · ·

JEANNE BARET
1740~1807

Botanist Jeanne Baret was the first woman ever to sail around the world, but since girls weren't permitted on board any naval ships at the time, she disguised herself as a boy and went anyway. A little "No girls allowed!" sign at the end of the ship's gangplank wasn't going to stop her from going where she wanted to go.

JEANNE AND ME

COUNT ALL THE THINGS YOU HAVE IN COMMON WITH JEANNE BARET.

- I want to see the world.
- I dream of what it would be like to live in other places.
- I like to look at plants.
- I love drawing pictures of flowers.
- I'm good at comparing things and seeing what's similar and what's different.
- I'm good at disguises.
- I don't believe some things are only for boys and others are only for girls.
- If a rule is unfair, I'll work to change it.
- I'm capable.
- I'm adventurous.

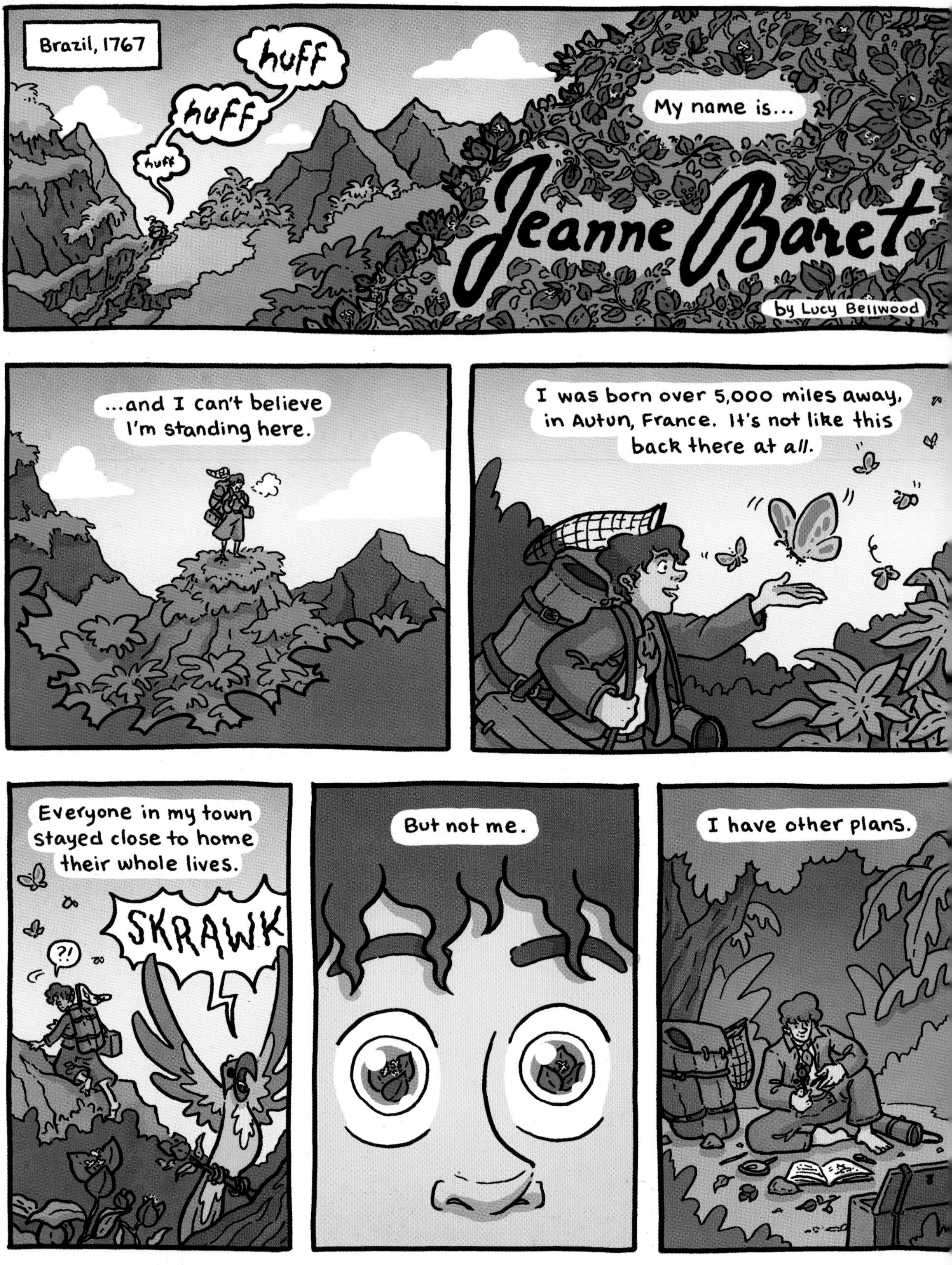
Brazil, 1767
huff
huff
huff
My name is...
Jeanne Baret
by Lucy Bellwood
...and I can't believe I'm standing here.
I was born over 5,000 miles away, in Autun, France. It's not like this back there at all.
Everyone in my town stayed close to home their whole lives.
SKRAWK
?!
But not me.
I have other plans.

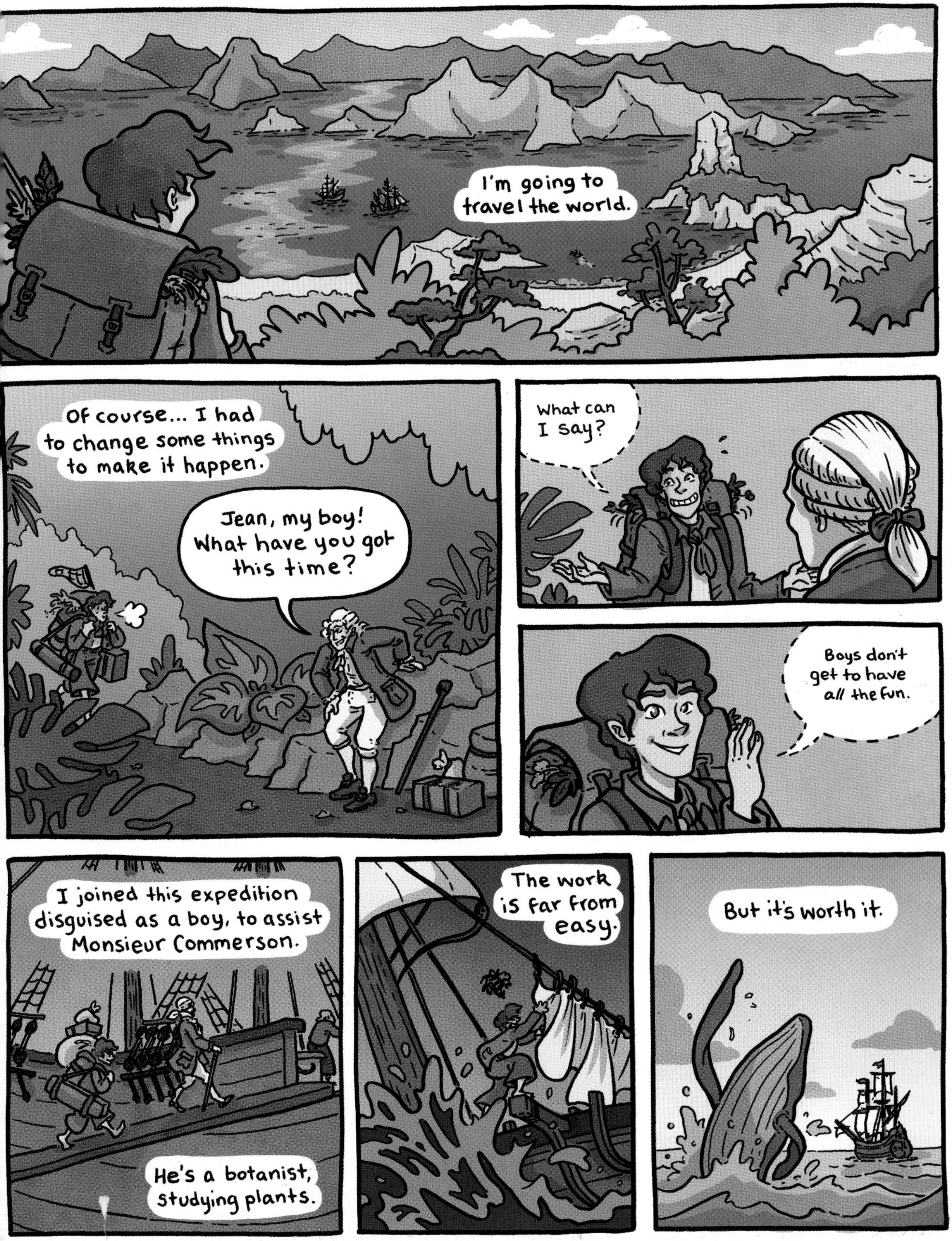
I'm going to travel the world.
Of course... I had to change some things to make it happen.
Jean, my boy! What have you got this time?
What can I say?
Boys don't get to have *all* the fun.
I joined this expedition disguised as a boy, to assist Monsieur Commerson.
He's a botanist, studying plants.
The work is far from easy.
But it's worth it.

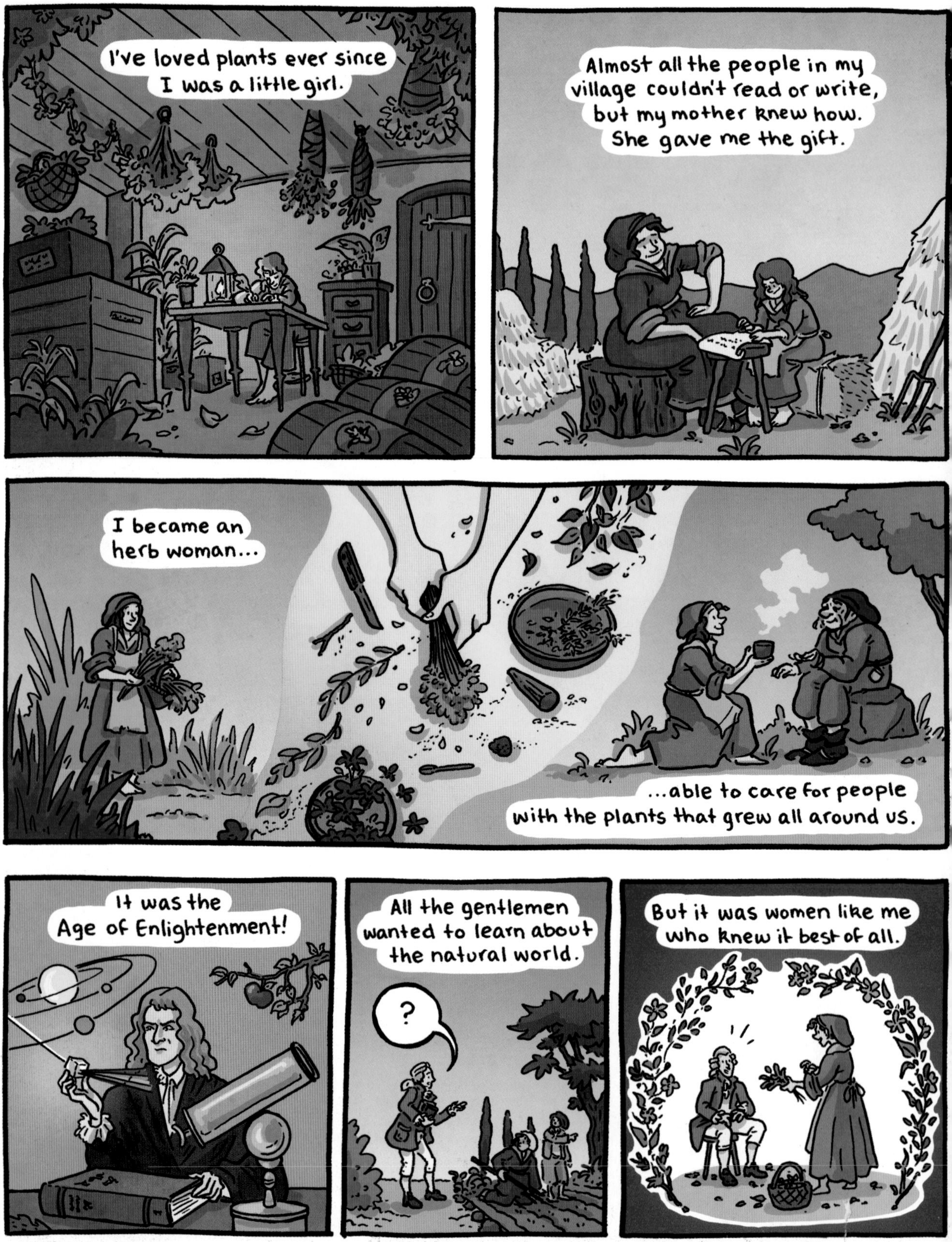

I've loved plants ever since I was a little girl.
Almost all the people in my village couldn't read or write, but my mother knew how. She gave me the gift.
I became an herb woman...
...able to care for people with the plants that grew all around us.
It was the Age of Enlightenment!
All the gentlemen wanted to learn about the natural world.
?
But it was women like me who knew it best of all.

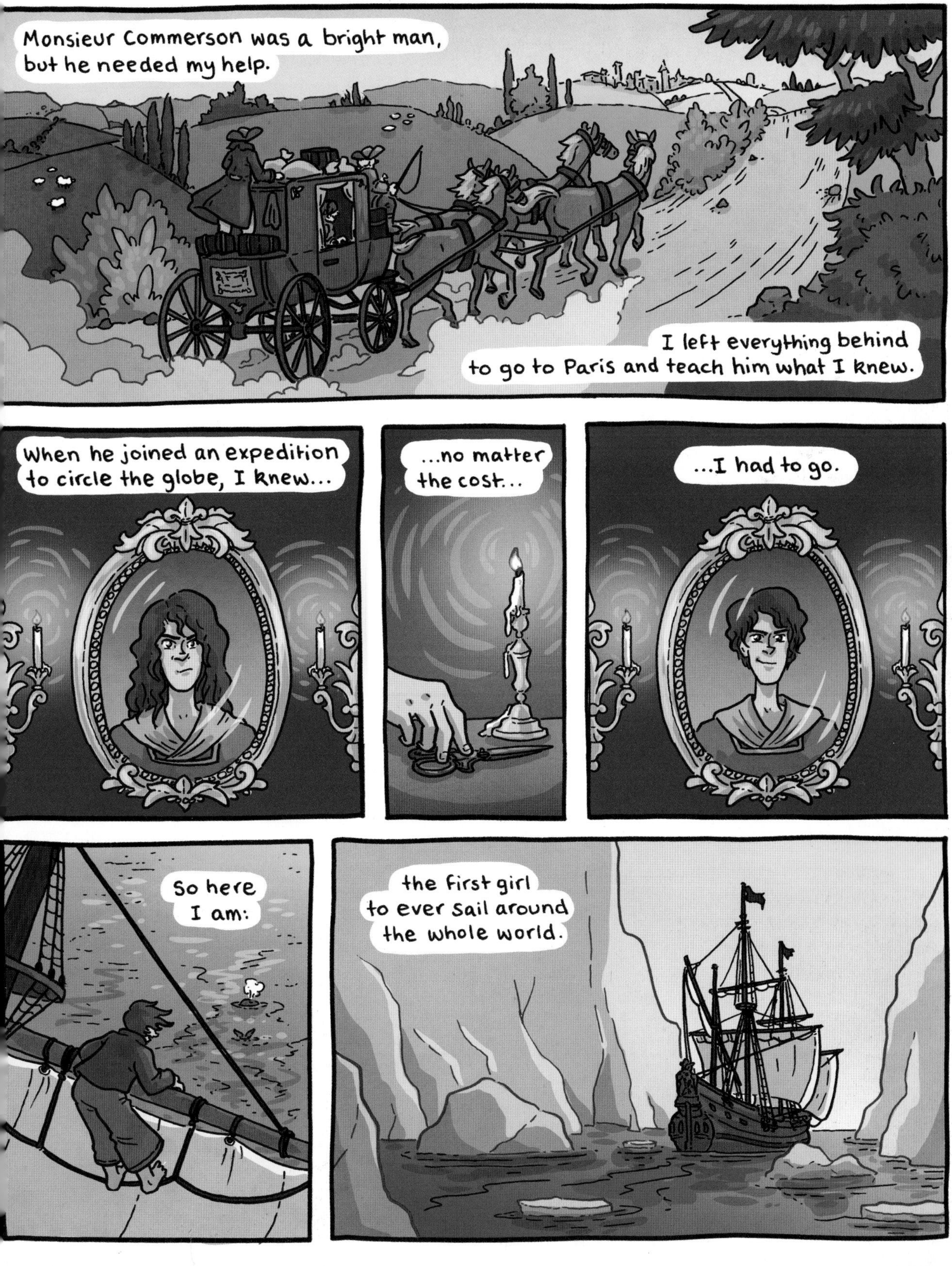
Monsieur Commerson was a bright man, but he needed my help.
I left everything behind to go to Paris and teach him what I knew.
When he joined an expedition to circle the globe, I knew...
...no matter the cost...
...I had to go.
So here I am:
the first girl to ever sail around the whole world.

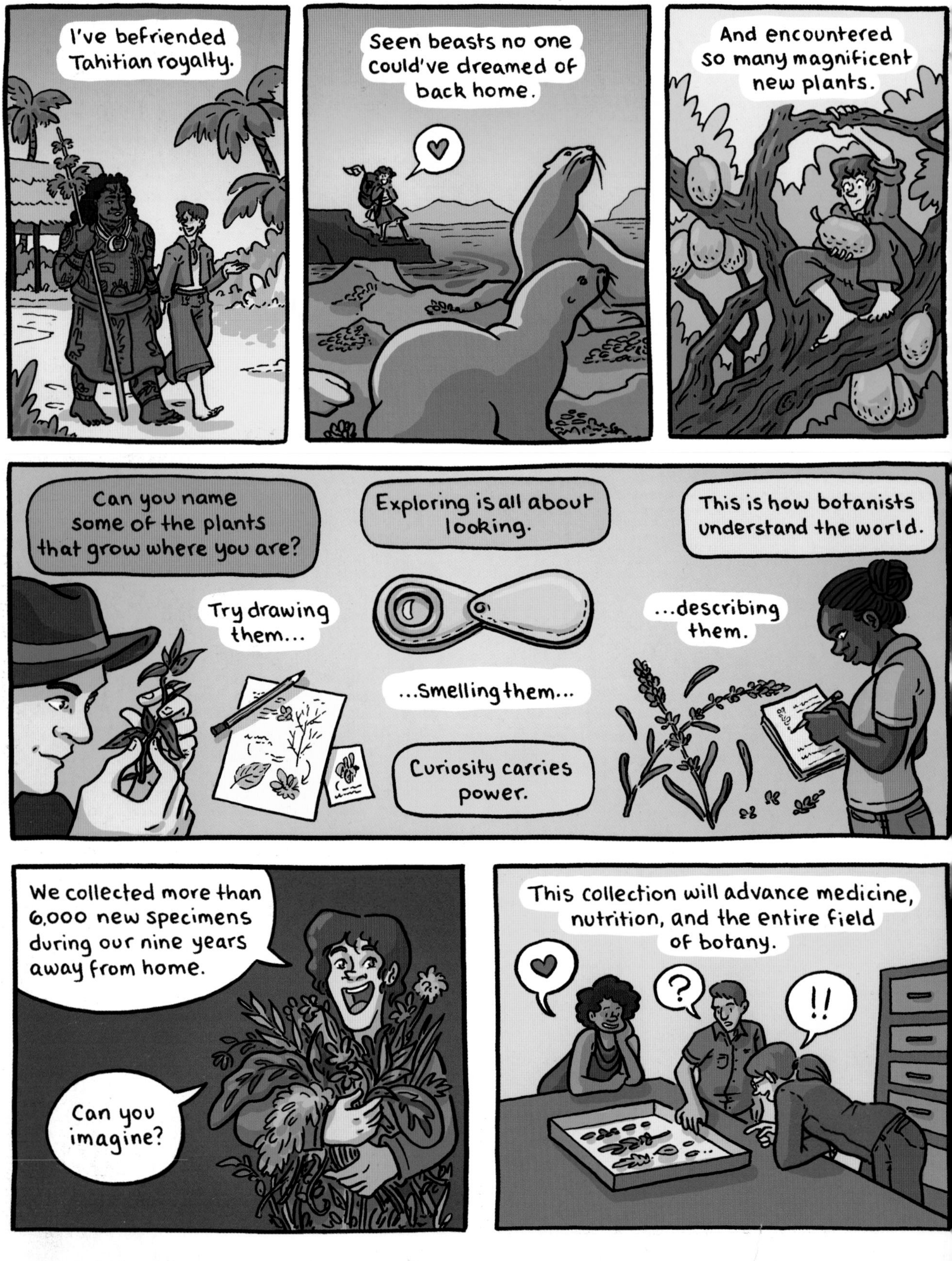

I've befriended Tahitian royalty.
Seen beasts no one could've dreamed of back home.
♥
And encountered so many magnificent new plants.
Can you name some of the plants that grow where you are?
Exploring is all about looking.
This is how botanists understand the world.
Try drawing them...
...describing them.
...smelling them...
Curiosity carries power.
We collected more than 6,000 new specimens during our nine years away from home.
Can you imagine?
This collection will advance medicine, nutrition, and the entire field of botany.
♥
?
!!

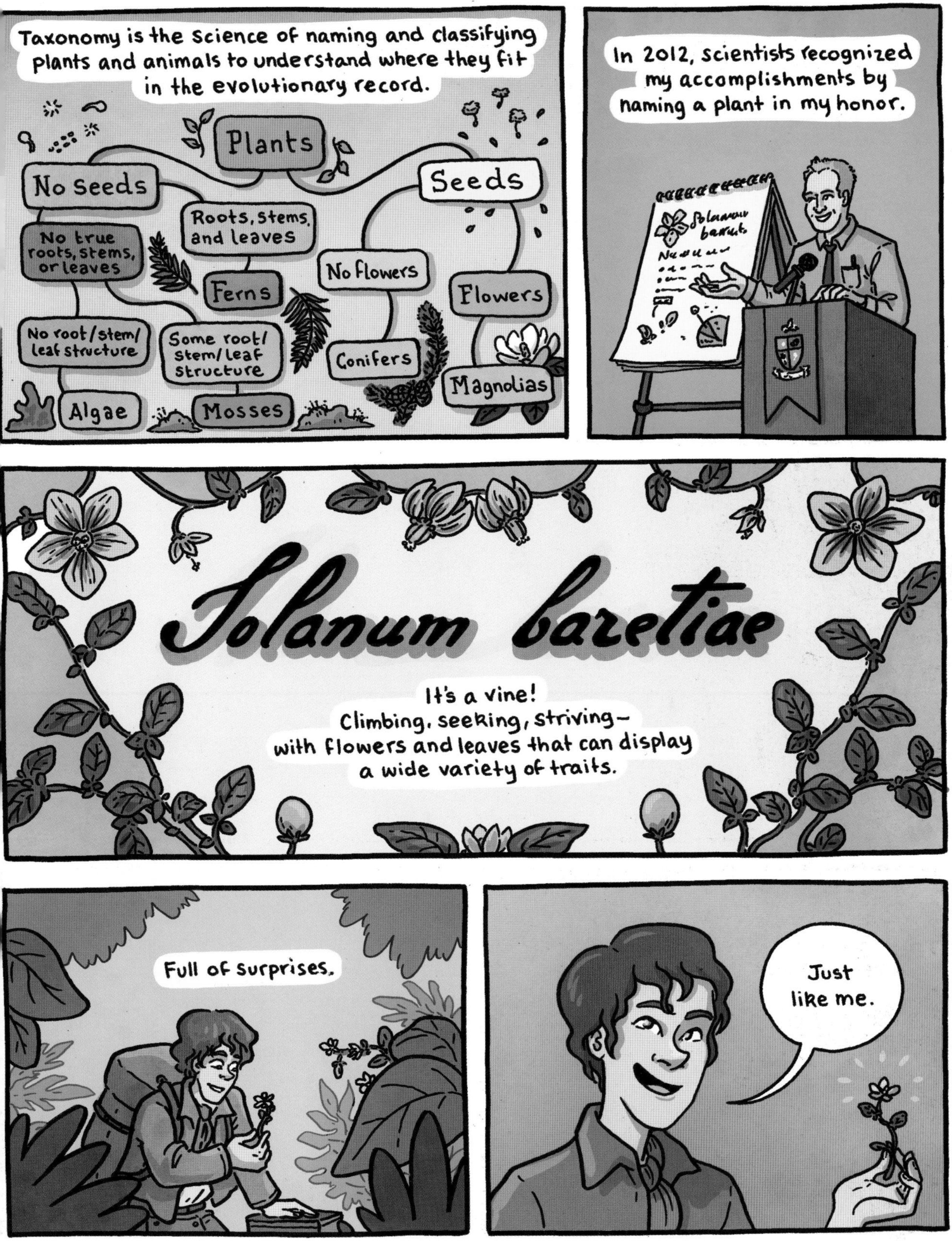
Taxonomy is the science of naming and classifying plants and animals to understand where they fit in the evolutionary record.
Plants
No seeds
Seeds
Roots, stems, and leaves
No true roots, stems, or leaves
Ferns
No flowers
Flowers
No root/stem/leaf structure
Some root/stem/leaf structure
Conifers
Magnolias
Algae
Mosses
In 2012, scientists recognized my accomplishments by naming a plant in my honor.
Solanum baretiae
It's a vine!
Climbing, seeking, striving—
with flowers and leaves that can display a wide variety of traits.
Full of surprises.
Just like me.

MEET THE ARTISTS

• • • •

WESHOYOT ALVITRE (Maria Tallchief) is an award-winning Tongva comic book artist, who, like Maria Tallchief, doesn't let preconceived notions stand in her way. She lives in Southern California with her husband and two daughters. Her first children's book, *At the Mountain's Base*, written by Traci Sorell (Kokila), is out now.

LUCY BELLWOOD (Jeanne Baret) is a professional adventure cartoonist based in Portland, Oregon, and the creator of *Baggywrinkles: A Lubber's Guide to Life at Sea* (Toonhound Studios), a memoir about her time working aboard tall ships, much like the one Jeanne Baret sailed.

MOLLY BROOKS (Kate Warne) is the Brooklyn-based author and illustrator of *Sanity & Tallulah* (Disney-Hyperion), a graphic novel about two girls in space. She loves watching vintage buddy-cop shows—Kate Warne would approve!— and making comics about knitting, hockey, and feelings.

CHAN CHAU (Caroline Herschel) is a Minnesota-born and -raised cartoonist, who's worked on the Emmy-winning *Danger & Eggs* series. When they're not making comics, they're making natal charts—based on the very same stars Caroline Herschel mapped—for their friends.

LITTLE CORVUS (Mary Anning) is an Eisner-nominated, queer, Latinx comic artist and illustrator, who spent their childhood on Washington's Puget Sound collecting jars full of shells and rocks, just like Mary Anning used to do. They have a BFA in Cartooning from the School of Visual Arts.

EMIL FERRIS (Mary Shelley) is the Chicago-based author of *My Favorite Thing Is Monsters* (Fantagraphics). Like Mary Shelley, she's a devotee of all things monstrous. She's also the winner of three Eisner Awards, two Ignatz Awards, and the Fauve D'Or.

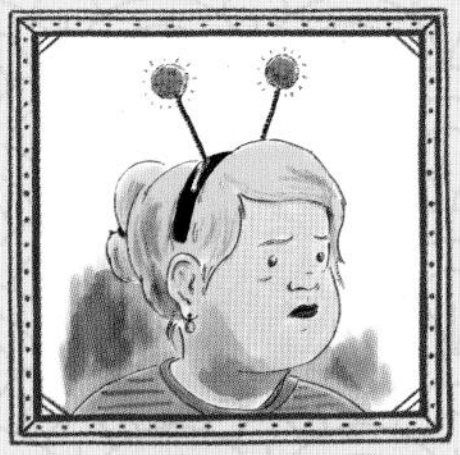

EMILY FLAKE (Eleanor Roosevelt) is a writer, illustrator, performer, and cartoonist, whose work often appears in the *New Yorker.* She lives in Brooklyn with her husband, their daughter, and a small orange cat. She wishes she could have attended one of Eleanor Roosevelt's ladies-only press conferences.

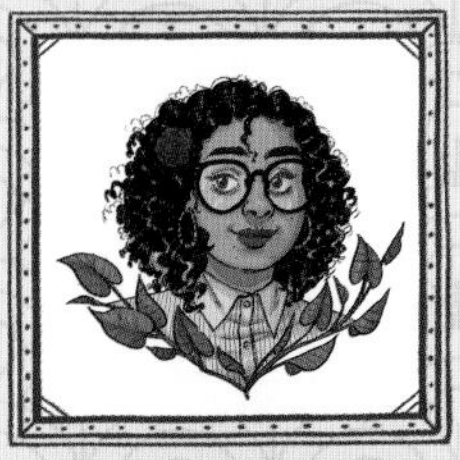

NAOMI FRANQUIZ (Frida Kahlo) is a Florida-based illustrator and comic book artist, who has published with Dark Horse, Image Comics, BOOM! Box, and Power & Magic Press. She loves animals—almost as much as her favorite artist, Frida Kahlo, did—and enjoys watching video compilations of rude cats.

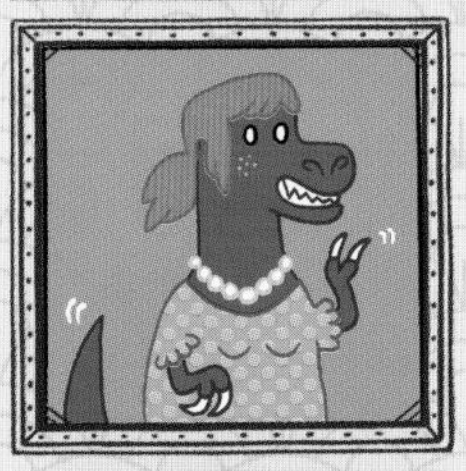

SOPHIE GOLDSTEIN (Mother Jones) is a cartoonist, illustrator, and comics instructor based in Tulsa, Oklahoma. She loves reading, drawing, and rock climbing and hopes every girl feels inspired to fight for a cause, just like Mother Jones.

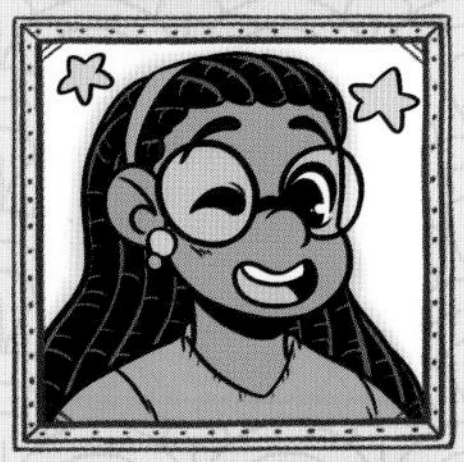

SHAUNA J. GRANT (Maya Angelou) is a Bronx-born and -bred cartoonist and illustrator with the magic power to create cuteness. Following in the footsteps of amazing black female artists such as Maya Angelou, she continues to pursue her dream of creating diverse artwork to ensure that every girl feels phenomenal.

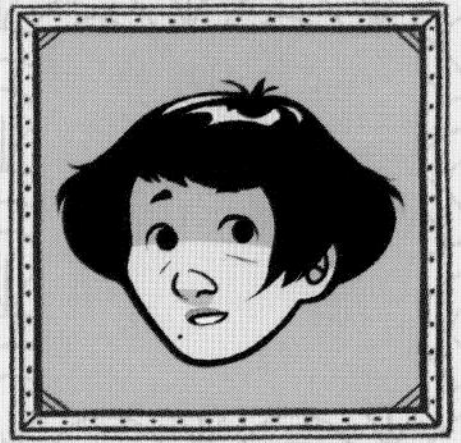

KIKU HUGHES (Emily Warren Roebling) is a Seattle-based comic artist and illustrator who attended school in New York City, where she spent many nights walking across the Brooklyn Bridge with her friends, talking about their futures. Like Emily Warren Roebling, she wants to help the women who come after her to succeed.

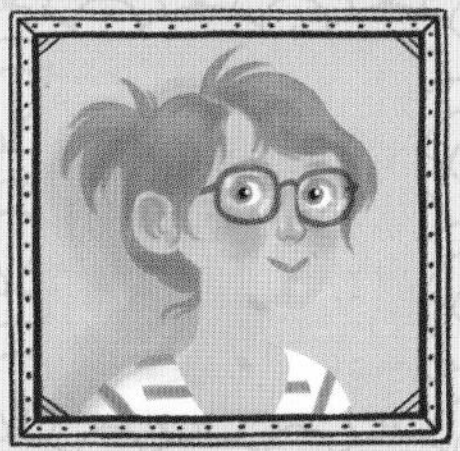

LUCY KNISLEY (Julia Child) is a critically acclaimed, award-winning comic creator, who loves French food almost as much as Julia Child. She specializes in personal, confessional graphic novels and travelogues, and her bestselling books include *French Milk* (Touchstone), *Relish* (First Second Books), and *Kid Gloves* (First Second Books). She lives in Chicago.

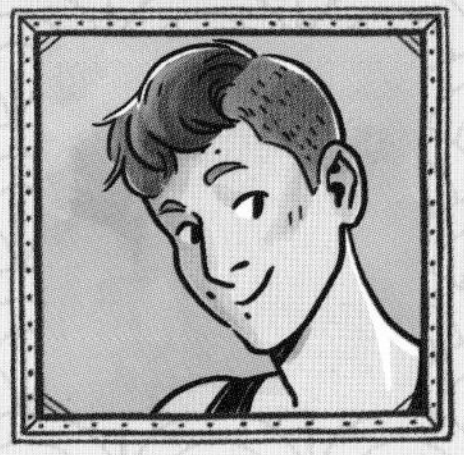

KAT LEYH (Annie Londonderry) is a GLAAD Award–winning comic writer and artist best known for her queer superhero comic series, Supercakes, and her graphic novel, *Snapdragon* (First Second Books). She's also the co-writer and cover artist of the all-ages series Lumberjanes (BOOM! Box). She lives in Chicago, where she gets around by bike—just like Annie!

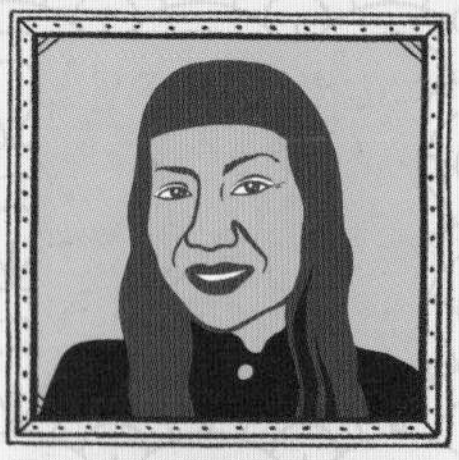

MARINAOMI (Junko Tabei) is an award-winning Japanese American cartoonist and the creator of the Cartoonists of Color and Queer Cartoonists databases. She lives in Los Angeles and admires Junko Tabei for her devotion to doing what she loves, regardless of what other people think.

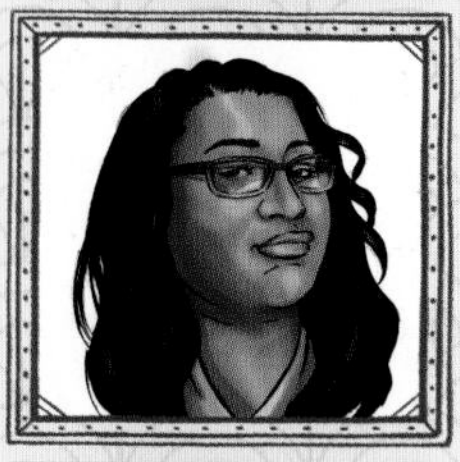

ALITHA E. MARTINEZ (Josephine Baker) is a New York City–based, Eisner-winning comic artist, who has worked on Marvel's *Iron Man*, as well as *Black Panther: World of Wakanda,* written by Roxane Gay and Ta-Nehisi Coates, among other titles. Learning about Josephine Baker inspired her to book a trip to France with her son.

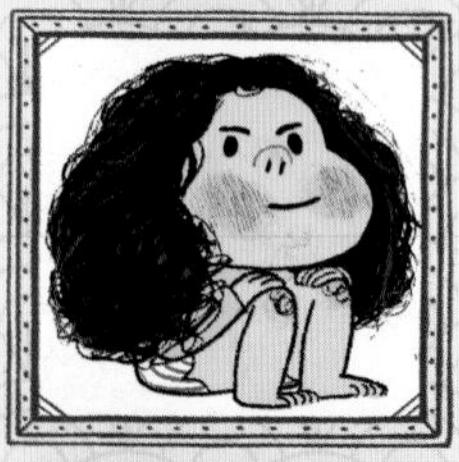

REBECCA MOCK (Ida Lewis) is a comic book artist and illustrator living in New York City. She is the artist of the Four Points graphic novel series. She especially loves drawing historical comics and comics about women, and she loves visiting old lighthouses like Ida Lewis's.

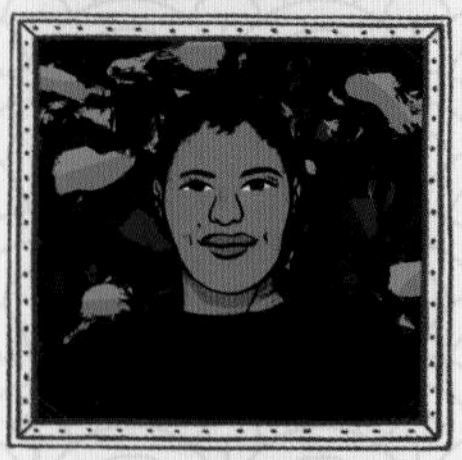

K. L. RICKS (Madam C. J. Walker) is a Massachusetts-based illustrator and cartoonist, whose work has appeared in the *New York Times* and the *New Yorker.* She has two upcoming graphic novels to be published by First Second Books. She aims to embody Madam C. J. Walker's courage, compassion, and empathy in the face of adversity every day.

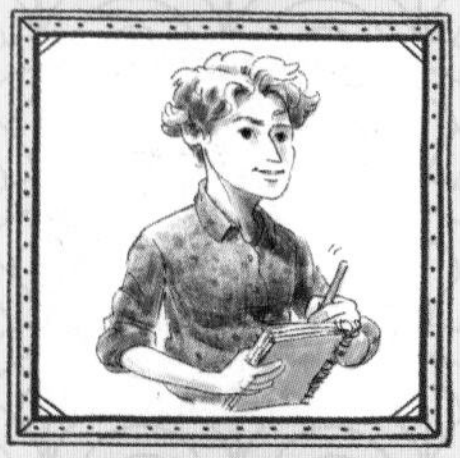

JACKIE ROCHE (Nellie Bly) is a Chicago-based cartoonist, whose work has appeared in the *Nib* and at Harvard University Library's Fair Use Week festivities. She also illustrated Samya Kullab's *Escape from Syria* (Firefly Books). Like Nellie Bly, Jackie exercises her curiosity to find interesting stories.

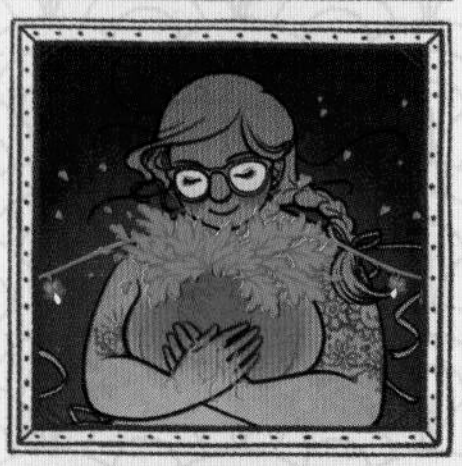

SARAH W. SEARLE (Hedy Lamarr) originally hails from spooky New England but currently lives in sunny Perth, Australia. She's the creator of *Sincerely, Harriet* (Graphic Universe) and *The Greatest Thing* (First Second Books), and she loves how Hedy pursued her dual passions of art and science to make the world a better place.

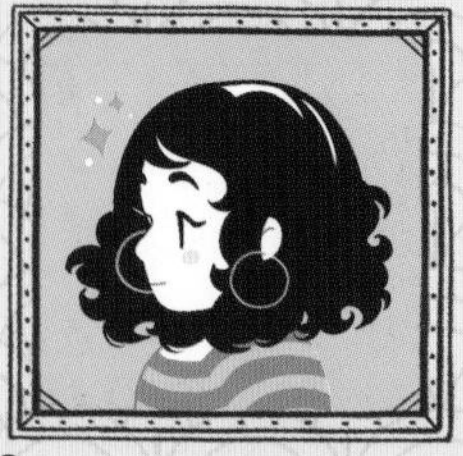

ROSEMARY VALERO-O'CONNELL (Hallie Daggett) is a Minneapolis-born, Zaragoza (Spain)–raised cartoonist and illustrator, who values independence as much as Hallie Daggett. She's the co-creator, with Mariko Tamaki, of *Laura Dean Keeps Breaking Up with Me* (First Second Books) and has worked with DC Comics and BOOM! Studios.

MARIS WICKS (Eugenie Clark) writes and draws comics about science when she's not scuba-diving with sharks. She's the author and illustrator of *Coral Reefs: Cities of the Ocean* (First Second Books) and *Human Body Theater* (First Second Books) and has worked with SpongeBob Comics, the Woods Hole Oceanographic Institution, the New England Aquarium, DC Comics, and Marvel. She lives in Somerville, Massachusetts.

BRITTNEY WILLIAMS (Wangari Maathai) is a former story intern at Walt Disney Animation Studios and a two-time GLAAD Award–nominated storyboard and comic book artist, whose clients include Marvel, Cartoon Network, and DreamWorks TV. She was so inspired by Wangari Maathai that she planted her own vegetable garden. She lives in Atlanta.

ASHLEY A. WOODS (Rosa Parks) is a Chicago-based illustrator and writer, who, inspired by Rosa Parks, stands in truth, despite any challenges that come with it. She illustrated the series *Niobe: She Is Life*, written by Amandla Stenberg and Sebastian A. Jones (Stranger Comics), and also *Ladycastle*, written by Delilah S. Dawson (BOOM! Studios).

SHANNON WRIGHT (Bessie Coleman) is an illustrator, cartoonist, and fanfiction enthusiast. Her work tends to explore social issues, like those Bessie Coleman faced, but she also enjoys depicting the mundane and fantastical aspects of life. Her clients include Google, the *New York Times*, *Time*, and *Mother Jones*. She lives in Fredericksburg, Virginia.

YAO XIAO (Raye Montague) is a China-born, New York City–based illustrator, who grew up building ship models because her grandmother was an engineer like Raye Montague. Her clients include Katy Perry, Google, the United Nations, *Vogue*, and the *New York Times*. Her work has also been recognized by the Kennedy Center for the Performing Arts.

kazoo is a new kind of print magazine for girls, ages 5 to 12, one that celebrates them for being strong, smart, fierce, and, above all, true to themselves. *Kazoo* has won two consecutive Parents' Choice Gold Awards and the 2019 National Magazine Award for General Excellence. To get it delivered to your door, subscribe at kazoomagazine.com and visit us on Twitter and Instagram.

To
ELLIE, BEA,
and
NOISEMAKERS EVERYWHERE

THIS IS A BORZOI BOOK PUBLISHED BY ALFRED A. KNOPF.

Copyright © 2020 by Kazoo Media LLC
Jacket art hand-lettering copyright © 2020 by Mye de Leon

All rights reserved. Published in the United States by Alfred A. Knopf,
an imprint of Random House Children's Books, a division of Penguin Random House LLC, New York.
"Your Name Is Hallie Daggett," by Rosemary Valero-O'Connell, originally published in *Kazoo* magazine by Kazoo Media LLC in 2016;
"Story of Bessie Coleman," by Shannon Wright, originally published in *Kazoo* magazine by Kazoo Media LLC in 2017;
"Josephine Baker: The Singing Spy," by Alitha E. Martinez, originally published in *Kazoo* magazine by Kazoo Media LLC in 2017;
"My Name Is Raye Montague and Have I Got a Story for You," by Yao Xiao, originally published in *Kazoo* magazine by
Kazoo Media LLC in 2017; "Keeper of the Light," by Rebecca Mock, originally published in *Kazoo* magazine by Kazoo Media LLC
in 2017; "Julia Child," by Lucy Knisley, originally published in *Kazoo* magazine by Kazoo Media LLC in 2018; "Planting Hope,"
by Brittney Williams, originally published in *Kazoo* magazine by Kazoo Media LLC in 2018; "A Small Brave Act: The Story of
Rosa Parks," by Ashley A. Woods, originally published in *Kazoo* magazine by Kazoo Media LLC in 2018; "Eleanor Roosevelt:
Lady Superhero" by Emily Flake, originally published in *Kazoo* magazine by Kazoo Media LLC in 2018; and "My Name Is . . .
Jeanne Baret" by Lucy Bellwood, originally published in *Kazoo* magazine by Kazoo Media LLC in 2019.

Knopf, Borzoi Books, and the colophon are registered trademarks of Penguin Random House LLC.
Visit us on the Web! rhcbooks.com
Visit *Kazoo* magazine on the Web: kazoomagazine.com
Educators and librarians, for a variety of teaching tools, visit us at RHTeachersLibrarians.com

Library of Congress Cataloging-in-Publication Data is available upon request.
ISBN 978-0-525-58017-1 (trade) — ISBN 978-0-525-58018-8 (trade pbk.) — ISBN 978-0-525-58020-1 (ebook)

The text of this book is set in 12-point Avenir LT Com.
Book design by Katrina Damkoehler. Interior hand-lettering by Mye de Leon

MANUFACTURED IN CHINA
February 2020
10 9 8 7 6 5 4 3 2 1
First Edition

Random House Children's Books supports the First Amendment and celebrates the right to read.

Image Credits

Courtesy of David Montague: Raye Montague (1987). Courtesy of the Green Belt Movement and UNEP: Wangari Maathai (2008).
Jaan Künnap: Junko Tabei (1985). Lynn Gilbert: Julia Child (1978)

PD-US

Mary Anning (1842), Caroline Herschel (1829), Emily Warren Roebling (1896), Hedy Lamarr (1944),
Madam C. J. Walker (1905), Annie Londonderry (1890), Maria Tallchief (1954), Frida Kahlo (1932), Josephine Baker (1950),
Maya Angelou (1993), Kate Warne (1864), Nelly Bly (1890), Eleanor Roosevelt (1933), Rosa Parks (1955),
Mother Jones (1902), Bessie Coleman (1921), Hallie Daggett (1913), Ida Lewis (1923), Jeanne Baret (1806)

Richard Rothwell: Mary Shelley (1840)

Photo by Tak Konstantinou. Courtesy of Mote Marine Laboratory & Aquarium: Eugenie Clark (2005)